Lecture Notes in Artificial Intelligence   7784

Subseries of Lecture Notes in Computer Science

Matteo Baldoni   Louise Dennis
Viviana Mascardi   Wamberto Vasconcelos (Eds.)

Declarative Agent Languages and Technologies X

10th International Workshop, DALT 2012
Valencia, Spain, June 4, 2012
Revised Selected Papers

 Springer

Series Editors

Randy Goebel, University of Alberta, Edmonton, Canada
Jörg Siekmann, University of Saarland, Saarbrücken, Germany
Wolfgang Wahlster, DFKI and University of Saarland, Saarbrücken, Germany

Volume Editors

Matteo Baldoni
Università degli Studi di Torino, Dipartimento di Informatica
Via Pessinetto, 12, 10149 Torino, Italy
E-mail: baldoni@di.unito.it

Louise Dennis
University of Liverpool, Department of Computer Science
Ashton Building, Liverpool, L69 3 BX, UK
E-mail: l.a.dennis@liverpool.ac.uk

Viviana Mascardi
Università degli Studi di Genova, DIBRIS, Dipartimento di Informatica
Via Dodecaneso, 35, 16146, Genova, Italy
E-mail: viviana.mascardi@unige.it

Wamberto Vasconcelos
University of Aberdeen, Department of Computing Science
Meston Building, Aberdeen, AB24 3UE, UK
E-mail: w.w.vasconcelos@abdn.ac.uk

ISSN 0302-9743   e-ISSN 1611-3349
ISBN 978-3-642-37889-8   e-ISBN 978-3-642-37890-4
DOI 10.1007/978-3-642-37890-4
Springer Heidelberg Dordrecht London New York

Library of Congress Control Number: 2013935526

CR Subject Classification (1998): I.2.11, I.2.0, I.2.2-4, F.3.1, D.2, D.1.6, F.1.3

LNCS Sublibrary: SL 7 – Artificial Intelligence

Typesetting: Camera-ready by author, data conversion by Scientific Publishing Services, Chennai, India

Printed on acid-free paper

Springer is part of Springer Science+Business Media (www.springer.com)

Preface

The Workshop on Declarative Agent Languages and Technologies (DALT), in its tenth edition in 2012, is a well-established forum for researchers and practitioners interested in exploiting declarative approaches for tackling the great challenges that today's distributed applications raise. Current distributed systems are usually made up of highly autonomous components working in open, dynamic, and unpredictable environments. A large, useful, practical, and popular subcategory of such distributed systems includes software agents and multi-agent systems (MASs). Designing, developing, testing, and maintaining such systems calls for models and technologies that ensure predictability and allow for the verification of critical properties, while still maintaining flexibility. Rapid prototyping and knowledge representation and management are often important in the design and development of such systems. Declarative approaches have the potential to offer solutions that satisfy the needs arising when engineering systems as complex as MASs. For this reason, declarative approaches have gained more and more attention in important application areas such as the Semantic Web, service-oriented computing, security, and electronic contracting.

This volume presents the latest developments in the area of declarative languages and technologies, which aim to provide rigorous frameworks for engineering autonomous interacting agents. These frameworks are based on computational logics and other formal methods such as mathematical models and game theoretical approaches that facilitate the development of agents reasoning and acting rationally, and support the formal verification of the agents' behavior against their specification.

In the tradition of DALT, the 2012 meeting was held as a satellite workshop of the 11th International Joint Conference on Autonomous Agents and Multiagent Systems (AAMAS 2012), in Valencia, Spain. Following the success of DALT 2003 in Melbourne (LNAI 2990), DALT 2004 in New York (LNAI 3476), DALT 2005 in Utrecht (LNAI 3904), DALT 2006 in Hakodate (LNAI 4327), DALT 2007 in Honolulu (LNAI 4897), DALT 2008 in Estoril (LNAI 5397), DALT 2009 in Budapest (LNAI 5948), DALT 2010 in Toronto (LNAI 6619), and DALT 2011 in Taiwan (LNAI 7169), DALT 2012 was organized as a forum in which theoreticians and practitioners could meet for scientific exchange on declarative approaches for specifying, verifying, programming, and running software agents and MASs.

This volume contains 13 contributions: four are revised and extended versions of short papers accepted at AAMAS 2012; and the remaining nine papers are original contributions presented at DALT 2012, revised and extended in light of our reviewers' comments. All the full papers have been carefully reviewed to check their originality, quality, and technical soundness. The DALT 2012 workshop received eight regular submissions and three position papers. Six papers and three position papers were selected by the Program Committee and are included in this volume. Each paper received at least three reviews. The position papers were an innovation introduced to celebrate DALT's 10th edition and the Alan Turing year. Each paper received two "light touch" reviews and was evaluated on the basis of its potential for stimulating discussion.

"Handling Change in Normative Specifications" by Duangtida Athakravi, Domenico Corapi, Alessandra Russo, Marina De Vos, Julian Padget, and Ken Satoh describes a (semi-)automated process for controlling the elaboration of normative specifications and demonstrates its effectiveness through a proof-of-concept case study. The methodology for elaborating normative specifications is based on use-cases to capture desirable and undesirable system behaviors, and inductive logic programming to justify why certain changes are better than others.

"Latest Developments of WADE to Support User-Centric Business Processes" by Federico Bergenti, Giovanni Caire, and Danilo Gotta presents the latest developments of WADE (Workflows and Agents Development Environment), aimed at enhancing its agent-based runtime platform by providing improved non-functional features and a better integration with the external software systems, and enabling the rapid and effective realization of user-centric business processes.

"Strong Planning in the Logics of Communication and Change" by Pere Pardo and Mehrnoosh Sadrzadeh discusses how to adapt backward plan search to the logics of communication and change (LCC). The proposed LCC planning system greatly expands the social complexity of scenarios involving cognitive agents that can be solved: for example, goals or plans may consist of a certain distribution of beliefs and ignorance among agents.

"Agent Deliberation via Forward and Backward Chaining in Linear Logic" by Luke Trodd, James Harland, and John Thangarajah explores how a BDI approach can be implemented in the Lygon logic programming language based on linear logic. The way backward and forward chaining techniques can be used to provide proactive and reactive agent behaviors is discussed, as well as extensions to Lygon to generate plans that achieve a given goal using abduction techniques, and to proactively check maintenance goals.

"Automatic Generation of Self-Monitoring MASs from Multiparty Global Session Types in Jason" by Davide Ancona, Sophia Drossopoulou, and Viviana Mascardi exploits global session types specifying multi-party interaction protocols to allow automatic generation of self-monitoring MASs. Such a generated MAS ensures that agents conform to the protocol at run-time, by adding a monitor agent that checks that the ongoing conversation is correct w.r.t. the global session type.

"A Generalized Commitment Machine for 2CL Protocols and Its Implementation" by Matteo Baldoni, Cristina Baroglio, Federico Capuzzimati, Elisa Marengo, and Viviana Patti proposes an operational semantics for the commitment protocol language 2CL. This semantics relies on an extension of Singh's Generalized Commitment Machine and has been implemented in Prolog by extending Winikoff, Liu, and Harland's implementation with a graphical tool that allows the analyst to explore all the possible executions, showing both commitment and constraint violations.

"Solving Fuzzy Distributed CSPs: An Approach with Naming Games" by Stefano Bistarelli, Giorgio Gosti, and Francesco Santini focuses on solving both Fuzzy Naming Games and Fuzzy Distributed Constraint Satisfaction Problems (DCSPs) with an algorithm inspired by Naming Games. With respect to classical Fuzzy DCSPs, the proposed system can react to small instance changes, and the algorithm does not require a pre-agreed agent/variable ordering.

"Commitment Protocol Generation" by Akin Gunay, Michael Winikoff, and Pınar Yolum faces the problem of generating commitment protocols on the fly to interact with other agents when no predefined protocols are available. The generation algorithm considers the agent's own goals and capabilities as well as its beliefs about other agents' goals and capabilities, in order to generate commitments that are more likely to be accepted by other agents.

"Goal-Based Qualitative Preference Systems" by Wietske Visser, Koen Hindriks, and Catholijn Jonker shows that qualitative preference systems (QPSs) provide a general, flexible, and succinct way to represent preferences based on goals. If the domain is not Boolean, preferences are often based on orderings on the possible values of variables. The paper shows that QPSs based on such multi-valued criteria can be translated into equivalent goal-based QPSs that are just as succinct, and that goal-based QPSs allow for more fine-grained updates than their multi-valued counterparts.

"SAT-Based BMC for Deontic Metric Temporal Logic and Deontic Interleaved Interpreted Systems" by Bożena Woźna-Szcześniak and Andrzej Zbrzezny considers MASs modeled by deontic interleaved interpreted systems and provides a new SAT-based bounded model checking (BMC) method for these systems. The properties of MASs are expressed by means of the metric temporal logic with discrete semantics and extended to include epistemic and deontic operators.

"Some Thoughts About Commitment Protocols (Position Paper)" by Matteo Baldoni and Cristina Baroglio deals with commitment protocols and, after more than ten years from their introduction, look at whether a "commitment to do something" is the only kind of regulative norm that we need in order to give social semantics to a physical action, and if commitment protocols realize what they promised.

"Semantic Web and Declarative Agent Languages and Technologies: Current and Future Trends" (Position Paper) by Viviana Mascardi, James Hendler, and Laura Papaleo reviews the state of the art in the integration of Semantic Web concepts in declarative agent languages and technologies and outlines what the authors expect the future trends of this research topic to be.

"Designing and Implementing a Framework for BDI-Style Communicating Agents in Haskell" (Position Paper) by Riccardo Traverso and Alessandro Solimando presents the design and prototypical implementation of a framework for BDI-style agents defined as Haskell functions, supporting both the explicit representation of beliefs and backtracking (at the level of individual agents), and asynchronous communication via message passing.

Given the exciting discussion carried out during the workshop and the high quality of the papers collected in this volume, the DALT 2012 organizers would like to thank all authors for their contributions, the members of the Steering Committee for the valuable suggestions and support, and the members of the Program Committee for their excellent work during the reviewing phase

January 2013   Matteo Baldoni
                                                          Louise Dennis
                                                       Viviana Mascardi
                                                 Wamberto Vasconcelos

Organization

Workshop Organizers

Matteo Baldoni   University of Turin, Italy
Louise Dennis   University of Liverpool, UK
Viviana Mascardi   University of Genova, Italy
Wamberto Vasconcelos   University of Aberdeen, UK

Programe Committee

Thomas Ågotnes   Bergen University College, Norway
Marco Alberti   Universidade Nova de Lisboa, Portugal
Natasha Alechina   University of Nottingham, UK
Cristina Baroglio   University of Turin, Italy
Rafael Bordini   Pontificia Universidade Católica do Rio Grande do Sul, Brazil
Jan Broersen   University of Utrecht, The Netherlands
Federico Chesani   University of Bologna, Italy
Flavio Correa Da Silva   Universidade de São Paulo, Brazil
Marina De Vos   University of Bath, UK
Francesco Donini   Università della Tuscia, Italy
Michael Fink   Vienna University of Technology, Austria
James Harland   RMIT University, Australia
Andreas Herzig   Paul Sabatier University, France
Koen Hindriks   Delft University of Technology, The Netherlands
Shinichi Honiden   National Institute of Informatics, Japan
João Leite   Universidade Nova de Lisboa, Portugal
Yves Lespérance   York University, Canada
Nicolas Maudet   University of Paris-Dauphine, France
John-Jules C. Meyer   Utrecht University, The Netherlands
Peter Novak   Czech Technical University in Prague, Czech Republic
Fabio Patrizi   Imperial College London, UK
Enrico Pontelli   New Mexico State University, USA
David Pym   University of Aberdeen, UK
Alessandro Ricci   University of Bologna, Italy
Michael Rovatsos   The University of Edinburgh, UK
Guillermo Simari   Universidad Nacional del Sur, Argentina
Tran Cao Son   New Mexico State University, USA

Steering Committee

Matteo Baldoni   University of Turin, Italy
Andrea Omicini   University of Bologna-Cesena, Italy
M. Birna van Riemsdijk   Delft University of Technology,
                             The Netherlands
Tran Cao Son   New Mexico State University, USA
Paolo Torroni   University of Bologna, Italy
Pınar Yolum   Bogazici University, Turkey
Michael Winikoff   University of Otago, New Zealand

Additional Reviewers

Michal Cap   Czech Technical University in Prague,
                            Czech Republic

Table of Contents

Invited Papers

Contributed Papers

Position Papers

Handling Change in Normative Specifications

Duangtida Athakravi[1], Domenico Corapi[1], Alessandra Russo[1], Marina De Vos[2],
Julian Padget[2], and Ken Satoh[3]

[1] Department of Computing
Imperial College London
{da407,d.corapi,a.russo}@imperial.ac.uk
[2] Department of Computing
University of Bath
{mdv,jap}@cs.bath.ac.uk
[3] Principles of Informatics Research Division
National Institute of Informatics
ksatoh@nii.ac.jp

Abstract. Normative frameworks provide a means to address the governance of
open systems, offering a mechanism to express responsibilities and permissions
of the individual participants with respect to the entire system without compromising their autonomy. In order to meet requirements careful design is crucial.
Tools that support the design process can be of great benefit. In this paper, we describe and illustrate a methodology for elaborating normative specifications. We
utilise use-cases to capture desirable and undesirable system behaviours, employ
inductive logic programming to construct elaborations, in terms of revisions and
extensions, of an existing (partial) normative specification and provide justifica-
tions as to why certain changes are better than others. The latter can be seen as
a form of impact analysis of the possible elaborations, in terms of critical consequences that would be preserved or rejected by the changes. The main contributions of this paper is a (semi) automated process for controlling the elaboration
of normative specifications and a demonstration of its effectiveness through a
proof-of-concept case study.

1 Introduction

Normative frameworks provide a powerful tool for governing open systems by providing guidelines for the behaviour of the individual components without regimentation [1]. Using a formal declarative language to specify the behaviour of a normative
system gives the system's designer a means to verify the compliance of the system with
respect to desirable behaviours or properties [2, 3]. When errors are detected, manually
identifying what changes to make in order to attain compliance with desired behaviours
is often difficult and error-prone: additional errors may be inadvertently introduced in
the specification as a result of misinterpretations, incompleteness or unexpected impact
of the manual changes. The availability of a systematic and automated framework for
elaborating and handling change in normative specifications would benefit the development process of such systems.

Corapi et al. [4] have shown how Inductive Logic Programming (ILP) can be used to
support the elaboration of partial normative specifications, modelled using Answer Set

M. Baldoni et al. (Eds.): DALT 2012, LNAI 7784, pp. 1–19, 2013.

Programming (ASP). The system designer provides intended behaviours in the form of use-cases. These are defined as specific (partial) scenarios of events and expected outcomes, and are used to validate the correctness of the specifications. Use-cases that fail the validation process are taken as positive examples (or *learning objectives*) for an inductive learning tool, which in turn constructs suggestions for improving the specification to guarantee the satisfiability of the failed use-cases. The learning of such suggestions (or *elaborations*) is performed within a search space defined by a given set of mode declarations that captures the format of possible changes that could be applied to a given formalised normative specification.

Use-cases are inherently partial descriptions of a system behaviour. While their sparse nature is well suited for the non-monotonicity of ASP, the learning process also becomes less restricted, thus causing the problem of *how to choose* among the multiple suggestions for change computed by the learner. For example, the failure to signal a violation when an agent tries to borrow a book from a library could be caused by the specification not correctly capturing any one of the following conditions: (i) the agent has already borrowed the maximum number of items allowed, (ii) the book is for reference only, or (iii) a combination of all these reasons. In general, to address any of these errors and establish the desired violations, there is more than one possible revision for the given specification, with each one having its own impact on the overall behaviour of the system. Thus, the problem with choosing the most appropriate revision is not the revision itself, but the effect of that revision when it is combined with the rest of the system and ensuring that desired system properties are maintained and undesired ones are not introduced.

The approach in [4] lacks criteria for selecting among a (possibly large) number of learned suggestions. This paper addresses this limitation and the general problem of how to choose between alternative changes to make to a (partial) normative specification, by providing an approach for analysing the impact of these changes. We make use of the notion of *relevant literals* as critical elements of the domain that are required to be positive or negative consequences in the intended specification, in order to discriminate between the suggested changes. The solution proposed in this paper provides also a general method for choosing among alternative hypotheses in the wider context of inductive learning.

The remainder of the paper is structured as follows: the next two sections provide background in the form of a summary of the formal and computational model (section 2) and an outline of the revision process (section 3) as described in detail in [4]; the method of test generation and the ranking of results is described in section 4 and then demonstrated in section 5 using the same file-sharing scenario as [4]. The paper ends with a discussion of some related work (section 6) and conclusions (section 7).

2 Normative Framework

Actions that we take in society are regulated by laws and conventions. Similarly, actions taken by agents or entities in open systems may be regulated or governed by the social rules of the system they operate in. It is the task of the normative framework to specify these rules and observe the interactions between the various entities with respect to these rules. The essential idea of normative frameworks is a (consistent) collection of rules whose purpose is to describe *A standard or pattern of social behaviour that is accepted in or expected of a group [OED]*. These rules may be stated in terms of events or actions, but specifically the events that matter for the functioning of the normative framework, based on its current state. In turn, each event/action can influence the normative state.

The control of an agent's or entity's power (effectiveness of an action) and permission to perform certain actions, its obligations and violations of the norms, needs to occur within the context of normative system. For example, raising a hand in class means something different than raising a hand during an auction. This relation between the physical and normative context is described by *Conventional Generation* [5] where an event in the physical world may correspond to an *normative event*. An example is clicking the "buy" button on Amazon, which *counts as* paying for the good.

2.1 The Formal Model

In this paper we use the model as set out in [2] based on the concept of *exogenous events* within the physical world and *normative states*, those within the framework's context. Events change the state of the normative system by acting on *normative fluents*, properties of the system that can be true at certain points in time.

The essential elements of the normative framework (summarised in Fig. 1(a)) are events ($\mathcal{E}$), which bring about changes in state, and fluents ($\mathcal{F}$), which characterise the state at a given instant. The function of the framework is to define the interplay between these concepts over time, in order to capture the evolution of a particular institution through the interaction of its participants. The model has two kinds of events: normative ($\mathcal{E}_{norm}$), that are the events defined by the framework, and exogenous ($\mathcal{E}_{ex}$), some of whose occurrence may trigger normative events in a direct reflection of "counts-as" [6], while the rest may have no relevance for a given framework. Normative events are further partitioned into normative actions ($\mathcal{E}_{act}$) that denote changes in normative state and violation events ($\mathcal{E}_{viol}$), that signal the occurrence of violations. Violations may arise either from explicit generation, (i.e. from the occurrence of a non-permitted event), or from the non-fulfilment of an obligation. The model also has two kinds of fluents: *normative fluents* that denote normative properties of the state such as *permissions* ($\mathcal{P}$), *powers* ($\mathcal{W}$) and obligations ($\mathcal{O}$), and *domain fluents* ($\mathcal{D}$) that correspond to properties specific to a particular normative framework.

A normative state is represented by the fluents that hold true in that state. Fluents that are not present are held to be false. Conditions on a state ($\mathcal{X}$) are expressed by a set of fluents that should be true or false. The normative framework is initialised with the state $\mathcal{I}$.

Changes in the normative state are specified by two relations: (i) the generation relation ($\mathcal{G}$), which implements counts-as by specifying how the occurrence of one (exogenous or normative) event generates another (normative) event, subject to the empowerment of the actor and the conditions on the state, and (ii) the consequence relation ($\mathcal{C}$), which specifies the initiation and termination of fluents, given a certain state condition and event.

The semantics of a normative framework is defined over a sequence, called a *trace*, of exogenous events. Starting from the initial state, each exogenous event is responsible

$\mathcal{N} = \langle \mathcal{E}, \mathcal{F}, \mathcal{C}, \mathcal{G}, \mathcal{I} \rangle$, where

1. $\mathcal{F} = \mathcal{W} \cup \mathcal{P} \cup \mathcal{O} \cup \mathcal{D}$
2. $\mathcal{G} : \mathcal{X} \times \mathcal{E} \to 2^{\mathcal{E}_{norm}}$
3. $\mathcal{C} : \mathcal{X} \times \mathcal{E} \to 2^{\mathcal{F}} \times 2^{\mathcal{F}}$

   where

   $C(X, e) =$
   $(\mathcal{C}^{\uparrow}(\phi, e), \mathcal{C}^{\downarrow}(\phi, e))$ where
   (i) $\mathcal{C}^{\uparrow}(\phi, e)$ initiates
       fluents
   (ii) $\mathcal{C}^{\downarrow}(\phi, e)$ terminates
        fluents

4. $\mathcal{E} = \mathcal{E}_{ex} \cup \mathcal{E}_{norm}$
   with $\mathcal{E}_{norm} = \mathcal{E}_{act} \cup \mathcal{E}_{viol}$
5. $\mathcal{I}$, initial instiutional state
6. State Formula: $\mathcal{X} = 2^{\mathcal{F} \cup \neg \mathcal{F}}$

$$p \in \mathcal{F} \Leftrightarrow \texttt{ifluent(p)}. \qquad (1)$$
$$e \in \mathcal{E} \Leftrightarrow \texttt{event(e)}. \qquad (2)$$
$$e \in \mathcal{E}_{ex} \Leftrightarrow \texttt{evtype(e, obs)}. \qquad (3)$$
$$e \in \mathcal{E}_{act} \Leftrightarrow \texttt{evtype(e, act)}. \qquad (4)$$
$$e \in \mathcal{E}_{viol} \Leftrightarrow \texttt{evtype(e, viol)}. \qquad (5)$$
$$\mathcal{C}^{\uparrow}(\phi, e) = P \Leftrightarrow \forall p \in P \ \texttt{initiated(p, T)} : - \qquad (6)$$
$$\texttt{occurred(e, I)}, EX(\phi, T). \qquad (7)$$
$$\mathcal{C}^{\downarrow}(\phi, e) = P \Leftrightarrow \forall p \in P \ \texttt{terminated(p, T)} : - \qquad (8)$$
$$\texttt{occurred(e, T)}, EX(\phi, T). \qquad (9)$$
$$\mathcal{G}(\phi, e) = E \Leftrightarrow \forall g \in E, \texttt{occurred(g, T)} : -$$
$$\texttt{occurred(e, T)},$$
$$\texttt{holdsat(pow(e), T)}, EX(\phi, T).$$
$$\qquad (10)$$
$$p \in \mathcal{I} \Leftrightarrow \texttt{holdsat(p, i00)}. \qquad (11)$$

(a)   (b)

Fig. 1. (a) Formal specification of the normative framework and (b) translation of normative framework-specific rules into $AnsProlog$

for a state change, through the eventual initiation and termination of fluents. This is achieved by a three-step process: (i) the transitive closure of $\mathcal{G}$ with respect to a given exogenous event determines all the generated (normative) events, (ii) to this, all violations of non-permitted events and non-fulfilled obligations are added, giving the set of all events whose consequences determine the new state, (iii) the application of $\mathcal{C}$ to this set of events identifies all fluents that are initiated and terminated with respect to the current state, so determining the next state. For each trace, the normative framework can determine a sequence of states that constitutes the model of the framework for that trace. This process is realised as a computational process using answer set programming.

2.2 Computational Model

The formal model described above is translated into an equivalent computational model using answer set programming (ASP) [7] with $AnsProlog$ as the implementation language[1]. $AnsProlog$ is a knowledge representation language that allows the programmer to describe a problem and the requirements for solutions declaratively, rather than specifying an algorithm to find the solutions to the problem. The mapping follows the naming convention used in the Event Calculus [8] and Action languages [9].

The basic components of the language are atoms, elements that can be assigned a truth value. An atom can be negated using *negation as failure* or classical negation. *Literals* are atoms a or classically negated atoms $-a$. Extended literals are literals 1 or negated literals not 1. The latter is true if there is no evidence supporting the truth of a. Atoms and (extended) literals are used to create rules of the general form: $a : -b_1, ..., b_m, \text{not } c_1, ..., \text{not } c_n$, where a, b_i and c_j are literals. Intuitively, this

---

[1] In this paper we use the SMODELS syntax for writing $AnsProlog$ programs.

means *if all literals* b_i *are known/true and no literal* c_j *is known/true, then* a *must be known/true*. a is called the head and $b_1, ..., b_m$, not $c_1, ..., $ not c_n the body of the rule. Rules with an empty body are called *facts*. Rules with an empty head are called *constraints*, indicating that no solution should be able to satisfy the body. A *(normal) program (or theory)* is a conjunction of rules and is also denoted by a set of rules. The semantics of *AnsProlog* is defined in terms of *answer sets*, that is, assignments of true and false to all atoms in the program that satisfy the rules in a minimal and consistent fashion. A program may have zero or more answer sets, each corresponding to a solution. They are computed by a program called an *answer set solver*. For this paper the solver we used was ICLINGO [10].

The mapping of a normative framework consists of two parts: an independent *base component* and the *framework-specific component*. The independent component deals with inertia of the fluents, the generation of violation events of non-permitted actions and of (un)fulfilled obligations.

The mapping uses the following atoms:

- ifluent(p) to identify fluents,
- evtype(e, t) to describe the type of an event,
- event(e) to denote the events,
- instant(i) for time instances,
- final(i) for the last time instance,
- next$(i1, i2)$ to establish time ordering,
- occurred(e, i) to indicate that the (normative) event happened at time i,
- observed(e, i) that the (exogenous) event was observed at time i,
- holdsat(p, i) to state that the normative fluent p holds at i, and finally
- initiated(p, i) and terminated(p, i) for fluents that are initiated and terminated at i.

Given that exogenous events are always empowered while normative events are not, the mapping must keep type information for the events, hence the evtype(e, t) atoms. Similarly, violation events are always permitted and empowered. However, all fluents, irrespective of type, are treated the same way so the mapping does not differentiate between them.

Figure 1(b) provides the framework-specific translation mechanism. An expression ϕ in the framework is translated into *AnsProlog* rule bodies as conjunction of literals, using negation as failure for negated expressions, denoted as $EX(\phi, T)$. The translation of the formal model is augmented with a trace program that specifies (i) the length of traces that the designer is interested in, and (ii) the property that each, except the final, time instant is associated with exactly one exogenous event (iii) specifics of the desired trace(s), for example length, or the occurrence of a specific event.

3 Revising Normative Rules

In this section we briefly summarise the approach described in [4] for computing elaborations of normative specifications through use-cases by means of non-monotonic inductive logic programming. Our proposed technique for analysing the impact that possible elaborations could have on a normative specification extends this approach with a formal mechanism for narrowing down the number of suggested elaborations based on a notion of *relevant literals*.

The development of a normative specification is captured in [4] by an iterative process that supports automated synthesis of new rules and revisions of existing one from given use-cases. The latter represent instances of executions that implicitly capture the desired behaviour of the system. They are defined as tuples $\langle T, O \rangle$ where T (trace) specifies a (partial) sequence of exogenous events (observed(e, t)), and O (output) describes the expected output as a set of holdsat and occurred literals that should appear in the normative state. The traces do not have to be complete (i.e. include an event for each time instance) and the expected output may contain positive as well as negative literals and does not have to be exhaustive. An existing (partial) normative specification N is validated against a use-case $\langle T, O \rangle$, specified by the designer, by using T as a trace program for N and adding a constraint that no answer set should be accepted that does not satisfy O. If no answer set is computed then the normative specification does not comply with the use-case and a learning step is performed to compute new rules and/or revisions of existing rules that guarantee the satisfiability of the use-case. This validity check can be extended to a set of use-cases U from which we derive the conjunction of all the traces T_U and outputs O_U (making sure that there is no conflict in the time points being used).

The learning step is in essence a Theory Revision [11] task, defined in terms of a non-monotonic inductive logic programming [12], and implemented in answer set programming using the learning system ASPAL [13], [14].

Within the context of our computational model of normative systems, this task is expressed as a tuple $\langle O_U, N_B \cup T_U, N_T, M \rangle$, where:

1. O_U is the set of expected outputs,
2. N_B is the part of the normative specification that is not subject to revisions (i.e. "static" background knowledge) augmented with the traces of the use-cases,
3. N_T is the part of the normative system that is subject to modification, and
4. M is the set of mode declarations that establish how rules in the final solution shall be structured. A mode declaration can be of the form $modeh(s)$ or $modeb(s)$, where s is the schema of the predicate that can be used in the head or body of a rule respectively.

These last define the literals that can appear in the head and in the body of a well-formed revision. The choice of the M is therefore crucial. Larger M with more mode declarations ensures higher coverage of the specification but increase the computation time. Conversely, smaller mode declarations improve performance but may result in partial or incorrectly formed solutions.

In [4] the mode declaration M is specified to allow the synthesis of new normative rules as well as revision of existing rules. To compute the first type of solutions, M allows predicates occurred, initiated and terminated to appear in the head of the learned rules and predicates holdsat and occurred to appear in the body of the learned rules. To compute revisions on existing rules the mode declaration M makes use of special predicates: exception(p, $\bar{v}$), where p is a reified term for a rule existing in the specification and $\bar{v}$ the list of variables in the rule that are involved in the change. This special predicate can appear in the head of a learned rule whose body gives the new literals that need to be added to the existing rule p with specific variables $\bar{v}$. Another special predicate is del(i, j), where i is the index of an existing rule and j the number of the literal in the body of the existing rule that needs to be removed. This is learned as a ground fact. By means of these two special predicates it is possible to learn rules that define what literals to add to and what literals to remove from existing rules of the normative specification N_T. The reader may refer to [4] for further details.

4   Handling Change

The approach proposed by [4] provides an automated way for computing suggestions of possible elaborations of a given normative specification. The designer must then choose the most appropriate revision from a (possibly large) set of alternative changes. In real applications this is impractical, as the number of suggested changes can be too large to work with. Informally, possible alternative revisions can be any combinations of addition of new literals and/or deletion of existing literals in any of the existing rules of the specification. Automated criteria for selecting solutions from the suggestions provided by the learning are therefore essential.

In the remainder of this paper, we show that analysing the impact of suggested changes, in terms of relevant literals that would be preserved or discarded, can be an effective criteria for revision selection. Considering all the consequences that each possible revision would give is clearly not a practical solution. What is needed is a mechanism for identifying key consequences that would allow to reject some suggested changes whilst preserving others. We propose that test generation can provide such a mechanism and show how the process can carried out in answer set programming to fit with both the inductive learner and the computational model of the normative frameworks.

4.1   Test Generation

A test normally defines the set of outcomes that have to be observed given certain *achievable information* in order to confirm or refute an hypothesis. Using the definitions from [15], a test can formally be defined as a pair (A, l) where A is a conjunction of achievable literals, the initial condition specified by the tester, and l is an observable, the outcome (l or $\neg l$) decided by the tester. Using this structure, we can define confirmation and refutation tests with respect to given background knowledge Σ.

Definition 1. *The outcome a of a test is said to* confirm *a hypothesis H iff $\Sigma \wedge A \wedge H$ is satisfiable and $\Sigma \wedge A \vDash H \rightarrow a$. The outcome a of a test is said to* refute *a hypothesis H iff $\Sigma \wedge A \wedge H$ is satisfiable and $\Sigma \wedge A \vDash H \rightarrow \neg a$.*

Hence, a refutation test has the power to eliminate the hypothesis when its outcome is not included in the consequence of $\Sigma \wedge A$ where H is true. Note that in this paper the symbol $\vDash$ is associated with the *skeptical stable model* semantics[2] in conformity with the underlying ASP framework.

---

[2] $P \vDash a$ if a is true in every answer set of P.

Using the notion of relevant test in [15], we define *relevant literals* as follows.

Definition 2. *(Relevant Literal) Let $\langle T, O \rangle$ be a use-case consisting of a partial trace T and desired outcome O, Σ a given (partial) normative specification, and HYP the set of hypotheses representing the suggested revisions of Σ that satisfy $\langle T, O \rangle$. A literal l is* relevant *if:*

1. *$\Sigma \wedge T \wedge O \wedge H_i$ is satisfiable, for all $H_i \in HYP$*
2. *$\Sigma \wedge T \wedge O \nvDash \bigvee_{H_i \in HYP} \neg H_i$*
3. *$T \wedge O \wedge l$ is an abductive explanation for $\bigvee_{H_i \in HYP} \neg H_i$*
4. *$T \wedge O \wedge l$ is not an abductive explanation for $\neg H_i$, for all $H_i \in HYP$*

Conditions 1 and 2 above state, respectively, that each suggested revision (H_i) satisfies the given use-case and is consistent with the normative specification and the use-case. Both these conditions are guaranteed by the correctness of the learning process [13]. Conditions 3 and 4 above ensure that some but not all suggested revisions are refuted by the relevant literal l. Thus should l be observed, at least one hypothesis may be rejected.

The automated generation of tests for specific objectives (e.g. eliminate some hypothesis H) can be formulated [15] in terms of an abductive problem [16] so that $\Sigma \cup (A, l) \vDash \neg H$. Informally, given an abductive problem $\langle B, Ab, G \rangle$, where B is a background knowledge, G is a goal, and Ab a set of abducibles, a conjunction of literals E in the language Ab, is an *abductive explanation* for G, with respect to B if and only if $B \wedge E$ is satisfiable and $B \wedge E \vDash G$.

4.2   The Approach

Our approach extends the work of [4] with an iterative process for computing relevant literals and discarding learned revisions that are refuted by the relevant literals. As illustrated in Fig. 2, once possible changes are learned, this iterative process is activated. At each iteration, the (remaining) learned revisions are "combined" with the existing normative specification as integrity constraints in order to capture conditions 3 and 4 above and ensure that the abduced relevant literals have the power to eliminate some suggested revisions. Traces of the given use-cases are included as achievable literals to guarantee that the abduced relevant literals conform with the use-cases. The abduced relevant literals are ranked according to how much information can be gained from them. The most highly ranked literal is then presented to the designer, who can then specify the truth value for the literal. Based on the designer's answer, suggested revisions that are refuted by the relevant literal are discarded. The process is repeated: new relevant literals and their scores are computed with respect to the remaining suggested revisions. This process is repeated until no further relevant literals can be identified. This is the inner loop of the process depicted in Fig. 2. The remaining learned revisions are then returned to the designer. If only one suggested revision remains, this is used to change the specification automatically and the revised normative description is returned.

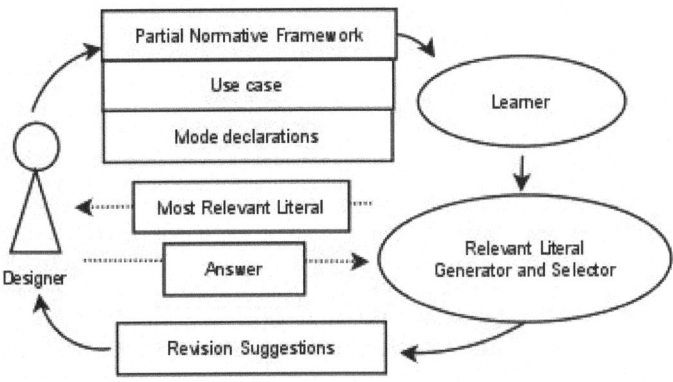

Fig. 2. Handling changes in normative specifications

Suggested Revisions as Hypotheses. Changes to our normative specifications can be one of three different varieties: addition of new rules, deletion of an existing rule, and addition or deletion of a body literal in an existing rule. These modifications correspond to the following facts in each solution:

1. $r \leftarrow c_1, \ldots, c_n$: A new rule is added to the revised specification.
2. $del(i, j)$: The condition j of rule r_i in N_T is deleted. If a rule has all of its condition deleted, then it is removed from the revised specification.
3. $xt(i, r_i) \leftarrow c_1, \ldots, c_n$: The condition of rule r_i in N_T is extended with the conditions $c_1, \ldots, c_n$. Should a solution contain two of such facts for extending the same rule, then the revised specification contains two different versions of the extended rule.

To abduce relevant literals, each modification in a learned solution is (automatically) combined with the static part of the background knowledge N_B. For each revisable rule r_i in solution S_k the following clause is added:

1. If r_i is deleted by S_k, then clauses corresponding to r_i are not added to N_B
2. $\neg \text{hyp}_k :- \textbf{not } \textbf{r}_i, c_1, \ldots, c_n, c_{n+1}, \ldots, c_m$
   If both $xt(i, r_i) \leftarrow c_1, \ldots, c_n$ and $del(i, j)$ facts are in S_k and $c_{n+1}, \ldots, c_m$ are the conditions of rule r_i from N_T that are not deleted by S_k
3. $\neg \text{hyp}_k :- \textbf{not } \textbf{r}_i, c_1, \ldots, c_m$
   If only $del(i, j)$ is in S_k, and $c_1, \ldots, c_m$ are conditions of rule r_i from N_T that are not deleted by S_k
4. $\neg \text{hyp}_k :- \textbf{not } \textbf{r}_i, c_1, \ldots, c_n, c_{n+1}, \ldots, c_m$
   If only $xt(i, r_i) \leftarrow c_1, \ldots, c_n$ is in S_k, and $c_{n+1}, \ldots, c_m$ are the conditions of r_i from N_T
5. $\neg \text{hyp}_k :- \textbf{not } \textbf{r}_i, c_1, \ldots, c_m$
   If S_k does not change r_i, and $c_1, \ldots, c_m$ are the conditions of r_i from N_T

For example, if we have the following N_T:

terminated(perm(shoot(A1, A2)), Time) : −initiated(peace, Time).
terminated(perm(shoot(A1, A2)), Time) : −holdsat(peace, Time).

...and three alternative suggested revisions:

1. Add: initiated(perm(shoot(A1, A2)), Time) : −initiated(war, Time). The following rules are added to the normative specification, with head predicate ¬hyp(1):

> ¬hyp(1) : − **not** initiated(perm(shoot(A1, A2)), Time),
>   initiated(war, Time).
> ¬hyp(1) : − **not** terminated(perm(shoot(A1, A2)), Time),
>   initiated(peace, Time).
> ¬hyp(1) : − **not** terminated(perm(shoot(A1, A2)), Time),
>   holdsat(peace, Time).

The first of the above rules represents the new rule added by the suggestion, while the latter two correspond to changes made by alternative revision suggestions but left unchanged by the current suggestion.

2. Change: terminated(perm(shoot(A1, A2)), Time) : −initiated(peace, Time). to: terminated(perm(shoot(A1, A2)), Time) : −terminated(war, Time). The following rules are added:

> ¬hyp(2) : − **not** terminated(perm(shoot(A1, A2)), Time),
>   terminated(war, Time).
> ¬hyp(2) : − **not** terminated(perm(shoot(A1, A2)), Time),
>   holdsat(peace, Time).

Similarly, the revised rule in the second suggestion is captured by the first rule above with head predicate ¬hyp(2), while the second of these represents the rule deleted by the third suggestion.

3. Remove: terminated(perm(shoot(A1, A2)), Time) : −holdsat(peace, Time). This results in the following rules been added to the normative specification:

> ¬hyp(3) : − **not** terminated(perm(shoot(A1, A2)), Time),
>   initiated(peace, Time).

The above rule, with head predicate ¬hyp(3), corresponds to the rule revised by the second revision suggestion.

Abducing Relevant Literals. Let $\langle T, O \rangle$ be the use-case that was used to learn the set R of suggested revisions, N_B be the part of the normative specification that R leaves unchanged, N_R the rules in the specification that one or more suggestions in R revise, $C_H/2$ be the function that transform rules by suggested revisions as described in section 4.2, and let *HYP* be the set of hypotheses in $C_H(N_R, R)$. The relevant literals are solutions of the abductive task $\langle B, Ab, G \rangle$ where:

$$B = N_B \cup T \cup C_H(N_R, R)$$
$$G = O \cup \neg(\bigwedge_{H_i \in HYP} \neg H_i) \cup \neg(\bigwedge_{H_i \in HYP} H_i)$$

and Ab is the set of ground instances of (possible) outcomes. The relevant literals is a set $E \subseteq Ab$ such that $B \cup E \vDash G$.

The above abductive task is computed using ASP and the solutions generated are answer sets containing relevant literals. To know the exact impact each relevant literal has on the hypothesis space, it is important to match it to the hypotheses it refutes. Algorithm 1 is used to extract relevant literals that refute a given suggested change (i.e. learned hypothesis) from the answer sets, using a series of set comparisons. The algorithm finds the differences between an answer set with a falsified hypothesis and another where it is not, then finds the smallest subsets of all these differences. The output of the algorithm are the smallest sets of literals that can refute the hypothesis. Note that while set intersection could potentially be used to extract such relevant literals, it would disregard the cases where a disjunction of literals $l_1 \vee l_2$ can falsify a hypothesis.

Scoring Relevant Literals. Ideally we want to be able to dismiss as many suggested revisions as possible. The number of hypotheses that could be discarded depends on the relevant literal's truth value: e.g. while we may be able to reject nearly all hypotheses if the literal is true, we may not be able to reject any should it be false. We use the number of minimum hypotheses that a relevant literal may reject as the score for comparing the literal against other relevant literals, using a fractional score when the literal can only falsify a hypothesis in conjunction with others. Thus, for each relevant literal l that rejects n suggested revisions when it is true, and m suggested revisions when it is false, $minimum(n, m)$ is the score for l. The most relevant literals are those with the highest value of these scores, and could be further ranked according to the maximum number of hypotheses each one falsifies.

5   Case Study

The case study is taken from [4]. The scenario describes a system of file sharing agents where:

> Agents are initialized to have ownership of a unique block of digital data, which all together comprise a digital object – a file of some kind. After the initial download of the unique block, an agent must share a copy of a block of data it possesses before acquiring the right to download a copy of a block from another agent. Violations and misuses are generated when an agent requests a download without having shared a copy of a block after its previous download, and a misuse terminates its empowerment to download blocks. However, if an agent has *VIP* status, it can download blocks without any restriction.

Algorithm 1. Extracting relevant literals of a given hypothesis

Input: answer sets ANS, hypothesis predicate h, and the set of hypothesis predicates HYP
Output: a set
REV of relevant literals that refute h

1: {Find the difference between S_i and answer sets that do not have relevant literals of h}
2: $DIFF = \emptyset$
3:
4: **for all** $S_i \in ANS$ **do**
5:     **if** $\neg h \in S_i$ **then**
6:         **for all** $S_j \in ANS$ **do**
7:             **if** $\neg h \notin S_j$ **then**
8:                 $NREV = S_j \cup HYP \cup \{\neg h : HYP\}$
9:                 $DIFF = DIFF \cup \{S_i - NREV\}$
10:            **end if**
11:        **end for**
12:    **end if**
13: **end for**
14:
15: {Find the smallest subsets from the sets in $DIFF$}
16: $REV = \emptyset$
17:
18: **for all** $D \in DIFF$ **do**
19:     $REV = REV - \{R : REV | R \supset D\}$
20:     **if** $D \notin REV$ and $\nexists R : REV(R \subset D)$ **then**
21:         $REV = REV \cup \{D\}$
22:     **end if**
23: **end for**
24:
25: **return** REV

Our existing normative specification includes the six revisable rules in Fig.3(a), that is N_T. The learner is supplied with the use-case comprising T (Fig.3(b)) and O (Fig.3(c)). This use-case shows how a violation is raised when *alice* downloads data consecutively without sharing any data in between. On the other hand, no violations are raised when *charlie* downloads data without sharing, as *charlie* is a VIP. For the system specification to comply with the use-case, the fourth and fifth rule need to be revised, so that VIP agent's empowerment will not be terminated after a download, and a syntactic error in the fifth rule corrected, where the first Y should be X in occurred(download(Y,Y,B),I).

For this particular use-case and six revisable rules, with a maximum of seven rules per solution the learner outputs 41 ways in which the rules could be revised. Due to the space limitations, we look only at 4 of the proposed 41 (see Fig. 4).

```
% Rule 1
initiated(hasblock(X,B),I) :-
    occurred(myDownload(X,B),I).
% Rule 2
initiated(perm(myDownload(X,B)),
    I) :-
    occurred(myShare(X),I).
% Rule 3
terminated(pow(
    extendedfilesharing,
    myDownload(X,B)),I) :-
    occurred(misuse(X),I).
% Rule 4
terminated(perm(
    myDownload(X,B2)),I) :-
    occurred(myDownload(X,B),I).
% Rule 5
occurred(myDownload(X,B),I) :-
    occurred(download(Y,Y,B),I),
    holdsat(hasblock(Y,B),I).
% Rule 6
occurred(myShare(X),I) :-
    occurred(download(Y,X,B),I),
    holdsat(hasblock(X,B),I).
```

(a)

$$T = \left\{ \begin{array}{l} \texttt{observed(start,i00)} \\ \texttt{observed(download(alice,bob,x3),} \\ \qquad \texttt{i01)} \\ \texttt{observed(download(charlie,bob,x3)} \\ \qquad \texttt{,i02)} \\ \texttt{observed(download(bob,alice,x1),} \\ \qquad \texttt{i03)} \\ \texttt{observed(download(charlie,alice,} \\ \qquad \texttt{x1),i04)} \\ \texttt{observed(download(alice,charlie,} \\ \qquad \texttt{x5),i05)} \\ \texttt{observed(download(alice,bob,x4),} \\ \qquad \texttt{i06)} \end{array} \right\}$$

(b)

$$O = \left\{ \begin{array}{l} \textbf{not } \texttt{viol(myDownload(alice,x3),} \\ \qquad \texttt{i01)} \\ \textbf{not } \texttt{viol(myDownload(charlie,x3),} \\ \qquad \texttt{i02)} \\ \textbf{not } \texttt{viol(myDownload(bob,x1),i03)} \\ \textbf{not } \texttt{viol(myDownload(charlie,x1),} \\ \qquad \texttt{i04)} \\ \textbf{not } \texttt{viol(myDownload(alice,x5),} \\ \qquad \texttt{i05)} \\ \texttt{viol(myDownload(alice,x4),i06)} \\ \texttt{occurred(misuse(alice), i06)} \end{array} \right\}$$

$$\bigcup$$

$$\left\{ \begin{array}{l} \textbf{not } \texttt{occurred(misuse(a), i)} \\ \mid a \in Agents, i \in Instances, i \neq i06 \end{array} \right\}$$

(c)

Fig. 3. Rules for revision (a), with use-case trace (b) and outputs (c)

5.1 Generating Relevant Literals

To form the background knowledge for the abductive task, rule 4 and rule 5 are removed from the current specification, and their suggested revisions included in the specifications following the representation described in section 4.2. Fig. 5 contains an extract from the ASP encoding of our abductive task for computing relevant literals regarding revisions for rule 4 and rule 5.

By adding the trace, as well as these hypotheses to the framework, the program can be used as the background data for the abduction task. The head of the suggested new and revised rules are used as abducible predicate symbols, while their revised conditions are used as constraints for these abducibles to avoid an explosion in the number of answer sets. The following integrity constraints capture conditions 2 and 4 of our test characterisation given in section 4.2

```
:- hyp(1), hyp(2), hyp(3), hyp(4).
:- -hyp(1), -hyp(2), -hyp(3), -hyp(4).
```

```
%---Suggestion 1
% New rule
occurred(misuse(A),I) :- occurred(viol(myDownload(A,C)),I).
% Revise rule 4
terminated(perm(myDownload(X,B2)),I) :- occurred(myDownload(X,B),I), not isVIP(X).
% Revise rule 5
occurred(myDownload(X,B),I) :-
   holdsat(hasblck(Y,B),I), occurred(download(X,Y,B),I).

%---Suggestion 2
% New rule
occurred(misuse(A),I) :- occurred(viol(myDownload(A,C)),I).
% Revise rule 4
terminated(perm(myDownload(X,B2)),I) :- occurred(myDownload(X,B),I), not isVIP(X).
% Revise rule 5
occurred(myDownload(X,B),I) :-
   holdsat(hasblck(Y,B),I), occurred(download(X,Y,B),I).
occurred(myDownload(X,B),I) :-
   holdsat(hasblck(Y,B),I), occurred(viol(myDownload(Y,B2)),I).

%---Suggestion 3
% New rule
occurred(misuse(A),I) :- occurred(viol(myDownload(A,C)),I).
% Revise rule 4
terminated(perm(myDownload(X,B2)),I) :- occurred(myDownload(X,B),I), not isVIP(X).
% Revise rule 5
occurred(myDownload(X,B),I) :- occurred(download(X,Y,B),I).

%---Suggestion 4
% New rule
occurred(misuse(A),I) :- occurred(viol(myDownload(A,C)),I).
% Revise rule 4
terminated(perm(myDownload(X,B2)),I) :- occurred(myDownload(X,B),I), not isVIP(X).
% Revise rule 5
occurred(myDownload(X,B),I) :-
   holdsat(hasblck(Y,B),I), occurred(download(X,Y,B),I).
occurred(myDownload(X,B),I) :-
   holdsat(hasblck(Y,B),I), occurred(viol(myDownload(X,B2)),I).
```

Fig. 4. 4 selected revision suggestions from the 41 proposed

However, since we use Algorithm 1 to identify the relevant literals, as explained in section 4.2 the constraint is relaxed to:

```
:- -hyp(1), -hyp(2), -hyp(3), -hyp(4).
```

The constraint above is still needed, as the algorithm searches for answer sets which includes -hyp/1 instances to extract relevant literals from. Thus, while the answer sets without any refuted hypothesis are excluded from the algorithm's output, answer sets with all hypotheses refuted will still be included.

Applying Algorithm 1 to the answer sets generated by the abductive task, the following relevant literals are computed:

Literals that can falsify both $hyp(2)$ and $hyp(4)$:

$$\left\{ \begin{array}{l} \neg \; \texttt{occurred(viol(myDownload(alice,x1)),i06),} \\ \neg \; \texttt{occurred(viol(myDownload(alice,x2)),i06),} \\ \neg \; \texttt{occurred(viol(myDownload(alice,x3)),i06),} \\ \neg \; \texttt{occurred(viol(myDownload(alice,x5)),i06),} \\ \neg \; \texttt{occurred(viol(myDownload(bob,x1)),i06),} \\ \neg \; \texttt{occurred(viol(myDownload(bob,x2)),i06),} \\ \neg \; \texttt{occurred(viol(myDownload(bob,x3)),i06),} \\ \neg \; \texttt{occurred(viol(myDownload(bob,x4)),i06),} \\ \neg \; \texttt{occurred(viol(myDownload(bob,x5)),i06)} \end{array} \right.$$

```
% New Rule
-hyp(H) :- not occurred(misuse(A),I), occurred(viol(myDownload(A,C)),I), hyp_id(H)
            .

% Rule 4
-hyp(H) :- not terminated(perm(myDownload(X,B2)),I), occurred(myDownload(X,B),I),
            not isVIP(X), hyp_id(H).

%---Suggestion 1
% Rule 5
-hyp(1) :- not occurred(myDownload(X,B),I), occurred(download(X,Y,B),I),
            holdsat(hasblck(Y,B),I).

%---Suggestion 2
% Rule 5
-hyp(2) :- not occurred(myDownload(X,B),I), occurred(download(X,Y,B),I),
            holdsat(hasblck(Y,B),I).
-hyp(2) :- not occurred(myDownload(X,B),I), occurred(viol(myDownload(Y,B2)),I),
            holdsat(hasblck(Y,B),I).

%---Suggestion 3
% Rule 5
-hyp(3) :- not occurred(myDownload(X,B),I), occurred(download(X,Y,B),I).

%---Suggestion 4
% Rule 5
-hyp(4) :- not occurred(myDownload(X,B),I), occurred(download(X,Y,B),I),
            holdsat(hasblck(Y,B),I).
-hyp(4) :- not occurred(myDownload(X,B),I), occurred(viol(myDownload(X,B2)),I),
            holdsat(hasblck(Y,B),I).
```

Fig. 5. Computing relevant literals

Literals that
can falsify
only $hyp(4)$:

```
occurred(misuse(bob),i06) ∧ occurred(viol(myDownload(bob,x1)),i06)
occurred(misuse(bob),i06) ∧ occurred(viol(myDownload(bob,x2)),i06)
occurred(misuse(bob),i06) ∧ occurred(viol(myDownload(bob,x3)),i06)
occurred(misuse(bob),i06) ∧ occurred(viol(myDownload(bob,x5)),i06)
```

However, $hyp(1)$ and $hyp(3)$ cannot be falsified as both revisions produce the same consequences using the current use-case.

5.2   Scoring the Relevant Literals

When scoring the literals such as `occurred(misuse(bob),i06)`, where the literal alone cannot refute a hypothesis, a fractional score is given corresponding to how many other literals are needed to reject the hypothesis. The scores for each relevant literal are given in Table 1, with the following four literals having highest score:

```
occurred(viol(myDownload(bob,x1)),i06)
occurred(viol(myDownload(bob,x2)),i06)
occurred(viol(myDownload(bob,x3)),i06)
occurred(viol(myDownload(bob,x4)),i06)
occurred(viol(myDownload(bob,x5)),i06)
```

Any of these literals can be returned to the designer as the most relevant. Should the designer consider the returned literal to be false, then both the second and fourth suggested revisions could be discarded. However, if the literal is considered to be true, the dependent literal `occurred(misuse(bob),i06)` is given to the designer. This is because the two literals are dependent as shown by the lists of relevant literals for each hypothesis given above.

Table 1. Scoring of relevant literals

Relevant literal	Truth value	
	True	False
occurred(viol(myDownload(alice,x1)),i06)	0.0	2.0
occurred(viol(myDownload(alice,x2)),i06)	0.0	2.0
occurred(viol(myDownload(alice,x3)),i06)	0.0	2.0
occurred(viol(myDownload(alice,x5)),i06)	0.0	2.0
occurred(viol(myDownload(bob,x1)),i06)	0.5	2.0
occurred(viol(myDownload(bob,x2)),i06)	0.5	2.0
occurred(viol(myDownload(bob,x3)),i06)	0.5	2.0
occurred(viol(myDownload(bob,x4)),i06)	0.5	2.0
occurred(viol(myDownload(bob,x5)),i06)	0.5	2.0
occurred(misuse(bob),i06)	0.0	0.5

6   Related Work

The literature on norm change and norm revision is quite diverse, but also quite thinly spread across a range of disciplines. Many normative frameworks include appeal to extrinsic normative frameworks, such as negotiation, argumentation, voting, or even fiat (dictatorship) to mediate norm change. These are not the concern of this paper. Our focus is on the specific nature of the revision: *what* needs to change, rather than *how* it shall be brought about. In human societies, the identification of what may be informal, or the outcome of an extensive evaluative study, along with proposals for which rules to revoke, which rules to add and an assessment of the consequences. This reflects work in the philosophy of law, the logic of norms, or the logic of belief change [17], where the drive has been the discovery of norm conflicts and their subsequent revision in the framework of deontic logic. However, this only explores the principle of norm conflict and norm inconsistency (concluding that they are in fact the same), and that it may be resolved by a process of norm revision in which the norm set is reduced and subsequently extended (consistently). Further theoretical studies can be found in [18–20]

Artikis [21] presents a formalization of a (run-time) process for changing the rules governing a protocol, central to which are the notions of stratification and degrees of freedom to determine a metric for the magnitude and hence feasibility of the change from the current rules to the new rules. However, fundamental to this scheme is that the state-space of alternatives be known *a priori*, so it is essentially limited to known-knowns, rather than the exploration of all possibilities to remedy shortcomings.

Campos et al. [22] propose a mechanism for the adaptation of a normative framework – which they call an electronic institution (EI) – in which the EI is goal-driven and utilizes a feedback mechanism to compare observations with expected goals in order to self-reconfigure using transition functions. The expected goals are quantitative constraints on values of observed properties, while actual performance is captured in an objective function comprising a weighted aggregation of observed properties. As with Artikis, above, the scope for adaptation is limited in that responses are pre-determined in the specification and may only affect parameters of norms.

Tinnemeier et al. [23] make clear that normative concepts should be used to affect which entities have the permission and the power to effect norm change, they also point out that norm-reasoning is typically beyond the competence of typical agency. In consequence of the latter, they choose for the normative framework to provide suitable norm-change operators for the agents to use that do not require detailed norm knowledge. While the scope of changes is more extensive than either Artikis or Campos, the rules for norm scheme change (sic) appear to depend both on domain knowledge and the foresight of the designer.

Thus, although there is a select literature which addresses norm change in various ways, it either suffers from an absence of a computational model, or has very restricted solution space which depends on prediction of what changes may be needed. In contrast, we provide technical support for a formal model of norm revision, as presented here and in our earlier paper [4], which can adapt the normative framework arbitrarily, to meet evolving requirements, expressed through goals, and is, we believe, entirely novel.

7 Conclusions

In this paper, we have tackled the problem of distinguishing between revisions of normative specifications through the use of test generation. While we have concentrated on problem of choosing between normative revisions, more generally our work for choosing between alternate hypotheses is applicable to any theory revision problem. As discussed in [11], there appears two ways of judging whether one revision is better than another. The first is by looking at how complete and consistent the revised theory would be by checking it satisfies a set of desired characteristics such as the AGM postulate (see Chapter 2 of [24]). As we depended on previous work for the correctness of the revision, this is not the directly related to our work. The second is by following the principle of minimal change which takes the revision that changes the original theory the least as the best solution. While this approach ensures that as much knowledge as possible is retained by the change, the minimal revision may not always reflect the specification that the designer wants. Thus, other criteria in addition to minimal changes should be used in a revision framework based on use-cases.

Although examining all possible revisions may give a more complete view of the changes made to the original partial specification, our approach can help the user by pointing out the key discriminating aspects between the different revisions. By identifying comparable consequences of the suggested revisions, we are able to use them as a rationale for rejecting possible changes. We have investigated how test generation can be applied, providing a notion of test characteristics for revisions, and used this characterisation to describe how abduction can be used to find such relevant literals. In [15], the *discriminating test* is mentioned as another type of test that could reject hypotheses regardless of its truth value. It is also mentioned that while they are ideal to use for rejecting hypotheses, their characteristics are too restrictive and thus relevant tests were discussed. For the relevant literals in this paper, the scoring mechanism ensures that relevant literals satisfying the characteristics of discriminating tests have higher priority.

Our case study demonstrates how our proposed approach could be integrated into an existing framework for normative refinement, where ASP can be used to compute relevant literals and score them in order to identify those that are most relevant. It also shows a situation where our approach may not discriminate all suggested revisions. While the revision suggestions are different, our approach could not find any relevant literals as the system trace used to find it does not describe a scenario in which the revisions would differ. As the revision process is designed to be carried out iteratively, use-cases from previous cycles could be kept either as additional constraints or as additional traces to use for generating relevant literals.

References

1. Grossi, D., Aldewereld, H., Dignum, F.: *Ubi Lex, Ibi Poena*: Designing Norm Enforcement in E-Institutions. In: Noriega, P., Vázquez-Salceda, J., Boella, G., Boissier, O., Dignum, V., Fornara, N., Matson, E. (eds.) COIN 2006 Workshops. LNCS (LNAI), vol. 4386, pp. 101–114. Springer, Heidelberg (2007)
2. Cliffe, O., De Vos, M., Padget, J.: Answer Set Programming for Representing and Reasoning About Virtual Institutions. In: Inoue, K., Satoh, K., Toni, F. (eds.) CLIMA VII. LNCS (LNAI), vol. 4371, pp. 60–79. Springer, Heidelberg (2007)
3. Artikis, A., Sergot, M., Pitt, J.: An executable specification of an argumentation protocol. In: Proceedings of Conference on Artificial Intelligence and Law, ICAIL, pp. 1–11. ACM Press (2003)
4. Corapi, D., Russo, A., Vos, M.D., Padget, J.A., Satoh, K.: Normative design using inductive learning. TPLP 11(4-5), 783–799 (2011)
5. Searle, J.R.: A Construction of Social Reality. Allen Lane, The Penguin Press (1955)
6. Jones, A.J., Sergot, M.: A Formal Characterisation of Institutionalised Power. ACM Computing Surveys 28(4es), 121 (1996) (read November 28, 2004)
7. Gelfond, M., Lifschitz, V.: Classical negation in logic programs and disjunctive databases. New Generation Computing 9(3-4), 365–386 (1991)
8. Kowalski, R., Sergot, M.: A logic-based calculus of events. New Gen. Comput. 4(1), 67–95 (1986)
9. Gelfond, M., Lifschitz, V.: Action languages. Electron. Trans. Artif. Intell. 2, 193–210 (1998)
10. Gebser, M., Kaminski, R., Kaufmann, B., Ostrowski, M., Schaub, T., Thiele, S.: Engineering an Incremental ASP Solver. In: Garcia de la Banda, M., Pontelli, E. (eds.) ICLP 2008. LNCS, vol. 5366, pp. 190–205. Springer, Heidelberg (2008)
11. Wrobel, S.: First order theory refinement (1996)
12. Sakama, C.: Induction from answer sets in nonmonotonic logic programs. ACM Trans. Comput. Log. 6(2), 203–231 (2005)
13. Corapi, D.: Nonmonotonic Inductive Logic Programming as Abductive Search. PhD thesis, Imperial College London (2012)
14. Corapi, D., Russo, A., Lupu, E.: Inductive Logic Programming in Answer Set Programming. In: Muggleton, S.H., Tamaddoni-Nezhad, A., Lisi, F.A. (eds.) ILP 2011. LNCS, vol. 7207, pp. 91–97. Springer, Heidelberg (2012)
15. Mcilraith, S.: Generating tests using abduction. In: Proceedings of the Fourth International Conference on Principles of Knowledge Representation and Reasoning, KR 1994, pp. 449–460. Morgan Kaufmann (1994)
16. Kakas, A.C., Kowalski, R., Toni, F.: Abductive logic programming. Journal of Logic and Computation 2(6), 719–770 (1992)
17. Alchourrón, C.E.: Conflicts of norms and the revision of normative systems. Law and Philosophy 10, 413–425 (1991), doi:10.1007/BF00127412

18. Ullmann-Margalit, E.: Revision of norms. Ethics 100(4), 756–767 (1990) Article Stable, http://www.jstor.org/stable/2381777 (retrieved March 20, 2012)
19. Boella, G., van der Torre, L.W.N.: Regulative and constitutive norms in normative multiagent systems. In: Dubois, D., Welty, C.A., Williams, M.A. (eds.) KR, pp. 255–266. AAAI Press (2004)
20. Governatori, G., Rotolo, A.: Changing legal systems: legal abrogations and annulments in defeasible logic. Logic Journal of the IGPL 18(1), 157–194 (2010)
21. Artikis, A.: Dynamic protocols for open agent systems. In: Sierra, C., Castelfranchi, C., Decker, K.S., Sichman, J.S. (eds.) AAMAS (1), pp. 97–104. IFAAMAS (2009)
22. Campos, J., López-Sánchez, M., Rodríguez-Aguilar, J.A., Esteva, M.: Formalising Situatedness and Adaptation in Electronic Institutions. In: Hübner, J.F., Matson, E., Boissier, O., Dignum, V. (eds.) COIN 2008. LNCS, vol. 5428, pp. 126–139. Springer, Heidelberg (2009)
23. Tinnemeier, N.A.M., Dastani, M., Meyer, J.J.C.: Programming norm change. In: van der Hoek, W., Kaminka, G.A., Lespérance, Y., Luck, M., Sen, S. (eds.) AAMAS, pp. 957–964. IFAAMAS (2010)
24. Gabbay, D.M., Rodrigues, O., Russo, A.: Revision, Acceptability and Context - Theoretical and Algorithmic Aspects. Cognitive Technologies. Springer (2010)

Latest Developments of WADE to Support User-Centric Business Processes

Federico Bergenti[1], Giovanni Caire[2], and Danilo Gotta[2]

[1] Università degli Studi di Parma, 43124, Parma, Italy
federico.bergenti@unipr.it
[2] Telecom Italia S.p.A., 10148, Torino, Italy
{giovanni.caire,danilo.gotta}@telecomitalia.it

Abstract. In this paper we present the latest developments of *WADE* (*Workflows and Agents Development Environment*) that provide concrete support for a better realization of the innovative paradigm of *agent-based BPM* (*Business Process Management*). First, we review and critique the basic ideas behind agent-based BPM and we focus on its innovative characteristics with respect to traditional BPM. Then, we describe the most recent developments of WADE that are intended to enhance its agent-based runtime platform by providing improved non-functional features and a better integration with the external software systems. Finally, we discuss the new functionality that WADE offers to enable the rapid and effective realization of *user-centric business processes*, i.e., business processes that are tightly integrated with the work of users and that are mainly driven by user interactions. Such processes are met frequently in practice and WADE seamlessly accommodates Web and Android users by means of dedicated views. We conclude this paper with a brief overview of notable mission-critical applications that are already using WADE and its new features.

Keywords: Agent-based BPM, user-centric business processes, WADE.

1 Introduction

Business Process Management (*BPM*) is now a consolidated trend in IT that has recently come up as a new discipline intended to unify related topics such as process modeling, workflows, enterprise application integration and business-to-business integration (see, e.g., [12]). BPM is today considered essential to the life of complex and dynamic enterprises and the research on the subject from IT and other perspectives is very active.

Despite the complexity of the subject that has been promoting interesting and longstanding debates, we can broadly refer to a business process as a set of interdependent activities that collectively realize a business objective or policy within the context of an organizational structure that defines the functional roles and the relationships between actors [22]. With this respect, BPM includes at least the following activities regarding business processes [15]:

M. Baldoni et al. (Eds.): DALT 2012, LNAI 7784, pp. 20–36, 2013.
© Springer-Verlag Berlin Heidelberg 2013

- Process description: every process must be described in some specification language in order to enumerate *(i)* the activities that need to be performed, *(ii)* the actors that perform them, and *(iii)* the interdependencies and related constraints that exist between activities; and
- Process execution and operational management: organizations typically use a software system, called BPM system, which is in charge of enacting the process description and turn it into practice.

Generally speaking, a BPM system enables a wide range of tasks like automating manual work, improving information and knowledge exchange among employees, controlling business processes in place, and assist in design and engineering of business processes. More in details, there are a few features that every BPM system must provide and that we consider of paramount importance (see also [12]):

- It should transparently support multiple instances of a given process and a given task;
- It should ensure that dependencies between the tasks are timely satisfied;
- It should allow the activities of users to be assigned appropriately; and
- It should smoothly integrate with the enterprise software tools required to complete the tasks.

While the importance of BPM systems in process execution is obvious, it is of equal importance to couple BPM systems with the models intended to express the complexities of business processes in the scope of their organizational context, and to support reasoning about processes for enabling future optimization and reengineering activities. It is often the case in the practice of BPM that the approach proposed by the adopted BPM system becomes the driving force of BPM and we often see business processes accustomed to systems and not vice versa. Such a counterintuitive approach is quite common practice in small and dynamic enterprises and this is the main reason why we believe that the role of the BPM systems in the large scope of BPM is often underestimated.

The introduction of a BPM system typically entails the adoption of appropriate workflows within the enterprise. A workflow, as defined in [22], is the automation of a business process–in whole or part–during which artifacts, information and/or tasks are passed from one actor to another according to a set of procedural rules.

Among the large variety of possible classification of business processes, it is worth noting that even the general definition of workflow that [22] proposes stresses the central role of actors in BPM. Then, if we match such a general definition with the everyday practice of BPM, we note that normally workflows are designed to ensure that the right people receive the right information at the right time. Workflows are often used to guide the work of people and we often witness workflows that are only meant to interact with the users of the BPM system. Such users are central subjects of BPM, exactly like BPM systems, and we strongly believe that they deserve a special treatment on their own.

In order to emphasize the role of users in the very general landscape of BPM and to justify the very frequent use of business processes to drive the work of people, we talk about *user-centric business processes* every time a business process is primarily intended to interact with the users of the BPM system in order to guide and provide assistance on his or her operative work.

User-centric business processes are so frequent in practice and their importance is so relevant for actual uses that modern BPM systems are requested to reserve a special treatment to them in order to enable specific functionality and promote optimizations. Unfortunately, little or no attention to such a kind of processes is paid by traditional BPM systems and interaction with users is often underestimated as yet another type of event. Such an approach is obviously very generic, but it misses a relevant part of the peculiarity of such processes, i.e., the need for the system to provide a means for users to effectively interact with the business processes. In the description of a user-centric business process we need to precisely describe the way users are presented the relevant information regarding the state of the process, i.e., the view that the user has on the process. Moreover, we also need to precisely describe the information that the user is expected to provide in order for the process to continue smoothly. Both such characteristics are of remarkable importance in practice and they deserve special care that traditional BPM systems do not always provide. Traditional BPM systems are high quality, mature tools intended primarily to manage business processes that are well structured and whose paths are identified a priori (see, e.g., [4]). However, the very high complexity and the intrinsic volatile and evanescent nature of today's business environment often make current BPM systems not sufficient. This has lead to the identification of a number of weaknesses of current BPM systems and the criticism against available BPM systems is now a solid movement (see, e.g., [15,17]). Therefore, we witness the rapid evolution of alternative approaches to traditional BPM that notably include *agent-based BPM*, and more generally, the adoption of the entire spectrum of agent technologies in the scope of BPM. The promise of agent technologies with this respect is to provide solid warranties for greater dynamism, agility and adaptability.

We already have a number of agent-based BPM systems available (see, e.g., [1,2,6,7,13,16,17]) and all such proposals share the common factor of using the autonomous and collaborative nature of agents to accommodate unexpected situations in dynamic business processes. This is a characteristic feature of agent-based BPM systems that is often used to motivate their adoption, but it is worth noting that agent technologies today provide so crucial advantages (e.g., in terms of non-functional features at runtime and effectiveness at design time) that their use should not be limited to the situations in which dynamism is a critical requirement.

In the practice of using agent-based BPM systems in real-world contexts (see, e.g., the concluding section and [7,21]) we noticed that users often appreciate them for their ease of use or for their robustness and dependability, rather than for their ability to cope with dynamic and unexpected situations, which are very rare and of marginal interest. The rest of this paper focuses on the weaknesses of traditional BPM systems that we have just emphasized and it presents a set of tools that effectively address them.

In the following section we describe the view of agent-based BPM that *WADE* (*Workflows and Agents Development Environment*) [7] promotes and we sketch a comparison with more traditional solutions. Then, Section 3 presents the most recent developments of WADE that have turned it into a full-featured agent-based BPM platform with improved non-functional characteristics and better interfaces with external software systems. All described features of WADE are available since version 3.1 (dated July 2012), which also includes a specific support for user-centric business processes, as described in Section 5. Finally, we close the paper with a brief summary of mission-critical systems based on WADE that are in everyday use in Telecom Italia.

2   Agent-Based BPM

In order to properly discuss the role of agent technologies in the scope of BPM, we must first review in details what a BPM system is and how it is expected to behave. The most relevant reference for this kind of systems is [22], which characterizes a BPM system as a software system that defines, creates and manages the execution of workflows that are running on one or more workflow engines. Such workflow engines are able to interpret the process definition, interact with workflow participants and, where required, invoke the use of other software.

Such BPM systems are typically modularized in a set of well-defined parts (see, e.g., [12]) as follows:

- Business process definition tools: they allow modeling the process in terms of workflows, actors, tasks, activities and their relationships and interdependencies. This is normally done using a graphical notation that typically resembles flowcharts.
- Business process servers: they are the software systems that provide the runtime execution of defined processes. They read process definitions and actually execute and track them.
- Business process clients: they are software systems that actors use to interact with the workflow. The application does not need to be part of the BPM system and it is typically a thin (Web) client that behaves as a front end to allow users to receive information and to submit events to the business process server.
- Business process monitoring and administration tools: they are intended to provide a real-time view of the state of execution of workflows and they provide means to manage unforeseen situations. They are valuable tools that give concrete help at runtime and that trace the information needed to optimization and reengineer processes.

Even if the modularization of typical BPM systems is well established and understood, in principle different systems can have different approaches to support the lifecycle of business processes.

Unfortunately, according to [22], the majority of current generation BPM systems share a common approach to structure the lifecycle of business processes. They all start modeling business process from activity analysis and they pay principal attention to business process tasks interdependences in order to correctly enact known sequence of the tasks [12]. All in all, such systems are adequate only in situations where a business process is fully understood and every conceivable outcome of tasks and activities can be considered and controlled beforehand.

As we briefly discussed before, not all business processes can be defined with such a fine level of control at design time. Real-world business processes are complex and continuously changing in order to accommodate the changes of their operative environment. Because of that, [12] provides a list of the major drawbacks and limitations of traditional BPM systems, which we review here taking into account recent developments in the field:

- Limited flexibility during process enactment;
- Inability to cope with dynamic changes in the availability of resources needed to accomplish activities and tasks, as existing systems tend to lack the necessary facilities to redistribute work items automatically as and when required;
- Inadequate handling of exceptional situations, especially when an exceptional case arises in a part of compound, yet possibly recoverable, tasks;
- Limited or even null ability to predict changes due to external events, in both the volume and the time distribution of activities; and
- Insufficient interoperability with other software systems, as the majority of existing BPM systems consist of centralized and monolithic systems that are meant to control their operative environment and that are not designed to cooperate with other, possibly unknown, controllers.

Even a superficial read of the mentioned drawbacks suggests that agent technologies are capable of addressing and effectively solving all such issues. If agent technologies are involved in the enactment of business processes, we benefit from the intrinsic dynamism and flexibility of agent-based systems and we rely on mature technologies that provide solid solutions to common software development issues. Moreover, the use of agent technologies can fruitfully enable a *declarative* approach to BPM that has already gained a significant interest for its inherent characteristics (see, e.g., [18,20]).

An agent-based BPM system is made of a set of software modules that meet the coarse grained criteria that define agenthood and that are involved in managing the flow of work throughout a business process [15,17]. The basic idea is to rethink the mentioned modules of a traditional BPM system in terms of interacting agents in charge of peculiar responsibilities and capable of predicting and reacting to unforeseen situations. This does not mean that we need to rethink the discussed modularization of a BPM system; rather agents give us the possibility of going deeper in the characterization of the parts of a BPM system. All such parts are then viewed as agents in order to benefit from the intrinsic characteristics of agents themselves.

Moreover, the use of agents enables another, orthogonal, modularization possibility, as suggested in [12]. An agent-based BPM system can split a business process into parts and trust the control over such parts to individual agents.

Given such a view of an agent-based BPM system we can sum up the major advantages of such an approach as follows [4,15]:

– Agents allow decentralized ownership of tasks, information and resources involved in business processes;
– The use of communicating agents, which also concerns about business logic, allows flexible and dynamic solution paths to the business process execution;
– The adoption of agents provides a high degree of natural concurrency when many interrelated tasks are running at any given point of the business process;
– The decoupling of the parts of the system that agents ensure allows them to be swapped out, replaced, or even added to the system without impacting other parts; and
– Agent technologies are today ready to build highly decentralized and distributed systems with notable non-functional features in terms of solidity and robustness.

Unfortunately the literature has already identified some disadvantages of the promising agent-based approach to the realization of BPM systems (see, e.g., [15]). We summarize the most prominent here for the sake of completeness:

– Agent-based systems have no overall system controller, which implies that the agent-based approach might not be the best choice for managing business processes with a lot of global constraints to be satisfied; and
– Agent-based systems have no global complete knowledge, i.e., an agent's actions are determined by that agent's local knowledge and this may mean that agents could make globally sub-optimal decisions.

It is worth noting that such issues are actually common to all agent-based software systems and they are not typical of BPM systems. All in all, such issues and their importance originate from the common understanding that considers agent-based systems useful only in a limited set of contexts that are characterized by intrinsic dynamism and uncertainty. This is no longer the case as the agent technologies of today have already proved their maturity and their valuable role in the design and realization of solid and robust software.

3   WADE as a BPM Platform

Obviously not all operative environments are so critical to make apparent the shortcomings of agent technologies and often the benefits that agent-based BPM brings are more relevant than the related issues. In fact, our experiences in real-world BPM suggest that agent technologies can work effectively in traditional settings and that they can provide notable benefits to common tasks of BPM. The work presented in this paper is precisely motivated by such a point of view: we think that agent technologies are now ready to deliver very solid, scalable and visually programmable software systems even in traditional environments where dynamism and uncertainty are not major issues.

3.1   Aims and Scope of WADE

We have been using agent technologies frequently in traditional operative environments and users appreciated such a choice for its maturity and effectiveness in the provision of non-functional features coupled with the possibility of visually programming complex behaviors. The heart of all our experience is *WADE* (*Workflow and Agent Development Environment*) [7], a software tool for the visual development of agents as workflow executors that since version 3.0 can be considered a first class agent-based BPM system. Actually, WADE has already been successfully adopted in a number of mission-critical software systems, as detailed further at the end of this paper, for the possibilities it provides in the visual realization of solutions with distinguished non-functional requirements in terms of scalability and robustness. The role of WADE agents in such systems is not only about exploiting the autonomy of agents in the management of dynamic and unforeseen situations; rather it is about providing developers with friendly tools that represent a robust shield against the complexity of non-functional requirements. Moreover, the tight integration of WADE with mainstream development technologies, like Java and Web services, allows developers incrementally adopting agent technologies in their systems. The parts of the system that can fruitfully empower the features of agents are easily developed using WADE, while other parts are still developed using mainstream technologies with no effort needed for integration.

More in details, WADE is an open-source framework meant to develop distributed and decentralized applications based on the agent paradigm and the workflow metaphor. It is built on top of JADE [3,14], the popular open-source middleware for the implementations of multi-agents systems in compliance with FIPA specifications [9]. WADE adds to JADE the possibility to define agent tasks in terms of workflows and a set of mechanisms to handle the complexity of administration and fault tolerance operations in a decentralized and distributed environment. In the view of a system that WADE advocates, each agent is equipped with a set of workflows and the principal duty of an agent is to enact the proper workflow depending on the dynamic situations it faces. Such workflows are normally described using the pleasant visual notation of the *WOLF* (*WOrkflow LiFe cycle management environment*) graphical editor (see also [1,2] for similar graphical languages for agent-based workflows). WOLF promotes a high-level view of workflows, i.e., of the tasks of agents, and it gives developers a friendly tool shown in Figure 1.

It is worth noting that the conception of WADE and related tools is always concerned about the smooth transition from mainstream technologies and agent technologies in order to ensure a proper management of all well/known issues related to a substantial paradigm shift. This is the reason why WOLF tightly couples the graphical view of a workflow with the underlying Java class that concretely implements it. The developer is free to work on either the graphical view or the Java class freely and he or she can change its work approach as easily as clicking on a tab because WOLF ensures a real-time roundtrip accordance of the two views. Moreover, the choice of implementing WOLF as Eclipse plug-in [8]

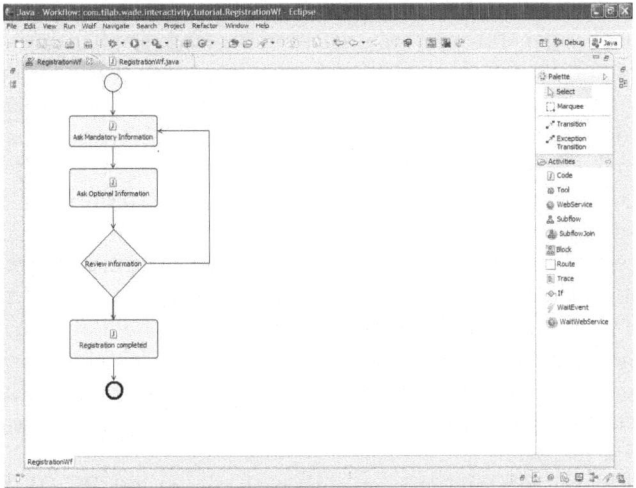

Fig. 1. WOLF visual editor for WADE workflows

that fully exploits the features of the Eclipse platform ensures that developers are allowed to work in one of the most appreciated environments available today.

Many advantages have been demonstrated to become effective once we decide to follow the WADE approach and, among them, it is worth mentioning the possibility of having a graphical representation of a workflow which is easily understandable by domain experts as well as by programmers. Because of the workflows expressiveness, domain experts can directly validate the system logics and, in some cases, they can even contribute to the actual development of the system with no need of programming skills.

3.2   BPM-Oriented Evolutions of WADE

WADE was initially conceived back in 2006 to exploit the workflow approach in the implementations of system internal logics that can be modeled in terms of short running processes. Such kind of processes are generally characterized by a short execution time (typically seconds or in some cases minutes) and a high CPU time consumption, and they can be defined in terms of the activities to be executed, the relations between such activities, which specify the execution flow, and the conditions of start-up and termination. Consistently with the aforementioned requirements regarding short-running processes, some design decisions have been taken. First, workflows are modeled in terms of Java code to ensure maximum efficiency and flexibility. In the literature several formalisms, e.g., XPDL, BPEL, WS-BPEL [19], can be found to describe workflows. However, if on the one hand they provide a clear and intuitive representation of the process execution flow, on the other hand they are not suitable to specify all the details involved in the implementation of a piece of the internal logic of a given software system. A general-purpose programming language like Java is definitely more powerful and flexible to deal with data transformations, computations and with the low level auxiliary operations that are often needed when specifying the internal logic of the system under development. Then, given that workflows start and terminate their executions in a short time, no persistency mechanism was considered necessary and workflows did not survive to the shutdown of their WADE platform.

Starting from 2010 new requirements from Telecom Italia WADE-based systems, as well as from the open-source community, showed that, though very effective for a particular type of applications, the advocated approach restricted too tightly the actual uses of WADE. In particular, more and more frequently the need to properly manage situations where a workflow could block waiting for external events that may happen in hours, days or even months was indicated as a mandatory feature.

To meet such ever growing requirements, with version 3.0, WADE had a strong evolution that, though preserving its distinctive characteristics, makes it now a tool that can effectively play a substantial role in agent-based BPM contexts.

Long-Running Workflows. The base for all WADE BPM-oriented features described in this section is the possibility of having workflows that survive to a system restart. Such workflows are identified as long-running. In details, if the platform is shut down just after a long-running workflow W has executed activity A_n, as soon as the platform starts up again, workflow W is automatically reloaded and forced to recover its execution starting from activity A_{n+1}. Under the hood WADE saves the state of a long-running workflow on a persistent storage after the execution of each activity. The persistent storage is implemented by a relational database accessed through Hibernate. The mechanism has been developed and tested with a number of different database management systems, e.g., H2, mySql and Oracle. A new administrator agent called *WSMA* (*Workflow Status Manager Agent*) has been introduced and it is responsible to manage all operations related to tracing, persisting and recovering the status of workflows.

Asynchronous Events. Another major step in the evolution of WADE is the introduction of an integrated event sub-system implemented as an agent called *ESA* (*Event System Agent*). When developing a workflow, besides regular activities, it is now possible to include new synchronization activities that, when reached, make the execution block until a given event happens. In details, when the process enters such a synchronization activity, the related agent thread is released to prevent resource consumption and the WSMA switches the workflow state from ACTIVE to SUSPENDED. A dedicated API is then provided to allow agents submitting events to the event system. As soon as an event matching the template specified in the synchronization activity is submitted, the workflow agent is resumed and the state of the workflow is switched back to ACTIVE. Furthermore, the information that the event bares is made available to the workflow for further processing. The event system stores received events for a configurable amount of time so that it is now possible to transparently deal with situations where a synchronization activity is reached after the expected event happened. In such cases the workflow does not even block and it immediately steps forward. It should be noted that the possibility of blocking to receive asynchronous events is not strictly related to long-running workflows however, if the system is restarted, long-running workflows will be recovered transparently and all suspended short-running workflows are immediately aborted.

Web Service Exposure. Since version 2.0 WADE includes a powerful embedded support to invoke Web services from within a workflow. In version 3.0 such a support is enriched with the dual possibility of exposing Web services. Such a new feature is twofold. First, it is possible to expose the operations specified in a given WSDL and block a workflow waiting for a given operation to be invoked. This is achieved by combining the new Web service exposure feature with the support for asynchronous event described previously. An ad-hoc *WaitWebService* synchronization activity is now available that, when reached, blocks the workflow until the event corresponding to the invocation of a previously exposed Web service operation happens. Internally, the code serving the Web service invocation encapsulates the operation parameters into an event that is submitted to the event system. Second, it is now possible to automatically expose a workflow as a Web service. The workflow name is mapped to the service name and a single execute operation is generated with input parameters matching workflow's ones. The code intended to serve the invocation triggers the execution of the workflow.

From the architectural point of view, the Web service exposure feature is implemented by a new component called *WadeServices*. This is a common Web application that can be executed within any servlet container, e.g., Apache Tomcat.

It is worth noting that this new feature of WADE is made available in WOLF by means of a simple point-and-click on the workflow Java class.

Administration Web Console. According to the new evolutions of WADE and in order to facilitate the administration of the platform, a Web monitor and configuration console was developed to allow performing both low level management operations, e.g., the start-up/shut-down of the platform, and high-level actions related to the business logics, e.g., browsing and launching a workflow. This new Web console was implemented using the ZK framework [23], an open source solution to develop Web applications based on AJAX machinery. In particular, the ZK framework has been extended to support new ZK components specifically intended to support WADE administration functionalities. Such components, developed for and used by the Web console, can be also reused inside custom Web applications that need to integrate WADE platform management functionality.

4   WADE User-Centric Workflows

The extensive use of WADE in mission-critical applications (see the concluding section and [7] for some examples) has witnessed the notable importance of user interactions in the scope of workflows. This is not surprising and we acknowledge that the idea of workflows has its origins in the management of the work of people. Nonetheless, we believe that the common approach of treating user interactions as yet another type of event does not adequately capture the importance and the high frequency of them. So called user-centric workflows are therefore introduced in WADE version 3.0 as a means to capture workflows that *(i)* frequently need to interact with users, and *(ii)* are mainly intended to gather information and provide feedback to users. WADE now lifts user interactions to a higher level and it provides specific tools and features to manage them effectively. The design guidelines for such a recent development of WADE are as follows:

- The description of the information to provide to users and the related input to acquire from users must be independent of the device that the user is concretely accessing;
- Any element of such a description must be extensible in order to let developers provide more specific descriptions of both input and output information;
- The software application that the user accesses must be replaceable by any custom application once the communication with the WADE platform is correctly performed; and
- No device is privileged and developers must be able to describe workflows in full generality, if they really want.

From such very generic guidelines we choose the *Model-View-Controller* (*MVC*) [10] architectural design pattern as the coarse grained model around which we designed the new interactivity package of WADE. Therefore, WADE version 3.0 adopts the following terminology:

- The model of the interaction is the abstract description of the information to provide to users and the related input expected from users; and
- The view of the interaction is the visual representation of the model realized by the application that the user adopts to connect to a workflow. In concrete terms, the new interactivity package of WADE provides the Java classes of the model and a number of visualizers intended to be integrated in the application shipped to users.

In order to fully exploit the power of user-centric business processes, the developer of a workflow should first inform WADE that the workflow itself needs to interact with users. This is accomplished by realizing a workflow class that extends the `InteractiveWorkflow` class rather than the common `Workflow` class. Such an `InteractiveWorkflow` class is a specific subclass of `Workflow` that provides the needed machinery to link a workflow instance to a visualizer. WADE ensures a one-to-one correspondence between a user and an instance of an `InteractiveWorkflow` and therefore an `InteractiveWorkflow` has just one user at a time. Multiple users can be accommodated into a single instance of a workflow by having the control of the workflow passed between users, just like we normally do in user-centric workflows.

When an `InteractiveWorkflow` is connected to a visualizer, it is requested to provide the visualizer with a description of the information to present to the user and with a related description of the possible user inputs. Such a mechanism is concretely driven by the workflow developer who can freely use the new method `interact()` that `InteractiveWorkflow` provides. Such a method is supplied with an `Interaction` object that contains the following parts:

- An abstract description of the information to be presented to the user with some abstract requirements on the way information is presented, e.g., by indicating how a set of labels should be aligned on the user screen;
- An abstract description of the information that the user is allowed to return in his or her response;
- An abstract description of the constraints that the user response must meet to be considered valid; and
- A list of possible abstract actions that the user is allowed to choose as valid responses.

Upon executing the `interact()` method, the workflows is put into a SUS-PENDED state to allow the corresponding visualizer to present the information to the user and to enable the user to provide feedback by means of one of the available response actions. The visualizer is on duty for showing the information in the best possible way and for allowing the user to provide its response. The visualizer is also responsible for the correctness of the provided response because it is in charge of checking the constraints that identify valid responses. Once the user has validly compiled its response and chosen one of the available response actions, the visualizer returns user response to the workflow instance in terms of a copy of the original `Interaction` object that now contains relevant user input and from which the developer can extract the user response easily. Such an approach allows developers retrieving response information from where they originally decided they should be contained. Moreover, it ensures no redundant information is sent back in responses.

The interaction between the workflow and the visualizer relies completely on WADE agents because *(i)* WADE ensures that any running workflow instance is associated with an agent; and *(ii)* visualizers are implemented by means of WADE agents that can interact with user devices.

How WADE agents are concretely connected with user devices is heavily dependent on the actual visualizer the user is accessing, as discussed briefly later in this section.

4.1   A Model of Interactions

In the WADE nomenclature an interaction is both an abstract description of the information to be provided to users and a means to allow users constructing responses. Therefore, WADE provides a set of Java classes that are used to describe interactions with such a dual meaning. Such classes are designed using the standard approach adopted in modern user interfaces and they are structured in a containment tree. Figure 2 sketches a class diagram of some of the classes that the developer can use to create a model. Such classes are divided into the following major groups:

- Passive elements, e.g., labels and pictures, that are leafs of the containment tree intended to describe the information to be provided to users;
- Information elements, e.g., text areas and menus of various types, that are leafs of the containment tree and that are meant to provide the user with a means to compile his or her responses;
- Containers, e.g., list and grid panels, that are designed to aggregate a group of children in order to describe their relative position in an abstract manner;
- Actions that describe the types of responses the user can select; and
- Constraints that concretely provide check procedures to ensure the correctness of the user responses.

With the notable exception of constraints, all such Java classes are purely descriptive and they are simple containers for information flowing between an InteractiveWorkflow and a visualizer. They are designed to maintain the clear separation of concerns of the MVC design pattern. All such classes describe the model of an interaction, while the relative controller is implemented by the adopted visualizer, which also generates on the fly the relative view. Such an approach ensures, among other things, that developers are free to add new visualizers and that no visualizer is privileged.

Constraints are peculiar in the scope of the MVC pattern because they are intended to validate user input. They represent a pluggable part of the controller because they are responsible for updating the view upon changes in the model, e.g., by marking invalid components with an error notification. WADE provides a set of general purpose constraints that can be used, e.g., to make sure a mandatory menu has at least an item selected or to warrantee that the text in a text field conforms to a given regular expression.

Finally, it is worth mentioning that WADE version 3.1 already provides descriptors for visual elements that are not supposed to be available to all visualizers. This is the case, e.g., of the `Position` and of the `Camera` classes that are now available only to the Android visualizer. This is not contradictory with the abstract and extensible approach that we enforced with the mentioned design guidelines. In fact, no visual element is guaranteed to be available to all visualizers even if the most common of them are likely to be always there. It is up to the developers of the application that integrates WADE workflows to ensure that workflows use components that are actually available.

4.2   Available Visualizers

At the time of writing WADE provides three visualizers meant to accommodate two important classes of users: Web users and Android users. Web users

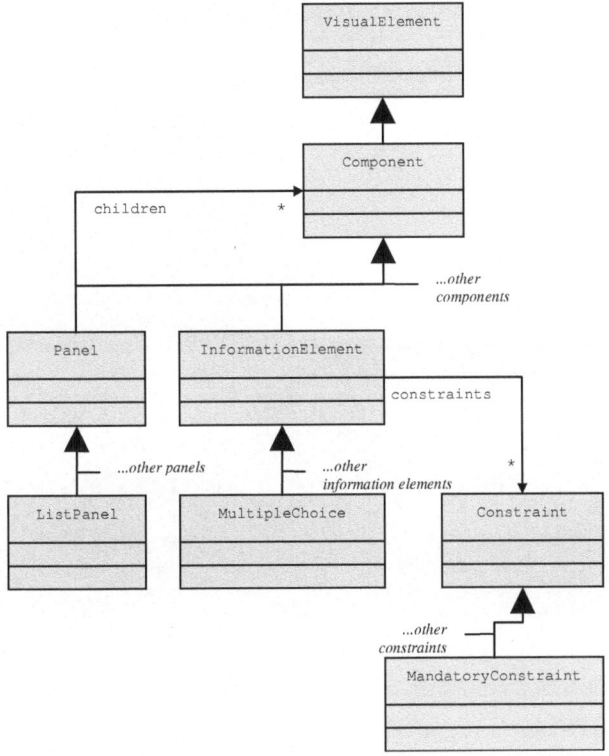

Fig. 2. Excerpt from WADE interactivity package

are allowed to activate new interactive workflows and to connect to suspended workflows by means of dedicated visualizers developed using the ZK toolkit [23] and the *GWT (Google Web Toolkit)* [11].

ZK is a very popular toolkit to develop AJAX applications in Java and it is easily interfaced with WADE[1]. The ZK visualizer instantiates one JADE agent on the server side of the Web application for each and every Web session and it ensures agents are properly connected with the WADE platform. The client side of the ZK application is meant to *(i)* present information to the user, *(ii)* provide selectable actions in terms of buttons, and *(iii)* ensure constraints are met before passing any response to workflow agents. The chosen approach ensures a lightweight client that is only in charge of realizing the user interface on the fly and of validating constraints. ZK provides a proprietary communication means between the client browser and the server side of the application that is completely hidden in the deep internals of ZK, thus becoming transparent to developers.

---

[1] The WADE administration Web console is also developed with ZK.

Fig. 3. Android emulator presenting the user interface of a WADE interactive workflow

GWT is the Google's proposal to develop highly interactive Web applications and it provides almost unique means to develop client-side Java code. The GWT visualizer is essentially a porting of the ZK visualizer, even if a clearer separation between the client code and server code can be accomplished. Just like any other GWT application, the visualizer is split into a client side that is responsible to provide a rich GUI to the user, and a server side that communicates with back-end agents and progresses workflows. The two side are linked via GWT RCP mechanism and JADE agents are confined on the server side. Therefore, the actual logic of the visualizer resides on the server side, while the client side is only responsible for building user interfaces and for collecting user input which is then passed back to workflows.

The Android visualizer is developed along the lines of the two Web visualizers and we ensured that the internals of the two visualizers are developed using the same architecture and adopting closely related classes. The major difference with Web visualizers is that the Android visualizer is a single Android application that hosts on the user terminal:

- A JADE container in split mode (see JADE documentation for details [14]) which is created in the scope of the WADE platform;
- The agent needed to connect the user with the workflow; and
- The visual components that are used to dynamically assemble and render the user interface.

No proprietary communication mechanism is needed in this case because the agent and the visual components share some memory of the terminal.

Figure 3 shows the Android emulator presenting the user interface of the sample interactive workflow depicted in Figure 1.

5   Conclusions

This paper presents recent developments of WADE in the larger scope of agent-based BPM. It gives an overview of the main concepts of agent-based BPM and it emphasizes the main features of it in comparison with traditional BPM. Even if we acknowledge the power and possibilities of agent-based BPM to tackle dynamic and unforeseen situations, we advocate the use of agent technologies in the development of BPM systems for their solid non-functional features and for their proven ease of use. Such features are easily understood and mastered by the personnel involved in BPM projects and they ensure a smooth transition from mainstream approaches to innovative technologies with minimal, or even null, issues. Actually, WADE has been appreciated in the development of mission critical agent-based BPM systems for the agile approach that it brings in. WADE provides a solid platform for the development of complex BPM systems that tightly integrate the power of a visual approach with scalability, robustness and interoperability with mainstream technologies. This has reduced the effort needed to develop effective demonstrators and prototypes that were fruitfully scaled up to the cores of real systems, thus reducing time-to-market and improving the overall qualities of systems and of development processes.

WADE is commonly used in Telecom Italia for a number of mission critical systems [7,21] that are now in everyday use with real users and in the scope of projects with real customers. The following is a brief list of the most notable initiatives that use WADE in Telecom Italia:

- NNEM implements a mediation layer between network elements and OSS systems for millions of Telecom Italia customers;
- Wizard provides step-by-step guidance to thousands Telecom Italia technicians performing installation and maintenance operations in the fields with more than 1 million documented assisted installation since 2007; and
- WeMash, a mash-up platform for service-oriented architectures, enables non-developer users to self-create simple applications and to share them within the team they are working in.

The results were so compelling that Telecom Italia chose WADE as the enabling middleware for a *SAAS (Software As A Service)* offer for Utilities customers in the fields of electricity, gas and water. This offer includes various systems based on the new functionalities of WADE 3.1 described in this paper with a fully functional service-oriented architecture based completely on open source components.

References

1. Bartocci, E., Corradini, F., Merelli, E.: Building a Multi-Agent System from a User Workflow Specification. In: Proc. Workshop "Dagli Oggetti agli Agenti". CEUR Workshop Proceedings, vol. 204 (2006)
2. Bartocci, E., Corradini, F., Merelli, E., Scortichini, L.: BioWMS: A Web-based Workflow Management System for Bioinformatics. BMC Bioinformatics 8(S-1) (2007)
3. Bellifemine, F.L., Caire, G., Greenwood, D.: Developing Multi-Agent Systems with JADE. John Wiley & Sons (2007)
4. Bolcer, G.A., Taylor, R.N.: Advanced Workflow Management Technologies. Software Process: Improvement and Practice 4(3), 125–171 (1998)
5. BPMN – Business Process Modeling Notation, http://www.bpmn.org
6. Cai, T., Gloor, P.A., Nog, S.: DartFlow: A Workflow Management System on the Web Using Transportable Agents. Technical Report, Dartmouth College (1997)
7. Caire, G., Gotta, D., Banzi, M.: WADE: A Software Platform to Develop Mission Critical Applications Exploiting Agents and Workflows. In: Proc. 7th Int'l Conf. Autonomous Agents and Multiagent Systems, pp. 29–36 (2008)
8. Eclipse, http://www.eclipse.org
9. FIPA – Foundation for Intelligent Physical Agents, http://www.fipa.org
10. Fowler, M.: Patterns of Enterprise Application Architecture. Addison-Wesley (2003)
11. Google Web Toolkit, http://code.google.com
12. Grundspenkis, J., Pozdnyakov, D.: An Overview of the Agent.Based Systems for the Business Process Management. In: Proc. Int'l Conf. Computer Systems and Technologies (2006)
13. Hawryszkiewycz, I., Debenham, J.: A Workflow System Based on Agents. In: Quirchmayr, G., Bench-Capon, T.J.M., Schweighofer, E. (eds.) DEXA 1998. LNCS, vol. 1460, pp. 135–144. Springer, Heidelberg (1998)
14. JADE – Java Agent Development framework, http://jade.tilab.com
15. Jennings, N.R., Faratin, P., Johnson, M.J., Norman, T.J., Wiegand, M.E.: Agent-Based Business Process Management. Int'l J. Cooperative Information Systems 5(2-3), 105–130 (1996)
16. Jin, W., Chang, S.T.: Agent-based Workflow: TRP Support Environment (TSE). Computer Networks and ISDN Systems 28(7-11), 1501–1511 (1996)
17. Pang, G.: Implementation of an Agent-Based Business Process. Technical Report, University of Zurich (2000)
18. Pesic, M., Schonenberg, H., Van der Aalst, W.M.P.: DECLARE: Full Support for Loosely-Structured Processes. In: Proc. 11th IEEE International Enterprise Distributed Object Computing Conference, p. 287 (2007)
19. Shapiro, R: A Comparison of XPDL, BPML and BPEL4WS (Rough Draft), Cape Vision (2002)
20. Telang, P.R., Singh, M.P.: Specifying and Verifying Cross-Organizational Business Models: An agent-Oriented Approach. IEEE Transactions on Services Computing 5(3), 305–318 (2012)
21. Trione, L., Long, D., Gotta, D., Sacchi, G.: Wizard, WeMash, WADE: Unleash the Power of Collective Intelligence. In: Proc. 8th Int'l Conf. Autonomous Agents and Multiagent Systems (2009)
22. Workflow Management Coalition. Workflow Management Coalition Terminology & Glossary, http://www.wfmc.org
23. ZK Open-Source Framework, http://www.zkoss.org

Strong Planning in the Logics of Communication and Change

Pere Pardo[1] and Mehrnoosh Sadrzadeh[2]

[1] Institut d'Investigació en Intel·ligència Artificial (IIIA - CSIC), Spain
[2] Dept. of Computer Science, University of Oxford, UK

Abstract. In this contribution we study how to adapt Backward Plan search to the Logics of Communication and Change (LCC). These are dynamic epistemic logics with common knowledge modeling the way in which announcements, sensing and world-changing actions modify the beliefs of agents or the world itself. The proposed LCC planning system greatly expands the social complexity of scenarios involving cognitive agents that can be solved. For example, goals or plans may consist of a certain distribution of beliefs and ignorance among agents. Our results include: soundness and completeness of backward planning (breadth first search), both for deterministic and strong non-deterministic planning.

1 Introduction

Practical rationality or decision-making is a key component of autonomous agents, like humans, and correspondingly has been studied at large. This research has been conducted from several fields: game theory, planning, decision theory, etc. each focusing on a different aspect (strategic decision-making, propositional means-ends analysis, and uncertainty, respectively).

While the different models are well-understood, they were (understandably) designed with a considerably low level of expressivity at the object language. For instance, game-theory does not represent the logical structure underlying the states, actions and goals; planning [5], on the other hand, represents part of it with atomic facts and negation, but it traditionally disregards other existing agents. All this contrasts with the area of logic, where logics for multi-agent systems (with increasing expressivity) have been characterized.

Specially relevant to the topic of cognitive agents are the notions of belief, action, goal, norm, and so on. The first two elements are the target of dynamic epistemic logics DEL [3], [15], [16], a recent family of logics which allow us to reason about agents' communications, observations and the usual world-changing actions. We focus on the so-called Logics of Communication and Change (LCC) [13], which generalize many previously known DEL logics, and hence include a rich variety of epistemic actions (in the DEL literature) and ontic actions (from the tradition on planning). Briefly, LCC logics are dynamic epistemic logics with common knowledge, ontic actions and several types of communicative actions (truthful or lying, public or private announcements).

Less consensus exists about representing and reasoning with motivational attitudes like goals, desires or intentions. On the one hand, logics in the BDI tradition (belief-desire-intention) [12] make them explicit in the language, e.g. one can express *agent a*

M. Baldoni et al. (Eds.): DALT 2012, LNAI 7784, pp. 37–56, 2013.

has goal φ; in the planning tradition, though, one only makes explicit their propositional content φ (what makes φ a goal is just its membership to the set of goals). Here we adopt the second (and less expressive) representation of goals.

In the present contribution, we describe a system for planning that accepts arbitrary epistemic formulas (e.g. common knowledge) as goals or state descriptions, and with ontic/epistemic actions given by Kripke-like action models. The language of LCC logics (used to this end) is further extended with action composition $\otimes$ and choice $\cup$, in order to study planning with non-deterministic actions. In this sense, we slightly generalize on previous results in [9] and [10], by dropping a technical restriction on the precondition of non-deterministic actions, and proposing slightly different plan structures. In summary, we define a breadth first search (BFS) algorithm for strong planning in the extended LCC logics. This search method is proved to be sound and complete: its outputs are (logically) successful plans and if such a successful plan exists, the algorithm terminates with some such solution. Finally, this algorithm easily extends to optimal plan search when each action is assigned some cost for its execution.

Motivating Example. Our aim, then, is to endow LCC logic based agents with planning capacities for this logic, so they can achieve their goals in scenarios where other agents have similar cognitive and acting abilities. In particular, LCC planning seems necessary for an agent whose goals consist in (or depend on) a certain distribution of knowledge and ignorance among agents. To illustrate the kind of rational behavior an LCC planner can exhibit, consider the following example:

Example 1. Agent a placed a bet with agent b that the next coin toss would be heads (h). Agent a knows she can toss the coin and detect its outcome, or flip the coin, without agent b knowing about it. Given a sensing action that tells a whether h holds or not, a successful plan seems to be: toss the coin; if sense that h, then show h to b; otherwise flip the coin and show h.

2   Related Work

Among logics for action guidance, the family of BDI [12] and related logics for intention are possibly the more popular. While these logics usually allow for considerable expressivity w.r.t. motivational attitudes (and their interaction with beliefs), they are not completely understood at a syntactic level. In fact, the use of planning methods has been suggested for an implementation of a BDI architecture. In particular, [4] suggest the use of LCC planning for the corresponding fragment of BDI logic. In this work [4] (see also [8]), the authors study LCC forward planning based on the semantics of update models; the BFS search algorithm is shown to be complete for LCC forward planning and in addition this problem (LCC forward planning) is shown to be semi-decidable in the general multi-agent case. An extension for (single-agent) conditional plan search in AND/OR-graphs can be found in [1]. The present work addresses the multi-agent case using instead a backward search approach (in OR-graphs). The motivation for this lies in the nature of communicative actions: while forward search is based on actions that are *executable*, backward search focuses on actions that are *relevant to the current goals*. This makes a difference in LCC since many actions will exist which are everywhere executable, so forward planning will typically face the state explosion problem.

Another work along the same lines is [2] (and related papers) where regression methods are introduced for the fragment of LCC without common knowledge. Regression can also be used as a (non-incremental) planning algorithm for LCC.

3   Preliminaries: The Logics of Communication and Change

Logics for agents with epistemic and communicative abilities have been developed in the recent years, ranging from epistemic logic [7] (for individual, group or common belief or knowledge), to logics of announcements [3], [15] (public or private, honest or dishonest), and finally to incorporating ontic actions (i.e. world-changing actions) [16]. All this has been unified within the single framework of Logics of Communication and Change [13], or LCC logics, formally a dynamic extension of epistemic logic using action models. This work proposes a general (translation-based) method that provides a complete axiomatization of an LCC logic from the specification of its particular action model. Since LCC logics are built by adding dynamic action models U on top of E·PDL (propositional dynamic logic PDL under an epistemic reading), we recall PDL first.

3.1   Epistemic PDL

Propositional dynamic logic [6] is a modal logic for reasoning about programs, with modalities $[\pi]$ (and $\langle \pi \rangle$) expressing *after executing program π it is necessarily (resp. possibly) the case that*. Using a semantics for programs π based on relations R_π (between the internal states of a machine running the program), the PDL programs π are built from basic actions a and the program constructors of composition $a; b$ (*do a then b*), choice $a \cup b$ (*either do a or b*), test $?\varphi$ (*test φ, and proceed if true or terminate*) and iteration a^* (*do a; repeat*) (the Kleene-star for the reflexive transitive closure). It was later suggested [13] that the dynamic modalities of PDL naturally admit an epistemic interpretation as well, called E·PDL, if we read the basic "program" $[a]$ as the modality for agent a's knowledge or belief; that is, $[a]\varphi$ reads: *a knows φ*, or *a believes φ*; and $\langle a \rangle$ reads: *a considers it possible that φ*. Note that epistemic PDL does not distinguish between knowledge and belief, as usually understood by the S5 and KD45 modal logics, respectively. And thus, at the abstract level of PDL we will indistinctly refer to $[a]$ as knowledge or belief. Within a particular model, though, we can properly refer to one or the other depending on the semantic properties, e.g. whether $[a]\varphi \to \varphi$ holds, etc.

Definition 1. *The language of* E·PDL, *denoted by* $\mathcal{L}_{\text{E·PDL}}$, *for a given sets of atoms* $p \in \text{Var}$ *and agents* $a \in \text{Ag}$ *consists of the following formulas φ and programs π:*

$$\varphi ::= p \mid \neg\varphi \mid \varphi_1 \wedge \varphi_2 \mid [\pi]\varphi \qquad \pi ::= a \mid ?\varphi \mid \pi_1; \pi_2 \mid \pi_1 \cup \pi_2 \mid \pi^*$$

The symbols $\bot, \vee, \leftrightarrow$ and $\langle \pi \rangle$ are defined from the above as usual. Under the epistemic reading, the PDL program constructors allow us to model, among others,

$[a; b]$	*agent a believes that b believes that*	(nested belief)
$[B]$, or $[a \cup b]$	*agents in $B = \{a, b\}$ believe that*	(group belief)
$[B^*]$, or $[(a \cup b)^*]$	*it is common knowledge among B that*	(comm. knowl.)

An E·PDL model $M = (W, \langle R_a \rangle_{a \in \text{Ag}}, V)$ does, as usual, contain a set of worlds W, a relation R_a in W for each agent a, and an evaluation $V : \text{Var} \to \mathcal{P}(W))$.

Definition 2. *The semantics of* E·PDL *consists of models* $M = (W, \langle R_a \rangle_{a \in \text{Ag}}, V)$, *containing: a set of worlds* W, *a relation* R_a *in* W *for each agent* a, *and an evaluation* $V : \text{Var} \to \mathcal{P}(W)$. *This map* V *extends to a map* $[\![\varphi]\!]^M$ *for each formula* φ *in* $\mathcal{L}_{\text{E·PDL}}$:

$$[\![\top]\!]^M = W \qquad\qquad [\![a]\!]^M = R(a)$$
$$[\![p]\!]^M = V(p) \qquad\qquad [\![?\varphi]\!]^M = \text{Id}_{[\![\varphi]\!]}$$
$$[\![\neg\varphi]\!]^M = W \setminus [\![\varphi]\!]^M \qquad [\![\pi_1;\pi_2]\!]^M = [\![\pi_1]\!]^M \circ [\![\pi_2]\!]^M$$
$$[\![\varphi_1 \wedge \varphi_2]\!]^M = [\![\varphi_1]\!]^M \cap [\![\varphi_2]\!]^M \quad [\![\pi_1 \cup \pi_2]\!]^M = [\![\pi_1]\!]^M \cup [\![\pi_2]\!]^M$$
$$[\![\pi^*]\!]^M = ([\![\pi]\!]^M)^*$$
$$[\![[\pi]\varphi]\!]^M = \{w \in W \mid \forall v((w,v) \in [\![\pi]\!]^M \Rightarrow v \in [\![\varphi]\!]^M)\}$$

where $\circ$ *and* * *are the composition and reflexive transitive closure of relations.*

Notice in particular that $[\![?\bot]\!]^M = \varnothing$ and $[\![?\top]\!]^M = \text{Id}_W$ (the identity relation on W). We recall the axioms/rules of E·PDL that provide a sound and complete axiomatization:

$$\begin{array}{rl}
(K) & \vdash [\pi](\varphi \to \psi) \to ([\pi]\varphi \to [\pi]\psi) \\
(test) & \vdash [?\varphi_1]\varphi_2 \leftrightarrow (\varphi_1 \to \varphi_2) \\
(sequence) & \vdash [\pi_1;\pi_2]\varphi \leftrightarrow [\pi_1][\pi_2]\varphi \\
(choice) & \vdash [\pi_1 \cup \pi_2]\varphi \leftrightarrow [\pi_1]\varphi \wedge [\pi_2]\varphi \\
(mix) & \vdash [\pi^*]\varphi \leftrightarrow \varphi \wedge [\pi][\pi^*]\varphi, \text{ and} \\
(induction) & \vdash \varphi \wedge [\pi^*](\varphi \to [\pi]\varphi)) \to [\pi^*]\varphi. \\
(Modus\ ponens) & \text{From } \vdash \varphi_1 \text{ and } \vdash \varphi_1 \to \varphi_2, \text{ infer } \varphi_2, \\
(Necessitation) & \text{From } \vdash \varphi, \text{ infer } \vdash [\pi]\varphi.
\end{array}$$

3.2   Action Models U, e

An LCC logic will add to an E·PDL language a set of modalities [U, e] for each pointed action model U, e with distinguished (actual) action e. These new operators [U, e] read *after each execution of action* e *it is the case that*. An action model is a tuple $U = (\text{E}, \text{R}, \text{pre}, \text{post})$ containing

- $\text{E} = \{e_0, \ldots, e_{n-1}\}$, a set of actions
- $\text{R} : \text{Ag} \to (\text{E} \times \text{E})$, a map assigning a relation R_a to each agent $a \in \text{Ag}$
- $\text{pre} : \text{E} \to \mathcal{L}_{\text{PDL}}$, a map assigning a precondition $\text{pre}(e)$ to each action e
- $\text{post} : \text{E} \times \text{Var} \to \mathcal{L}_{\text{PDL}}$, a map assigning a post-condition $\text{post}(e)(p)$, or $p^{\text{post}(e)}$, to each $e \in \text{E}$ and $p \in \text{Var}$

Let us fix the above enumeration $e_0, \ldots, e_{n-1}$ which will be used throughout the paper, unless stated otherwise. During plan search, in particular, when we refine a plan with some new action, the different alternatives will be considered according to this ordering: the refinement with e_0 will be considered before the refinement with e_1, and so on.

Definition 3. *The language of the* LCC-*logic for an action model* U *extends the formulas of* E·PDL *(for the same set of variables* Var *and agents* Ag*) with modalities for pointed action models* U, e, *giving the following sets of formulas* φ *and programs* π:

$$\varphi ::= p \mid \neg\varphi \mid \varphi_1 \wedge \varphi_2 \mid [\pi]\varphi \mid [\mathsf{U}, \mathsf{e}]\varphi \qquad \pi ::= a \mid ?\varphi \mid \pi_1; \pi_2 \mid \pi_1 \cup \pi_2 \mid \pi^*$$

The new modalities $[\mathsf{U}, \mathsf{e}]\varphi$ represent *"after the execution of* e, φ *will hold"*. The semantics of LCC computes $M, w \models [\mathsf{U}, \mathsf{e}]p$ in terms of the product update of M, w and U, e. This product update is (again) an E·PDL pointed model $M \circ \mathsf{U}, (w, \mathsf{e})$, with

$$M \circ \mathsf{U} = (W', \langle R'_a \rangle_{a \in \mathsf{Ag}}, V') \qquad \text{where}$$

- the set W' consists of those worlds (w, e) such that $M, w \models \mathsf{pre}(\mathsf{e})$
  (so executing e will lead to the corresponding state (w, e).)
- the relation $(w, \mathsf{e})R'_a(v, \mathsf{f})$ holds iff both wR_av and $\mathsf{e}R_a\mathsf{f}$ hold; and
- the valuations are $V'(p) = \{(w, \mathsf{e}) \in W' \mid M, w \models \mathsf{post}(\mathsf{e})(p)\}$,
  (the truth-value of p after e depends on that of $\mathsf{post}(\mathsf{e})(p)$ before the execution)

An updated model $(W', \langle R'_a \rangle_{a \in \mathsf{Ag}}, V')$ will be denoted $(W^{M \circ \mathsf{U}}, \langle R_a^{M \circ \mathsf{U}} \rangle_{a \in \mathsf{Ag}}, V^{M \circ \mathsf{U}})$.

Example 2. Several types of announcement (that φ by agent a) can be expressed. As purely epistemic actions, they are assigned the trivial post-condition $\mathsf{post}(\cdot)(p) = p$.

- a (successful) *truthful* announcement to sub-group $X \subseteq \mathsf{Ag}$, denoted $[\mathsf{U}, \varphi!_X^a]$, with

$$\mathsf{pre}(\varphi!_X^a) = \varphi \quad \text{and} \quad R_b(\varphi!_X^a, \mathsf{e}) \Leftrightarrow \begin{cases} \mathsf{e} = \varphi!_X^a & \text{if } b \in X \cup \{a\} \\ \mathsf{e} \in \{\varphi!_X^a, \mathsf{skip}\} & \text{if } b \notin X \cup \{a\} \end{cases}$$

- a (successful) *lying* announcement to X, denoted $\mathsf{U}, \varphi\dagger_X^a$, is defined by the same accessibility relation but with precondition $\mathsf{pre}(\varphi\dagger_X^a) = \neg\varphi$.
  (Here skip is the null action defined $\mathsf{pre}(\mathsf{skip}) = \top$, and $\mathsf{post}(\mathsf{skip})(p) = p$.)

From here on we assume that post-conditions $\mathsf{post}(\mathsf{e})(p)$ are restricted to the elements $\{p, \top, \bot\}$, rather than $\mathsf{post}(\mathsf{e})(p)$ being an arbitrary formula. This restriction was studied in [16] for logics similar to LCC, with epistemic modalities for agents $[a]$ and group common knowledge $[B^*]$ for $B \subseteq \mathsf{Ag}$. The authors show that the logic resulting after this restriction on post-conditions is as expressive as the original where post-conditions are arbitrary formulas.

Later, we recover this expressivity by introducing a non-deterministic choice operator for actions. Let us remark that choice is more general than arbitrary post-conditions φ, since it can model the toss of a coin without describing which conditions φ would result in the coin landing heads.

This restriction makes the truth-value of p after e to be either of the following:

if $\mathsf{post}(\mathsf{e})(p) = \ldots$	then the truth-value of p after e is $\ldots$
$\top$	true (since $\top$ is always true, hence true before e)
p	its truth-value before the execution of e
$\bot$	false (since $\bot$ is always false)

3.3   Logics of Communication and Change

The PDL semantics $[\![\cdot]\!]$ for E·PDL-formulas extends to a semantics for LCC by adding:

$$[\![[\mathsf{U},\mathsf{e}]\varphi]\!]^M = \{w \in W \mid \text{ if } M, w \models \mathsf{pre}(\mathsf{e}) \text{ then } (w, \mathsf{e}) \in [\![\varphi]\!]^{M \circ \mathsf{U}}\}.$$

In [13], the authors define program transformers $T_{ij}^{\mathsf{U}}(\pi)$ that provide a mapping between E·PDL programs (see Def. 4). Given any combination of actions in a model U the transformers provide a complete set of reduction axioms, reducing LCC to E·PDL. In a sketch, the U, e-modalities are pushed inside the formula, up to the case $[\mathsf{U}, \mathsf{e}]p$.

Definition 4. *Let an action model* U *with* $\mathsf{E} = \{\mathsf{e}_0, \ldots, \mathsf{e}_{n-1}\}$ *be given. The* program transformer *function* T_{ij}^{U} *is defined as follows:*

$$T_{ij}^{\mathsf{U}}(a) = \begin{cases} ?\mathsf{pre}(\mathsf{e}_i); a & \text{if } \mathsf{e}_i \mathsf{R}(a) \mathsf{e}_j, \\ ?\bot & \text{otherwise} \end{cases}$$

$$T_{ij}^{\mathsf{U}}(?\varphi) = \begin{cases} ?(\mathsf{pre}(\mathsf{e}_i) \wedge [\mathsf{U}, \mathsf{e}_i]\varphi), & \text{if } i = j \\ ?\bot & \text{otherwise} \end{cases}$$

$$T_{ij}^{\mathsf{U}}(\pi_1; \pi_2) = \bigcup_{k=0}^{n-1}(T_{ik}^{\mathsf{U}}(\pi_1); T_{kj}^{\mathsf{U}}(\pi_2))$$

$$T_{ij}^{\mathsf{U}}(\pi_1 \cup \pi_2) = T_{ij}^{\mathsf{U}}(\pi_1) \cup T_{ij}^{\mathsf{U}}(\pi_2)$$

$$T_{ij}^{\mathsf{U}}(\pi^*) = K_{ijn}^{\mathsf{U}}(\pi).$$

where K_{ijn}^{U} is inductively defined as follows:

$$K_{ij0}^{\mathsf{U}}(\pi) = \begin{cases} ?\top \cup T_{ij}^{\mathsf{U}}(\pi) & \text{if } i = j \\ T_{ij}^{\mathsf{U}}(\pi) & \text{otherwise} \end{cases}$$

$$K_{ij(k+1)}^{\mathsf{U}}(\pi) = \begin{cases} (K_{kkk}^{\mathsf{U}}(\pi))^* & \text{if } i = k = j \\ (K_{kkk}^{\mathsf{U}}(\pi))^*; K_{kjk}^{\mathsf{U}}(\pi) & \text{if } i = k \neq j \\ K_{ikk}^{\mathsf{U}}(\pi); (K_{kkk}^{\mathsf{U}}(\pi))^* & \text{if } i \neq k = j \\ K_{ijk}^{\mathsf{U}}(\pi) \cup (K_{ikk}^{\mathsf{U}}(\pi); (K_{kkk}^{\mathsf{U}}(\pi))^*; K_{kjk}^{\mathsf{U}}(\pi)) & \text{if } i \neq k \neq j \end{cases}$$

A calculus for the LCC logic of a given action model U is given by the following:

the axioms and rules for E·PDL

$[\mathsf{U}, \mathsf{e}]\top \leftrightarrow \top$	(top)
$[\mathsf{U}, \mathsf{e}]p \leftrightarrow (\mathsf{pre}(\mathsf{e}) \rightarrow \mathsf{post}(\mathsf{e})(p))$	(atoms)
$[\mathsf{U}, \mathsf{e}]\neg\varphi \leftrightarrow (\mathsf{pre}(\mathsf{e}) \rightarrow \neg[\mathsf{U}, \mathsf{e}]\varphi)$	(negation)
$[\mathsf{U}, \mathsf{e}](\varphi_1 \wedge \varphi_2) \leftrightarrow ([\mathsf{U}, \mathsf{e}]\varphi_1 \wedge [\mathsf{U}, \mathsf{e}]\varphi_2)$	(conjunction)
$[\mathsf{U}, \mathsf{e}_i][\pi]\varphi \leftrightarrow \bigwedge_{j=0}^{n-1}[T_{ij}^{\mathsf{U}}(\pi)][\mathsf{U}, \mathsf{e}_j]\varphi$	(E·PDL-programs)
if $\vdash \varphi$ then $\vdash [\mathsf{U}, \mathsf{e}]\varphi$	(Necessitation)

The completeness for this calculus is shown by reducing LCC to E·PDL. The translation, simultaneously defined for formulas $t(\cdot)$ and programs $r(\cdot)$ is

$$
\begin{array}{llll}
t(\top) & = \top & r(a) & = a \\
t(p) & = p & r(B) & = B \\
t(\neg\varphi) & = \neg t(\varphi) & r(?\varphi) & = ?t(\varphi) \\
t(\varphi_1 \wedge \varphi_2) & = t(\varphi_1) \wedge t(\varphi_2) & r(\pi_1; \pi_2) & = r(\pi_1); r(\pi_2) \\
t([\pi]\varphi) & = [r(\pi)]t(\varphi) & r(\pi_1 \cup \pi_2) & = r(\pi_1) \cup r(\pi_2) \\
t([\mathsf{U},\mathsf{e}]\top) & = \top & r(\pi^*) & = (r(\pi))^* \\
t([\mathsf{U},\mathsf{e}]p) & = t(\mathsf{pre}(\mathsf{e})) \to p^{\mathsf{post}(\mathsf{e})} \\
t([\mathsf{U},\mathsf{e}]\neg\varphi) & = t(\mathsf{pre}(\mathsf{e})) \to \neg t([\mathsf{U},\mathsf{e}]\varphi) \\
t([\mathsf{U},\mathsf{e}](\varphi_1 \wedge \varphi_2)) & = t([\mathsf{U},\mathsf{e}]\varphi) \wedge t([\mathsf{U},\mathsf{e}]\varphi_2) \\
t([\mathsf{U},\mathsf{e}_i][\pi]\varphi) & = \bigwedge_{j=0}^{n-1} [T_{ij}^{\mathsf{U}}(r(\pi))]t([\mathsf{U},\mathsf{e}_j]\varphi) \\
t([\mathsf{U},\mathsf{e}][\mathsf{U},\mathsf{e}']\varphi) & = t([\mathsf{U},\mathsf{e}]t([\mathsf{U},\mathsf{e}']\varphi))
\end{array}
$$

These translation functions t and r will be part of the backward planning algorithms presented in the next sections.

4 Backward Deterministic Planning in LCC

We proceed to introduce search algorithms for planning domains expressible in some LCC logic. In this section we study the deterministic case. The first step is to adapt the basic elements of planning systems:

- the goal and initial state are formulas of E·PDL (the static fragment of LCC).
- the set of available actions $A \subseteq \mathsf{E}$, among those in the action model U
- an available action is a pointed action model U, e where $\mathsf{e} \in A$

A deterministic plan is an executable sequence of actions in A that necessarily leads from any initial state to some goal state.

As we said, the proposed search methods for LCC planning are based on the above reduction of LCC into E·PDL. Given a (goal) formula φ for the current plan π and some action e, we want to compute the minimal conditions ψ (upon an arbitrary state) that would make φ to hold after e. After refinement of π with e, this minimal condition ψ will be the new goal replacing φ. More formally, we say $\psi \in \mathcal{L}_{\mathrm{PDL}}$ is the *weakest precondition* for a formula $[\mathsf{U}, \mathsf{e}]\varphi$, iff (in LCC)

$$\models \psi \leftrightarrow [\mathsf{U}, \mathsf{e}]\varphi.$$

This notion generalizes the definition in classical planning of open goals after refinement. Recall in classical planning, the different variables (or literals) p, q are logically independent, so the total effects of an action simply decompose into the individual effects w.r.t. each variable.

The weakest precondition for e to cause an arbitrary formula φ is the formula:

$$t([\mathsf{U}, \mathsf{e}]\varphi \wedge \langle \mathsf{U}, \mathsf{e} \rangle \top)$$

extracted from the reduction to E-PDL by way of translation using t, r. Indeed, the correctness of the translation based on t, r makes

$$\models t([\mathsf{U}, \mathsf{e}]\varphi \wedge \langle \mathsf{U}, \mathsf{e}\rangle \top) \leftrightarrow [\mathsf{U}, \mathsf{e}]\varphi \wedge \langle \mathsf{U}, \mathsf{e}\rangle \top$$

These functions t, r can then be seen as goal-transforming functions: a current goal φ is mapped into $t([\mathsf{U}, \mathsf{e}]\varphi \wedge \langle \mathsf{U}, \mathsf{e}\rangle \top)$, which becomes the new goal after we refine the plan with e.

Definition 5. *Given some LCC logic for an action model U, a planning domain is a triple* $\mathbb{M} = (\varphi_T, A, \varphi_G)$, *where* φ_T, φ_G *are consistent E-PDL formulas describing, resp., the initial and goal states; and* $A \subseteq \mathsf{E}$ *is the subset of a actions available to the agent.*

A solution to $\mathbb{M}$ *is a sequence* $\mathsf{f}_1, \ldots, \mathsf{f}_m \in A^{<\omega}$ *of actions in A, such that*

$$\models \varphi_T \to [\mathsf{U}, \mathsf{f}_1] \ldots [\mathsf{U}, \mathsf{f}_m]\varphi_G \quad and \quad \models \varphi_T \to \langle \mathsf{U}, \mathsf{f}_1\rangle \ldots \langle \mathsf{U}, \mathsf{f}_m\rangle \top$$

The subset $A \subseteq \mathsf{E}$ denotes those actions that are actually available to our planner-executor agent a. The reason to distinguish A from E is that some other agent $b \in \mathsf{Ag}$ might attribute our agent a some abilities which a does not actually possess, or b might fail to attribute a some of her actual abilities (and attribute her instead a decaffeinated version of some of these abilities). Thus, on the one hand, we want to distinguish the beliefs of b after an execution of some action e as depending on how b interpret this action e. On the other, we want to make explicit which abilities does our agent possess, in order to build realistic plans.

From here on, π will denote a deterministic plan, i.e. a sequence of actions e in decreasing order of execution (rather than an arbitrary epistemic PDL program as before). Plans are denoted by a pair (*action sequence, open goals*)

Definition 6. *Given some planning domain* $\mathbb{M} = (\varphi_T, A, \varphi_G)$, *the (initial) empty plan is the pair* $\pi_\varnothing = (\varnothing, \varphi_G)$ *and if* $\pi = (\pi, \varphi_{\mathsf{goals}(\pi)})$ *is a plan, then* $\pi(\mathsf{e}) = (\pi^\cap\langle\mathsf{e}\rangle, \varphi_{\mathsf{goals}}(\pi(\mathsf{e})))$, *defined by the goal* $\varphi_{\mathsf{goals}(\pi(\mathsf{e}))} = t([\mathsf{U}, \mathsf{e}]\varphi_{\mathsf{goals}(\pi)} \wedge \langle \mathsf{U}, \mathsf{e}\rangle \top)$, *is also a plan. A plan π is a* leaf *iff* $\varphi_{\mathsf{goals}(\pi(\mathsf{e}))}$ *is inconsistent, or* $\models \varphi_{\mathsf{goals}(\pi(\mathsf{e}))} \to \varphi_{\mathsf{goals}(\pi)}$.

Leafs are plans not worth considering, either because (a) when we add the last action refinement e, the resulting plan demands an inconsistent precondition $\varphi_{\mathsf{goals}(\pi(\mathsf{e}))}$ (and hence the plan cannot be executed) or (b) because e does not contribute to delete part of the previous goals $\varphi_{\mathsf{goals}(\pi)}$. The search space for the proposed planning algorithm (see below) is the set sequences $(\mathsf{f}_1, \ldots, \mathsf{f}_m) \in A^{<\omega}$. (These sequences are read in decreasing order of execution, i.e. as the sequence of operators $\mathsf{U}, \mathsf{f}_m, \ldots, \mathsf{U}, \mathsf{f}_1$.) Then, the planning algorithm explores just a fragment of this space, since it will not bother to generate/evaluate further refinements of leaf plans. A breadth first search (henceforth, BFS) algorithm for deterministic planning in LCC is given in Figure 1.

Actions $\mathsf{e} \in \mathsf{E}$, as defined above, are deterministic, in the sense that $\models [\mathsf{U}, \mathsf{e}]\varphi \vee \psi \leftrightarrow ([\mathsf{U}, \mathsf{e}]\varphi \vee [\mathsf{U}, \mathsf{e}]\psi)$. Thus, deterministic plans consist of actions $\mathsf{e} \in \mathsf{E}$ in our current action models U. Later we will extend LCC with composition $\otimes$ and choice $\cup$ to study the non-deterministic case. There we will fully recover the expressivity of actions

---

Input : $\mathsf{M} = (\varphi_T, A, \varphi_G)$.
LET Plans $= \langle \pi_\varnothing \rangle$ and $\pi = \pi_\varnothing$
WHILE $\not\models \varphi_T \to \varphi_{\text{goals}(\pi)}$
    DELETE π FROM Plans
    SET Plans $=$ Plans $\cap \langle \pi(\mathsf{e}) \mid \mathsf{e} \in A$ and $\pi(\mathsf{e})$ not a leaf $\rangle$
    SET $\pi =$ the first element of Plans
Output : π (i.e. the sequence $[\mathsf{U}, \mathsf{e}_1] \ldots [\mathsf{U}, \mathsf{e}_k]$)

Fig. 1. BFS algorithm for backward deterministic planning in LCC

defined by arbitrary post-conditions $p^{\text{post}(\mathsf{e})} = \varphi$ of [13], i.e. actions with conditional effects: *if φ then (after e) p.* The first contribution of this paper is the following result:[1]

Theorem 1. *BFS is sound and complete for LCC backward planning: the output π of the algorithm in Fig. 1 is a solution for $(\varphi_T, A, \varphi_G)$; conversely, if a solution exists, then the algorithm terminates (with a solution output).*

5   An Extension of LCC with Action Composition and Choice

In this section we propose an extension of LCC logic with bounded composition and choice, denoted $\text{LCC}_{\cup \otimes n}$. To this end, we first expand any LCC logic with the composition of at most n actions, denoted $\otimes n$, and later we add choice $\cup$. Both operations map two actions e, f to a new action denoted, resp., $\mathsf{e} \otimes \mathsf{f}$ and $\mathsf{e} \cup \mathsf{f}$, interpreted as follows:

- $\mathsf{e} \otimes \mathsf{f}$ models an execution of e followed by an execution of f, and
- $\mathsf{e} \cup \mathsf{f}$ models non-deterministic actions: each execution of $\mathsf{e} \cup \mathsf{f}$ either instantiates as an execution of e or as an execution of f.

For the composition of actions, the resulting action models are shown equivalent to a bounded number of updates with the previous simple actions. The logic of the former action updates, denoted $\text{LCC}_{\otimes n}$ reduces to the corresponding LCC logic.

Then we introduce choice $\cup$ into these models $\mathsf{U}^{\leq n}$. The semantics for non-deterministic actions $\mathsf{e} \cup \mathsf{f}$ is presented in terms of multi-pointed models (w, e) and (w, f), one for each possible realization of the former action. Again we extend the language and axioms accordingly for this logic $\text{LCC}_{\cup \otimes n}$, and reduce this logic again to E·PDL. In the next section, we will study non-deterministic planning problems in terms of plan solutions expressible in this $\text{LCC}_{\cup \otimes n}$ logics.

5.1   Update with the Product of n Actions in U^n

To define the composition of actions, we simply consider the product of an action model by itself, $\mathsf{U}_1 \otimes \cdots \otimes \mathsf{U}_k$, for each $k \leq n$. Here n denotes the maximum number of

---

[1] Proofs for results in this paper can be found at the first author's webpage
www.iiia.csic.es/en/individual/pere-pardo.

compositions allowed in the resulting logic $\text{LCC}_{\otimes n}$. An obvious requirement is that these action models are defined for the same set of variables Var and agents Ag.

We define first action models of the form $U^n = U_1 \otimes \cdots \otimes U_n$ and study them from a semantic point of view. This action model U^n just contains arbitrary products of exactly n actions: $f_1 \otimes \cdots \otimes f_n$.

Note that, in the next definition, the pre' functions of the product action model U^n are defined in terms of the corresponding functions pre from U, and pre' from $U^2, \ldots, U^{n-1}$. From here on, we let $\overrightarrow{f}$ denote some sequence $f_1 \otimes \cdots \otimes f_k$, also written $f_1, \ldots, f_k$, for an appropriate k.

Definition 7. *Let* $U = (E, R, \text{pre}, \text{post})$ *be an action model. We define the* product action model

$$U^n = (E', R', \text{pre}', \text{post}')$$

inductively as follows:

$$E' = E^n = \{(f_1, \ldots, f_n) \mid f_1, \ldots, f_n \in E\}$$
$$R'_a = \{\langle (e, \ldots, e'), (f, \ldots, f') \rangle \mid eR_a f \text{ and } \ldots \text{ and } e'R_a f'\}$$
$$\text{pre}'(e \otimes f) = \text{pre}(e) \wedge [U, e]\text{pre}(f) \qquad \text{for the case } n = 2$$
$$\text{pre}'(f_1 \otimes \overrightarrow{f}) = \text{pre}(e) \wedge [U, e]\text{pre}(\overrightarrow{f})$$
$$\text{post}'(f_1 \otimes \cdots \otimes f_n) = \begin{cases} \text{post}(f_k)(p) & \text{if } \text{post}(f_k)(p) \neq p = \\ & = \text{post}(f_{k+1})(p) = \ldots = \text{post}(f_n)(p) \\ \text{post}(f_1)(p) & \text{if } \text{post}(f_1)(p) = \ldots = \text{post}(f_n)(p) = p \end{cases}$$

More formally, in Def. 7 we should rather define inductively (from the case $n = 2$)

$$\text{pre}'(e \otimes \overrightarrow{f}) = \text{pre}(e) \wedge t([U, e]\text{pre}'(\overrightarrow{f}))$$

in order to comply with the condition upon action models: $\text{pre} : E \to \mathcal{L}_{\text{PDL}}$. But for the sake of simplicity, we will keep the above notation. Also note that in U^n the product of actions $f \otimes \cdots \otimes f'$ treats p just as the latest action in this tuple satisfying $\text{post}(\cdot)(p) \neq p$ (i.e. the latest action non-trivial w.r.t. p). Finally, observe that some combinations $e \otimes f$ in the product action model will never be applicable, e.g. when $\models [U, e]\neg\text{pre}(f)$. For the purpose of planning, one can forget about the existence of these actions in the resulting model $U \otimes U$.

It can be seen by direct inspection that the so-called product action model U^n is indeed an action model, provided U is. Moreover, the update of an E-PDL model M by a product action model, say $U \otimes U$, reduces to a sequence of updates with the simpler action model, e.g. $(M \circ U) \circ U$. With more detail, updating a state w with an action $e \otimes f$ is semantically equivalent to updating w with e first, and then updating again with f. We first check this is the case for $U^2 = U \otimes U$.

Lemma 1. *We have the following isomorphism*

$$M \circ (U \otimes U) \cong (M \circ U) \circ U.$$

This isomorphism extends to the valuations of arbitrary formulas and programs.

Corollary 1. *For each formula φ in the language of* $U \otimes U$:

$$(w, (\mathsf{e}, \mathsf{f})) \in [\![\varphi]\!]^{M \circ U^2} \Leftrightarrow ((w, \mathsf{e}), \mathsf{f}) \in [\![\varphi]\!]^{(M \circ U) \circ U}$$

Also, note that the proof of Lemma 1 does not depend upon the assumption that the two action models are the same. More generally, we have the following result for different action models U, U'.

Corollary 2. *Let* U, U' *be action models defined on the same sets of variables* Var *and agents* Ag. *Then,* $M \circ (U \otimes U') \cong (M \circ U) \circ U'$. *Moreover,* $[\![\varphi]\!]^{M \circ (U \otimes U')} = [\![\varphi]\!]^{(M \circ U) \circ U'}$, *for each* φ *in the language of* $U \otimes U'$.

Before proceeding to the generalization of this lemma, we need the claim that the update with an action model U preserves isomorphisms.

Lemma 2. *If* $M \cong M'$ *are isomorphic epistemic models, and* U *is an action model, then* $M \circ U \cong M' \circ U$.

The previous Corollary 2 for the basic case $n = 2$ extends to an arbitrary finite number $n \geq 2$ of actions $\mathsf{f}_1, \ldots, \mathsf{f}_n$. That is, it extends to updates with products of arbitrary n actions taken from a given action model U.

Corollary 3. *We have* $M \circ U^n \cong (M \circ U_1) \cdots \circ U_n$

5.2 Update with the Produce of $\leq n$ Actions in $U^{\leq n}$

Finally, we can define the action model $U^{\leq n}$ for the product of at most n actions (from a fixed action model U) in terms of the product action models $U, U^2, \ldots, U^n$ previously defined.

Definition 8. *Let* U *be an action model and let* $U_1 = \ldots = U_n (= U)$ *be* n *different copies of* U, *denoted* $U_k = (E_k, R_k, \mathsf{pre}_k, \mathsf{post}_k)$ *for each* $1 \leq k \leq n$. *We define* $U^{\leq n} = (E^{\leq n}, R^{\leq n}, \mathsf{pre}^{\leq n}, \mathsf{post}^{\leq n})$ *as follows*

$$E^{\leq n} = \bigcup_{k \leq n} E_k \qquad \mathsf{pre}^{\leq n} = \bigcup_{k \leq n} \mathsf{pre}_k$$
$$R^{\leq n}(a) = \bigcup_{k \leq n} R_k(a) \quad \mathsf{post}^{\leq n} = \bigcup_{k \leq n} \mathsf{post}_k$$

In parallel, the sequence *of at most* n *updates on a model* M, *denoted*

$$(M \circ U_1) \cdots \circ U_{\leq n} = (W^{(M \circ U_1) \cdots \circ U_{\leq n}}, R^{(M \circ U_1) \cdots \circ U_{\leq n}}, V^{(M \circ U_1) \cdots \circ U_{\leq n}})$$

can be defined in a straightforward way from each product action model $(M \circ U_1) \cdots \circ U_k$.

$$W^{(M \circ U_1) \cdots \circ U_{\leq n}} = \bigcup_{k \leq n} W^{(M \circ U_1) \cdots \circ U_k}$$
$$R^{(M \circ U_1) \cdots \circ U_{\leq n}}(a) = \bigcup_{k \leq n} R^{(M \circ U_1) \cdots \circ U_k}(a)$$
$$V^{(M \circ U_1) \cdots \circ U_{\leq n}} = \bigcup_{k \leq n} V^{(M \circ U_1) \cdots \circ U_k}$$

It can be observed that $U^{\leq n}$ is an action model; and also that $(M \circ U_1) \cdots \circ U_{\leq n}$ is an E·PDL model. Moreover, we can extend Corollary 3 to the present case:

Corollary 4. *If* U *is an action model, then*

$$M \circ U^{\leq n} \cong (M \circ U_1) \cdots \circ U_{\leq n}$$

5.3   The Logic $\text{LCC}_{\otimes n}$ of the Action Model $U^{\leq n}$

Let U be again a fixed action model and consider the corresponding product action model $U^{\leq n}$. The language $\mathcal{L}_{\text{LCC}_{\otimes n}}$ of the logic $\text{LCC}_{\otimes n}$ for this action model $U^{\leq n}$ is simply the language of LCC, but now with action modalities of the form $[U^{\leq n}, f_1 \otimes \cdots \otimes f_k]$, for each $f_1 \otimes \cdots \otimes f_k \in E^{\leq n}$ in the present action model $U^{\leq n}$.

The semantics of updates with pointed action model $U^{\leq n}, (f_1, \ldots, f_k)$ is also that of simple action models U. In the present case, we have

$$M, w \models [U^n, e \otimes \cdots \otimes f]\varphi \text{ iff } M, w \models \text{pre}(e \otimes \cdots \otimes f) \text{ implies}$$
$$M \circ U^n, (w, (e \otimes \cdots \otimes f)) \models \varphi$$

A complete axiom system for $\text{LCC}_{\otimes n}$, the logic of (bounded) product action models $U^{\leq n}$, is obtained by extending the previous LCC axioms and rules with reduction axioms for the new product actions $f_1 \otimes \cdots \otimes f_k$.

---

the LCC reduction axioms and rules for $[U, e]\varphi$ formulas with $\varphi \in \mathcal{L}_{\text{LCC}_{\otimes n}}$

plus

$$[U^{\leq n}, (f_1, f_2, \ldots, f_k)]\varphi \leftrightarrow [U^{\leq n}, f_1][U^{\leq n}, (f_2, \ldots, f_k)]\varphi \qquad \text{(Product)}$$

Fig. 2. The axioms and rules for $\text{LCC}_{\otimes n}$

These axioms suffice for the introduction of composition. They induce again a translation function t which splits product actions $[U^{\leq n}, e \otimes f]$ into a sequence of updates $[U^{\leq n}, e][U^{\leq n}, f]$ and proceeds as the translation for LCC for the remaining cases.

Lemma 3. *The product axiom is sound:*

$$\models [U^{\leq n}, f_1 \otimes f_2 \otimes \cdots \otimes f_k]\varphi \leftrightarrow [U^{\leq n}, f_1][U^{\leq n}, f_2 \otimes \cdots \otimes f_n]\varphi$$

As we said, we extend the previous translation $\mathcal{L}_{\text{LCC}} \to \mathcal{L}_{\text{E·PDL}}$ into a translation $\mathcal{L}_{\text{LCC}_{\otimes n}} \to \mathcal{L}_{\text{E·PDL}}$ with the help of an additional clause

$$t([U^{\leq n}, (f_1, f_2, \ldots, f_n)]\varphi) = t([U^{\leq n}, f_1]t([U^{\leq n}, (f_2, \ldots, f_k)]\varphi))$$

Theorem 2. *For each formula $\varphi \in \mathcal{L}_{\text{LCC}_{\otimes n}}$, we have*

$$\models \varphi \Leftrightarrow \vdash \varphi$$

Proof. ($\Leftarrow$) Soundness is established by the corresponding result for LCC in [13] plus the above result for the reduction axiom for product actions. These results also establish the correctness of the extended translation function: each formula in $\text{LCC}_{\otimes n}$ is logically equivalent (in LCC) to an E·PDL-formula $t(\varphi)$.

($\Rightarrow$) E·PDL is complete, and each formula in $\mathcal{L}_{\text{LCC}_{\otimes n}}$ is equivalent to some $\mathcal{L}_{\text{E·PDL}}$ formula.

In addition, the LCC reduction axioms that would correspond to product modalities (except for the case of E·PDL-programs) are also sound.

Proposition 1. *Except for the* LCC *axiom on* E·PDL-*programs, the* LCC *reduction axioms are sound for product action modalities* $[U^{\leq n}, f_1 \otimes \cdots \otimes f_k]$ *are sound.*

In contrast to the previous section on deterministic planning, we cannot fix a priori which action model $U^{\leq n}$ (and logic) are we working with, when solving a given planning domain based on U. It is only after the planning algorithm terminates with a solution, that we (a posteriori) discover for which n the action model $U^{\leq n}$ (actually $U^{\cup \leq n}$, see below) will suffice to check that this plan is indeed a solution. Non-deterministic solutions are more naturally expressed if we further extend the logics $LCC_{\otimes n}$ with non-deterministic choice.

5.4 $LCC_{\cup \otimes n}$: Choice and Non-deterministic Actions

In this section we extend the LCC-logics of bounded composition with the operator choice, that maps some pairs of actions e, f into a new action $e \cup f$. The latter expression denotes an action with indeterminate effects: an execution of $e \cup f$ will turn either as an execution of e or as an execution of f. It is an external agent, the environment (nature) in principle, who chooses the particular outcome after each execution of $e \cup f$. (This is called *demonic* non-determinism, in opposition to so-called *angelic* non-determinism where the planner agent itself selects a course of actions e rather than another one f, if both are executable.) Choice will be indistinctly represented as follows $E_d, \{e, \ldots, f\}$ or $e \cup \ldots \cup f$.

The language of $LCC_{\cup \otimes n}$ adds to that of $LCC_{\otimes n}$ a clause for action modalities of the form

$$[U^{\leq n}, E_d]\varphi$$

where $E_d \subseteq E^{\leq n}$ is an arbitrary (but non-empty) set of product actions $(f_1 \otimes \cdots \otimes f_k)$. The new actions, say,

$$\begin{aligned} E_d &= \{(f_1 \otimes \cdots \otimes f_k), \ldots, (f'_1 \otimes \cdots \otimes f'_{k'})\} \quad \text{are also denoted} \\ &= (f_1 \otimes \cdots \otimes f_k) \cup \ldots \cup (f'_1 \otimes \cdots \otimes f'_{k'}). \end{aligned}$$

The presence of post-conditions in LCC actions prevents us from modeling the new non-deterministic actions, e.g. $e \cup f$, as full-fledged actions in the action model (as we did for product $e \otimes f \in E^{\leq n}$). The problem is that for actions like *tossing a coin*, the post-condition for *heads*, say the variable h, will be at each execution either $\top$ or $\bot$; hence the post-condition for h is not a unique formula, and post cannot be a map.

This contrasts with the match between $U^{\leq n}$ and $LCC_{\otimes n}$ above, and also with the purely epistemic action models [3]. In these logics, each action operator in the language is associated an element in the action model. In this sense, even if our set of actions in the model is the same $E^{\leq n}$ that we had for $LCC_{\otimes n}$ logics, each constructible non-deterministic plans will be shown "equivalent" to some E_d modality. For example, the plan -informally written as- $e \otimes (f \cup f')$ will be associated the modality $[U, (e \otimes f) \cup (e \otimes f')]$.

As suggested in [13] non-deterministic actions are introduced with the help of multi-pointed semantics.

Definition 9. *Given an epistemic model M and an action model U, let $W_d \subseteq W$ and $\mathsf{E}_d = \{\mathsf{f}_1, \ldots, \mathsf{f}_k\} \subseteq \mathsf{E}$. Then M, W_d and U, E_d are multi-pointed models. We define*

$$M, W_d \models \varphi \qquad \textit{iff } M, w \models \varphi \quad \textit{for each } w \in W_d$$
$$M, w \models [\mathsf{U}, \mathsf{E}_d]\varphi \; \textit{iff } M \circ \mathsf{U}, \{(w, \mathsf{f}), \ldots, (w, \mathsf{f}')\} \models \varphi$$
$$\textit{for each } (w, \mathsf{f}), \ldots, (w, \mathsf{f}') \in W^{M \circ \mathsf{U}} \textit{ with } \mathsf{f}, \ldots, \mathsf{f}' \in \mathsf{E}_d$$

In other words, this semantics for $[\mathsf{U}, \mathsf{E}_d]$ modalities simply amounts to the semantics of the operators $[\mathsf{U}, \mathsf{f}]$ for each $\mathsf{f} \in \mathsf{E}_d$. That is,

$$M, w \models [\mathsf{U}, \mathsf{E}_d]\varphi \quad \textit{iff} \quad \textit{for each } f \in \mathsf{E}_d, \quad M, w \models \mathsf{pre}(\mathsf{f}) \textit{ implies } M \circ \mathsf{U}, (w, \mathsf{f}) \models \varphi$$

For the reasons pointed above, non-deterministic actions $\mathsf{e} \cup \mathsf{f}$ or E_d are not actions in the action model, only their components e and f are. In other words, the action model is just $\mathsf{U}^{\leq n}$. In summary, we just add the modalities $[\mathsf{U}, \mathsf{E}_d]$ and expand the semantics to the multi-pointed case, rather than expanding the action models themselves.

In [13], the additional reduction axiom listed next is suggested for non-deterministic choice. Here we add it to the previous system $\mathrm{LCC}_{\otimes n}$:

the reduction axioms and rules of $\mathrm{LCC}_{\otimes n}$

plus

$$[\mathsf{U}, \mathsf{E}_d]\varphi \; \leftrightarrow \; \bigwedge_{\mathsf{e} \in \mathsf{E}_d} [\mathsf{U}, \mathsf{e}]\varphi \qquad\qquad \textit{(choice)}$$

Fig. 3. The axioms and rules for $\mathrm{LCC}_{\cup \otimes n}$

It is straightforward that the reduction axiom *(choice)* for $[\mathsf{U}, \mathsf{E}_d]\varphi$ is sound w.r.t. the semantics above. This allows us to extend once more the translation function t from $\mathrm{LCC}_{\otimes n}$ to $\mathrm{LCC}_{\cup \otimes n}$ with the clause

$$t([\mathsf{U}^{\leq n}, \mathsf{e} \cup \ldots \cup \mathsf{f}]\varphi) \;=\; t([\mathsf{U}^{\leq n}, \mathsf{e}]\varphi) \wedge \ldots \wedge t([\mathsf{U}^{\leq n}, \mathsf{f}]\varphi)$$

The resulting translation function t splits the new modalities $[\mathsf{U}, \mathsf{E}_d]$ and then proceeds as in the case of $\mathrm{LCC}_{\otimes n}$. The soundness of the axiom *(choice)* preserves the soundness of the expanded translation function, again reducing the language of $\mathrm{LCC}_{\cup \otimes n}$ to that of E·PDL and giving the next completeness result.

Corollary 5. *The logic $\mathrm{LCC}_{\cup \otimes n}$ is sound and complete.*

Fact 1. *The LCC axioms for $[\mathsf{U}, \mathsf{e}]$ that do not involve preconditions $\mathsf{pre}(\cdot)$ are also sound for $[\mathsf{U}, \mathsf{e} \cup \mathsf{f}]$ modalities. That is, all the LCC axioms except for* (atoms) *and* (partial functionality)*.*

Also notice that the executability of non-deterministic actions $\mathsf{e} \cup \mathsf{f}$ only requires that some action e or f (or both) is executable.

Lemma 4. *The following holds:* $\models \langle \mathsf{U}, \mathsf{E}_d \rangle \top \leftrightarrow \bigvee_{\mathsf{e} \in \mathsf{E}_d} \mathsf{pre}(\mathsf{e})$.

6 Non-deterministic Plans in LCC

Now we turn into non-deterministic planning, for planning domains containing actions with disjunctive effects are available to the agent, e.g.

$$\models [U, f_0 \cup f_1] \, p \vee q, \quad \text{but with} \quad \not\models [U, f_0 \cup f_1] p \ \text{ and } \ \not\models [U, f_0 \cup f_1] q$$

as given by the post-conditions postconditions $\mathsf{post}(f_0)(p) = \mathsf{post}(f_1)(q) = \top$, and $\mathsf{post}(f_0)(q) = q$ and $\mathsf{post}(f_1)(p) = p$).

In particular, we focus on strong non-deterministic planning. Recall a strong solution for a given planning domain is a plan such that all of its possible executions in the initial state lead to a goal state. Thus, ignoring preconditions, the above action $f_0 \cup f_1$ is a strong solution to $(\varphi_T, \{f_0 \cup f_1\}, \varphi_G)$, for the goal $\varphi_G = p \vee q$; and it is a weak solution when the goal is $\varphi_G = p$.)

Example 3. Consider the action *toss a coin*. This can be seen as a non-deterministic choice between the two deterministic actions of *toss heads* and *toss tails*. Let (resp.) toss_h and $\mathsf{toss}_{\neg h}$ denote these actions, with assigned post-conditions

$$\mathsf{post}(\mathsf{toss}_h) : h \longmapsto \top, \quad \text{and} \quad \mathsf{post}(\mathsf{toss}_{\neg h}) : h \longmapsto \bot$$

Note that the executing agent a cannot distinguish whether she executes toss_h or $\mathsf{toss}_{\neg h}$ (at least until the coin has landed and the agent proceeds to observe the result). This indistinguishability, formally given by $R_a(\mathsf{toss}_h, \mathsf{toss}_{\neg h})$ and viceversa, is called *runtime* indistinguishability in [4]. Even if the agent intends the toss to result in heads (i.e. the agent intends toss_h), the action really available to a is

$$\mathsf{toss}_h \cup \mathsf{toss}_{\neg h} \quad \text{computed as} \quad \bigcup \{e \in E \mid R_a(\mathsf{toss}_h, e)\}$$

Randomness is not essential feature to non-deterministic actions, as the next example illustrates.

Example 4. Consider for instance, the action of pressing a button on the wall, which will switch the light *on* or *off* (the latter denoting $\neg on$). Let the corresponding deterministic actions be denoted on and off, defined by similar post-conditions:

$$\mathsf{post}(\mathsf{on}) : on \longmapsto \top, \quad \text{and} \quad \mathsf{post}(\mathsf{off}) : on \longmapsto \bot$$

In contrast to the coin example, these two actions have different (in fact, mutually inconsistent) preconditions:

$$\mathsf{pre}(\mathsf{on}) = off \quad \text{and} \quad \mathsf{pre}(\mathsf{off}) = on$$

Suppose first our executing agent a is blind (or blind-folded), so she cannot distinguish on from off at run-time (during execution). See Figure 4 (Top). Notice that on $\cup$ off has a trivial precondition: $on \vee \neg on$, given by $\mathsf{pre}(\mathsf{on}) \vee \mathsf{pre}(\mathsf{off})$.

Secondly, suppose instead that the agent can see (or has been told) whether the light is initially *on*, Figure 4(Mid). She knows which of the two actions on* or off* is executable (has a true precondition), so we can model them separately as two deterministic actions.

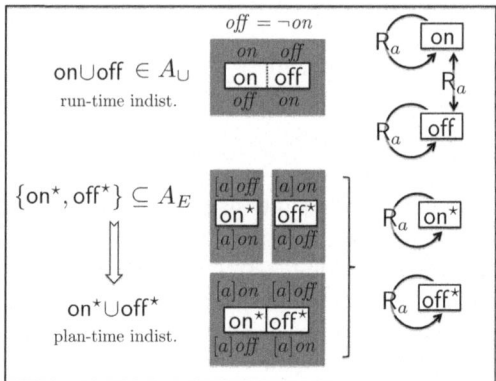

Fig. 4. (Top) A blind agent pressing the light button: on $\cup$ off. (Mid) Switching the light on (while seeing): on*. Similarly for off*. (Bottom) Pressing the light button (while seeing), during the planning phase.

Along this line, the planner agent a might not know (during planning) whether she will find the light *on* or *off*, when she switches it (this being a planned action). Figure 4 (Bottom). This is called *plan-time* indistinguishability in [4], since only at execution time the agent will know whether whether she is going to turn the light on or off. This kind of actions, modeled as a choice on$^\star \cup$ off*.

After this review on the effects of partial observability of states and actions, we proceed to the task of plan search. As these examples show, the previous notions of *available actions A*, *plan* and *solution* must be redefined for the present non-deterministic case. For the sake of simplicity, we will only consider the choice between two actions $f_0 \cup f_1$. The definitions and results in this paper can be generalized to the choice of finitely many actions $f_0 \cup f_1 \cup \cdots \cup f_k$.

From here on, we abstract from any particular bound n upon the length of plans, so in the following we will just write the action model as U rather than as a fixed action model $\mathsf{U}^{\leq n}$. With this remark in mind, recall the set of action sequences definable in $\mathrm{LCC}_{\mathsf{U} \otimes n}$ is any sequence of action modalities

$$[\mathsf{U}, \mathsf{E}_1] \ldots [\mathsf{U}, \mathsf{E}_k] \quad \text{(also written } (\mathsf{E}_0, \ldots, \mathsf{E}_k))$$

Concerning the basic actions available to the agent, we have: (1) a set A_e of actions e from E; and (2) a set of $A_\cup$ containing pairs of actions, denoted e $\cup$ f, with again e $\in$ E and f $\in$ E. For an example of these basic actions, we have on*in A_E and on$^\star \cup$ off* and toss$_h \cup$ toss$_{\neg h}$ in $A_\cup$. The following definition replace the old set A from Definition 5 by the new set $A_\mathsf{E} \cup A_\cup$.

Definition 10. *A* non-deterministic planning domain *in* U *is a triple*

$$\mathbb{M} = (\varphi_T, A_\mathsf{E} \cup A_\cup, \varphi_G)$$

with $A_\mathsf{E} \subseteq \mathsf{E}$, *and* $A_\cup \subseteq \mathsf{E} \times \mathsf{E}$.

Not all of the above action sequences $[U, E_1] \ldots [U, E_k]$ in the language of $LCC_{\cup \otimes n}$ denote action sequences that are available to the agent according to a planning domain M. The latter sub-class is defined next.

Definition 11. *We say $[U, e]$ and $[U, e \cup f]$ are M-sequences whenever $e \in A_E$ and $e \cup f$ in $A_\cup$. Moreover, if $e' \otimes \cdots \otimes e''$ and $f' \otimes \cdots \otimes f''$ are elements of $A_E^{\leq \omega}$ and $e \cup f \in A_\cup$ satisfies $(e, f), (f, e) \notin R_a$, then*

$$[U, (e \otimes e' \otimes \cdots \otimes e'') \cup (f \otimes f' \otimes \cdots \otimes f'')] \quad \text{is an } M\text{-sequence}$$

Finally, any finite sequence $[U, E_k] \ldots [U, E_1]$ of M-sequences is an M-sequence.

The idea of M-sequences is to minimally constrain (within the limits of $\mathcal{L}_{LCC_{\cup \otimes n}}$) how much freedom an agent is allowed after executing a non-deterministic action $e \cup f$ (while preserving epistemic control):

- if the components e and f are run-time indistinguishable according to R_a, the next action after executing $e \cup f$ must be uniquely specified (though it can be another non-deterministic action),
- if the components e and f are run-time distinguishable, one can execute alternative (deterministic) actions, say e' or f', depending on whether the execution of $e \cup f$ instantiated, resp., as e or as f.

Example 5. (Cont'd) Recall the sets of available actions $A_E = \varnothing$ and $A_\cup = \{toss_h \cup toss_{\neg h}\}$ from Example 3. Read the tossing action as causing the coin to land into agent a's hand. And expand these sets with a sensing action in $A_\cup$ (feeling in your hand whether the coin landed heads) and a flip (into heads) action in A_E:

$$feel_h \cup feel_{\neg h} \quad \begin{array}{ll} pre(feel_h) = h & pre(feel_{\neg h}) = \neg h \\ post(feel_h) = id_{Var} & post(feel_{\neg h}) = id_{Var} \\ R_a(feel_h, feel_{\neg h}) & R_a(feel_{\neg h}, feel_h) \end{array}$$

$$flip_h \quad \begin{array}{l} pre(flip_h) = \neg h \\ post(flip_h) : h \mapsto \top \end{array}$$

Then, the following is an M-sequence leading to a *heads* result in any execution.

$$[U, toss_h \cup toss_{\neg h}] \; [U, (feel_h \cup (feel_{\neg h} \otimes flip_h)]$$
tossing the coin, sensing it, and if tails flip it to heads

Definition 12. *We say that an M-sequence $[U, E_1], \ldots, [U, E_r]$ is a solution to the planning domain $M = (\varphi_T, A_E \cup A_\cup, \varphi_G)$ iff*

$$\begin{array}{ll} \models \varphi_T \rightarrow [U, E_1] \ldots [U, E_r] \varphi_G & \text{(success)} \\ \models \varphi_T \rightarrow \langle U, E_1 \rangle \ldots \langle U, E_r \rangle \top & \text{(executability)} \end{array}$$

It can be shown that the M-sequence from Ex. 5 is a solution for the planning domain

$$M = (\top, \{toss_h \cup toss_{\neg h}, feel_h \cup feel_{\neg h}, flip_h, skip\}, [(a \cup b)^*]h)$$

7   A Search Algorithm for Non-deterministic Planning in LCC

Let us then proceed to the study of search algorithms for arbitrary planning domains $\mathbb{M}$. These planning algorithms search for solutions in the space of plans, defined below. The idea is to reduce a non-deterministic plan into a sequence of pairs of deterministic plans, each pair motivated by the introduction of a non-deterministic action. These plans are a triple consisting of: (1) a (possibly empty) $\mathbb{M}$-sequence $[U, E_k], \dots [U, E_1]$, (possibly) prefixed by an operator-like expression $[U, \cdot]$ (denoting the operator under construction); and formulas for (2) an initial state and (3) open goals corresponding to (1).

$$\text{plan } \pi \ = \ (\ \text{operator} + \mathbb{M}\text{-sequence},\ \text{init. state } \varphi_{\text{init}(\pi)},\ \text{open goals } \varphi_{\text{goals}(\pi)}\ )$$

Again we abuse notation and refer to (1) with the label π of the plan it belongs to.

Definition 13. *Given a planning domain* $\mathbb{M} = (\varphi_T, A_{\mathsf{E}} \cup A_{\cup}, \varphi_G)$, *the* empty plan *for* $\mathbb{M}$ *is the pair* $\pi_\varnothing = (\varnothing, \varphi_G)$. *For a given plan* $\pi_k = [U, E_k] \dots [U, E_1]$ *and its refinement with some* $\mathsf{e} \in A_{\mathsf{E}}$, *denoted* $\pi = \pi_k(\mathsf{e}) = [U, \mathsf{e}]\pi_k$, *we define the refinements* $\pi(\cdot)$ *with* $\mathsf{f} \in A_{\mathsf{E}}$ *or a run-time dist. action* $\mathsf{f} \cup \mathsf{f}' \in A_{\cup}$ *as:*

$$\pi(\mathsf{f}) = [U, \mathsf{f} \otimes \mathsf{e}]\pi_k \qquad\qquad \pi(\mathsf{f} \cup \mathsf{f}') = [U, (\mathsf{f} \otimes \mathsf{e}) \cup (\mathsf{f}' \otimes \mathsf{x})]\pi_k$$
$$\varphi_{\text{init}(\pi(\mathsf{f}))} = \varphi_T \qquad\qquad \varphi_{\text{init}(\pi(\mathsf{f} \cup \mathsf{f}'))} = \text{``}[U, \mathsf{f}'](\cdot)\text{''}$$
$$\varphi_{\text{goals}(\pi(\mathsf{f}))} = t([U, \mathsf{f}]\varphi_{\text{goals}(\pi)} \wedge \langle U, \mathsf{f}\rangle \top) \qquad \varphi_{\text{goals}(\pi(\mathsf{f} \cup \mathsf{f}'))} = \varphi_{\text{goals}(\pi_k)}$$

Given a plan π *of the form* $\pi = (\ [U, (\mathsf{f} \otimes \mathsf{e}) \cup (\mathsf{f}' \otimes \mathsf{x} \otimes \mathsf{e}')]\pi_k,\ \text{``}[U, \mathsf{f}'](\cdot)\text{''},\ \varphi_{\text{goals}(\pi)}\ )$, *and an action* $\mathsf{e}'' \in A_{\mathsf{E}}$ *we define the refinement* $\pi(\mathsf{e}'')$ *as*

$$\pi(\mathsf{e}'') = \begin{cases} [U, (\mathsf{f} \otimes \mathsf{e}) \cup (\mathsf{f}' \otimes \mathsf{x} \otimes \mathsf{e}'' \otimes \mathsf{e})]\pi_k & \text{if } \not\models [U, \mathsf{f}'][U, \mathsf{e}'' \otimes \mathsf{e}]\varphi_{\text{goals}(\pi_k)} \\ [U, (\mathsf{f} \otimes \mathsf{e}) \cup (\mathsf{f}' \otimes \mathsf{e}'' \otimes \mathsf{e})] & \text{otherwise} \end{cases}$$

$$\varphi_{\text{init}(\pi(\mathsf{e}''))} = \begin{cases} \varphi_{\text{init}(\pi(\mathsf{e}''))} & \text{if } \not\models [U, \mathsf{f}'][U, \mathsf{e}'' \otimes \mathsf{e}]\varphi_{\text{goals}(\pi_k)} \\ \varphi_T & \text{otherwise} \end{cases}$$

$$\varphi_{\text{goals}(\pi(\mathsf{e}''))} = \begin{cases} t([U, \mathsf{e}'']\varphi_{\text{goals}(\pi)} \wedge \langle U, \mathsf{e}''\rangle \top) & \text{if } \not\models [U, \mathsf{f}'][U, \mathsf{e}'' \otimes \mathsf{e}]\varphi_{\text{goals}(\pi_k)} \\ t([U, (\mathsf{f} \otimes \mathsf{e}) \cup (\mathsf{f}' \otimes \mathsf{e}'' \otimes \mathsf{e})]\varphi_{\text{goals}(\pi_k)} \\ \qquad \wedge \langle U, (\mathsf{f} \otimes \mathsf{e}) \cup (\mathsf{f}' \otimes \mathsf{e}'' \otimes \mathsf{e})\rangle \top) & \text{otherwise} \end{cases}$$

Finally, if $\mathsf{f} \cup \mathsf{f}'$ *is run-time indistinguishable to the agent, i.e.* $(\mathsf{f}, \mathsf{f}'), (\mathsf{f}', \mathsf{f}) \in R_a$, *we define the refinement of* π_k *with* $\mathsf{f} \cup \mathsf{f}'$ *as:*

$$\pi(\mathsf{f} \cup \mathsf{f}') = [U, \mathsf{f} \cup \mathsf{f}']\pi_k$$
$$\varphi_{\text{init}(\pi(\mathsf{f} \cup \mathsf{f}'))} = \varphi_T$$
$$\varphi_{\text{goals}(\pi(\mathsf{f} \cup \mathsf{f}'))} = t([U, \mathsf{f} \cup \mathsf{f}']\varphi_{\text{goals}(\pi_k)} \wedge \langle U, \mathsf{f} \cup \mathsf{f}'\rangle \top)$$

Given a plan π *and a refinement of it* $\pi(\cdot)$, *we say* $\pi(\cdot)$ *is a* leaf *iff either* $\varphi_{\pi(\cdot)}$ *is inconsistent or* $\models \varphi_{\text{goals}(\pi(\cdot))} \rightarrow \varphi_{\text{goals}(\pi)}$. *The* Terminating Condition *for a plan* π *is*

$$\varphi_{\text{init}(\pi)} = \varphi_T \quad \text{and} \quad \models \varphi_{\text{init}(\pi)} \rightarrow \varphi_{\text{goals}(\pi)}$$

After a run-time indistinguishable action, e.g. coin tossing, conditional plans can be made depending on the outcome of an observation. Let us finally address the properties of non-deterministic planning based on BFS.

Input : $\mathbb{M} = (\varphi_T, A_E \cup A_U, \varphi_G)$.
LET Plans $= \langle \pi_\varnothing \rangle$ and $\pi = \pi_\varnothing$
WHILE π does not satisfy Terminating Condition
    DELETE π FROM Plans
    SET Plans $=$ Plans$^\cap \langle \pi' \mid \pi'$ refines π and π' not a leaf $\rangle$.
    SET $\pi =$ the first element of Plans
Output : π (i.e. the $\mathbb{M}$-sequence defined by π)

Fig. 5. BFS algorithm for backward non-deterministic planning in $\mathrm{LCC}_{\cup \otimes n}$

Theorem 3. *Let the output of the BFS algorithm in Fig. 5 be* $[\mathsf{U}, \mathsf{E}_1] \ldots [\mathsf{U}, \mathsf{E}_k]$ *for a planning domain* $\mathbb{M}$. *Then,* $[\mathsf{U}, \mathsf{E}_1] \ldots [\mathsf{U}, \mathsf{E}_k]$ *is an* $\mathbb{M}$-*sequence and a solution for* $\mathbb{M}$.

Theorem 4. *For a given planning domain* $\mathbb{M}$, *if some* $\mathbb{M}$-*sequence exists that is a solution to* $\mathbb{M}$, *then the BFS algorithm in Fig. 5 terminates (with a solution).*

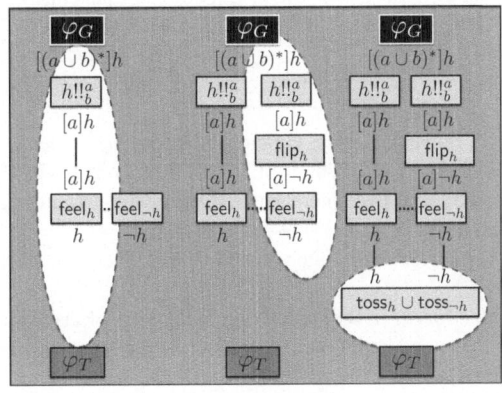

Fig. 6. Plan search in Example 1. Incremental construction of a solution for the coin example.

Example 6. Recall Example 1, where the planner agent a must show heads, denoted h, to win the prize. The action flip_h is secret in the sense of $(\mathrm{flip}_h, \mathrm{skip}) \in R_b$, i.e. agent b believes nothing is happening; this secrecy is known by a provided flip_h is only R_a-related to itself. The construction of a solution is shown in Figure 6, where: (Left) a deterministic plan is being built, consisting of a's demonstration $h!!_b^a$ that h to b (with a knowing a priori that h); a plan-time indistinguishable action $\mathrm{feel}_h \cup \mathrm{feel}_{\neg h}$ is added. (Center) The planner proceeds to solve the rightmost case where $\mathrm{feel}_{\neg h}$ is executed (due to a $\neg h$ state). This planning sub-problem is solved by a flip_h action, followed by the same demonstration $h!!_b^a$. (Right) Finally, the algorithm stops after adding the run-time indistinguishable action of tossing $\mathrm{toss}_h \cup \mathrm{toss}_{\neg h}$. Note the remaining of the plan is executable no matter the result of the coin toss. The slightly different plan construction from [10] can also be built with two deterministic sensing actions (for h and $\neg h$).

8 Conclusions and Future Work

We presented backward planning algorithms for a planner-reasoner agent enabling her to find deterministic or (non-deterministic) strong plans in multi-agent scenarios. We considered dynamic epistemic logics with ontic actions, further extended with composition and choice. Planners in these logics are sensitive to others' beliefs and may contain communications and observations as well as the usual fact-changing actions. As for future work, we would like to study more complex plan structures, or new kinds of actions like belief revision announcements. Another direction would be the study of (logical) heuristics to improve the performance of LCC planners.

Acknowledgements. This work has been funded by projects AT (CSD 2007-022), AR-INF (TIN2009-14704-C03-03); and grants 2009-SGR-1434 and EPSRC EP/J002607/1.

References

1. Andersen, M.B., Bolander, T., Jensen, M.H.: Conditional Epistemic Planning. In: del Cerro, L.F., Herzig, A., Mengin, J. (eds.) JELIA 2012. LNCS (LNAI), vol. 7519, pp. 94–106. Springer, Heidelberg (2012)
2. Aucher, G.: DEL-sequents for progression. Journal of Applied Non-Classical Logics 21(3-4), 289–321 (2011)
3. Baltag, A., Moss, L., Solecki, S.: The logic of public announcements, common knowledge and private suspicions. In: Proc. of 7th Conf. TARK 1998, pp. 43–56 (1998)
4. Bolander, T., Andersen, M.: Epistemic planning for single- and multi-agent systems. Journal of Applied Non-Classical Logics 21(1), 9–34 (2011)
5. Ghallab, M., Nau, D., Traverso, P.: Automated Planning: Theory and Practice. Morgan Kaufmann (2004)
6. Harel, D., Kozen, D., Tiuryn, J.: Dynamic Logic. MIT Press, Massachusetts (2000)
7. Hintikka, J.: Knowledge and belief: an introduction to the logic of the two notions. Cornell University Press (1962)
8. Löwe, B., Pacuit, E., Witzel, A.: Planning based on dynamic epistemic logic (2010)
9. Pardo, P., Sadrzadeh, M.: Planning in the Logics of Communication and Change. In: Proc. of AAMAS 2012 (2012)
10. Pardo, P., Sadrzadeh, M.: Backward Planning in the Logics of Communication and Change. In: Proc. of Agreement Technologies AT 2012 (2012)
11. Pearl, J.: Heuristics: Intelligent Search Strategies for Computer Problem Solving. Addison-Wesley (1984)
12. Rao, A., Georgeff, M.: Modeling rational agents within a BDI-architecture. In: Proc. of Principles of Knowledge Representation and Reasoning (KR), pp. 473–484 (1991)
13. van Benthem, J., van Eijck, J., Kooi, B.: Logics of Communication and Change. Information and Computation 204, 1620–1662 (2006)
14. van der Hoek, W., Wooldridge, M.: Tractable Multiagent Planning for Epistemic Goals. In: Proc. of AAMAS 2002, pp. 1167–1174 (2002)
15. van Ditmarsch, H., van der Hoek, W., Kooi, B.: Dynamic Epistemic Logic. Springer (2008)
16. van Ditmarsch, H., Kooi, B.: Semantic results for ontic and epistemic change. In: Bonanno, van der Hoek, Wooldridge (eds.) LOFT 7, pp. 87–117 (2008)

Agent Deliberation via Forward and Backward Chaining in Linear Logic

Luke Trodd, James Harland, and John Thangarajah

School of CS & IT, RMIT University
GPO Box 2476
Melbourne, 3001, Australia
{luke.trodd,james.harland,johnt}@rmit.edu.au

Abstract. Agent systems are designed to work in complex dynamic environments, which requires an agent to repeatedly deliberate over its choice of actions. A common way to achieve this is to use agent architectures based on the Belief-Desire-Intention (BDI) model, in which an agent continuously deliberates over the best way to achieve its goals in the current environment. In this paper we explore how a BDI approach can be implemented in Lygon, a logic programming language based on linear logic. In particular, we show how backward and forward chaining techniques can be used to provide proactive and reactive agent behaviours. We discuss some extensions to Lygon which allow us to use abduction techniques to generate plans to achieve a given goal, as well as an addition to the syntax of Lygon which greatly simplifies the specification of a sequence of goals to be achieved. We also show how a simple addition to the backward chaining process allows us to specify proactive checking of maintenance goals.

1 Introduction

Intelligent agents are often used to determine software solutions to problems that occur in complex dynamic environments. Three common properties of agents in such environments are being *situated, reactive* and *proactive* [19]. Being *situated* means that the agent is embedded in the environment, and can both sense it and act on it. This means that the agent needs to be able to take input from the environment and use it to determine an appropriate course of action. Being *reactive* means that it needs to be able to adapt its behaviour to changes in the environment. This means that the agent needs to continually monitor the environment and potentially change what it has previously decided to do. Being *proactive* means that the agent has a particular agenda that it is trying to achieve.

For example, consider a robot vacuum cleaner in an office building, which is instructed to ensure that a particular set of offices is clean. This robot has sensors which enable it to tell whether a given room is clean or dirty, and has a vacuum action that can be performed to convert a dirty room into a clean one. The robot can also only clean the room that it is currently located in, so that to clean another room, it must move to the other room first. The robot must also maintain a certain minimum of battery energy, and if the level falls below a certain amount, it must return to the charging station and recharge before proceeding. As people and other robots can come and go within the

M. Baldoni et al. (Eds.): DALT 2012, LNAI 7784, pp. 57–75, 2013.

building, the status of each room can vary from clean to dirty and vice-versa, due to human interaction (clean to dirty) or a helpful fellow robot (dirty to clean). This robot is *situated*, as it can sense the status of the rooms, and perform actions (vacuum, move, charge) which will update the environment. This robot will need to be *reactive*, as rooms originally thought to be dirty can turn out to be clean and vice-versa. This robot will also need to be *proactive*, in that it will need to find a way to clean its allocated offices. It will also need to monitor its battery usage, and recharge whenever necessary to maintain its minimum level of battery power.

Agent solutions to this kind of problem are often based on the *Belief-Desire-Intention (BDI)* paradigm [15,19]. *Beliefs* represent what the agent believes to be the current state of the world. *Desires* specify the proactive behaviour of the agent, in that the agent works to make these true. Often desires can be mutually exclusive or contradictory, requiring the agent to select from among them. For example, our cleaning robot may desire to clean multiple rooms but can only clean one at any given time. For this reason BDI implementations often use *goals*, which can be thought of as desires with some restrictions on them (such as requiring goals to be consistent, feasible and not yet achieved). There can be several types of goals, including *achievement goals*, such as cleaning a room (which is dropped once it is achieved), and *maintenance goals*, such as maintaining a minimum level of charge (which is an ongoing process). *Intentions* are plans of action that the agent has selected to achieve its current goals. Often there are many ways to achieve a set of goals that the agent is working on, implying the need for a mechanism to choose between them.

Implementations of BDI systems are usually based around an *observe-think-act* cycle, in which an agent will observe the current environment, which may have changed since the last observation, determine which goals it should be pursuing and what plans should be used to achieve them, and choose a particular action to perform. Note that while the number of actions performed in the *act* phase is not specified, it is intended to be relatively small, so that the agent will be able to detect changes in the environment (which is only done in the *observe* phase) and respond to them within an appropriate amount of time. Hence a fundamental feature of BDI systems is the manner in which they provide both proactive (or goal-directed) and reactive behaviour.

In this paper, we consider how we may adapt existing logical inference techniques to implement a BDI architecture. Using logic as a basis for the architecture will mean that we can develop methods for formal analysis of agent systems via logical inference, as well as being able to exploit existing automated reasoning technologies to develop applications. In particular, we will investigate the use of *linear logic* [5] for such systems. Linear logic has the potential to offer many advantages in the agent context over other logics due to its resource-oriented nature. Linear logic is able to specify actions cleanly and intuitively [12], can effectively express resource oriented problems and has a native notion of concurrency appropriate for agent architectures. Linear logic has also been recently applied to agent negotiation [14], and adaptive narratives [1]. This suggests that there is significant potential for the development of BDI agents based on linear logic. In particular, the existence of logic programming languages based on linear logic, such as Lygon [6] and Lolli [9] make such languages a natural starting point for this investigation.

Our BDI agent architecture will be based on Lygon technology. This means that we proceed in a bottom-up manner, *i.e.* commencing with what can be readily implemented in Lygon, identifying where extensions are needed, adding these to Lygon and eventually developing a BDI deliberation cycle. This has been implemented and applied to various problems (including the gold mining problem used in the CLIMA agent programming contest[1]). Our focus is hence not so much on the design of (yet another) agent programming language, nor on the formal analysis of such a language, but on the similarities and differences between what is provided in linear logic programming languages such as Lygon and what is required by a BDI agent architecture. Once this is done, we intend to use our implementation experience to develop both appropriate language features and a formal analysis of their properties.

One of the key features of a BDI architecture is the distinction between the *think* phase and the *act* phase. In order to support the latter phase, we have developed and implemented a forward-chaining inference mechanism (see Section 2.3 for more details) to complement Lygon's existing backward-chaining mechanism. This provides a natural method for implementing reactive behaviour. We demonstrate a variety of enhancements that extend upon the existing Lygon architecture, facilitating agent oriented programming. We introduce new concepts and connectives which significantly simplify the expression of some typical agent programs. We introduce a novel, simple but effective technique for proactive checking of maintenance goals [4] in a generic manner. We describe a novel BDI agent deliberation cycle that accommodates the mentioned reactive and deliberative behaviours. We have implemented these techniques in Lygon and have developed and tested a number of applications.

This paper is organised as follows. In Section 2, we discuss linear logic and backward- and forward-chaining methods, and in Section 3, we discuss how we describe our extensions to Lygon. In Section 4, we present our version of the BDI deliberation cycle, and we discuss our implementation with a detailed example in Section 5 highlighting the advantages of this approach. Finally in Section 6, we present our conclusions.

2 Background

2.1 Linear Logic

There is a vast literature on linear logic [5] and its variants, and we do not attempt a general introduction here. However, we give an overview of the main features relevant to this paper.

Linear logic is often described as being "resource-sensitive", in its ability to control the duplication of formulae. A defining difference between linear and classical logic is that in linear logic by default each formula can be used only once. This means that differences in resources, such as having two dollars rather than one, can be captured simply by having two copies of an appropriate formula rather than one. This property means that linear logic is a natural way in which to specify *fluents*, which is appropriate for many practical agent scenarios. As discussed by Masseron et al. [12], this makes it simple to represent actions and hence plans in linear logic. Linear logic also allows the

---

[1] http://centria.di.fct.unl.pt/~clima

default behaviour to be overridden by operators known as exponentials, which means that it is possible to use classical reasoning if desired. There are two versions of and conjunction (denoted $\otimes$ and $\&$) and disjunction (denoted $\invamp$ and $\oplus$), the first one of which accumulates resources (*multiplicative* $\otimes$ and $\invamp$) and another which does not (*additive* $\&$ and $\oplus$).

The $\otimes$ operator can intuitively be thought of as combining two resources together. As an example, consider a situation in which we visit a restaurant to order a meal. We might represent a meal in the form *Burger $\otimes$ Fries $\otimes$ Coke*, indicating that we will receive the three food 'resources' together. Intuitively we can think of the $\&$ operator as a choice that we can make. In a statement *Burger $\&$ Fries*, the choice between a *Burger* or *Fries* is arbitrary and we can be sure that both are valid choices. The $\oplus$ operator resembles $\vee$ in classical logic, encoding a choice which is not ours to make. A statement *Burger $\oplus$ Fries* implies that we will receive either a *Burger* or *Fries* but have no say in the matter (the choice is made by the restaurant). The par operator $\invamp$ is the dual of the $\otimes$ operator, but has less intuitive definition. In practice it defines a concurrent operation whereby the context can be split between both sides of the operator, allowing us to share resources.

The operator $\multimap$ is the linear version of classical implication. The fundamental difference between this and classical implication is that a resource must be consumed in the process. The linear implication *Money $\multimap$ Coke* tells us that given *Money* we can obtain a *Coke*, but that we must "consume" *Money* to get it. Note that from the statement *Money $\multimap$ Coke* we can infer by backward-chaining that if we want *Coke*, we need first acquire *Money*, and that by forward-chaining we can infer that from *Money* we can acquire *Coke*.

Linear logic also has a negation $(^{\perp})$ which can be used to represent supply or debt. For example to represent the perspective of the restaurant providing the above meal we can write $Burger^{\perp} \invamp Fries^{\perp} \invamp Coke^{\perp}$.

2.2 Lygon

Lygon is a logic programming language based on linear logic [6,17]. Lygon is a strict extension of pure Prolog that incorporates linear logic reasoning capabilities. Lygon by default allows resources to be used only once during a computation. This makes it an excellent tool for problem domains which are resource-oriented.

Lygon maps each of the linear logic connectives as follows:

$$\text{Logic } \otimes \& \invamp \oplus \multimap F^{\perp}$$
$$\text{Lygon } * \& \# @ \to \text{neg } F$$

For example, t o specify a program which exchanges two dollars for a meal we may write:

```
meal <- dollar * dollar
```

where * is the ASCII for $\otimes$ and we write $\multimap$ 'backwards' à la Prolog as <-. To specify that buying a meal consumes two dollars and provides a burger, fries and coke we might define the clause:

```
meal <- dollar * dollar * (neg burger # neg fries # neg coke).
```

This same pattern can be used for agent actions, in that the above rule can be interpreted as an action `meal` with pre-conditions `dollar * dollar` and post-conditions `burger * fries * coke`.

The most significant difference between Lygon and Prolog is that in Lygon a program context must be maintained, which may vary from step to step. For example, given a goal such as $G_1 * G_2$, it is necessary to split the (linear part of) the program into two mutually exclusive and exhaustive parts P_1 and P_2 such that $P_1 \vdash G_1$ and $P_2 \vdash G_2$. In Prolog, as formulae can be arbitrarily copied, this is not necessary. In Lygon (and other implementations, such as Lolli [9]) the implementation of * will provide the entire context to G_1, and if it succeeds, the remaining unused context is passed to G_2. Hence the transmission of the program context is fundamental in Lygon, and as we shall see, this is a critical property for BDI agent systems.

2.3 Inference and Abduction

The requirement for an agent to use a combination of both proactive and reactive behaviour corresponds in automated reasoning to a combination of both *backward-chaining* and *forward-chaining* inference [7,2,11]. Backward-chaining involves reasoning backwards from a goal towards known truths, whereas forward-chaining involves using what is known to be true to infer new results. Harland and Winikoff [8] have proposed a BDI system based on linear logic, in which the proactive behaviour of the agent is provided by backward-chaining methods and the reactive behaviour of the agent is provided by forward-chaining methods. In terms of the BDI cycle mentioned above, this means that the *think* phase would be implemented by backward-chaining techniques and the *act* and *observe* phases by forward-chaining ones. Backward-chaining methods have been the basis of logic programming languages based on linear logic, such as Lygon [6] and Lolli [9]. Forward-chaining methods have also been used [7], and techniques to combine both methods into one system have also been studied [2,11]. However, there has been comparatively little work on applying such methods to agent systems. In addition, the work of Harland and Winikoff was purely a design; no precise execution method was given and no implementation was developed.

Backward-chaining has long been the standard technique in logic programming, theorem provers and other applications. Given a set of formulae and a goal, backward-chaining seeks to find a proof by starting at the goal and recursively decomposing it into subgoals, attempting to resolve them using depth-first recursion and backtracking. Consider the formulae below.

```
X flies -> X has wings
X has a beak -> X is a bird
X has wings -> X is a bird
```

Given these rules we may wish to prove `X is a bird`, given that we know it flies. We would then select the second and third rules, since `X is a bird` is the conclusion of these rules. Following the inference backwards from the conclusion to the premise, we then determine that either X has a beak or X has wings imply our goal. By following a similar process, we determine that X has wings is implied by X flies, and so we have proved our result. In a linear logic context, a backward-chaining proof tells us that we can achieve some state (or resources) G, given some initial state or resources and a set of valid exchanges. The backward-chaining approach is usefully applied to many applications such as the querying of databases and solving a set of constraints. In an agent context, backward-chaining may be viewed as a method for finding plans, as it allows us to ask "what if?"questions about the world, and hence provides means of implementing proactive behaviour.

Backward-chaining is very closely related to another technique known as *abduction*. Logical deduction can be considered a projection forward from cause to effects that enable us to predict the logical outcome of a set of inferences. Abduction on the other hand allows us to project backwards from effects to causes to abduce possible explanations for our observations [16]. A classic example of this is demonstrated by the following [3]:

```
grass is wet ← rained last night
grass is wet ← sprinkler was on
shoes are wet ← grass is wet
```

Given the above rules, we may observe that our shoes are wet and attempt to abduce an explanation for why this is so. By recursively computing explanations for our observations we determine that our shoes may be wet because it rained last night or because the sprinkler was on.

Forward-chaining essentially uses modus ponens as an inference rule. For example, consider the following rules:

```
There is smoke -> There is a fire
There is a fire -> There is an emergency
```

Given these implications, if we observe smoke we can conclude there is a fire and can therefore conclude there is an emergency. One useful application of forward chaining to agent systems is its natural resemblance to reactive behaviours. Given some situation, we can define a rule that reactively applies some action or plan. For example we may define a reactive rule:

```
There is fire − > Sound alarm
```

This makes it straightforward to include such rules in an agent, to allow for strictly reactive behaviour such as an emergency response or performing safely-critical actions such as braking. A reactive system may be made up of many forward chaining rules, which can be seen as a collection of stimulus-response, in-out or condition-action rules [10].

3   Agents in Lygon

Our general strategy is to map each phase of the *observe-think-act* cycle to a particular paradigm. In the *observe* phase, the beliefs of the agent are updated, depending on the output from the agent's sensors or other means of perceiving the environment. As we shall see, this may also involve some forward-chaining computation. In the *think* phase, we apply backward-chaining techniques to our current goals, to determine the appropriate actions to be taken. In the *act* phase, we apply forward-chaining techniques to perform the chosen actions, which will generally involve updating the agent's beliefs in a corresponding manner.

3.1   Actions

We now describe our extensions to Lygon to make it feasible to use as a BDI agent programming system. To make our discussion concrete, we will first specify Lygon rules for the actions in the vacuum cleaner example. We assume that the robot has a maximum of 100 units of energy, and a single move action costs 10 units. A vacuum action can only take place when the room the robot is in is dirty, and this takes 20 units of energy. The rules for the move, vacuum and charge actions are below. These, modulo some simple syntactic sugar, can be directly used in Lygon.[2] We prefix actions with the reserved word act. The general form of rules for action is

```
act Name: Preconditions -> Postconditions.
```

```
act move(Y): at(X)*energy(C) -> at(Y)*energy(C-10).
act charge: at(charger)*energy(C) -> at(charger)*energy(100).
act vacuum(X): at(X)*dirty(X)*energy(C) ->
                            at(X)*clean(X)*energy(C-20).
```

Fig. 1. Vacuum cleaner actions

One of the first issues that arises is that Lygon is designed as a logic programming language, and hence goals are queries, which result in an answer of "yes" or "no". In an agent system, goals are not only assumed not to be true, but the point of performing computation on goals is to determine a particular set of actions that will make the goal true. Hence our first step is to extend Lygon with abductive capabilities, so that the result of a computation is not just an answer, but is a set of actions to be performed (possibly empty, corresponding to a "yes") in order to make the goal true. The *abducibles*, i.e. the results of the abduction process, are constrained here to be actions, which is why the action rules are preceded by the keyword act.

Consider the example above if the robot is in room 1, room 2 is dirty, the robot has 70 units of energy, and has a goal of clean(2). The rules above can be used to show that the robot needs to achieve the goal at(2) before it can perform the action vacuum(2), which will result in the goal being achieved. To achieve at(2), the rules above also show that it will need to perform move(2). As there are no more goals to be achieved, it has determined that the sequence of actions move(2) then vacuum(2) will achieve the goal.

---

[2] This and many other details can be found in a detailed technical report available from http://www.cs.rmit.edu.au/~jah/agents-in-lygon. Lygon code and the extensions described herein can be found at the same URL.

3.2   The >> Operator

The basic idea is to write actions and plans as rules in Lygon, and to use backward-chaining together with abduction to determine a set of actions that will achieve the goal. A subtlety here that may not be immediately apparent is that there is a need to specify sequences of goals, i.e. goals and actions that must be performed in a particular order. In the above example, it is clear that the move action must be performed before the vacuum action, as a post-condition of the move action (i.e. being in room 2) is a pre-condition of the vacuum action. This means that subgoal at(2) must be achieved before the action vacuum(2) is performed. Moreover, it is common for plans to require that a particular set of actions be performed in a specific order, sometimes intermixed with subgoals [18]. This means that in order to implement a BDI-style system, we need to be able to specify a sequential order in which actions, plans and goals are to be executed or achieved. This is nothing more or less than a reflection of the fact that the actions required to achieve a particular goal are usually constrained to work in a particular sequence.

Unfortunately there is no (simple) way to use existing Lygon connectives to do this. One promising possibility is to use *, which does something related, but as discussed by Winikoff [17], this does not work, as * can only distribute existing resources. Given a goal $G_1 * G_2$ any new information generated in the solution of G_1 (and in particular the postconditions of an executed action) cannot be passed onto G_2. Using $G_1 \# G_2$ does allow this, but does not restrict the computation of G_1 to be performed before G_2 (and in fact allows both goals to be pursued concurrently). Another possibility is to use the "continuation-passing style" mechanism proposed by Winikoff, which adds a continuation argument to each rule, and splits each rule into a number of rules. However, this is unwieldy, and the number of rules can potentially grow very large and hence difficult to maintain, especially due to the recursive nesting of rules that is required.

Hence we introduce a new connective >> (read 'then'), in order to succinctly state what is required. Intuitively, an agent wanting to sequentially achieve goals G_1 and G_2 will first perform actions to achieve G_1, and, having noted the updates to the world that these actions have made, make plans for achieving G_2 from that updated world. Hence a program and goal $P, G_1 >> G_2$ results in the program and goal P_1, G_2 where P_1 is the result of actions A_1 which convert P to P_1 and for which $P_1 \vdash G_1$.

The >> operator defines an intuitive notion of a sequence of formulae. When combined with the agent paradigm it can be used to define sequences of actions or plans whose outcomes rely on those that come before. Implicit in this definition is the need for the connective to pass state between its left and right sides, in which the output state after achieving the left side should feed into the right side. For example, we may wish to specify that plan A be executed to accomplish some state in the world, followed by plan B to give us a final state. This can be represented as plan A >> plan B.

Note that much of the effort in implementing logic programming languages based on linear logic is centred on the management of context [9,6,17]. Computation involves updating these contexts, and possibly passing them onto other goals according to particular management rules (based on the rules of inference of linear logic). From an agent perspective, this is very similar to updating the state of world after an action is performed. What the above discussion shows is that the management of agent contexts requires an approach that does not correspond directly to those already in use in linear logic programming languages.

In some cases we may wish to specify a sequence, but are not concerned with the order in which that sequence occurs. For example, we may wish to specify that our vacuum robot should clean the lounge and bedroom in some sequence but we do not care which comes first. With a simple extension to the >> operator we can achieve this behaviour, defining the operator <> with the semantics (A >> B @ B >> A).

3.3   Reasoning about Agents

The >> mechanism makes it straightforward to specify agent behaviours. It also seems intuitively simple, although it in some ways combines both forward- and backward-chaining. Consider a program P_0 and the goal $G_1 >> G_2 >> \ldots >> G_n$. This asks the agent system to find, if possible, actions $A_1, A_2 \ldots A_n$ such that $P_{i-1} \xmapsto{A_i} P_i$ (i.e. the actions A_i will convert P_{i-1} to P_i) and $P_i \vdash G_i$. If at any point, such an A_i cannot be found, backtracking occurs to see if some alternatives can be found for earlier goals (meaning that there can be many such A_i for each G_i). In other words, solving for each goal G_i results in a backward-chaining computation to find A_i, and the results of each action are propagated forwards to the next goal. The relationship between >> and combinations of forward- and backward-chaining [2] is beyond the scope of this paper, and is an item of future work.

It is important to note that the backward-chaining phase, including >>, is a planning phase only; no actual changes are made at this point (i.e. no actions are performed). The agent is at this point exploring future options, and it is possible that a number of potential alternatives are investigated, from which the agent will select the most appropriate one. It should also be noted that this process of determining an appropriate course of action will be repeated at each *think* phase of the BDI cycle (see Section 4).

A pleasing by-product of this approach is that as the above mechanism requires the generation of potential future states, it is straightforward to perform proactive checking of *maintenance goals* [4]. These are goals which are intended to remain true, and so if they become false, the agent must take action to restore them. As discussed by Duff *et al.* [4], it is generally sensible to check these proactively, i.e. before attempting a goal which may violate a maintenance goal. For example, our cleaning robot is required to ensure that its battery never becomes fully discharged during the cleaning process. So we specify a maintenance goal that requires the energy level to be at least 10 at all times. A reactive approach would wait until the energy drops to 10 (or less), and then interrupt the robot and require it to recharge. A proactive method would look at the robot's plans, and only allow it to consider plans in which the energy is always 10 or more throughout the execution of the plan. Hence a proactive approach will eliminate action sequences which will violate maintenance goals (although it is sensible to combine this with a reactive approach, in case some unforeseen circumstances occur).

It is straightforward to implement both reactive and proactive checking of maintenance goals in this framework. The reactive approach can be implemented by adding appropriate rules which are evaluated during the *observe* phase by forward-chaining. The proactive approach can be implemented during the *think* phase, as this involves the explicit construction of the future states that the agent foresees as a result of its actions. Hence we can incorporate a procedure into this generation that will check for constraints that each such state should satisfy. In the case of maintenance goals, this constraint will be that no maintenance goal is violated by the state. If so, execution continues as normal. If not, (*i.e.* some maintenance goal is violated), failure occurs and the system backtracks to attempt to find some alternatives.

In the case of our robot, we can thus enforce a constraint that it always maintains at least 10 units of energy by simply adding a constraint that no state is allowed in which this condition is violated.

3.4   Vacuum Example

To see how this works, consider the code in Figure 2, which should be considered in conjunction with the rules for the actions move, vacuum and charge in Figure 1. Note that see (G) simply tests whether G is true, whereas G by itself means an achievement goal.

```
plan clean(X): see(at(X))*see(dirty(X)) -> act vacuum(X).
plan clean(X): see(at(Y))*see(dirty(X)) ->
    act move(X) >> act vacuum(X).
plan cleanall: not(dirty(_)).
plan cleanall: see(at(X))*see(dirty(X)) ->
    plan clean(X) >> plan cleanall.
plan cleanall: see(dirty(X)) ->
    plan clean(X) >> plan cleanall.
plan cleanall: see(energy(C))*lt(C,100) ->
    act move(charger) >> act charge >> plan cleanall.
discharged <- see(energy(C))*lt(C,10).
constrain plan cleanall: not(discharged).
```

Fig. 2. Vacuum code

The first two rules specify plans for achieving the goal clean(X), which can be done by either cleaning the room the robot is currently in (first rule) or moving to another room and cleaning it (second rule). The next four rules specify a plan for cleaning all rooms. If there are no dirty rooms, there is nothing to do. Otherwise, if the robot can see that the current room is dirty, it cleans it, and then reconsiders the rooms (i.e. this is a recursive rule). Otherwise, it will clean any dirty room it can see, and, lastly, it will recharge itself by moving to the charger, recharging and then reconsidering what needs to be done. The last two rules specify the constraint that during the computation of plan cleanall, all states are required to have not(discharged) true, i.e. that the maintenance goal must be proactively maintained.

Once a potential sequence of actions has been found, we then enter the *act* phase of the cycle, which performs the given actions, and evaluates any appropriate rules along the way. This is done in a straightforward manner using forward-chaining. It should be noted that the *observe* phase is also executed in a forward-chaining manner, in that once the input to the agent is received (in the form of sensors or events or other means), it can be useful to perform some processing of these inputs.

For example, imagine that our robot has fire extinguishing capabilities. We could define an event that activates a fire extinguishing mode when a fire is detected. This could be expressed as

```
event alarm: see(fire(X)) -> plan respond(X).
plan respond(X): see(fire(X)) -> act move(X) >> act hose.
```

This event overrides the current goal of the agent with `plan respond(X)` when a fire is detected in room X. When the plan is evaluated, it moves to the appropriate room and activates its `hose` action to put out the fire. The execution clause of an event can be any valid Lygon clause that can be decomposed into a series of actions. The specified clause replaces the current goal in the BDI cycle, such that the agent will now work towards achieving it rather than its original goal. The agent will return to its original goal only when the new goal completes or is unachievable.

We present and discuss a more detailed example in Section 5.

4   BDI Deliberation Cycle

In this section we give a (necessarily brief) overview of our version of the BDI cycle. The operation of the cycle can be summarised as follows: Given an expected world state E, current intentions I and a goal G:

1. Observe the world to obtain current beliefs W.
2. Sequentially test each event (if events are active).
   - If the event rule applies, recursively call BDI cycle with the event body as goal, deactivating events.
   - Reobserve the world to obtain updated beliefs W
3. If expected world E ≠ observed world W
   - Construct a new plan of action with goal G, replacing I. If construction fails, terminate indicating failure
4. If I is empty, terminate cycle, indicating success
5. Otherwise
   - Obtain the first action A in intentions I
   - Simulate action A on current beliefs W to get E2
   - Execute action A
   - If action A execution fails
     - Restart cycle with E & I empty and with goal G
   - Otherwise
     - Remove A from intentions, getting I2
     - Restart cycle with E2, I2, goal G

Steps 1 and 2 correspond to the *observe* phase, steps 3 and 4 to the *think* phase and step 5 to the *act* phase.

This cycle has a number of important properties.

- The observation function obtains the current state of the world from the world state store. This enables states to persist between cycles and allows users to specify a state at command line, or integrate external sensors in a relatively simple way.

- Events are evaluated before planning occurs. This emphasises the reactive nature of events; they always take priority over the current goal. Events can be deactivated, for example if we are currently processing an event in the cycle we do not want to introduce infinite recursion.
- The execution of an event recursively spawns its own BDI cycle. This effectively takes over the current BDI cycle, trying to achieve the execution clause of the event. It is important to note that although the execution clause is evaluated using the abductive planning mechanism, this does not significantly compromise responsiveness for simple action bodies. Where the clause contains actions only, the planning mechanism will deterministically generate an action list from the specified action clause. At the end of the new BDI cycle we are returned to the original cycle and hence the original goal.
- Constructing a plan of action fully decomposes the goal into a sequence of atomic actions. This guarantees its validity and allows the application of constraints described later.
- It is possible that no solution can be found to achieve goal G, given the current world W. In this case we terminate the cycle with a failure indication.
- The plan of action that is determined to achieve our goal constitutes our current intentions. Success is determined when there are no more actions left to do (we have no intentions). A world in which goal G is already accomplished will return an empty plan of action if it is evaluated.
- Unnecessary replanning is avoided by maintaining an expected state of the world. This expected state is obtained by simulating the present action on current beliefs and collecting the resulting state using the clause `act theAction >> collect`. Where the world is equivalent to the expected state, our current intentions are still valid. External changes to the world may cause us to discard current intentions (which are no longer achievable) and generate a new valid set of intentions.
- Actions can fail, which is handled by re-evaluating the original goal.
- The cycle is reiterated after the execution of each action. This means that events have the opportunity to interrupt execution in between each action.

The mechanisms that have been discussed in this paper have been implemented in an extended version of Lygon. Our extensions to Lygon have added around 1100 lines (of sparsely arranged and duly commented code) to the original Lygon interpreter of 720 lines. The current implementation has been developed and tested using SWI-Prolog.

5   Features

5.1   Detailed Rules

The brevity and expressive power of the Lygon extensions we have implemented become apparent when used in tandem and applied to complex agent problems. The syntax allows us to express complex scenarios in a very concise and highly abstracted fashion. This affords us clear productivity advantages over more prevalent imperative languages such as JACK. A decisive advantage of the Lygon extensions are its ability to express complex high level abstractions using expressive and concise syntax. This makes the tool suitable for rapid prototyping scenarios.

To investigate the power of this approach, we have used it to develop solutions for two problems:

- An extended version of the vacuum cleaner example
- The gold mining problem used in the CLIMA programming contest[3].

Due to space limitations, we only discuss the vacuum cleaner example here. Whilst this involves a fair bit of detail, we believe that doing so will provide a much better illustration of our approach than an abstract discussion of programming language features.

We extend the the robot cleaner program to accommodate more complex behaviour as follows:

- We accommodate vacuuming of multiple rooms in appropriate sequence.
- We enable the robot to remove obstacles preventing movement (by vaporizing them).
- We must maintain battery charge to prevent the robot running flat.
- We reactively detect and respond to intruders by activating an alarm.
- We detect and respond to presence of fire by replacing the current goal, and allow for excessive battery discharge in this case.

An implementation that demonstrates these requirements is outlined in Figure 3.

The cleaner program demonstrates a variety of features of the implemented extensions in Lygon. It has reactive and proactive properties, making use of deliberative planning techniques to determine appropriate action sequences, and events to respond to dynamic changes in the environment. It applies constraints in both the proactive planning phase to prevent inappropriate behaviour, and dynamically to react to exceptional conditions. The program also demonstrates the integration of standard Lygon clauses to define common functionality shared between components.

The cleaner program specifies a number of atomic actions which characterise the agents interaction with the environment. The move rule allows the robot to change its location to an arbitrarily defined position. In practice the implementation of such an action will be encapsulated in an external system which handles all appropriate logic. For the purposes of determining its outcome, we presume that a single movement consumes 10% of the current charge. In a more precise implementation, we might specify less generic movement actions with unique discharge rates that reflect the relative distances between locations. For example, we may wish to specify that moving between the lounge and bedroom consumes 12 units of energy and between the bedroom and kitchen 9 units, like so:

```
act move(lounge, bedroom): at(lounge)*energy(C) -> at(bedroom)*energy(C-12).
act move(bedroom, kitchen): at(bedroom)*energy(C) -> at(kitchen)*energy(C-9).
```

Internal action failures are modelled as complete failures if they report failure without making any changes to the state of the world. For exampe, a move action may fail to complete, leaving the robot in its original location. When such a failure occurs, the BDI cycle responds by immediately restarting the cycle for re-planning and results in the

---

[3] http://centria.di.fct.unl.pt/~clima

```
act move(Y): at(_)*energy(C)*is(C2,C-10) -> at(Y)*energy(C2).
act vacuum(X): at(X)*dirty(X)*energy(C)*is(C2,C-20) -> at(X)*clean(X)*energy(C2).
act charge: at(charger)*energy(C) -> at(charger)*energy(100).
act fastcharge: at(charger)*energy(C)*is(C2,50) -> at(charger)*energy(C2).
act extinguish: fire(X)*at(X) -> smoke(X)*at(X).
act soundalarm: alarm(_) -> alarm(on).
act stopalarm: alarm(_) -> alarm(off).
act vaporize(X): at(X)*obstacle(X)*energy(C)*is(C2,C-20) -> at(X)*energy(C2).

event fire: see(fire(X)) -> act soundalarm >> plan firerespond(X).
event intruder: see(intruder(X)) -> act soundalarm.
event lowbattery: batterylow -> act move(charger) >> act(charge).
event safe: see(alarm(on))*not(fire(_))*not(intruder(_)) -> act stopalarm.

plan clean(X): see(at(X))*see(obstacle(X)) -> act vaporize(X) >> act vacuum(X).
plan clean(X): see(at(X))*see(dirty(X))*not(obstacle(X)) -> act vacuum(X).
plan cleanall: not(dirty(_)).
plan cleanall: see(dirty(X))*see(at(X)) -> plan clean(X) >> plan cleanall.
plan cleanall: see(dirty(X))*not(at(X)) ->
                 act move(X) >> plan clean(X) >> plan cleanall.
plan cleanall: see(energy(C))*lt(C,100) ->
                 act move(charger) >> act charge >> plan cleanall.
constrain plan cleanall: not(batterylow).
plan firerespond(X): not(fire(X)).
plan firerespond(X): see(fire(X))*see(at(X)) -> act extinguish.
plan firerespond(X): see(fire(X))*see(at(Y)) -> act move(X) >> act extinguish.
plan firerespond(X): see(energy(C))*lt(C,100) ->
                 act move(charger) >> act fastcharge >> plan firerespond(X).
constrain plan firerespond(X): not(discharged).

discharged <- see(energy(C))*lt(C,1).
batterylow <- see(energy(C))*lt(C,25).
```

Fig. 3. Detailed rules for vacuum

construction of a plan identical to the previous (since the world has not changed). In the case of partial failure (for example a movement action between the bedroom and kitchen may fail halfway, leaving the robot in the lounge) the BDI cycle will re-plan given the new state of the world generating a new plan that accommodates the partial state changes made by the action.

A requirement of our robot is the maintenance of battery charge, which is consumed by the various actions it can execute. This implies means to recharge the battery, we use the charge and fastcharge actions (the latter for use in emergency situations at the cost of reduced battery life). In order to remove obstacles from our path we use the vaporize(X) action.

Our robots emergency handling requirements specify that it must be able to put out fires (extinguish action) and respond to intruders with the sounding of an alarm (soundalarm and stopalarm actions).

5.2 Execution

To initiate the specified program, we specify the command execute(plan cleanall). The cleanall plan represents the top level goal seeking to ensure all rooms have been appropriately vacuumed and are free of obstacles. The plan is defined recursively, cleaning a single room and calling itself to deal with any additional dirty rooms. The terminating condition is specified first and activated when there are no dirty rooms observed, triggering the success of the plan. Two cases are identified for cleaning requirements: when we are currently in a dirty room, and when there is a dirty room elsewhere that requires us to travel. The ordering of these plans is specified such that when the robot is cleaning the room it is currently in, this action will take precedence over cleaning external rooms. Each of these rules calls the subplan clean(X) to handle both cleaning and obstacle removal in the current room.

The clean(X) plan is called when we would like to clean the room that we are currently in. It identifies two cases: one when we are blocked by an obstacle (requiring it to be vaporized), and where we are free to clean. An alternative implementation to the program we have specified might be to require the user to specify an order in which to clean rooms using goals of the form

$$clean(lounge) <> clean(kitchen) <> \ldots$$

Considering such an implementation we might imagine a scenario in which a requested goal is unachievable. For example we may specify that the lounge, kitchen, bedroom and bathroom be cleaned in any order. Unfortunately it is not possible to have enough charge to complete four consecutive rooms, and is thus unachievable.

A more useful response may be a description of why the goal cannot be achieved. For example, we may indicate that the goal is unachievable because all planning paths fail when charge is determined to fall below 0, preventing the calling of additional actions. Given a list of reasons for failure (extracted from the various failure paths during abduction), it may even be possible to determine how to best partially achieve the specified goal (choosing the least undesirable failure). For example we could determine that we can clean the lounge and kitchen but not the bedroom and bathroom.

An important consideration when specifying proactive constraints is the realisation that in their present form they are a solution trimming feature. In the context of our batterylow constraint, this means that any combination of actions leading to a low battery level will cause the current plan decomposition to fail. For this reason we must provide additional plan options that enable the cleaning decomposition to continue even when the battery becomes low. This motivates the addition of a fourth cleanall plan option:

```
plan cleanall: see(energy(C))*lt(C,100) ->
     act move(charger) >> act charge >> plan cleanall
```

When planning decomposition has generated sufficient actions to cause the battery constraint to fail, the cleanall plan will be unable to continue cleaning rooms until it is recharged. This will lead to the failure of the first three plan cases. Backtracking will eventually reach the fourth plan option, enabling the robot to perform a recharge before continuing with the cleanall plan. This approach can be used as a general mechanism to accomplish constraint recovery in most circumstances [4].

---

[4] One limitation of this approach however is in the presence of nested plans. When nesting plans, all constraints are inherited and will therefore continue to trim solutions, however the additional parent plan options are not available for recovery. This can lead to the complete failure of the sub-plan even where recovery is possible by appropriate actions. The solution when this is a problem is to duplicate the additional plan options on subplans, in the same way that we did for the parent plans.

5.3   Reactive Rules

In addition to the proactive approach, we also specify a reactive constraint in the form of the `batterylow` event, which may seem redundant. In an ideal world a purely proactive constraint approach would be sufficient. However in the practical scenarios there may be circumstances in which the battery becomes low in ways that we cannot plan for. For example the owner may install a new battery that is mostly depleted or an action execution may consume more charge than expected. In such cases replanning may not be the best approach, firstly because it consumes significant resources which will consume additional battery charge, and secondly because assumptions about the amount of battery charge consumed may be incorrect. This rule takes care of such situations by reactively overriding the robots current plan and moving it to the charger to perform a recharge. In essence, this event can be considered a fail-safe mechanism that compensates for the imperfect nature of planning. Using a combination of pro-active and reactive maintenance goals ensures a robust system that is able to handle a variety of failure scenarios.

A subtle limitation of the current battery maintenance constraint on the `cleanall` plan can be seen during analysis of the programs behaviour. It can be observed that plans which reduce the battery charge below 35% and then attempt to recharge will fail, even though we might expect them to succeed providing charge stays above 25%. This situation arises due to the implementation of the recharge option in the `cleanall` plan. This plan consists of two actions, i.e. moving to the charger and then charging. Because the constraint still applies during the execution of this plan, constraints are enforced immediately after the movement action. Since movement costs 10% charge, by the time the robot arrives at the charger it is expected to have a low battery and thus the constraint indicates that the plan should fail. A simple solution in this case is to enable the constraint to succeed if we are currently at the charger, like so:

```
constraint plan cleanall: not(batterylow) @ at(charger)
```

This constraint ensures that the `batterylow` constraint only applies when we are not currently at the charger. Although conceptually simple, the updated constraint is a little unintuitive. A improved approach might be a mechanism which excludes constraints in certain scenarios, or to specify a clause that is executed in response to a constraint violation (on which the constraint itself is not enforced).

The cleaning robot can deal with a number of dynamic scenarios through the use of reactive events, defined in order of priority. An important function for our agent is the handling of emergency situations. At the highest priority is the handling of fires when they occur. The fire event responds by activating the alarm and then calling upon the `fireresponse(X)` plan. Recalling our discussion on the implemented BDI cycle, events always take priority over proactive plans, replacing whatever plan the agent is currently pursuing and asserting the `fireresponse(X)` plan. This provides an intuitive mechanism for prioritising goals. Given some initial goal, events can replace that goal when certain conditions arise, returning to the original goal only when event goals have been achieved. Since events are evaluated in definition order, the programmer can specify their priority by the order in which events are defined.

The `fireresponse` plan identifies three scenarios

- there is no fire (in which case we just succeed)
- there is a fire in the current room
- there is a fire in an external room

This plan makes use of the `extinguish` action to put out the fire, the expected outcome of which will be the consumption of the fire fact, but generation of smoke. Like the `cleanall` plan, this plan is constrained to prevent discharging of the battery. In this case we would like to allow maximum discharge to fight the fire due to the emergency situation (we obviously don't want to attempt an unnecessary recharge whilst a fire is raging). Hence, we specify that charge should not fall below 1%.

An important property to notice about this implementation is the possibility for the `cleanall` rule to become unachievable in circumstances where a fire event occurs. When the fire event is triggered, the robot responds by executing the `firerespond(X)` plan. Although the constraints on the plan ensure that we will not fully discharge the battery during the fire fighting process, it does allow the circumstance where the battery can become close to depleted by the time the fire is put out. In some circumstances the battery may be discharged below 10%, a level at which the robot does not have enough power to move to the charger on conclusion of the fire-fighting plan. This behaviour is reasonable in the given circumstances, as we do not wish to attempt a battery recharge during fire fighting unless the charge is critical. In practice, the `lowbattery` event will attempt a recharge once fire-fighting is complete, but this is potentially unachievable, leading to the robot becoming stuck (a small price to pay for putting out the fire). The presented scenario demonstrates the subtle interaction of multiple constrained plans in the presence of events. Although a constraint should ensure the maintenance of that condition throughout planning, it does not guarantee that the final state achieved won't lead to the violation of constraints in other plans. This subtle behaviour should be considered when specifying multiple plans that contain constraints.

In addition to the `fire` event, we also specify an `intruder` event. This event simply activates the alarm when an intruder is detected. Since it only performs a single action, it is highly reactive, able to offer timeliness guarantees. Its immediate effect is to replace the agents current intentions with the `soundalarm` action. Events of this form are suitable for real-time interactions. Since no planning is required, they are a purely forward-chaining mechanism. As a final reactive measure, to accommodate the switching off of the alarm we define the `safe` event. This event is activated when the alarm is on but there is no longer a threat (fire or intruder). This enables the automatic deactivation of the alarm at the end of an emergency.

6   Conclusions and Further Work

We have seen how a BDI system can be constructed from the integration of proactive and reactive components based on backward- and forward-chaining techniques within a linear logic based agent system. Linear logic offers an intuitive and powerful framework for modelling many agent concepts such as actions and plans. We believe that the implementation we have developed shows conclusively that the framework proposed by Harland and Winikoff [8] is not only feasible, but has many valuable properties for agent systems. The syntax we implemented on top of the Lygon interpreter offers an intuitively simple yet very powerful framework for specifying agent behaviours. Linear logic has proven to be an effective framework for application to agent oriented programming, effectively modelling actions and resource oriented logic suitable for agents. Specifying plans in linear logic turns out to be relatively intuitive once the appropriate tools have been specified. Reactive behaviours have been effectively modelled in the form of events, enabling a powerful synergy of agent behaviours suitable for many applications. One of the more pleasing artefacts of the implemented agent extensions was the relatively straightforward means by which proactive constraints could be implemented on top of the framework. Proactive constraints provide an extremely powerful mechanism for arbitrarily restricting agent behaviours in an intuitive way. The constraint mechanism effectively implements many of the ideals proposed by Duff at al. [4] for proactive maintenance goals in an agent context.

As future work, the precise relationship between the $>>$ operator and the increasingly sophisticated proof-theoretic combinations of backward- and forward-chaining [2,11] requires further investigation. The definition of the $>>$ operator itself is in some sense orthogonal to the issues of backward- and forward-chaining, but the way in which it is used in agent programs seems to imply that further analysis will be rewarding. Given that $G_1 >> G_2$ specifies a particular order in which G_1 and G_2 must be used, non-commutative versions of linear logic may be an appropriate starting point [13]. The key technical issue is finding an appropriate interaction between the non-commutative connective $>>$ and the other commutative connectives, as distinct from having only commutative or non-commutative properties alone.

Another aspect of future work is to incorporate maintenance goals into the planning mechanism. This would mean that the generation of actions would also include the possibility to generate actions designed to restore maintenance goals after a predicated violation. Hence rather than just avoid situations where violations occur, the agent can take actions to recover from violations.

Another direction for further work involves further sophistication of our BDI cycle, and in particular in the ability of an agent to develop several alternative plans and to be able to choose between them. We also intend to investigate how much forward-chaining we should allow in the *act* phase. Currently we cease this phase after one action. This is conservative, in that this means the agent has a chance to re-observe the world after each update. However, it may be sensible in some circumstances to allow more actions to execute, on the grounds that we can often predict that no changes to our plans will result from the execution of these actions.

References

1. Bosser, A.-G., Cavazza, M., Champagnat, R.: Linear logic for non-linear storytelling. In: Proceedings of the European Conference on Artificial Intelligence, Lisbon (August 2010)
2. Chaudhuri, K., Pfenning, F., Price, G.: A logical characterization of forward and backward chaining in the inverse method. Journal of Automated Reasoning 40, 133–177 (2008)
3. Denecker, M., Kakas, A.C.: Abduction in Logic Programming. In: Kakas, A.C., Sadri, F. (eds.) Computational Logic: Logic Programming and Beyond. LNCS (LNAI), vol. 2407, pp. 402–436. Springer, Heidelberg (2002)

4. Duff, S., Harland, J., Thangarajah, J.: On proactivity and maintenance goals. In: Proceedings of the International Conference on Autonomous Agents and Multi-Agent Systems, Hakodate, pp. 1033–1040 (2006)
5. Girard, J.-Y.: Linear logic. Theoretical Computer Science 50(1), 1–102 (1987)
6. Harland, J., Pym, D., Winikoff, M.: Programming in Lygon: An Overview. In: Nivat, M., Wirsing, M. (eds.) AMAST 1996. LNCS, vol. 1101, pp. 391–405. Springer, Heidelberg (1996)
7. Harland, J., Pym, D., Winikoff, M.: Forward and backward chaining in linear logic. In: CADE-17 Workshop on Proof-Search in Type-Theoretic Systems, Pittsburgh (June 2000)
8. Harland, J., Winikoff, M.: Agents via mixed-mode computation in linear logic. Annals of Mathematics and Artificial Intelligence 42(1), 167–196 (2004)
9. Hodas, J., Miller, D.: Logic programming in a fragment of intuitionistic linear logic. Information and Computation 110(2), 327–365 (1994)
10. Kowalski, R., Sadri, F.: Towards a Unified Agent Architecture that Combines Rationality with Reactivity. In: Pedreschi, D., Zaniolo, C. (eds.) LID 1996. LNCS, vol. 1154, pp. 135–149. Springer, Heidelberg (1996)
11. Liang, C., Miller, D.: Focusing and polarization in linear, intuitionistic, and classical logic. Theoretical Computer Science 410(46), 4747–4768 (2009)
12. Masseron, M., Tollu, C., Vauzeilles, J.: Generating plans in linear logic i: Actions as proofs. Theoretical Computer Science 113(2), 349–370 (1993)
13. Polakow, J.: Linear logic programming with an ordered context. In: Principles and Practice of Declarative Programming, Montreal (September 2000)
14. Porello, D., Endriss, U.: Modelling multilateral negotiation in linear logic. In: Proceedings of the European Conference on Artificial Intelligence, Lisbon, p. 939 (August 2010)
15. Rao, A.S., Georgeff, M.P.: An abstract architecture for rational agents. In: Proceedings of the International Conference on Principles of Knowledge Representation and Reasoning, pp. 439–449 (1992)
16. Shanahan, M.: Prediction is deduction but explanation is abduction. In: Proceedings of the International Joint Conference on Artificial Intelligence, pp. 1055–1060 (1989)
17. Winikoff, M.: Logic Programming With Linear Logic. PhD Thesis, University of Melbourne (1997)
18. Winikoff, M., Padgham, L., Harland, J., Thangarajah, J.: Declarative and procedural goals in intelligent agent systems. In: Proceedings of the International Conference on Principles of Knowledge Representation and Reasoning, Toulouse (April 2002)
19. Woolridge, M.: Intelligent Agents. MIT Press, Cambridge (1999)

Automatic Generation of Self-monitoring MASs from Multiparty Global Session Types in Jason

Davide Ancona[1], Sophia Drossopoulou[2], and Viviana Mascardi[1]

[1] DIBRIS, University of Genova, Italy
{davide.ancona,viviana.mascardi}@unige.it
[2] Imperial College, London, UK
scd@doc.ic.ac.uk

Abstract. Global session types are behavioral types designed for specifying in a compact way multiparty interactions between distributed components, and verifying their correctness. We take advantage of the fact that global session types can be naturally represented as cyclic Prolog terms - which are directly supported by the Jason implementation of AgentSpeak - to allow simple automatic generation of self-monitoring MASs: given a global session type specifying an interaction protocol, and the implementation of a MAS where agents are expected to be compliant with it, we define a procedure for automatically deriving a self-monitoring MAS. Such a generated MAS ensures that agents conform to the protocol at run-time, by adding a *monitor* agent that checks that the ongoing conversation is correct w.r.t. the global session type.

The feasibility of the approach has been experimented in Jason for a non-trivial example involving recursive global session types with alternative choice and fork type constructors. Although the main aim of this work is the development of a unit testing framework for MASs, the proposed approach can be also extended to implement a framework supporting self-recovering MASs.

1   Introduction

A protocol represents an agreement on how participating systems interact with each other. Without a protocol, it is hard to do a meaningful interaction: participants simply cannot communicate effectively.
The development and validation of programs against protocol descriptions could proceed as follows:
- *A programmer specifies a set of protocols to be used in her application.*
...
- *At the execution time, a local monitor can validate messages with respect to given protocols, optionally blocking invalid messages from being delivered.*

This paper starts with a few sentences drawn from the manifesto of Scribble, a language to describe application-level protocols among communicating systems

M. Baldoni et al. (Eds.): DALT 2012, LNAI 7784, pp. 76–95, 2013.

initially designed by Kohei Honda and Gary Brown[1]. The team working on Scribble involves both scientists active in the agent community and scientists active in the session types one. Their work inspired the proposal presented in this paper where multiparty global session types are used on top of the Jason agent oriented programming language for runtime verification of the conformance of a MAS implementation to a given protocol. This allows us to experiment our approach on realistic scenarios where messages may have a complex structure, and their content may change from one interaction to another.

Following Scribble's manifesto, we ensure runtime conformance thanks to a Jason monitor agent that can be automatically generated from the global session type, represented as a Prolog cyclic term. Besides the global session type, the developer must specify the type of the actual messages that are expected to be exchanged during a conversation.

In order to verify that a MAS implementation is compliant with a given protocol, the Jason code of the agents that participate in the protocol is extended seamlessly and automatically. An even more transparent approach would be possible by overriding the underlying agent architecture methods of Jason responsible for sending and receiving messages, which could intercept all messages sent by the monitored agents, and send them to the monitor which could manage them in the most suitable way. In this approach message "sniffing" would have to occur at the Java (API) level, gaining in transparency but perhaps loosing in flexibility.

In this paper we show the feasibility of our approach by testing a MAS against a non-trivial protocol involving recursive global session types with alternative choice and fork type constructors.

The paper is organized in the following way: Section 2 provides a gentle introduction to the global session types we used in our research; Section 3 discusses our implementation of the protocol testing mechanism; Section 4 presents the results of some experiments we have carried out; Section 5 discusses the related literature and outlines the future directions of our work.

2   A Gentle Introduction to Global Session Types for Agents

In this section we informally introduce global session types (global types for short) and show how they can be smoothly integrated in MASs to specify multiparty communication protocols between agents. To this aim, we present a typical protocol that can be found in literature as our main running example used throughout the paper.

Our example protocol involves three different agents playing the roles of a seller s, a broker b, and a client c, respectively. Such a protocol is described by the FIPA AUML interaction diagram [17] depicted in Figure 1: initially, s communicates to b the intention to sell a certain item to c; then the protocol

---

[1] http://www.jboss.org/scribble/

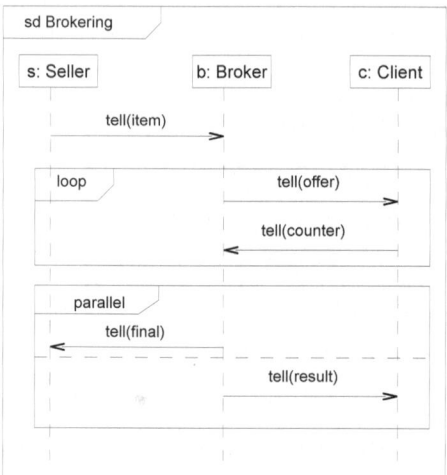

Fig. 1. The Brokering interaction protocol in FIPA AUML

enters a negotiation loop of an arbitrary number n (with $n \geq 0$) of iterations, where b sends an offer to c and c replies with a corresponding counter-offer. After such a loop, b concludes the communication by sending in an arbitrary order the message of type `result` to c, and of type `final` to s.

Even though the AUML diagram of Figure 1 is very intuitive and easy to understand, a more compact and formal specification of the protocol is required to perform verification or testing of a MAS, in order to provide guarantees that the protocol is implemented correctly. Global session types [8,14] have been introduced and studied exactly for this purposes, even though in the more theoretical context of calculi of communicating processes. A global type describes succinctly all sequences of sending actions that may occur during a correct implementation of a protocol.

Depending on the employed type constructors, a global type can be more or less expressive. Throughout this paper we will use a fixed notion of global type, but our proposed approach can be easily adapted for other kinds of global types. The notion of global type we adopt is a slightly less expressive version of that proposed by Deniélou and Yoshida [10] (which, however, allows us to specify the protocol depicted in Figure 1), defined on top of the following type constructors:

– *Sending Actions*: a sending action occurs between two agents, and specifies the sender and the receiver of the message (in our case, the names of the agents, or, more abstractly, the role they play in the communication), and the type of the performative and of the content of the sent message; for instance, `msg(s, b, tell, item)` specifies that agent s (the seller) sends the **tell** performative to agent b (the broker) with content of type `item`.

– *Empty Type*: the constant end represents the empty interaction where no sending actions occur.
– *Sequencing*: sequencing is a binary constructor allowing a global type t to be prefixed by a sending action a; that is, all valid sequences of sending actions denoted by seq(a,t) are obtained by prefixing with a all those sequences denoted by t. For instance,

```
seq(msg(alice,bob,tell,ping),
    seq(msg(bob,alice,tell,pong),end))
```

specifies the simple interaction where first alice sends **tell**(ping) to bob, then bob replies to alice with **tell**(pong), and finally the interaction stops.
– *Choice*: the choice constructor has variable arity[2] n (with $n \geq 0$) and expresses an alternative between n possible choices. Because its arity is variable we use a list to represent its operands. For instance,

```
choice([
    seq(msg(c,b,tell,counter),end),
    seq(msg(b,s,tell,final),end),
    seq(msg(b,c,tell,result),end)
])
```

specifies an interaction where either c sends **tell**(counter) to b, or b sends **tell**(final) to s, or b sends **tell**(result) to c.
– *Fork*: the fork binary[3] constructor specifies two interactions that can be interleaved. For instance,

```
fork(
    seq(msg(b,s,tell,final),end),
    seq(msg(b,c,tell,result),end)
)
```

specifies the interaction where first b sends **tell**(final) to s, and then b sends **tell**(result) to c, or the other way round.

Recursive types: the example types shown so far do not specify any interaction loop, as occurs in the protocol of Figure 1. To specify loops we need to consider recursive global types; for instance, the protocol consisting of infinite sending actions where first alice sends **tell**(ping) to bob, and then bob replies **tell**(pong) to alice, can be represented by the recursive type T s.t.

```
T = seq(msg(alice,bob,tell,ping),
        seq(msg(bob,alice,tell,pong),T))
```

If we interpret the equation above syntactically (that is, as a unification problem), then the unique solution is an infinite term (or, more abstractly, an infinite tree) which is *regular*, that is, whose set of subterms is finite. In practice, the unification problem above is solvable in most modern implementations of Prolog,

---

[2] Arity 0 and 1 are not necessary, but make the definition of predicate next simpler.
[3] For simplicity, the operator has a fixed arity, but it could be generalized to the case of n arguments (with $n \geq 2$) as happens for the choice constructor.

where cyclic terms are supported; this happens also for the Jason implementation, where Prolog-like rules can be used to derive beliefs that hold in the current belief base[4]. As another example, let us consider the type T2 s.t.

```
T2 = seq(msg(alice,bob,tell,ping),
         seq(msg(bob,alice,tell,pong),choice([T2,end])))
```

Such a type contains the infinite interaction denoted by T above, but also all finite sequences of length $2n$ (with $n \geq 1$) of alternating sending actions msg(alice,bob, tell,ping) and msg(bob,alice,tell,pong).

We are now ready to specify the Brokering protocol with a global type BP, where for sake of clarity we use the auxiliary types OffOrFork, Off, and Fork:

```
BP          = seq(msg(s,b,tell,item),OffOrFork),
OffOrFork   = choice([Off,Fork])
Off         = seq(msg(b,c,tell,offer),
                  seq(msg(c,b,tell,counter),OffOrFork))
Fork        = fork(seq(msg(b,s,tell,final),end),
                  seq(msg(b,c,tell,result),end))
```

Note that for the definition of global types we consider in this paper, the fork constructor does not really extend the expressiveness of types: any type using fork can be transformed into an equivalent one without fork. However, such a transformation may lead to an exponential growth of the type .To see this, let us consider the following type F:

```
F           = fork(AliceBob,CarolDave),
AliceBob    = seq(msg(alice,bob,tell,ping),
                  seq(msg(bob,alice,tell,pong),AliceBob))
CarolDave   = seq(msg(carol,dave,tell,ping),
                  seq(msg(dave,carol,tell,pong),CarolDave))
```

Type F is equivalent to the following type AC that does not contain any fork:

```
AC = choice([seq(msg(alice,bob,tell,ping),BC),
             seq(msg(carol,dave,tell,ping),AD)]),
BC = choice([seq(msg(bob,alice,tell,pong),AC),
             seq(msg(carol,dave,tell,ping),BD)]),
AD = choice([seq(msg(alice,bob,tell,ping),BD),
             seq(msg(dave,carol,tell,pong),AD)]),
BD = choice([seq(msg(bob,alice,tell,pong),AD),
             seq(msg(dave,carol,tell,pong),BC)])
```

Formal Definitions

Figure 2 defines the abstract syntax of the global session types that will be used in the rest of the paper. As already explained in the previous section, global types are defined coinductively: GT is the greatest set of regular terms defined by the productions of Figure 2.

---

[4] Persistency of cyclic terms is supported by the very last version of Jason; since testing of this feature is still ongoing, it has not been publicly released yet.

$$GT ::= \text{choice}([GT_1,\ldots, GT_n]) \ (n \geq 0) \ |$$
$$\text{seq}(SA, GT) \ |$$
$$\text{fork}(GT1, GT1) \ |$$
$$\text{end}$$
$$SA \ ::= \text{msg}(AId_1, AId_2, PE, CT)$$

Fig. 2. Syntax of Global Types

The meta-variables AId, PE and CT range over agent identifiers, performatives, and content types, respectively. Content types are constants specifying the types of the contents of messages.

The syntactic definition given so far still contains global types that are not considered useful, and, therefore, are rejected for simplicity. Consider for instance the following type NC:

```
NC = choice([NC,NC])
```

Such a type is called *non contractive* (or *non guarded*), since it contains an infinite path with no seq type constructors. These kinds of types pose termination problems during dynamic global typechecking. Therefore, in the sequel we will consider only *contractive* global types (and we will drop the term "contractive" for brevity), that is, global types that do not have paths containing only the choice and fork type constructors. Such a restriction does not limit the expressive power of types, since it can be shown that for every non contractive global type, there exists a contractive one which is equivalent, in the sense that it represents the same set of sending action sequences. For instance, the type NC as defined above corresponds to the empty type end.

Interpretation of global types. We have already provided an intuition of the meaning of global types. We now define their interpretation, expressed in terms of a next predicate, specifying the possible transitions of a global type. Intuitively, a global type represents a state from which several transition steps to other states (that is, other global types) are possible, with a resulting sending action. Consider for instance the type F defined by

```
fork(seq(msg(b,s,tell,final),end),
     seq(msg(b,c,tell,result),end))
```

Then there are two possible transition steps: one yields the sending action msg(b,s,tell,final) and moves to the state corresponding to the type

```
fork(end,
     seq(msg(b,c,tell,result),end))
```

while the other yields the sending action msg(b,c,tell,result) and moves to the state corresponding to the type

```
fork(seq(msg(b,s,tell,final),end),
     end)
```

Predicate `next` is defined below, with the following meaning: if `next(GT1,SA,GT2)` succeeds, then there is a one step transition from the state represented by the global type GT1 to the state represented by the global type GT2, yielding the sending action SA. The predicate is intended to be used with the mode indicators `next(+,+,-)`, that is, the first two arguments are input, whereas the last is an output argument.

```
1  next(seq(msg(S, R, P, CT),GT),msg(S, R, P, C),GT) :-
       has_type(C, CT).
2  next(choice([GT1|_]),SA,GT2) :- next(GT1,SA,GT2).
3  next(choice([_|L]),SA,GT) :- next(choice(L),SA,GT).
4  next(fork(GT1,GT2),SA,fork(GT3,GT2)) :- next(GT1,SA,GT3).
5  next(fork(GT1,GT2),SA,fork(GT1,GT3)) :- next(GT2,SA,GT3).
```

We provide an explanation for each clause:

1. For a sequence `seq(msg(S, R, P, CT),GT)` the only allowed transition step leads to state GT, and yields a sending action `msg(S, R, P, C)` where C is required to have type CT; we assume that all used content types are defined by the predicate `has_type`, whose definition is part of the specification of the protocol, together with the initial global type.
2. The first clause for `choice` states that there exists a transition step from `choice([GT1|_])` to GT2 yielding the sending action SA, whenever there exists a transition step from GT1 to GT2 yielding the sending action SA.
3. The second clause for `choice` states that there exists a transition step from `choice([_|L])` to GT yielding the sending action SA, whenever there exists a transition step from `choice(L)` (that is, the initial type where the first choice has been removed) to GT yielding the sending action SA.
   Note that both clauses for `choice` fail for the empty list, as expected (since no choice can be made).
4. The first clause for `fork` states that there exists a transition from `fork(GT1,GT2)` to `fork(GT3,GT2)` yielding the sending action SA, whenever there exists a transition step from GT1 to GT3 yielding the sending action SA.
5. The second clause for `fork` is symmetric to the first one.

We conclude this section by a claim stating that contractive types ensure termination of the resolution of `next`.

Proposition 1. *Let us assume that* `has_type`(c, ct) *always terminates for any ground atoms c and ct. Then,* `next`(gt, sa, X) *always terminates, for any ground terms gt and sa, and logical variable X, if gt is a contractive global type.*

Proof. By contradiction, it is straightforward to show that if `next`(gt, sa, X) does not terminate, then gt must contain a (necessarily infinite) path with only `choice` and `fork` constructors, hence, gt is not contractive.

3   A Jason Implementation of a Monitor for Checking Global Session Types

As already explained in the Introduction, the main motivation of our work is a better support for testing the conformance of a MAS to a given protocol, even though we envisage other interesting future application scenarios (see Section 5). From this point of view our approach can be considered as a first step towards the development of a unit testing framework for MASs where testing, types, and – more generally – formal verification can be reconciled in a synergistic way.

In more detail, given a Jason implementation of a MAS[5], our approach allows automatic generation[6] of an extended MAS from it, that can be run on a set of tests to detect possible deviations of the behavior of a system from a given protocol. To achieve this the developer is required to provide (besides the original MAS, of course) the following additional definitions:

- The Prolog clauses for predicate next defining the behavior of the used global types (as shown in Section 2); such clauses depend on the notion of global type needed for specifying the protocol; depending on the complexity of the protocol, one may need to adopt more or less expressive notions of global types, containing different kinds of type constructors, and for each of them the corresponding behavior has to be defined in terms of the next predicate. However, we expect the need for changing the definition of next to be a rare case; the notion of global type we present here captures a large class of frequently used protocols, and it is always possible to extend the testing unit framework with a collection of predefined notions of global types among which the developer can choose the most suitable one.
- The global type specifying the protocol to be tested; this can be easily defined in terms of a set of unification equations.
- The clauses for the has_type predicate (already mentioned in Section 2), defining the types used for checking the content of the messages; also in this case, a set of predefined primitive types could be directly supported by the framework, leaving to the developer the definition of the user-defined types.

The main idea of our approach relies on the definition of a centralized *monitor* agent that verifies that a conversation among any number of participants is compliant with a given global type, and warns the developer if the MAS does not progress. Furthermore, the code of the agents of the original MAS requires minimal changes that, however, can be performed in an automatic way.

In the sequel, we describe the code of the monitor agent, and the changes applied to all other agents (that is, the participants of the implemented protocol).

3.1   Monitor

We illustrate the code for the monitor by using our running brokering example. The monitor can be automatically generated from the global type specification in a trivial way. The global type provided by the developer is simply a conjunction *UnifEq* of unification equations of the form $X = GT$, where X is a logical variable, and GT is a term (possibly containing logical variables) denoting a global type. The use of more logical variables is allowed for defining auxiliary

---

[5] We assume that the reader is familiar with the AgentSpeak language [20].

[6] Its implementation has not been completed yet.

types that make the definition of the main type more readable. Then from *UnifEq* the following Prolog rule is generated:

```
initial_state (X)  :- UnifEq.
```

where X is the logical variable contained in *UnifEq* corresponding to the main global type. The definition of the type of each message content must be provided as well. In fact, the protocol specification defines also the expected types (such as item, offer, counter, final and result) for the correct content of all possible messages. For example, the developer may decide that the type offer defines all terms of shape offer(Item, Offer), where Item is a string and Offer is an integer; similarly, the type item corresponds to all terms of shape item(Client, Item) where both Client and Item are strings.

Consequently, the developer has to provide the following Prolog rules that formalize the descriptions given above:

```
has_type (offer (Item,  Offer),  offer)  :-
    string (Item) & int (Offer).
has_type (item (Client,  Item),  item)  :-
    string (Client) & string (Item).
```

The monitor keeps track of the runtime evolution of the protocol by saving its current state (corresponding to a global type), and checking that each message that a participant would like to send, is allowed by the current state. If so, the monitor allows the participant to send the message by explicitly sending an acknowledgment to it. We explain how participants inform the monitor of their intention to send a message in Section 3.2.

The correctness of a sending action is directly checked by the next predicate, that also specifies the next state in case the transition is correct. In other words, verifying the correctness of the message sent by S to R with performative P and content C amounts to checking if it is possible to reach a NewState from the CurrentState, yielding a sending action msg(S, R, P, C) (type_check predicate).

```
/* Monitor's initial beliefs and rules */

// user-defined predicates
initial_state(Glob)  :-
   Merge = choice([Off,Fork]) &
   Off= seq(msg(b, c, tell, offer),
            seq(msg(c, b, tell, counter), Merge)) &
   Fork= fork(seq(msg(b, s, tell, final),end),
              seq(msg(b, c, tell, result),end)) &
   Glob = seq(msg(s, b, tell, item),Merge).

has_type(offer(Item, Offer), offer) :-
    string(Item) & int(Offer).
has_type(counter(Item, Offer), counter) :-
    string(Item) & int(Offer).
has_type(final(Res, Client, Item, Offer), final) :-
    string(Res) & string(Client) & string(Item) & int(Offer).
has_type(result(Res, Item, Offer), result) :-
    string(Res) & string(Item) & int(Offer).
has_type(item(Client, Item), item) :-
    string(Client) & string(Item).
// end of user-defined predicates

timeout(4000).
```

```
type_check(msg(S, R, P, C), NewState) :-
   current_state(CurrentState) &
   next(CurrentState, msg(S, R, P, C), NewState).

// Rules defining the next predicate follow
........
```

The monitor prints every information relevant for testing on the console with the .print internal action. The .send(R, P, C) internal action implements the asynchronous delivery of a message with performative P and content C to agent R.

A brief description of the main plans follow.

- Plan test is triggered by the initial goal !test that starts the testing, by setting the current state to the initial state.
- Plan move2state upgrades the belief about the current state.
- Plan successfulMove is triggered by the !type_check_message(msg(S, R, P, C)) internal goal. If the type_check(msg(S, R, P, C), NewState) context is satisfied, then S is allowed to send the message with performative P and content C to R. The state of the protocol changes, and monitor notifies S that the message can be sent.
- Plan failingMoveAndProtocol is triggered, like successfulMove, by the !type_check_message(msg(S, R, P, C)) internal goal. It is used when successfulMove cannot be applied because its context is not verified. This means that S is not allowed to send message P with content C to R, because a dynamic type error has been detected: the message does not comply with the protocol.
- Plan messageReceptionOK is triggered by the reception of a tell message with msg(S, R, P, C) content; the message is checked against the protocol, and the progress check is activated (!check_progress succeeds either if a message is received before a default timeout, or if the timeout elapses, in which case !check_progress is activated again: .wait(+msg(S1, R1, P1, C1), MS, Delay) suspends the intention until msg(S1, R1, P1, C1) is received or MS milliseconds have passed, whatever happens first; Delay is unified to the elapsed time from the start of .wait until the event or timeout).

All plans whose context involves checking the current state and/or whose body involves changing it are defined as atomic ones, to avoid problems due to interleaved check-modify actions.

```
/* Initial goals */

!test.

/* Monitor's plans */

@test[atomic]
+!test : initial_state(InitialState)
   <- +current_state(InitialState).

@move2state[atomic]
```

```
+!move_to_state(NewState) : current_state(LastState)
   <- -current_state(LastState);
      +current_state(NewState).

@successfulMove [atomic]
+!type_check_message(msg(S, R, P, C)) : type_check(msg(S, R, P, C), NewState)
   <- !move_to_state(NewState);
      .print("\nMessage ", msg(S, R, P, C), "\nleads to state ", NewState, "\n");
      .send(S, tell, ok_check(msg(S, R, P, C))).

@failingMoveAndProtocol
+!type_check_message(msg(S, R, P, C)) : current_state(Current)
   <- .print("\n*** DYNAMIC TYPE-CHECKING ERROR ***\nMessage ", msg(S, R, P, C),
      "\ncannot be accepted in the current state ", Current, "\n");
      !move_to_state(failure).

@messageReceptionOK
+msg(S, R, P, C)[source(S)]: true
   <- -msg(S, R, P, C)[source(S)];
      !type_check_message(msg(S, R, P, C));
      !check_progress.

+!check_progress : timeout(MS)
   <- .wait({+msg(S1, R1, P1, C1)}, MS, Delay);
      !aux_check_progress(Delay).

+!aux_check_progress(Delay) : timeout(MS) & Delay < MS.

+!aux_check_progress(Delay) : timeout(MS) & current_state(Current) & Delay >= MS
   <- .print("\n*** WARNING ***\nNo progress for ", Delay, " milliseconds
      in the current state ", Current, "\n");
      !check_progress.
```

3.2 Participants

We assume that participants interact via asynchronous exchange of messages with `tell` performatives.

To keep the implementation as general and flexible as possible, in the participants' code extended as explained below we use the `Perf` logical variable where the message performative is expected. Under the assumption that only `tell` performatives will be used, `Perf` will always be bound to the `tell` ground atom.

Only two changes are required to the code of participants:

1. `.send` is replaced by `!my_send` and
2. two plans are added for managing the interaction with the monitor.

The first plan is triggered by the `!my_send` internal goal; `my_send` has the same signature as the `.send` internal action, but, instead of sending a message with performative `Perf` and `Content` to `Receiver`, it sends a `tell` message to the monitor in the format `msg(Sender, Receiver, Perf, Content)`. When received, this message will be checked by the monitor against the global type, as explained in Section 3.1.

The second plan is triggered by the reception of the monitor's message that allows the agent to actually send `Content` to `Receiver`, by means of a message with performative `Perf`. In reaction to the reception of such a message, the agent sends the corresponding message to the expected agent.

```
/* Plans for runtime type checking */

+!my_send(Receiver, Perf, Content) : true
    <- .my_name(Sender);
       .send(monitor, tell, msg(Sender, Receiver, Perf, Content)).

+ok_check(msg(Sender, Receiver, Perf, Content))[source(monitor)] : true
    <- -ok_check(msg(Sender, Receiver, Perf, Content))[source(monitor)];
       .send(Receiver, Perf, Content).
```

3.3 Discussion

Alternative implementations. We opted to implement the proof-of-concept of our approach by extending the code of the existing participants rather than modifying the code of the Jason interpreter, because this was the simplest and quickest solution we could devise for developing a prototype, and easily experimenting different design choices. However, the same results could be obtained by directly modifying the .send internal action by overriding the underlying agent architecture methods of Jason responsible for sending and receiving messages.

This solution would not require any modification of the code of the participants, and would allow the monitor to forward the message, when correct, directly to the recipient agent, thus reducing the number of interactions required among agents.

Another interesting solution would consist in creating a monitor agent for each agent participating to the interaction, thus avoiding the communication problems of the centralized approach where the unique monitor is required to exchange a large amount of messages with the other agents; however, this solution requires to project the global session type to end-point types (a.k.a. local types), specifying the expected behavior of each single agent involved in the interaction. Depending on the considered notion of global type, it might be non trivial to find an efficient and complete projection algorithm.

Global type transition. We have already shown that the next predicate is ensured to terminate on contractive global types; however, a developer may erroneously define a non contractive type for testing its system. Fortunately, there exist algorithms for automatically translating a non contractive global type into an equivalent contractive one.

Another issue concerns non deterministic global types, that is, global types where transitions are not deterministic. Consider for instance the following global type:

```
fork(seq(msg(alice,bob,tell,ping),
         seq(msg(bob,alice,tell,pong),end)),
     seq(msg(alice,bob,tell,ping),
         seq(msg(alice,bob,tell,bye),end)))
```

In this case the next predicate has to guess which of the two operand types must progress upon reception of the message matching with msg(alice,bob,tell,ping); this means that in case of non deterministic global types the monitor may detect false positives. To avoid this problem one could determinize the type, but depending on the considered notion of global type, it would not be easy, or even possible, to devise a determinization algorithm. Alternatively, the monitor could store the whole sequence of received sending actions to allow backtracking in case of failure, thus making the testing procedure much less efficient.

Finally, it is worth mentioning that the proposed approach makes an efficient use of memory space if the initial global type does not contain loops with the fork constructor. In this case the space required by a global type representing an intermediate state is bounded by the size of the initial global type; since only one type at a time is kept in the belief base of the monitor, this implies a significant space optimization when the total number of all possible states is exponential w.r.t. the size of the initial global type. As already pointed out, this consideration does not apply to types with loops involving the fork constructor, like in the following example:

```
T = fork(seq(msg(alice,bob,tell,ping),T),
         seq(msg(bob,alice,tell,pong),T)).
```

In this case the term grows at each transition step (and there are cases where the type cannot be simplified to a smaller one); however, we were not able to come up with examples of realistic protocols that require types with fork in a loop to be specified.

4   The Framework at Work

In this section we show the actual functioning of our framework by discussing the experiments we made with the brokering global type. We show the correct code of seller (s), broker (b) and client (c) apart from the fragments common to all of them and discussed in Section 3, and omitting the definition of intuitive predicates, and then we discuss how the framework works with both correct and buggy code.

Seller. The seller starts the conversation (it has a !start initial goal) by sending a message to the broker telling that it wants to sell orange to c. It has a plan triggered by the reception of the final result of the negotiation, whose body is empty, and no initial beliefs.

```
/* Plans */

+!start : true
    <- !my_send(b, tell, item(c, orange)).

+final(Res, Client, Item, Offer)[source(Broker)] : true.
```

Broker. The broker has no initial goals and its policy is the following:

- whatever the item to trade, and the client with whom trading, it proposes to sell it at an initial price stored in its belief base (10 euros for a crate of oranges when trading with c).
- Depending on the counter offer it receives, three situations may take place:

1. The counter offer is in a range that leaves room for negotiation. The broker makes an offer with price decremented by one with respect to the previous offered one (first plan triggered by +counter(Item, Offer)).
2. The counter offer is too low and there is no room for negotiating. The final decision (noDeal) is sent both to the seller and to the client (second plan triggered by +counter(Item, Offer)).
3. The counter offer can be accepted. The final decision (ok) is sent both to the seller and to the client. We do not show the plan for this case, since it is very similar to the previous one.

```
/* Initial beliefs and rules */

initial_offer(c, orange, 11).
acceptable_offer(c, orange, 6).

/* Plans */

+item(Client, Item)[source(s)] : initial_offer(Client, Item, Offer)
   <- +current_offer(Client, Item, Offer);
      !my_send(Client, tell, offer(Item, Offer)).

+counter(Item, Offer)[source(Client)] : acceptable_offer(Client, Item, Min)
                                        & Offer < Min & Offer > Min-4
   <- !decrement(Client, Item, NewOffer);
      !my_send(Client, tell, offer(Item, NewOffer)).

+counter(Item, Offer)[source(Client)] : acceptable_offer(Client, Item, Min)
                                        & Offer <= Min-4
   <- !my_send(Client, tell, result(noDeal, Item, Offer));
      !my_send(s, tell, final(noDeal, Client, Item, Offer)).
```

Client. The client has a reactive behavior: whatever the offer it receives, the client answers with a counter offer depending on the initial_counter_offer belief in its belief base, and increments it by one at any interaction step, until it receives the result of the negotiation.

```
/* Initial beliefs and rules */

initial_counter_offer(b, orange, 3).

/* Plans */

+offer(Item, Offer)[source(Broker)] : initial_counter_offer(Broker, Item, Initial)
   <-  -initial_counter_offer(Broker, Item, Initial);
       -offer(Item, Offer)[source(Broker)];
       +current_counter_offer(Broker, Item, Initial);
       !my_send(Broker, tell, counter(Item, Initial)).

+offer(Item, Offer)[source(Broker)] : true
   <- -offer(Item, Offer)[source(Broker)];
      !increment(Broker, Item, NewOffer);
      !my_send(Broker, tell, counter(Item, NewOffer)).

+result(Res, Item, Offer)[source(Broker)]: true.
```

4.1   Running the Example

When running the MAS consisting of agents monitor, s, b, and c, we obtain console messages like those shown below (we only show the first operators of the

printed states, for space constraints; we use "_" for the dropped text, since ". . ."
is part of the cyclic term representation; Msg -> St means that the agent moves
to state St upon reception of Msg). The conversation complies with the global
type and a state that is equivalent to end is reached. Since we do not model
the notion of protocol termination, the monitor cannot know that the protocol
terminated successfully, and keeps watching the conversation and issues warning
messages every M seconds. The developer can easily verify that no messages are
sent because no more messages had to be sent in state fork(end,end).

```
[monitor]
msg(s,b,tell,item(c,orange)) -> choice([...seq(msg(b,c,tell,offer),_)
....

[monitor]
msg(b,c,tell,offer(orange,9)) -> seq(msg(c,b,tell,counter),choice([_]))

[monitor]
msg(c,b,tell,counter(orange,5)) -> choice([...seq(msg(b,c,tell,offer),_)])

[monitor]
msg(b,c,tell,offer(orange,8)) -> seq(msg(c,b,tell,counter),choice([_]))

[monitor]
msg(c,b,tell,counter(orange,6)) -> choice([...seq(msg(b,c,tell,offer),_)])

[monitor]
msg(b,c,tell,result(ok,orange,6)) -> fork(seq(msg(b,s,tell,final),end),end)

[monitor]
msg(b,s,tell,final(ok,c,orange,6)) -> fork(end,end)

[monitor]
*** WARNING ***
No progress for 4001 milliseconds in the current state fork(end,end)
```

Bug 1. Let us suppose that the second plan for dealing with offers in the client's
code, is the following:

```
+offer(Item, Offer)[source(Broker)] : true
    <- -offer(Item, Offer)[source(Broker)];
       !increase(Broker, Item, NewOffer);
       !my_send(Broker, tell, offer(Item, NewOffer));
       !my_send(Broker, tell, anotherOffer(Item, NewOffer)).
```

Instead of sending a counter offer, the client sends an offer followed by a message with unknown type. The console messages we obtain in this case are shown
below.

```
...

[monitor]
msg(b,c,tell,offer(orange,8)) -> seq(msg(c,b,tell,counter),choice([_]))

[monitor]
*** DYNAMIC TYPE-CHECKING ERROR ***
msg(c,b,tell,offer(orange,4)) cannot be accepted in
seq(msg(c,b,tell,counter), choice([_]))

[monitor]
*** DYNAMIC TYPE-CHECKING ERROR ***
msg(c,b,tell,anotherOffer(orange,4)) received when no ongoing protocol
```

The monitor notifies two dynamic type checking errors: the first one due to the unexpected offer message, and the second one due to the message received after the protocol testing failed. The message that caused the failure and the current global type state are shown. When a protocol fails, warnings about lack of progress are suppressed.

The developer can either fix the code of the agent that sent the message or the specification of the global type, depending on where the error was.

Bug 2. The client has a !start initial goal, hence it autonomously starts to interact with the broker before the previous messages that the protocol enforces have been sent:

```
/* Plans */

+!start : initial_counter_offer(Broker, Item, Initial)
   <-  -initial_counter_offer(Broker, Item, Initial);
        +current_counter_offer(Broker, Item, Initial);
        !my_send(Broker, tell, counter(Item, Initial)).
```

The monitor prints out the following message:

```
[monitor]
*** DYNAMIC TYPE-CHECKING ERROR ***
msg(c,b,tell,counter(orange,3)) cannot be accepted in
seq(msg(s,b,tell,item),choice([_]))
```

Bug 3. We deleted all the plans triggered by the reception of +counter(Item, Offer)[source(Client)] from the broker's code, making the broker agent unable to react to a counter offer. The state of the protocol printed out by the monitor in its warning message helps the MAS developer in identifying the agent that is expected to send a message at that point of the conversation.

```
[monitor]
msg(s,b,tell,item(c,orange)) -> state choice([...seq(msg(b,c,tell,offer),_])

[monitor]
msg(b,c,tell,offer(orange,11)) -> state seq(msg(c,b,tell,counter),choice([_]))

[monitor]
msg(c,b,tell,counter(orange,3)) -> state choice([...seq(msg(b,c,tell,offer),_])

[monitor]
*** WARNING ***
No progress for 4000 ms in choice([...seq(msg(b,c,tell,offer),_)])
```

We run the MAS with different values for the broker's initial and acceptable offers, and with various communication errors besides those described in the paragraphs above, always obtaining the expected result.

5   Related and Future Work

Our work represents a first step in two directions: extending an existing agent programming language with session types, and supporting testing of protocol conformance within a MAS. In this section we consider the related works in both areas, discuss the (lack of) proposals of integrating session types in existing MASs frameworks, and outline possible extensions of our work.

Session types on top of existing programming languages. The integration of session types into existing languages is a recent activity, dating back to less than ten years ago for object oriented calculi, and less than five years for declarative ones. The research field is very lively and open, with the newest proposals published just a few months ago.

Session types have been integrated into object calculi starting from 2005 [11,12]. The first full implementation of a language and run-time for session-based distributed programming on top of Java, featuring asynchronous message passing, delegation, session subtyping and interleaving, combined with class downloading and failure handling, dates back to 2008 [16]. More recently, a Java language extension has been proposed, that counters the problems of traditional event-based programming with abstractions and safety guarantees based on session types [15].

Closer to our work on declarative languages, the paper [21] discusses how session types have been incorporated into Haskell as a standard library that allows the developer to statically verify the use of the communication primitives provided without an additional type checker, preprocessor or modification to the compiler. A session typing system for a featherweight Erlang calculus that encompasses the main communication abilities of the language is presented in [19]. Structured types are used to govern the interaction of Erlang processes, ensuring that their behavior is safe with respect to a defined protocol.

Protocol representation and verification in MASs. Because of the very nature of MASs as complex systems consisting of autonomous communicating entities that must adhere to a given protocol in order to allow the MAS correct functioning, the problem of how representing interaction protocols has been addressed since the dawning of research on MASs (one of the most well known outcomes being FIPA AUML interaction diagrams [17]), and the literature on protocol conformance verification is extremely rich.

Although a bit dated, [6] still represents one of the most valuable contributions to *verification of a priori conformance.* In that paper the authors propose an approach based on the theory of formal languages to formally prove the interoperability of two policies (the actual protocol implementations), each of which is compliant with a protocol specification.

The problem of *verifying the compliance of protocols at run time* has been tackled – among others – within the SOCS project[7], where the SCIFF computational logic framework [1] is used to provide the semantics of social integrity constraints. Such a semantics is based on abduction: expectations on the possibly observable, yet unknown, events are modeled as abducibles and social integrity constraints are represented as integrity constraints. To model MAS interaction, expectation-based semantics specifies the links between the observed events and the expected ones. The recent paper "Modelling Interactions via Commitments and Expectations" [23] discusses that and related approaches. Although aimed at testing run-time conformance of an actual conversation with respect to a given protocol, our approach differs from the expectation-based one in many respects,

---

[7] http://lia.deis.unibo.it/research/projects/SOCS/

including the lack of notion of expectation in the agent language, and the implementation of the testing mechanism in a seamless way on top of an existing and widespread agent-oriented programming language. As far as formalisms for representing agent interaction protocols are concerned, the reader may find a concise but very good survey in Section 4 of [22] where the authors propose a commitment-based semantics of protocols.

Our approach is currently limited to the runtime verification of the MAS compliance to the interaction protocol, but the exploitation of session types as the formalism to represent protocols allows us to take advantage of all the results achieved in the session types research field, which include session subtyping and algorithms for static verification of protocol properties such as safety and liveness. The ability to specify the type of messages (has_type(c, ct) predicate) in order to relate actual messages to messages specified in the protocol, usually given at a more abstract level, is a characterizing feature of our approach and seems to be supported by none of the proposals mentioned above.

Session Types and MASs. As demonstrated for example by the Scribble language mentioned in the Introduction and by [13], using session types to represent and verify protocol conformance inside MASs is not a new idea but, to the best of our knowledge, no attempts of taking advantage of global session types to verify MASs programmed in some widespread agent oriented programming languages had been made so far, and our proposal is an original one.

Future extensions. Some extensions to our work have already been implemented in the last few months: in [2] we explored the theoretical foundations of our framework and we introduced a concatenation operator that allows a significant enhancement of the expressive power of our global types. In [3] we further empowered our formalism with a mechanism for easily expressing constrained shuffle of message sequences like the alternating bit protocol discussed in [10]; accordingly, we modified the semantics of the new introduced feature, and showed the expressive power of these "constrained global types". With respect to this extension, we are currently exploring the work of Baier, et al. on Constraint Automata [4,5] that offers a transition system using synchronization constraints and data constraints to specify behavior and concurrent protocols as automata models. Constraint Automata are compositional, i.e., more complex protocols/behaviors can be constructed as a composition of simpler protocols/behaviors, which is a common goal with our work.

Our work can be further extended in many ways. Besides the specific issues mentioned in Section 3, and the fully automatic generation of the monitor and participants code, our short term goals include analyzing how our approach could be extended to other Prolog-based agent-programming languages, such as GOAL [7] or 2APL [9], and designing more complex protocols to stress-test our system and provide a quantitative assessment of its runtime behavior and scalability.

In the medium term, we plan to work for evolving our mechanism towards a framework supporting self-recovering MASs. This evolution would require to modify the way we extend the code of the participant agents, in order to automatically select other messages to send in the current state, if any, in case the monitor realizes that the chosen one does not respect the protocol. Default recovery actions for the situation where no other choices are available, should be defined as well. In such a context – more oriented towards verification of interoperability of deployed systems rather than testing of systems-to-be –, agents might advertise to the monitor the services they offer and the protocols to follow in order to obtain them. Besides ensuring the protocol's compliance, the monitor could then act as a repository of *<service specification, protocol specification>* couples, helping agents to locate services in an open MAS in a similar way the Universal Description, Discovery and Integration (UDDI) registry does for web services.

In the long term, the integration of ontology-based meaning into protocol specifications, leading to "ontology-aware session types", will be addressed. Our previous work on CooL-AgentSpeak [18] will represent the starting point for that extension.

Acknowledgments. We are grateful to J. F. Hübner and R. H. Bordini for their effort in making cyclic terms in Jason belief base persistent, thus making the implementation of our monitor agent possible. We also thank the anonymous reviewers for their careful reading of the paper and for the valuable suggestions provided to improve its quality.

References

1. Alberti, M., Gavanelli, M., Lamma, E., Mello, P., Torroni, P.: The *SCIFF* Abductive Proof-Procedure. In: Bandini, S., Manzoni, S. (eds.) AI*IA 2005. LNCS (LNAI), vol. 3673, pp. 135–147. Springer, Heidelberg (2005)
2. Ancona, D., Barbieri, M., Mascardi, V.: Global Types for Dynamic Checking of Protocol Conformance of Multi-Agent Systems (Extended Abstract). In: Massazza, P. (ed.) ICTCS 2012, pp. 39–43 (2012)
3. Ancona, D., Barbieri, M., Mascardi, V.: Constrained global types for dynamic checking of protocol conformance in multi-agent systems. In: SAC 2013. ACM (to appear, 2013)
4. Arbab, F., Baier, C., de Boer, F.S., Rutten, J.J.M.M.: Models and temporal logical specifications for timed component connectors. Software and System Modeling 6(1), 59–82 (2007)
5. Baier, C., Sirjani, M., Arbab, F., Rutten, J.J.M.M.: Modeling component connectors in Reo by constraint automata. Sci. Comput. Program. 61(2), 75–113 (2006)
6. Baldoni, M., Baroglio, C., Martelli, A., Patti, V.: Verification of Protocol Conformance and Agent Interoperability. In: Toni, F., Torroni, P. (eds.) CLIMA VI. LNCS (LNAI), vol. 3900, pp. 265–283. Springer, Heidelberg (2006)
7. Braubach, L., Pokahr, A., Moldt, D., Lamersdorf, W.: Goal Representation for BDI Agent Systems. In: Bordini, R.H., Dastani, M., Dix, J., El Fallah Seghrouchni, A. (eds.) PROMAS 2004. LNCS (LNAI), vol. 3346, pp. 44–65. Springer, Heidelberg (2005)
8. Carbone, M., Honda, K., Yoshida, N.: Structured Communication-Centred Programming for Web Services. In: De Nicola, R. (ed.) ESOP 2007. LNCS, vol. 4421, pp. 2–17. Springer, Heidelberg (2007)

9. Dastani, M.: 2APL: a practical agent programming language. Autonomous Agents and Multi-Agent Systems 16(3), 214–248 (2008)
10. Deniélou, P.-M., Yoshida, N.: Multiparty Session Types Meet Communicating Automata. In: Seidl, H. (ed.) ESOP 2012. LNCS, vol. 7211, pp. 194–213. Springer, Heidelberg (2012)
11. Dezani-Ciancaglini, M., Mostrous, D., Yoshida, N., Drossopoulou, S.: Session Types for Object-Oriented Languages. In: Thomas, D. (ed.) ECOOP 2006. LNCS, vol. 4067, pp. 328–352. Springer, Heidelberg (2006)
12. Dezani-Ciancaglini, M., Yoshida, N., Ahern, A., Drossopoulou, S.: A Distributed Object-Oriented Language with Session Types. In: De Nicola, R., Sangiorgi, D. (eds.) TGC 2005. LNCS, vol. 3705, pp. 299–318. Springer, Heidelberg (2005)
13. Grigore, C., Collier, R.: Supporting agent systems in the programming language. In: WI/IAT, pp. 9–12. IEEE Computer Society (2011)
14. Honda, K., Yoshida, N., Carbone, M.: Multiparty asynchronous session types. In: POPL 2008, pp. 273–284. ACM (2008)
15. Hu, R., Kouzapas, D., Pernet, O., Yoshida, N., Honda, K.: Type-Safe Eventful Sessions in Java. In: D'Hondt, T. (ed.) ECOOP 2010. LNCS, vol. 6183, pp. 329–353. Springer, Heidelberg (2010)
16. Hu, R., Yoshida, N., Honda, K.: Session-Based Distributed Programming in Java. In: Vitek, J. (ed.) ECOOP 2008. LNCS, vol. 5142, pp. 516–541. Springer, Heidelberg (2008)
17. Huget, M.-P., Bauer, B., Odell, J., Levy, R., Turci, P., Cervenka, R., Zhu, H.: FIPA modeling: Interaction diagrams. Working Draft Version (July 02, 2003), http://www.auml.org/auml/documents/ID-03-07-02.pdf
18. Mascardi, V., Ancona, D., Bordini, R.H., Ricci, A.: CooL-AgentSpeak: Enhancing AgentSpeak-DL agents with plan exchange and ontology services. In: IAT 2011, pp. 109–116. IEEE Computer Society (2011)
19. Mostrous, D., Vasconcelos, V.T.: Session Typing for a Featherweight Erlang. In: De Meuter, W., Roman, G.-C. (eds.) COORDINATION 2011. LNCS, vol. 6721, pp. 95–109. Springer, Heidelberg (2011)
20. Rao, A.S.: AgentSpeak(L): BDI Agents Speak Out in a Logical Computable Language. In: Perram, J., Van de Velde, W. (eds.) MAAMAW 1996. LNCS, vol. 1038, pp. 42–55. Springer, Heidelberg (1996)
21. Sackman, M., Eisenbach, S.: Session types in Haskell: Updating message passing for the 21st century. Technical report, Imperial College, Department of Computing (2008), http://spiral.imperial.ac.uk:8080/handle/10044/1/5918
22. Singh, M.P., Chopra, A.K.: Correctness Properties for Multiagent Systems. In: Baldoni, M., Bentahar, J., van Riemsdijk, M.B., Lloyd, J. (eds.) DALT 2009. LNCS, vol. 5948, pp. 192–207. Springer, Heidelberg (2010)
23. Torroni, P., Yolum, P., Singh, M.P., Alberti, M., Chesani, F., Gavanelli, M., Lamma, E., Mello, P.: Modelling interactions via commitments and expectations. In: Handbook of Research on Multi-Agent Systems: Semantics and Dynamics of Organizational Models. IGI Global (2009)

A Generalized Commitment Machine for 2CL Protocols and Its Implementation

Matteo Baldoni, Cristina Baroglio, Federico Capuzzimati,
Elisa Marengo, and Viviana Patti

Università degli Studi di Torino
Dipartimento di Informatica
c.so Svizzera 185, I-10149 Torino, Italy
name.surname@unito.it

Abstract. This work proposes an operational semantics for the commitment protocol language 2CL. This semantics relies on an extension of Singh's Generalized Commitment Machine, that we named 2CL-Generalized Commitment Machines. The 2CL-Generalized Commitment Machine was implemented in Prolog by extending Winikoff, Liu and Harland's implementation. The implementation is equipped with a graphical tool that allows the analyst to explore all the possible executions, showing both commitment and constraint violations, and thus helping the analyst as well as the protocol designer to identify the risks the interaction could encounter. The implementation is part of an Eclipse plug-in which supports 2CL-protocol design and analysis.

Keywords: Commitment protocols, constraints among commitments, commitment machine, commitment machine implementation.

1 Introduction and Motivation

Agent interaction is generally specified by defining *interaction protocols* [21]. For communicating with one another, agents must follow the schema that the protocol shapes. Different protocol models can be found in the literature, this work concerns *commitment-based protocols* [19,24]. This kind of protocols relies on the notion of commitment, which in turn encompasses the notions of debtor and creditor: when a commitment is not fulfilled, the debtor is liable for that violation but as long as agents reciprocally satisfy their commitments, any course of action is fine.

In many practical contexts where protocols model *business interactions* (e.g. trading, banking), designers must be able to regulate and constrain the possible interactions as specified by *conventions, regulations, preferences* or *habits* [2,5]. Some proposals address the issue of introducing similar regulations inside commitment protocols [4,11,7,17], but none of them developed tools for visualizing and analyzing how regulations or constraints impact on the interactions allowed by a commitment-based protocol. The availability of intuitive and possibly graphical tools of this kind would support the identification of possible

M. Baldoni et al. (Eds.): DALT 2012, LNAI 7784, pp. 96–115, 2013.

violations, thus enabling an *analysis of the risks* the interaction could encounter. As a consequence, it would be possible to raise alerts concerning possible violations before the protocol is enacted, and to reduce risks by defining proper operational strategies, like regimentation (aimed at preventing the occurrence of violations) or enforcement (introduction of warning mechanisms) [14].

The work presented in this paper aims at filling this gap. To this purpose, we started from the commitment protocol language 2CL described in [4], whose key characteristic is the extension of the regulative nature of commitments by featuring the definition of patterns of interaction as sets of *constraints*. Such constraints declaratively specify either conditions to be achieved or the order in which some of them should be achieved. The first contribution is, therefore, a formal, operational semantics for the proposal in [4], which relies on the Generalized Commitment Machine in [20]. We named our extension 2CL-Generalized Commitment Machines (2CL-GCM for short). On top of this, it was possible to realize the second contribution of this work: a Prolog implementation for 2CL-GCM, which extends the implementation in [22], and is equipped with a graphical tool to explore all the possible executions, showing both commitment and constraint violations. The implementation is part of a plug-in Eclipse which supports 2CL-protocol design and analysis.

The chief characteristic of our solution is that it performs a *state evaluation* of protocol constraints, rather than performing path evaluation (as, instead, done by model checking techniques). State evaluation allows considering each state only once, labeling it as a state of violation if some constraint is violated in it or as a legal state when no constraint is violated. This is a great difference with respect to path evaluation, where a state belonging to different paths can be classified as a state of violation or not depending on the path that is considered. The advantage is practical: state evaluation allows to easily supply the user an overall view of the possible alternatives of action, highlighting those which will bring to a violation and those that will not. State evaluation, however, is possible only by making some restriction on the proposal in [4]. Specifically, we assume that the domain is expressed in terms of positive facts only.

The paper is organized as follows. Section 2 briefly summarizes 2CL interaction protocol specification. Section 3 describes the formalization of 2CL-GCM. Section 4 presents a Prolog implementation of 2CL-GCM. Section 5 describes the 2CL Tools that supply features for supporting the protocol design and analysis. Section 6 discusses Related Work and Conclusions. Along the paper we use as a running example the well-known NetBill interaction protocol.

2   Background: 2CL Interaction Protocols

Let us briefly recall the main characteristics of commitment protocols, as defined in [4]. In this approach, commitment protocols are extended with a set of temporal constraints the interaction should respect. Constraints relate *commitments*. By $C(x, y, r, p)$ agent x commits to an agent y to bring about the consequent condition p when the antecedent condition r holds. When r equals *true*, we use

Table 1. 2CL operators and their meaning

	Relation	Operator	Repr.	LTL formula
Relation Operators	Correlation	A correlate B	$A \bullet\!\!- B$	$\Diamond A \supset \Diamond B$
		A not correlate B	$A \bullet\!\!\not- B$	$\Diamond A \supset \neg\Diamond B$
	Co-existence	A co-exist B	$A \bullet\!\!-\!\!\bullet B$	$A \bullet\!\!- B \wedge B \bullet\!\!- A$
		A not co-exist B	$A \bullet\!\!\not-\!\!\bullet B$	$A \bullet\!\!\not- B \wedge B \bullet\!\!\not- A$
Temporal Operators	Response	A response B	$A \bullet\!\!-\!\!\rightarrow B$	$\Box(A \supset \Diamond B)$
		A not response B	$A \bullet\!\!\not\!\!\rightarrow B$	$\Box(A \supset \neg\Diamond B)$
	Before	A before B	$A \rightarrow\!\!\bullet B$	$\neg B \cup A$
		A not before B	$A \not\!\!\rightarrow\!\!\bullet B$	$\Box(\Diamond B \supset \neg A)$
	Cause	A cause B	$A \bullet\!\!-\!\!\rightarrow\!\!\bullet B$	$A \bullet\!\!-\!\!\rightarrow B \wedge A \rightarrow\!\!\bullet B$
		A not cause B	$A \bullet\!\!\not\!\!\rightarrow\!\!\bullet B$	$A \bullet\!\!\not\!\!\rightarrow B \wedge A \not\!\!\rightarrow\!\!\bullet B$

the short notation $C(x, y, p)$. Commitments are used to define the *social effects* of the protocol actions.

Definition 1 (Interaction protocol). $\mathcal{P} = \langle$Ro, F, s_0, A, Cst$\rangle$ *An interaction protocol* $\mathcal{P}$ *is a tuple* $\langle$Ro, F, s_0, A, Cst$\rangle$, *where* Ro *is a set of roles, identifying the interacting parties*, F *is a set of facts and commitments that can occur in the social state*, s_0 *is the set of facts and commitments in the initial state of the interaction*, A *is a set of actions, and* Cst *is a set of constraints.*

The set of social actions A, defined on F and on Ro, forms the *constitutive specification* of the protocol. The social effects are introduced by the construct *means*, which amounts to a *counts-as* relation [18,14]: by means of it, a physical event is given a social meaning. An *if* condition denotes the context in which a counts-as relation holds. For instance, consider the action *sendGoods* reported in Table 1. Its social meaning is that it makes the facts *goods* true (the goods were delivered to the customer) and creates the commitment $C(m, c, pay, receipt)$ that corresponds to a promise by the merchant to send a receipt after the customer has paid. Further examples can be found in the first part of Table 1, which reports all the actions of the NetBill protocol. The formalization is inspired by those in [24,22].

2CL constraints Cst, defined on F and on Ro as well. Constraints express what is mandatory and what is forbidden without the need of listing the possible executions extensionally. The syntax is "dnf_1 **op** dnf_2", where dnf_1 and dnf_2 are disjunctive normal forms of facts and commitments, and **op** is one of the 2CL operators, reported in Table 1 together with their Linear-time Temporal Logic [10] interpretation and with their graphical notation.

Constraints can either be *relational* or *temporal*. The former kind expresses constraints on the co-occurrence of conditions (if a condition is achieved then also another condition must be achieved, but the order of the two achievements does not matter). For instance, one may wish to express that both the payment for some item and its delivery must occur without constraining the order of the

Action Definitions

(a1) *sendRequest* **means** *request* **if** $\neg quote \wedge \neg goods$

(a2) *sendQuote* **means** $quote \wedge create(\mathsf{C}(m, c, \mathsf{C}(c, m, goods, pay), goods))$
$\wedge \ create(\mathsf{C}(m, c, pay, receipt))$

(a3) *sendAccept* **means** $create(\mathsf{C}(c, m, goods, pay))$ **if** $\neg pay$

(a4) *sendGoods* **means** $goods \wedge create(\mathsf{C}(m, c, pay, receipt))$

(a5) *sendEPO* **means** pay

(a6) *sendReceipt* **means** $receipt$ **if** pay

Constraints

(c1) $quote \dashrightarrow\bullet \mathsf{C}(c, m, goods, pay) \vee \mathsf{C}(c, m, pay)$

(c2) $\mathsf{C}(m, c, pay, receipt) \wedge goods \dashrightarrow\bullet pay$

(c2) $pay \bullet\!\!\dashrightarrow\bullet receipt$

Fig. 1. Actions and constraints for the NetBill protocol: m stands for merchant while c stands for customer

two conditions: no matter which occurs first, when one is met, also the other must be achieved. Temporal constraints, instead, capture the relative order at which different conditions should be achieved. Fig. 1 reports the constraints imposed by the NetBill protocol: *(c1)* means that a quotation for a price must occur before a commitment to pay or a conditional commitment to pay given that some goods were delivered; *(c2)* that the conditional commitment to send a receipt after payment and the delivery of goods must occur before the payment is done; *(c3)* that after payment a receipt must be issued and if a receipt is issued a payment must have occurred before.

Only interactions which respect the constraints are *legal*. Violations amounting to the fact that a constraint is not respected can be detected *during the execution*.

3   2CL Generalized Commitment Machine

The semantics of 2CL commitment protocols is given based on the 2CL *generalized commitment machine* (2CL-GCM). In turn, 2CL-GCM relies on the notion of *generalized commitment machine* (GCM) (introduced in [20]), extending it with a proper account of 2CL constraints. Below we introduce the technical elements on top of which the definition of a 2CL-GCM will be given.

Propositions. Propositions are meant to capture conditions of interests (e.g. the fact that a payment has occurred or that a request for quote has been made) and social relationships among the interacting parties. We represent them in terms of facts and commitments, whose meaning is assumed to be known and agreed by all the agents. Let us assume **true** and **false** to be part of this set, representing respectively the *true* and the *false* values of propositional logic.

States. The evolution of an interaction is represented by means of states: each state captures a snapshot on a particular moment of the interaction. According to [20], a GCM features a set S of possible *states*, each of which is represented by a logical expression defined on a set of propositions.

Example 1. Considering NetBill, $goods \wedge$ C(c, m, pay) represents one possible configuration of the social state, i.e. it is a state in S. This expression means that the goods were shipped and that there is a commitment from c (customer) to m (merchant) to pay for them.

Initial state. Denoted by s_0, it is the state from which the interaction starts.

Example 2. In the NetBill example, if we assume the commitment C($m, c,$ *pay, goods*) to be part of the initial state it represents that, when accepting the role of merchant, the agent is also taking the engagement to send the goods when these are paid.

Good States. We identify a set $G \subseteq S$ as the set of *good states*. Intuitively, they capture desired possible endings of the interaction. For instance, they may be those that do not contain unsatisfied active commitments, or those satisfying a condition of interest (e.g. payment done and goods shipped).

Physical Events. The interaction evolves as the consequence of the occurrence of physical events. We denote by L_A their set.

Action Theory. Given the definition of an action a, and two states s and s', it is possible to determine whether a transition between the two can be inferred as a consequence of the occurrence of a physical event a. As in [20], in 2CL-GCM transitions between the states are logically inferred on the basis of an action theory, that contains a set of axioms of the kind $p \overset{a}{\hookrightarrow} q$, meaning that q is a consequence of performing action a in a state where p holds. When q is false the meaning is that a is impossible if p holds. Only transitions that find correspondence in an axiom of the action theory can be inferred. In the following E is the conjunction of E_F, which is a logical expression (possibly true) concerning facts only, and E_{op}, which is a logical expression (possibly true) concerning operations on commitments only.

Definition 2 (Action theory). *An action axiom $s \overset{a}{\hookrightarrow} s'$ belongs to the action theory Δ of a protocol $\mathcal{P} = \langle Ro, F, s_0, A, Cst \rangle$ iff there exists a definition "a means E if Cond" in A s.t. $s \vdash Cond$ and:*

(a) *$\forall e_{op}$ s.t. $E_{op} \vdash e_{op}$ and given $z \overset{e_{op}}{\hookrightarrow} z'$ according to commitment operations' axioms (see [20, Section 2.2]) then if $s \vdash z$ then $s' \vdash z'$; and*

(b) *$\forall e_F$ s.t. $E_F \vdash e_F$ then $s' \vdash e_F$ and:*

   (b.1) *if $s \vdash C(x, y, e, e_F)$ (with e possibly true) then $s' \vdash \neg C(x, y, e, e_F)$ and*

   (b.2) *if $s \vdash C(x, y, e_F, e')$ then:*

      if $s' \nvdash e'$ then $s' \vdash \neg C(x, y, e_F, e') \wedge C(x, y, e')$; otherwise $s' \vdash \neg C(x, y, e_F, e') \wedge \neg C(x, y, e')$.

where $\vdash$ *and* $\equiv$ *represent respectively the logical consequence and the logical equivalence of propositional logic.*

Given two states, in order to determine whether the latter can be a consequence of the occurrence of a physical event in the former, it is necessary to consider the definition of the corresponding action 'a **means** E **if** $Cond$'. A transition labelled by 'a' can be inferred only if the condition $Cond$ can be derived in the starting state. In this case it is necessary to consider the effects E of the action and whether they can be derived on the target state. The target state should derive all the facts in E_F while for the operations on commitments E_{op} we apply the rules defined in [20, Section 2.2]. Finally, conditions *(b.1)* and *(b.2)* in Definition 2 check the *discharge* and the *detach* of commitments, due to facts derived from E_F.

Example 3. The action *sendAccept*, performed by the customer to accept a quote by the merchant, is defined as *sendAccept* **means** CREATE($\mathsf{C}(c, m, goods, pay)$) **if** $\neg pay$. The corresponding axiom is $\neg pay \overset{sendAccept}{\hookrightarrow} \mathsf{C}(c, m, goods, pay)$. Note that, given a state, in which $\neg pay \wedge quote$ holds, it is also possible to infer the axiom $\neg pay \wedge quote \overset{sendAccept}{\hookrightarrow} \mathsf{C}(c, m, goods, pay)$.

Constraints. A 2CL-GCM accounts for a set of constraints Cst that coincides with that defined in the corresponding protocol. These constraints will be taken into account for determining whether an interaction can be considered as a path of the machine.

We now have all the elements for defining a 2CL-GCM. The definition adopts the same notation in [20].

Definition 3 (2CL-GCM of a protocol). *A* 2CL-GCM *of a protocol* $\mathcal{P} = \langle$Ro, F, s_0, A, Cst$\rangle$ *is a tuple* $\mathbf{P} = \langle$S, $\mathsf{L_A}$, s_0, Δ, G, Cst$\rangle$ *where:*

- *S is a set of states represented as logical expressions;*
- *$\mathsf{L_A}$ is a set of physical events s.t. $a \in \mathsf{L_A}$ iff $\exists a$ **means** E **if** $Cond \in$ A ;*
- *$s_0 \in S$ and represents the initial state;*
- *Δ is an action theory s.t. $\forall s, s' \in$ S, $s \overset{a}{\hookrightarrow} s' \in \Delta$ iff there exists a **means** E **if** $Cond \in$ A s.t. $s \overset{a}{\hookrightarrow} s'$ is an action axiom of 'a' according to Definition 2;*
- *G $\subseteq$ S is a set of good states;*
- *Cst is a set of 2CL constraints.*

Moreover:

- *$\forall s, s' \in$ S, $s \not\equiv s'$, i.e. members of S are logically distinct;*
- *false $\notin$ S; and*
- *$\forall s \in$ G, $s' \in$ S : $(s' \vdash s) \Rightarrow (s' \in$ G), i.e. any state that logically derives a good state is also good.*

Notice that by varying the sets S and G different 2CL-GCMs associated to the same protocol can be obtained: when S contains all the states that can be reached from s_0, applying the protocol actions, the machine can infer all the possible interactions; when S is smaller, only a subset of the possible interactions is determined.

3.1   Path of a 2CL-GCM

Interactions between agents can be seen as paths traversing states, the transitions among which are labeled by the physical events which caused them. We denote a path τ as the sequence $\langle(\tau_0, a_0, \tau_1), (\tau_1, a_1, \tau_2), \dots\rangle$. In order for a path to be part of a 2CL-GCM it must respect some conditions:

1. The path must be infinite;
2. All the transitions of the path must be inferable by the machine; and
3. All constraints must be satisfied in the path.

It is not restrictive to focus on infinite paths. Indeed, all finite paths can be transformed into infinite ones by adding a transition from the last state of the finite path towards an artificial new state with a self loop [20]. In 2CL-GCM we assume that the action axioms that allow inferring such transitions are part of Δ.

2CL constraints verification can be done by exploiting the LTL formula associated to each of them. In particular, a constraint is satisfied in a path when it is verified in the *transition system* corresponding to the path. Given a path, the corresponding transition system can be derived quite straightforwardly.

Definition 4 (Transition System). *A transition system $T(\tau)$ of a path $\tau = \langle(\tau_0, a_0, \tau_1), (\tau_1, a_1, \tau_2), \dots\rangle$ is a tuple $\langle S_\tau, \delta_\tau, L_\tau\rangle$ where:*

- $S_\tau = \{\tau_i | \ \tau_i \ is \ a \ state \ in \ \tau\}$;
- $\delta_\tau : S_\tau \to S_\tau$ *is a transition function s.t.* $\delta(\tau_j) = \tau_k$ *iff* (τ_j, a, τ_k) *is in* τ;
- $L : S_\tau \to 2^F$ *is a labelling function, s.t. F is a set of facts and commitments and* $L(\tau_i) = \{e | \tau_i \vdash e\}$.

To define a 2CL-GCM path, we extend the definition of GCM path by additionally requiring the satisfaction of all the constraints of the 2CL-GCM.

Definition 5 (2CL-GCM path). *A path $\tau = \langle(\tau_0, a_0, \tau_1), (\tau_1, a_1, \tau_2) \dots\rangle$ is a path of a 2CL-GCM $\mathbf{P} = \langle S, L_A, s_0, \Delta, G, Cst\rangle$ when:*

i. $\forall(\tau_i, a_i, \tau_{i+1})$ *in τ then $\tau_i, \tau_{i+1} \in S$, $a_i \in L_A$, and $\tau_i \overset{a_i}{\hookrightarrow} \tau_{i+1} \in \Delta$; and*
ii. *being $inf(\tau)$ the set of states that occur infinitely often in τ, then $inf(\tau) \cap G \neq \emptyset$; and*
iii. *being $T(\tau)$ the transition system of τ according to Definition 4, $\forall c \in Cst$: $T(\tau), \tau_0 \models_{LTL} c$.*

where the LTL satisfaction relation $\models_{LTL}$ is the one defined in [1].

In the above definition, *(i)* and *(ii)* are the conditions for a path to be generated. Condition *(i)* requires that each state in the path is a state of the 2CL-GCM, that the action that causes the transition from a state to the subsequent one in the path is an action of the 2CL-GCM, and that the transition is inferable according to the axioms in Δ. Condition *(ii)* requires that at least one *good state* occurs infinitely often in the path. Condition *(iii)* accounts for the evaluation of the constraints. According to the LTL semantics, $T(\tau), \tau_0 \models_{LTL} c$ amounts to checking if c is satisfied in all the paths of the transition system, corresponding to τ. By construction $T(\tau)$ is a transition system made only of *one* linear path, whose starting state is the starting state of τ.

4   Implementation of the 2CL Commitment Machine

This section describes a Prolog implementation that allows exploring all the possible executions of an interaction protocol, showing the *regulative violations* – i.e. both those states in which some constraint is violated and those that contain unsatisfied commitments. We also prove the soundness of the implementation w.r.t. the 2CL-GCM formalization presented in the previous sections.

We used *tuProlog*[1] in our implementation, starting from the *enhanced commitment machine* by Winikoff et al. [22]. By relying on it, we inherit the mechanisms for the computation of the possible interactions. Specifically, the enhanced commitment machine features the generation of the reachable states, the transitions among them and the management of commitments (like the operations of discharge, creation and so on). Our extension equips it with the possibility of evaluating 2CL constraints.

The main characteristic of our tool is that it provides an overall graphical view of the possible interactions, highlighting those that will bring to a violation and those that will not. To this aim, constraints are used as a means to classify the possible interactions, rather than to prune the search space. The interacting parties, indeed, are not prevented from entering in illegal paths (due to the agent's autonomy), but they are made aware of the risks they are encountering and that they may incur in penalties as a consequence of the violations they caused [5]. This is a difference compared with those proposals where only the set of legal paths is shown, or with other proposals that aim at properties verification. In these cases, the verification ends when a path that does not satisfy the property is found. Alternatively, only one path at a time is considered [6,9]. Thus, none of these proposals provide an overview of possible interactions.

Starting from a protocol specification, our implementation determines the set of reachable states by applying a depth-first search (as in [22]). Specifically, given a state the program finds the set of applicable actions and computes the set of successors. A state is added to the graph only if it is new, otherwise only the transition is added. For what concerns the evaluation of protocol constraints, we implemented it as a *state evaluation*, that is to say that given a constraint its evaluation can be done on a state by considering its content only. In this way, each possible state (reachable given the starting state and the protocol actions) is considered only once and it is classified as a state of violation if some constraint is violated in it or as a legal state when no constraint is violated. This is a great difference with respect to path evaluation, where a state belonging to different paths can be classified as a state of violation or not depending on the path that is considered. The advantage is practical: given the set of reachable states, the user is able to immediately determine which of them are legal and which violate some constraints. Moreover, the overall representation results to be more compact because each state appears only once.

In order to perform the *state evaluation* we consider states whose content is given in terms of commitments and positive facts only. The characteristic of a

---

[1] http://www.alice.unibo.it/xwiki/bin/view/Tuprolog/

fact is that it is false until it becomes invariably true. In this setting, the evaluation of 2CL constraints can be made on single states. For instance, if in a state b holds but a does not, we can infer that the constraint 'a *before* b' is violated. Moreover, besides facts asserted by the protocol actions, in our implementation we additionally consider a set of facts associated to the operations performed on commitments. Specifically, along the line of Mallya *et al.* [15], whenever an operation is performed on a commitment, a corresponding predicate is automatically asserted in the state. For instance, when a commitment $C(x, y, r, p)$ is created, the predicate CREATED($C(x, y, r, p)$) is added to the state; when it is discharged, the predicate DISCHARGED($C(x, y, r, p)$) is added, and so forth for the other operations. Notice that these predicates are not meant to express whether a commitment is active or not. For instance, CREATED does not mean that the commitment is active in the state but simply that the corresponding operation has been performed on the commitment. 2CL constraints can be defined by considering these facts also.

In order to achieve the benefits of a state evaluation while guaranteeing the soundness of the verification with the theoretical framework presented in the previous section, we need to make some assumptions on the way protocols are specified:

1. Actions should be defined in such a way to do not retract facts;
2. The condition involved in constraints must involve conditions that persist (i.e. that involve DNFs of facts without negation);
3. Constraints expressed on commitments are to be opportunely transformed into constraints concerning operations preformed on commitments.

For the sake of clarity, we use the symbol $\mathbf{P_I}$ to refer to a protocol that respects these assumptions.

4.1   Generation of the Labeled Graph and Its Soundness

Let us consider a protocol $\mathbf{P_I}$. As reported in Listing 1.1, the exploration of the search space is made as a depth-first-search (as in [22]). Specifically, given a state, explore and nextstate find the set of possible successors, obtained by considering the set of actions in $\mathbf{P_I}$. For those actions whose preconditions are satisfied in the state, nextstate determines the resulting state by adding the facts which constitute their social meaning, executing the operations performed on commitments according to the commitments' life cycle and asserting the corresponding facts concerning such operations. Once the successor states are obtained they are added to the set of reachable states together with the corresponding transitions. The computation is rooted in the initial state. In our program, states are represented as predicates.

Definition 6 (State). *The predicate* state(ID, Content, Label) *represents a state in the implementation where:* ID *is a unique identifier associated to the state,* Content *is a list of facts and commitments and* Label $\subseteq$ {*final,not-final, violation, pending*} *is a list of labels that captures the absence (*final*) or the*

```
 1  explore(StateNum,Free,NextFree) :- state(StateNum,State,_),
 2    findall(t(StateNum,A,S2),nextstate(State,A,S2),Ts),
 3    add_states(Ts,Free,NextFree), add_transitions(Ts).
 4
 5  nextstate(State,Action,Result) :- happens(Action,State),
 6    findall(Add,initiates(Action,Add,State), AddS),
 7    findall(Del,terminates(Action,Del,State), DelS),
 8    merge_addList(AddS,State,NewState),
 9    findall(StableProp,initiates_stable_prop(Action,
10            StableProp,State,NewState), StablePropS),
11    merge_addList(AddS,StablePropS,AddList),
12    compute_next_state(State,AddList,DelS,New),
13    remove_duplicates(New,Result).
14
15  add_states([],N,N).
16  add_states([t(_,_,S)|Ss],N,N1) :-
17    state(_,St,_), seteq(St,S), !, add_states(Ss,N,N1).
18  add_states([t(_,_,S)|Ss],N,N3) :-
19    labels(S,L), assert(state(N,S,L)),
20    N1 is N+1, explore(N,N1,N2), add_states(Ss,N2,N3).
21
22  add_transitions([]).
23  add_transitions([t(S1,A,S2)|Ss]) :- transition(S1,A,Ss2),
24    seteq(S2,Ss2), !, add_transitions(Ss).
25  add_transitions([t(S1,A,S2)|Ss]) :- state(N2,Ss2,_), seteq(Ss2,S2),
26    assert(transition(S1,A,N2)), add_transitions(Ss).
27
28  subsumes(P,P).
29  subsumes(P,c(_,_,PP)) :- subsumes(P,PP).
30  subsumes(P,cc(_,_,_,PP)) :- subsumes(P,PP).
31  subsumes(c(X,Y,P),cc(X,Y,_Q,PP)) :- subsumes(P,PP).
32
33  happens(E,T) :- isAction(E), precond(E,P), implied(P,T).
34
35  initiates(E,P,T) :- happens(E,T), isFluent(P), causes(E,P).
36  initiates(E,c(X,Y,P),T) :- causes(E,create(c(X,Y,P))), happens(E,T),
37      \+(implied(P,T)).
38  initiates(E,c(X,Y,P),T) :- causes(E,create(cc(X,Y,Q,P))),
39      happens(E,T), implied(Q,T), \+(implied(P,T)).
40  initiates(E,cc(X,Y,P,Q),T) :- causes(E,create(cc(X,Y,P,Q))),
41      happens(E,T), \+(implied(Q,T)), \+(implied(P,T)).
42  initiates(E,c(X,Y,Q),T) :- holdsAt(cc(X,Y,P,Q),T), happens(E,T),
43      subsumes(PP,P), initiates(E,PP,T).
44
45  terminates(E,c(X,Y,P),T) :- holdsAt(c(X,Y,P),T), happens(E,T),
46      subsumes(PP,P), initiates(E,PP,T).
47  terminates(E,cc(X,Y,P,Q), T) :- holdsAt(cc(X,Y,P,Q),T), happens(E,T),
48      subsumes(QP,Q), initiates(E,QP,T).
49  terminates(E,cc(X,Y,P,Q), T) :- holdsAt(cc(X,Y,P,Q),T), happens(E,T),
50      subsumes(PP,P),  initiates(E,PP,T).
```

Listing 1.1. Prolog clauses that compute the set of reachable states and that assert the corresponding transitions The complete program can be downloaded at the URL http://di.unito.it/2cl.

presence (not-final) of unsatisfied active commitments, the presence of pending *constraints or the* violation *of a constraint.*

Notice that according to the clause add_state reported in Listing 1.1 (line 16), a state is added only if it is new, that is to say: there are no existing states with the same content.

Table 2. State conditions corresponding to 2CL operators

Relation	State Condition
Correlation	$\psi(A \,\bullet\!\!- B) = A \wedge B$
	$\psi(A \,\bullet\!\!\not- B) = \neg(A \wedge B)$
Co-existence	$\psi(A \,\bullet\!\!-\!\!\bullet B) = \psi(A \,\bullet\!\!- B) \wedge \psi(B \,\bullet\!\!- A)$
	$\psi(A \,\bullet\!\!\not-\!\!\bullet B) = \psi(A \,\bullet\!\!\not- B) \wedge \psi(B \,\bullet\!\!\not- A)$
Response	$\psi(A \,\bullet\!\!-\!\!\twoheadrightarrow B) = A \wedge B$
	$\psi(A \,\bullet\!\!\not\!\!\twoheadrightarrow B) = \neg(A \wedge B)$
Before	$\psi(A \,-\!\!\twoheadrightarrow B) = \neg(B \wedge \neg A)$
	$\psi(A \,\not\!\!\twoheadrightarrow B) = \neg(A \wedge B)$
Cause	$\psi(A \,\bullet\!\!-\!\!\twoheadrightarrow B) = \psi(A \,\bullet\!\!-\!\!\twoheadrightarrow B) \wedge \psi(A \,-\!\!\twoheadrightarrow B)$
	$\psi(A \,\bullet\!\!\not\!\!\twoheadrightarrow B) = \psi(A \,\bullet\!\!\not\!\!\twoheadrightarrow B) \wedge \psi(A \,\not\!\!\twoheadrightarrow B)$

Also transitions are represented by means of predicates, expressing the starting and the target state and the physical events that caused them.

Definition 7 (Transition). *The predicate* `transition(ID1,A, ID2)` *represents a transition where* `ID1` *and* `ID2` *correspond to the identifiers of existing states, and* `A` *is the action responsible for the transition.*

Before adding a state, this is labeled according to the constraints it satisfies or violates and to the commitments holding in it. Thanks to the assumptions that constraints are defined in terms of positive facts that persist along the interaction, the LTL formulas associated to the operators can be simplified. The resulting formulas are reported in Table 2 (a proof of their soundness can be found in [16, Chapter 6]. Below we provide an intuition).

Given a constraint c, we denote by $\psi(c)$ the corresponding condition to be verified on one state at a time (*state condition*). Consider, for instance, the *before* operator ($-\!\!\twoheadrightarrow$): it requires that A is met before or in the same state of B. So, given a run π, if in π there is a state j such that B holds while A does not, that is a state where a violation occurred, in formulas: $\pi_i \models_{LTL} A \,-\!\!\twoheadrightarrow B \Leftrightarrow \neg \exists j \geq i$ s.t. $\pi_j \models_{LTL} (B \wedge \neg A)^2$.

The other 2CL operators can be divided in two cases. *Correlation* ($\bullet\!\!-$) and *response* ($\bullet\!\!-\!\!\twoheadrightarrow$) are tackled in a similar way. $A \,\bullet\!\!- B$ requires that if A is achieved in a run, then also B is achieved in the same run (before or after A is not relevant). If B is achieved before A it will remain true also after. Therefore, in those cases in which the constraint is satisfied, from a certain time onwards both conditions will hold. In formulas: $\pi_i \models_{LTL} A \,\bullet\!\!- B \Leftrightarrow \neg \exists j \geq i$ s.t. $\pi_j \models_{LTL} A$ and $\forall j' \geq j$, $\pi_{j'} \models_{LTL} (A \wedge \neg B)$. The same equivalence holds for $\pi_i \models_{LTL} A \,\bullet\!\!-\!\!\twoheadrightarrow B$. In 2CL $A \,\bullet\!\!-\!\!\twoheadrightarrow B$ requires that when A is met, B is achieved at least once later (even if it already occurred in the past) but under our assumptions it can be checked in

---

^{2} Notice that since the second formula does not contain temporal operators it is verified in the current state. Thus it is verified in all the states of the path.

the same way of correlation. The state condition amounts to verifying whether a state satisfies A but does not satisfy B. Notice that states that satisfy the test cannot be marked as states of violation because the constraint does not require B to hold *whenever* A holds. A state of violation is signaled when the interaction does not continue after it: we say that there is a *pending* condition.

Negated correlation, response and *before* correspond to the same formula: $\pi_i \models_{LTL} A \text{ op } B \Leftrightarrow \neg\exists j \geq i \text{ s.t. } \pi_j \models_{LTL} (A \wedge B)$ where $\text{op} \in \{\not\leftrightarrow, \not\leftrightarrow, \not\leftrightarrow\}$. Intuitively, a constraint of the kind $A \not\leftrightarrow B$ (negative correlation) requires that if A holds, B is not achieved. Since facts persist, this amounts to check that the two conditions do not hold in the same state, otherwise a violation occurs. *Negative response (negative before)* adds a *temporal aspect* to not-correlation: if A holds, B cannot hold later (before, respectively). Since facts persist, the first achieved condition will remain true also after the other becomes true. Also in this case we only need to check that the two conditions do not hold together.

Derived operators are decomposed and the reasoning made for the operators, from which they derive, is applied. For instance, *cause* ($\bullet\!\!-\!\!\bullet$) derives from *before* and *response*. If a state does not satisfy the response part of the cause, it is marked as "pending"; if it violates the before part, it is marked as a "violation". Both labels are applied when the state does not satisfy any of the two.

Summarizing, given a constraint formula and a state in which to verify it, we have three possible outcomes: *(i)* the state satisfies the formula; *(ii)* the state does not satisfy the formula and this leads to a violation; and *(iii)* the state does not satisfy the formula but the violation is potential, depending on future evolution. Considering all the constraints of a protocol, a state can both violate some constraint and have pending conditions. Moreover, states are also evaluated based on the presence of unsatisfied active commitments.

In our implementation, constraints are represented with predicates. For instance, `before(A,B,Id)` represents a constraint of kind *before* whose antecedent and consequent conditions are are respectively `A` and `B` and `Id` is a unique identifier for the constraint. The predicates for the other kinds of constraints are similar, where `before` is substituted with the operator name. Constraints verification is implemented as previously described. Listing 1.2 reports, as an example, the verification of a *response* and of a *before*. The clause *check_pending* that is reported verifies response constraints: it is satisfied if there is a constraint of kind response, whose antecedent condition can be derived in the state, while the consequent condition cannot. In this case, the label *pending* is added to the list of labels of the state. A similar clause checks the correlation constraint. Instead, the clause *check_violation*, checks constraints of kind before, which are violated if the consequent condition can be derived in the state while their antecedent cannot. Other similar clauses, checking different conditions, are defined for the other operators. Finally, the program checks the presence of unsatisfied commitments (*check_commitments*) and adds the label *final* or *not-final* accordingly. The result of running this program on a protocol specification is an annotated graph of the reachable states.

```
 1  labels(State,Labels) :- find_labels(State,[],Labels).
 2
 3  find_labels(S,L1,R) :- check_violation(S,L1,L2),
 4     check_pending(S,L2,L3), check_commitments(S,L3,R).
 5
 6  check_pending(State,L,[pending(Constr)|L]) :- response(A,B,Constr),
 7     consequence(A,State), \+consequence(B,State).
 8
 9  check_violation(State,L,[violation(Constr)|L]) :- before(A,B,Constr),
10     consequence(B,State), \+consequence(A,State).
11
12  check_commitments(State,L,[final|L]) :- \+member(c(_,_,_),State).
13  check_commitments(State,L,[non-final|L]) :- member(c(_,_,_),State).
```

Listing 1.2. Prolog clauses checking constraints and adding the corresponding labels to the states

On the basis of the labels associated to a state, that are a consequence of constraints verification, we can define a legal path.

Definition 8 (Legal path). *Let* $\mathbf{P_I} = \langle \mathsf{Ro}, \mathsf{F}, s_0, \mathsf{A}, \mathsf{Cst} \rangle$ *be a protocol. A legal path* π *for* $\mathbf{P_I}$ *is a sequence* $\langle (0, a_0, 1), \ldots, (n-1, a_{n-1}, n) \rangle$ *where* $\forall i\ 0 \leq i \leq n$, i *represents the identifier of a state,* a_i *is an action in* A *and* π *is such that:*

i. $\forall (i, a_i, i+1)$ *in* π, *there exist* state(i, π_i, Label$_i$) *and* state(i+1, π_{i+1}, Label$_{i+1}$) *and* transition(i, a_i, i+1)*; and*

ii. state(n, π_n, Label$_n$) *is such that final* $\in$ Label$_n$ *and* $\{violation, pending\}$ $\cap$ Label$_n = \emptyset$*; and*

iii. $\nexists i$ *in* π *s.t.* state(i, π_i, Label$_i$) *and violation* $\in$ Label$_i$.

In words, a sequence of states and transitions is a legal path for a program when *(i)* each state in the path can be reached from the initial state by applying the actions (and in the specified order) identified by the sequence; *(ii)* the last state of the path does not contain unsatisfied active commitments or pending constraints; and *(iii)* none of the states in the path violates constraints.

In order to prove the soundness of our implementation we have to show that a legal path for our implementation is also a legal path for the corresponding 2CL-GCM. This latter, however, works on infinite paths where states are represented as logical formulas rather then as sets of facts and commitments. Along the line of [20], we define an equivalent infinite path π^∞ for a path π.

Definition 9 (Equivalent infinite path). $\pi^\infty = \langle (\pi_0, a_0, \pi_1), \ldots \rangle$ *is the equivalent infinite path corresponding to the finite path* $\pi = \langle (0, a_0, 1), \ldots, (n-1, a_{n-1}, n) \rangle$ *iff:*

i. $\forall i,\ 0 \leq i \leq n$, *given* state(i, π_i, Label$_i$) $\pi_i^\infty \vdash f$ *iff* $f \in \pi_i$*; and*

ii. $\forall i,\ 0 \leq i < n\ (\pi_i^\infty, a_i, \pi_{i+1}^\infty)$ *is in* π^∞ *iff* $(i, a_i, i+1)$ *is in* π*; and*

iii. $\forall i \geq n\ (\pi_i^\infty, a_i, \pi_{i+1}^\infty)$ *in* π^∞ *is such that* $\pi_i^\infty \equiv \pi_n^\infty$ *and* $\pi_{i+1}^\infty \equiv \pi_n^\infty$ *and* a_i *is the action 'act **means** true if* π_n^∞*'.*

Intuitively, the infinite path is obtained by adding a self loop on the last state of the finite path. Now we have all the elements for proving soundness.

Theorem 1 (Soundness). *Consider a protocol* $\mathbf{P_I} = \langle \mathsf{Ro}, \mathsf{F}, \mathsf{s}_0, \mathsf{A}, \mathsf{Cst} \rangle$. *Let* $\pi = \langle (0, a_0, 1), \ldots, (n-1, a_{n-1}, n) \rangle$ *be a path and let* π^∞ *be the corresponding infinite path. Let* $\mathbf{P} = \langle \mathsf{S}_\pi^\infty, \mathsf{L_A}, \mathsf{s}_0, \Delta, \mathsf{G}, \mathsf{Cst} \rangle$ *be a 2CL-GCM of* $\mathbf{P_I}$ *such that* $\mathsf{S}_\pi^\infty = \{\pi_i^\infty | \pi_i^\infty$ *is in* $\pi^\infty\}$ *and* $\mathsf{G} = \{\pi_i^\infty | \nexists C(x, y, p)$ *s.t.* $\pi_i^\infty \vdash C(x, y, p)\}$. *If* π *is a legal path for* $\mathbf{P_I}$, *then* π^∞ *is a path of* $\mathbf{P}$.

Given a protocol and the program representing it, if a path is legal according to this latter, then there exists a 2CL-GCM for which the corresponding infinite path is a path according to Definition 5. More precisely a 2CL-GCM of the protocol for which this condition holds is the one obtained by considering as set of states the states that are part of the path. As good states we consider those that do not contain unsatisfied active commitments.

Proof. In order for π^∞ to be a path of the 2CL-GCM $\mathbf{P} = \langle \mathsf{S}_\pi^\infty, \mathsf{L_A}, \mathsf{s}_0, \Delta, \mathsf{G}, \mathsf{Cst} \rangle$ it must satisfy the conditions *(i)–(iii)* of Definition 5:

i. $\forall (\pi_i^\infty, a_i, \pi_{i+1}^\infty)$ in π^∞ then (i.1) $\pi_i^\infty, \pi_{i+1}^\infty \in \mathsf{S}_\pi^\infty$, (i.2) $a_i \in \mathsf{L_A}$, and (i.3) $\pi_i^\infty \overset{a_i}{\hookrightarrow} \pi_{i+1}^\infty \in \Delta$. Condition (i.1) holds by construction of $\mathbf{P_I}$. Condition (i.2) holds trivially by definition of $\mathbf{P}$ (see Definition 3). Condition (i.3). Let us assume, by absurd, that $\pi_i^\infty \overset{a_i}{\hookrightarrow} \pi_{i+1}^\infty \notin \Delta$. This is possible when one of the conditions in Definition 2 is not satisfied. For construction of π^∞ then $\exists (i, a_i, i+1) \in \pi$ and consequently $\pi_i^\infty \vdash Cond$ of a_i. Condition *(a)* holds because each commitment's axiom is translated into a corresponding clause (see [20, Section 2.3]). Condition *(b)* holds because of clause `initiates` at Line 35 in Listing 1.1. Conditions *(b.1)* and *(b.2)* are verified respectively by clauses at Lines 45 and 47-49 of Listing 1.1. Therefore, $\pi_i^\infty \overset{a_i}{\hookrightarrow} \pi_{i+1}^\infty \in \Delta$.

ii. $inf(\tau) \cap \mathsf{G} \neq \emptyset$. Being π a legal path for $\mathbf{P_I}$ then there exits `state`$(n, \pi_n, \mathrm{Label}_n)$ such that *final* $\in \mathrm{Label}_n$, thus there are no active commitments in π_n. For construction of π^∞, $\pi_n^\infty \in \mathsf{G}$ and $\pi_n^\infty \in inf(\pi^\infty)$.

iii. $\forall c \in \mathsf{Cst}: T(\tau), \tau_0 \models_{LTL} c$. Being π a legal path for $\mathbf{P_I}$ then $\nexists i \in \pi$ such that `state`$(i, \pi_i, \mathrm{Label}_i)$ and *violation* $\in \mathrm{Label}_i$. Moreover, *pending* $\notin$ `state`$(n, \pi_n, \mathrm{Label}_n)$. Thus, for construction of π^∞, $\nexists c \in \mathsf{Cst}$ s.t. $T(\pi^\infty), \pi_0^\infty \not\models_{LTL} c$.

$\square$

5   2CL Tool for Protocol Design and Analysis

Based on the described technical framework, we developed a tool which supports the user in two different ways: *(i)* it features two graphical editors for specifying the protocol actions and the constraints; *(ii)* it generates different kinds of graphs for supporting the user in the analysis of the possible interactions and in understanding which of them are legal. The system is realized as an Eclipse plug-in, available at the URL `http://di.unito.it/2cl`. The functionalities that the system supports can be grouped into three components: *design, reasoning* and *visualization* (see Fig. 2).

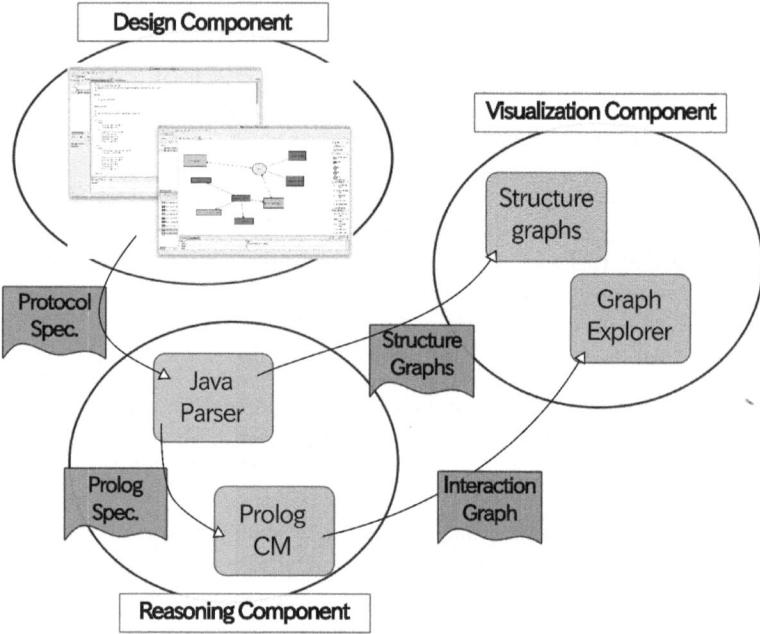

Fig. 2. Components and functionalities supplied by the system

Design Component. The design component provides the tools that are necessary for defining the protocol. It supplies two editors: one for the definition of the actions and one for the definition of constraints (Fig. 3). The *action definition* editor is basically a text editor. The *regulative specification editor* allows the user to graphically define a set of constraints. Constraints are represented by drawing facts, connecting them with 2CL arrows (following the graphical representation of Table 1) or with logical connectives so as to design DNF formulas. The advantage of having a graphical editor is that it supplies a global view of constraints, thus giving the perception of the *flow* imposed by them, without actually specifying any rigid sequence (no-flow-in-flow principle [3]). Fig. 3 shows a snapshot of the constraint editor with a representation of the NetBill constraints. On the right the user can select the element to introduce in the graph. By editing the properties (bottom of the figure), instead, he/she can specify the name of facts and other graphical aspects.

Reasoning Component. The reasoning component consists of a Java Parser and of the Prolog implementation of the commitment machine described in Section 4. The former generates different kinds of graphs as well as the Prolog program corresponding to the protocol specification. The latter is the input of the Prolog implementation of the commitment machine for the generation of the labeled graph. As explained, the labeled graph represents all the possible interactions where each state is labeled according to the evaluation of the protocol constraints. The graphical conventions is: *(i)* a state of violation is represented as

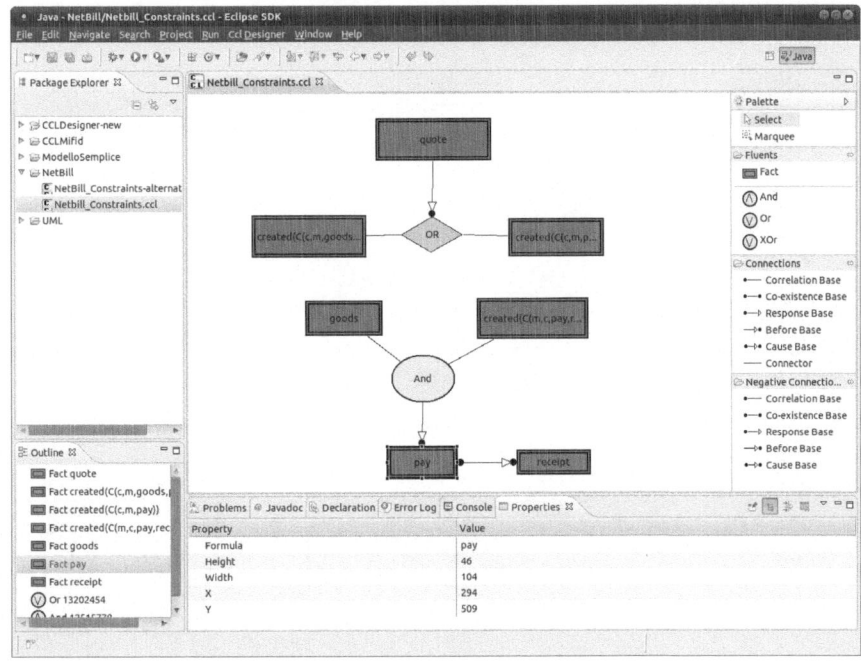

Fig. 3. Editor for constraint specification

a red diamond, with an incoming red dashed arrow (e.g. states 54, 57, 108 in Fig. 4); *(ii)* a state in which there is a pending condition is yellow[3] (e.g. states 45, 53, 108); *(iii)* a state with a single outline, independently from the shape (e.g. 49, 57, 60), is a state that contains unsatisfied commitments; *(iv)* a state with a double outline, independently from the shape, does not contain active commitments (e.g. 41, 108). Graphical notations can be combined, e.g. a yellow diamond with single outline is a state where there are unsatisfied active commitments, where a constraint is violated and where there is a pending condition (e.g. 53, 57, 114).

Visualization Component. All the graphs produced by the reasoning component can be visualized as images. *Labelled graph*, however, can be explored by means of the tool *Graph Explorer*, which is implemented in Java and relies on iDot (Incremental Dot Viewer) – an open source project that uses the prefuse[4] visualization framework for Dot graph display. The Graph Explorer supplies different functionalities, like the visualization of the shortest path given a source and a target state, and the visualization of legal (or illegal) paths only. The user can add or delete a node in a path; search a state starting from its label; and search all the states that contain a certain fact or commitment. Moreover, the

---

[3] Light gray states in black and white printing.

[4] http://prefuse.org/

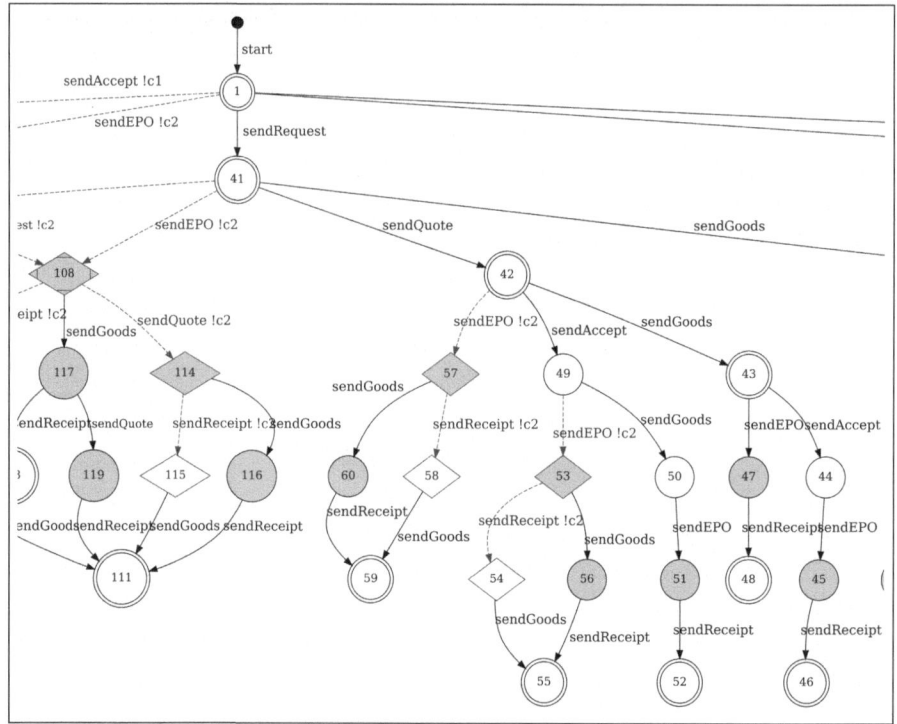

Fig. 4. Part of the labelled Graph for NetBill

tool allows the exploration of the graph one state at a time, by choosing which node to expand. Fig. 4 reports part of the labeled graph for NetBill.

Protocol Analysis. The tool can be used as a support in protocol analysis [5]. Particularly interesting is the possibility of exploring the labeled graph by means of the Graph Explorer, which can be used to predict whether performing a certain sequence of actions results in a violation and, in this case, if there is a way to return on a legal path. For what concerns the designer, it is not always easy, when specifying a protocol, to individuate which constraints to introduce but, with the help of the tool, it becomes easy to identify misbehaviors and revise the constraints so as to avoid them. Moreover, a designer can decide, by analyzing the graph, to modify the specification so as to regiment some of the patterns expressed as constraints, or to remove some of them. For instance, considering the running example, from Fig. 4 it is possible to infer that the protocol does not allow the customer to pay (*sendEPO*) before the merchant sends the goods. This is due to the constraint CREATED($C(m, c, pay, receipt)$) $\land$ *goods* $\rightarrow\!\!\bullet$ *pay*. If this behavior was not in the intention of the designer, he/she can discover it and, e.g., relax the *before* constraint ($\rightarrow\!\!\bullet$) transforming it into a *co-existence* ($\bullet\!\!-\!\!\bullet$). If, instead, that is exactly the desired behavior, one may decide to regiment *sendEPO* so as to enable the payment only after the goods have been sent.

The complete NetBill protocol encoding and the corresponding labeled graph together with further examples, like 2CL specifications of classical agent interaction protocols (CNet) and of real-life protocols (OECD guidelines and MiFID [5]) are available at http://di.unito.it/2cl (section Examples).

6   Related Work and Conclusions

This work provides an operational semantics of 2CL protocols [3,4], based on an extension of the Generalized Commitment Machine [20], and describes a Prolog implementation of this formalization, where the constraint evaluation is performed thanks to state conditions rather than by considering paths. Our aim was to enrich commitment machines with a mechanism for constraint evaluation, in a way that is suitable to creating tools which are useful in application domains. The provided formalization allows the creation of compact and annotated graphs, which provide a global overview of the possible interactions, showing which are legal and which cause constraint (or commitment) violations. The aim was to support an implementation, which enables the verification of exposure to risk on the graph of the possible executions, and taking decisions concerning how to behave or to modify the protocol in order to avoid such a risk. Due to this aim, we decided to base our implementation on [22], rather than on formalizations which support, for instance, model checking. The reason is that this work already is along the same line of ours, the intent being to give a global view on desirable and undesirable states. Winikoff et al. [22], however, propose to cope with undesired paths or undesired final states by adding ad-hoc preconditions to the actions, or by adding active commitments to states that are desired not to be final. This, however, complicates the reuse and the adaptation of the specification to different domains. On the contrary, the proposal in [4] results to be easily adaptable and customizable so as to address different needs of different domains, and it also allows for the specification of more expressive patterns of interaction, given as 2CL constraints.

Concerning model checking, in [8] it is possible to find a proposal of a branching-time logic that extends CTL*, used to give a logical semantics to the operations on commitments. This approach was designed to perform verifications on commitment-protocol ruled interactions by exploiting symbolic model checking techniques. The properties that can be verified are those that are commonly checked in distributed systems: fairness, safety, liveness, and reachability. It would be interesting to integrate in this logical framework the 2CL constraints in order to combine the benefits of both approaches: on the one hand, the possibility to embed in the protocols expressive regulative specification, and, on the other hand, the possibility to exploit the logical framework to perform the listed verifications.

For what concerns the semantics of commitment protocols, the literature proposes different formalizations. Some approaches present an operational semantics that relies on commitment machines to specify and execute protocols [24,23,22]. Some others, like [12], use interaction diagrams, operationally specifying commitments as an abstract data type, and analyzing the commitment's life cycle as a trajectory in a suitable space. Further approaches rely on temporal logics to give a formal semantics to commitments and to the protocols defined upon them. Among these, [13] uses DLTL. All these approaches allow the inference of the possible executions of the protocol, but, differently than [4], all of them consider as the only regulative aspect of the protocol the regulative value of the commitments.

Acknowledgements. The authors would like to thank the reviewers for their valuable comments. This research was partially funded by "Regione Piemonte" through the project ICT4LAW.

References

1. Baier, C., Katoen, J.-P.: Principles of Model Checking. MIT Press (2008)
2. Baldoni, M., Baroglio, C.: Some Thoughts about Commitment Protocols (Position Paper). In: Baldoni, M., Dennis, L., Mascardi, V., Vasconcelos, W. (eds.) DALT 2012. LNCS (LNAI), vol. 7784, pp. 190–196. Springer, Heidelberg (2013)
3. Baldoni, M., Baroglio, C., Marengo, E.: Behavior-Oriented Commitment-based Protocols. In: Proc. of ECAI. Frontiers in Artificial Intelligence and Applications, vol. 215, pp. 137–142. IOS Press (2010)
4. Baldoni, M., Baroglio, C., Marengo, E., Patti, V.: Constitutive and Regulative Specifications of Commitment Protocols: a Decoupled Approach. ACM Trans. on Int. Sys. and Tech., Spec. Iss. on Agent Communication 4(2) (2013)
5. Baldoni, M., Baroglio, C., Marengo, E., Patti, V.: Grafting Regulations into Business Protocols: Supporting the Analysis of Risks of Violation. In: Antón, A., Baumer, D., Breaux, T., Karagiannis, D. (eds.) Forth International Workshop on Requirements Engineering and Law (RELAW 2011), Held in Conjunction with the 19th IEEE International Requirements Engineering Conference, Trento, Italy, August 30, pp. 50–59. IEEE Xplore (2011)
6. Chesani, F., Mello, P., Montali, M., Torroni, P.: Commitment Tracking via the Reactive Event Calculus. In: Boutilier, C. (ed.) IJCAI, Pasadena, California, USA, pp. 91–96 (July 2009)
7. Chopra, A.K., Singh, M.P.: Constitutive Interoperability. In: Padgham, L., Parkes, D.C., Müller, J., Parsons, S. (eds.) Proc. of 7th International Joint Conference on Autonomous Agents and Multiagent Systems (AAMAS 2008), Estoril, Portugal, vol. 2, pp. 797–804. IFAAMAS (May 2008)
8. El-Menshawy, M., Bentahar, J., Dssouli, R.: Verifiable Semantic Model for Agent Interactions Using Social Commitments. In: Dastani, M., El Fallah Segrouchni, A., Leite, J., Torroni, P. (eds.) LADS 2009. LNCS, vol. 6039, pp. 128–152. Springer, Heidelberg (2010)
9. El-Menshawy, M., Bentahar, J., Dssouli, R.: Symbolic Model Checking Commitment Protocols Using Reduction. In: Omicini, A., Sardina, S., Vasconcelos, W. (eds.) DALT 2010. LNCS, vol. 6619, pp. 185–203. Springer, Heidelberg (2011)
10. Emerson, E.A.: Temporal and Modal Logic, vol. B. Elsevier, Amsterdam (1990)
11. Fornara, N., Colombetti, M.: Defining Interaction Protocols using a Commitment-based Agent Communication Language. In: Rosenschein, J.S., Sandholm, T., Wooldridge, M., Yokoo, M. (eds.) Proc. of the Second International Joint Conference on Autonomous Agents & Multiagent Systems (AAMAS 2003), Melbourne, Australia, pp. 520–527. ACM (July 2003)

12. Fornara, N., Colombetti, M.: A Commitment-Based Approach To Agent Communication. Applied Artificial Intelligence 18(9-10), 853–866 (2004)
13. Giordano, L., Martelli, A., Schwind, C.: Specifying and Verifying Interaction Protocols in a Temporal Action Logic. Journal of Applied Logic 5(2), 214–234 (2007)
14. Jones, A.J.I., Sergot, M.: On the Characterization of Law and Computer Systems:
the Normative Systems Perspective, pp. 275–307. John Wiley & Sons, Inc., New
York (1994)
15. Mallya, A.U., Singh, M.P.: Modeling Exceptions via Commitment Protocols. In:
Dignum, F., Dignum, V., Koenig, S., Kraus, S., Singh, M.P., Wooldridge, M. (eds.)
AAMAS, Utrecht, The Netherlands, pp. 122–129. ACM (July 2005)
16. Marengo, E.: 2CL Protocols: Interaction Patterns Specification in Commitment
Protocols. PhD thesis, Università degli Studi di Torino, Research Doctorate in
Science and High Technology, Specialization in Computer Science (October 2012),
http://www.di.unito.it/~emarengo/Thesis.pdf
17. Marengo, E., Baldoni, M., Baroglio, C., Chopra, A.K., Patti, V., Singh, M.P.:
Commitments with Regulations: Reasoning about Safety and Control in REGULA.
In: Sonenberg, L., Stone, P., Tumer, K., Yolum, P. (eds.) AAMAS, Taipei, Taiwan,
vol. 1–3, pp. 467–474. IFAAMAS (May 2011)
18. Searle, J.R.: The construction of social reality. Free Press, New York (1995)
19. Singh, M.P.: An Ontology for Commitments in Multiagent Systems. Artificial Intelligence and Law 7(1), 97–113 (1999)
20. Singh, M.P.: Formalizing Communication Protocols for Multiagent Systems. In:
Veloso, M.M. (ed.) IJCAI, Hyderabad, India, pp. 1519–1524. AAAI Press (January
2007)
21. Weiss, G. (ed.): Multiagent Systems: A Modern Approach to Distributed Artificial
Intelligence. The MIT Press (1999)
22. Winikoff, M., Liu, W., Harland, J.: Enhancing Commitment Machines. In: Leite,
J., Omicini, A., Torroni, P., Yolum, p. (eds.) DALT 2004. LNCS (LNAI), vol. 3476,
pp. 198–220. Springer, Heidelberg (2005)
23. Yolum, P., Singh, M.P.: Designing and Executing Protocols Using the Event Calculus. In: Agents, pp. 27–28. ACM, New York (2001)
24. Yolum, P., Singh, M.P.: Commitment Machines. In: Meyer, J.-J.C., Tambe, M.
(eds.) ATAL 2001. LNCS (LNAI), vol. 2333, pp. 235–247. Springer, Heidelberg
(2002)

Solving Fuzzy Distributed CSPs: An Approach with Naming Games[*,**]

Stefano Bistarelli[1,2], Giorgio Gosti[3], and Francesco Santini[1,4]

[1] Dipartimento di Matematica e Informatica, Università di Perugia
{bista,francesco.santini}@dmi.unipg.it
[2] Istituto di Informatica e Telematica (CNR), Pisa, Italy
stefano.bistarelli@iit.cnr.it
[3] Institute for Mathematical Behavioral Sciences, University of California,
Irvine, USA
ggosti@uci.edu
[4] Contraintes, INRIA - Rocquencourt, France
francesco.santini@inria.fr

Abstract. Constraint Satisfaction Problems (CSPs) are the formalization of a large range of problems that emerge from computer science. The solving methodology described here is based on *Naming Games (NGs)*. NGs were introduced to represent N agents that have to bootstrap an agreement on a name to give to an object (i.e., a word). In this paper we focus on solving both Fuzzy NGs and Fuzzy Distributed CSPs (Fuzzy DCSPs) with an algorithm inspired by NGs. In this framework, each proposed solution is associated with a preference represented as a fuzzy score. We want the agents to find the solution, which is associated with the highest preference value among all solutions. The two main features that distinguish this methodology from classical Fuzzy DCSPs algorithms are that *i)* the system can react to small instance changes, and *ii)* the fact the algorithm does not require a pre-agreed agent/variable ordering.

1 Introduction

In this paper we present a distributed algorithm to solve *Fuzzy Distributed Constraint Satisfaction Problems (Fuzzy DCSPs)* [14,18,11,12,17] that comes from a generalization of the *Naming Game* paradigm *(NG)* [15,1,13,10].

In Fuzzy DCSPs algorithms, the aim is to design a distributed architecture of processors, or more generally a group of agents, which cooperate to solve a particular Fuzzy DCSP instantiation. In the framework presented here, we see the Fuzzy DCSP solution search as a dynamic system, and we set the stable

---

[*] This work was carried out during the tenure of the ERCIM "Alain Bensoussan" Fellowship Programme, which is supported by the Marie Curie Co-funding of Regional, National and International Programmes (COFUND) of the European Commission.
[**] Research partially supported by MIUR PRIN 2010-2011 2010FP79LR project: "Logical Methods of Information Management".

M. Baldoni et al. (Eds.): DALT 2012, LNAI 7784, pp. 116–135, 2013.

states of the system as the solutions to our Fuzzy DCSP. To do this we design each agent so that it moves towards a stable local state. This system may be called "self-stabilizing" whenever the global stable state is obtained through the reinforcement of the local stable states [7]. The system settles to a global stable state when all agents are in stable local state, When the system finds this global stable state the DCSP instantiation is solved. A protocol designed in this way is resistant to damage and external threats, since it can react to small changes in the original problem instance. Moreover, in our approach all agents have the same probability to reveal private information, and for this reason such algorithm is unbiased (i.e., "fair") with respect to privacy.

The NG paradigm defines a set of problems where a number of agents bootstrap a commonly agreed name for one or more objects [15,1,13,10]. In this paper we discuss a NG generalization in which agents have individual fuzzy preferences over words. This is a straightforward generalization of the NG, because this paradigm naturally models the endogenous agents preferences and the attitudes towards a given naming system. These preferences may be driven by pragmatic or rational reasons: same words may be associated to different objects, same words may be too long or too complex, or may be easy to confuse and, therefore, less suitable as a solution for name assignments.

In Sec. 4, we define Fuzzy NG which are a generalization of the NG that introduces agent preferences. To model agents preferences we associate individual fuzzy levels with each word in the agents domain. In this way, the new game may be interpreted as an optimization problem. The Fuzzy NG we obtain can be seen as a particular instance of a Fuzzy DCSP with fuzzy unary constraints and crisp binary constraints which impose that the possible solutions are the ones in which all the agents connected by a communication link share the same word as a naming convention. Then we extend the works in [3] and [4] in order to consider agent preferences. Within this set of candidate solutions, the real solutions are the ones that optimize the overall preference for the agreed name. All the agents agree on the same word, which is the best possible according to the composition of the preferences of all the participating agents. Since we use fuzzy preferences, values are in the interval $[0, 1]$, they are aggregated with the min operator, and to optimize means to find the word with the maximum preference possible (with the max operator).

The algorithm is defined through an asymmetric interaction among agents, in which one peer is the "speaker" and the other involved agents are called "listeners". To let this interaction occur, our algorithm uses a central scheduler that randomly draws a speaker at each round. This may be interpreted as a "central blind orchestrator" scheme, anyhow this central scheduler has no information on the DCSP instance, and has no pre-determined agent/variable ordering: therefore, it preserves the privacy of the agents.

In Sec. 5 we explain how the algorithm in Sec. 4.1 can be extended to solve a generic instance of a Fuzzy DCSP, that is a DCSP problem where both unary and binary constraints are associated with a fuzzy preference. Fuzzy DSCPs can be used to deal with resource allocation, collaborative scheduling and distributed negotiation [11].

In summary, the main contributions of this paper are two. First, we discuss how individual preferences can be modeled in the NG with the use of the Fuzzy NG, and how we can use a distributed algorithm to solve this problem. Second, we discuss ho a similar algorithm can be used to solve more the more general class of Fuzzy DCSPs.

The paper extends preliminary work in [5], by refining the distributed algorithm and sketching a sample execution of the algorithm, to better understand its functioning. The paper is organized as follows: in Sec. 2 we respectively present the background on Fuzzy DSCPs and NGs, while Sec. 3 summarizes the related work. Section 4 presents an algorithm that solves Fuzzy NGs. Section 5 shows how to extend the algorithm in Sec. 4 in order to solve generic Fuzzy DCSPs. Then, in Sec. 6 we show a simple example on how the algorithm in Sec. 5 works, and Sec. 7 presents the tests and the results for the Fuzzy NG algorithm. Finally, in Sec. 8 we draw our conclusions and explain our future work.

2   Background

2.1   Distributed Constraint Satisfaction Problem (DCSP)

A classical constraint can be seen as the set of value combinations for the variables in its scope that satisfy the constraint. In the fuzzy framework, a constraint is no longer a set, but rather a fuzzy set [14]. This means that, for each assignment of values to its variables, we do not have to say whether it belongs to the set or not, but how much it does so. In other words, we need to use a graded notion of membership. This allows us to represent the fact that a combination of values for the constraint variables is partially permitted. A Fuzzy CSP is defined as a triple $P = \langle X, D, C \rangle$, where X is the set of variables and D is the set of corresponding variable domains (we suppose a single domain for all the variables). C is a set of fuzzy constraints. A fuzzy constraint is defined by a function c_V on a sequence of variables V, which is called the *scope* (or *support*) of the constraint, that is the set of variables on which the constraint is defined on.

$$c_V : \prod_{x_i \in V} D_i \to [0, 1]$$

The function c_V indicates to what extent an assignment of the variables in V satisfies the constraint [14]. In fuzzy constraints, 1 usually corresponds to the best preference, and 0 to the worst preference value. The combination $c_V \otimes c_W$ of two fuzzy constraints c_V and c_W is a new fuzzy constraint $c_{V \cup W}$ defined as

$$c_{V \cup W}(\eta) = min(c_V(\eta), c_W(\eta))$$

where η is a complete assignment of the variables in the problem, i.e., an assignment of the variables in X:

$$\eta \in \prod_{x_i \in X} D_i$$

If $c_1\eta > c_2\eta$ (e.g., $c_1\eta = 0.8$ and $c_2\eta = 0.4$), it means that the assignment η satisfies c_1 better than c_2. In the following of the paper we will use the expression $c\eta[x_i := d]$ to denote a constraint assignment in which variable $x_i \in X$ takes the value $d \in D$.

We can now define the preference of the complete set C of constants in the problem, by performing a combination of all the fuzzy constraints. Given any complete assignment η we have

$$(\bigotimes_{c_V \in C} c_V)(\eta) = \min_{c_V \in C} c_V(\eta)$$

Thus, the optimal solutions of a fuzzy CSP are the complete assignments whose satisfaction degree is maximum over all the complete assignments, that is,

$$OptSol(P) = \{\eta \mid \max_{\eta} \min_{c_V \in C} c_V(\eta)\}$$

In the description of our algorithm in Sec. 4 we will also need a definition of *projection* for fuzzy constraints: given a fuzzy constraint $c_V \in C$ and a variable $v \in V$, the *projection* [2] of c_V over v, written as $c_V \Downarrow_v$, is a fuzzy constraint c' such that $c'\eta = \max(c\eta[x_1 := d_1]\ldots[x_k := d_k])$, where $d_1\ldots d_k \in D$ and $x_1\ldots x_k \in (V\backslash\{v\})$. For instance, if $V = \{v\}$, then $c_V \Downarrow_v = c_V$. Informally, projecting means to eliminate the influence of all the variables $V\backslash\{v\}$ over a constraint (i.e., to remove the variables in $V\backslash\{v\}$ from its scope), by considering the assignment that maximises the preference of c.

In DCSPs [18,14], the main difference to a classical CSP is that each variable is controlled by a corresponding agent, meaning that this agent sets the variable's value. Formally, a DCSP is a tuple $\langle X, D, C, A \rangle$, i.e., a CSP with a set A of n agents. We suppose the number of variables m to be greater/equal than the number of agents n, i.e., $m \geq n$. When an agent controls more than one variable, this can be modeled by a single variable whose values are the combinations of values of the original variable. It is further assumed that an agent knows the domain of its variable and all the constraints involving its variable, and that it can reliably communicate with all the other agents which share the same constraints. The main challenge is to develop distributed algorithms that solve the CSP by exchanging messages among the agents. Fuzzy DCSPs features both all the features described in this section, i.e., fuzziness and distributivity.

2.2 Introduction to Naming Games

The NG model [15,1,13,10] describes a set of problems in which a number of agents bootstrap a commonly agreed name for one or more objects.

The game is played by a population of n agents which play pairwise interactions in order to negotiate conventions, that is associations between forms and meanings, and it is able to describe the emergence of a global consensus among them. For the sake of simplicity this model does not take into account the possibility of homonymy, so that all meanings are independent and one can work with only one of them, without loss of generality. An example of such a game is a population that has to reach a consensus on the name (i.e., the form) to assign to an object (i.e., the meaning), by exploiting local interactions only. However, the same model is appropriate to address all those situations in which negotiation rules a decision process (e.g., opinion dynamics) [1].

Each NG is defined by an interaction protocol. There are two important aspects in NGs:

- The agents randomly interact and use a simple set of rules to update their state.
- The agents converge to a consistent state in which all the objects of the set have a uniquely assigned name, by using a distributed social strategy.

Generally, two agents are randomly extracted at each round to perform the role of the "speaker" and the "listener" (or "hearer", as used in [15,1]). The interaction between speaker and listener determines the update of the internal state of the agents. DCSPs and NGs share a variety of common features, as already introduced in [3,4].

2.3   Self-stabilizing Algorithms

The definition of *self-stabilizing algorithm* in distributed computing was first introduced in [7]. A system is *self-stabilizing* whenever each system configuration associated with a *solution* is an absorbing state (global stable state), and any initial state of the system is in the basin of attraction of at least one *solution*.

In a self-stabilizing algorithm, we program the agents of our distributed system to interact with their neighbors. The agents update their state through these interactions by trying to find a stable state in their neighborhood. Since the nature of these algorithms is distributed, many legal configurations of agents states and their neighbors states start arising sparsely. Not all of these configurations are mutually compatible, and, thus, they form mutually inconsistent potential cliques. A self-stabilizing algorithm must find a way to make the global legal state emerge from the competition among these potential cliques. Dijkstra [7] and Collin [6] suggest that an algorithm designed in this way may not always converge, and a special agent is needed to break the system symmetry. [4] shows how a different strategy based on the concept of random behavior and probabilistic transition function can solve specific distributed constraint satisfaction problems with a probability of one. Moreover, [4] shows empirically how this approach can be used on a variety of CSP instances. In Sec. 4.2 we discuss how this later strategy is implemented on Fuzzy CSP instances.

3   Related Work

This paper extends the results in [3,4], in which some of the authors of this paper have solved (crisp) DCSPs with an algorithm inspired by the NG model. Whilst a number of approaches have been proposed to solve DCSPs [14,18] or centralized Fuzzy CSP [14] alone, there is less work in the literature related to solution schemes able to solve CSP instances that are both fuzzy and distributed.

It is important to notice the fundamental difference, with respect to this work, with the DCSP algorithms designed by Yokoo [18]. Yokoo addresses three fundamental kinds of DCSP algorithms: *Asynchronous Backtracking*, *Asynchronous weak-commitment Search* and *Distributed Breakout Algorithm*, all of them also presented in a survey article [18]. Although these algorithms share the property of being asynchronous, they require a pre-agreed agent/variable ordering. The algorithm presented in this paper does not need this initial condition. Therefore, we do not require a pre-processing phase where the ordering is defined, and it also allows for a more dynamic execution, since agents may leave and join without redefining the ordering.

Fuzzy DCSPs has been of interest to the Multi-Agent System community, especially in the context of distributed resource allocation, collaborative scheduling, and negotiation (e.g., [11]). Those works focus on bilateral negotiations and when many agents take part, a central coordinating agent may be required.

For example, the work in [11] promotes a rotating coordinating agent which acts as a central point to evaluate different proposals sent by other agents. Hence, the network model employed in those work is not totally distributed. One more important note is that this work focuses on competitive negotiation, where agents try to outsmart each other (i.e., opposed to our collaborative negotiation).

In [12] the authors propose two approaches to solve these problems: an iterative method and an adaptation of the *Asynchronous Distributed constraint OPTimisation* algorithm (*ADOPT*) for solving Fuzzy DCSP. They also present experiments on the performance comparison between the two approaches, showing that ADOPT is more suitable for low density problems; density is equivalent to the number of links divided by the number of agents.

Finally, in [16,17] the authors define the fuzzy GENET model for solving binary Fuzzy CSPs with a neural network model. Through transforming Fuzzy CSPs into $[0, 1]$ integer programming problems, the authors display the equivalence between the underlying working mechanism of fuzzy GENET and the discrete Lagrangian method. Benchmarking results confirm its feasibility in tackling Fuzzy CSPs, and flexibility in dealing with over-constrained problems. After a number of cycles, the network settles in a stable state. In this stable state, if the obtained fuzzy preference is greater/equal than a predefined threshold α_0, an acceptable solution is considered to be found. Otherwise, the network is trapped in a local minimum. Even if this termination conditions can be implemented in our self-stabilizing algorithm as shown in the tests over the $n \times (n-1)$-queens problem in Sec. 7. In the implementation we propose in Sec. 4 we let the algorithm search for the best optimum of the problem (i.e., without a lower threshold).

4   An Algorithm for Fuzzy Naming Games

In this section we extend classical NGs to take into account fuzzy scores associated with words, therefore, we propose an algorithm that solves Fuzzy NGs. Since we deal with fuzzy values associated only with words, we can consider Fuzzy NGs as particular Fuzzy DCSP instances, $P = \langle X, D, C, A \rangle$ (see Sec. 2.1). In this problem we have fuzzy unary constraints describing the preferences over the possible words, and binary crisp constraints that are satisfied only if the words chosen from two neighboring agents are the same (i.e., $x = y$). In Sec. 5 we further extend the algorithm in order to consider fuzzy binary constraints among agents, and consequently, to solve plain Fuzzy DCSPs.

At each round, the algorithm is based on two kinds of entities. The first is a single *speaker*, which communicates its choice on the word and the related fuzzy preference. The second is a set of *listeners*, which are the speaker's neighboring agents. These neighbors are those agents that can directly communicate with the speaker, through the communication network over the agents. At each round r, an agent is drawn with uniform probability to be the speaker. In the following of this section we describe in detail each step of the interaction scheme that defines the behavior between the speaker and the listeners: we consider three phases, *i) broadcast*, *ii) feedback* and *iii) update*. Each agent marks the element that it expects to be the final shared name in order to recall it when necessary.

4.1   Interaction Protocol

Broadcast. The speaker $a_s \in A$ executes the broadcast protocol. We suppose that each speaker a_s manages a variable $s \in X$. The speaker checks if the marked variable assignment $b \in D$ is in top, where top is the set of current best assignment, $top = \{x_s | x_s = \arg\max_x[(\bigotimes c_{V_s} \eta[s := x]) \Downarrow_s]\}$. The $\bigotimes$ composition is performed over all the constraints that include s in their support V_s, that is $s \in V_s$; then, the result is projected over s (see Sec. 2) in order to obtain a constraint over s only, and, finally, we consider the best preference associated with this constraint (with max). If the current marked variable assignment is not in top, the the agent selects a new variable assignment b from top with uniform probability, and marks it. The agent recalls the value $u = (\bigotimes c_{V_s} \eta[s := b]) \Downarrow_s$. and broadcasts the couple $\langle b, u \rangle$ to all its listeners, that is, it sends its subjective preference for the name of s.

Notice that, even if in this case we only have one unary fuzzy constraint over s, we perform the $\bigotimes$ composition to enforce the consistency w.r.t. not allowed values of s imposed by crisp binary constraints over it. As a remind, crisp binary constraints impose equality among the variables of different agents.

Feedback. All the listeners receive the broadcast message $\langle b, u \rangle$ from the speaker. Each listener $a_l \in A$, which controls variable l, computes the value $(\bigotimes c_{V_l} \eta[s := b][l := d_k]) \Downarrow_l$ for all possible d_k values, where d_k is any possible assignment for variable l, and c_{V_l} is any constraint with a scope that includes variable l. In other words, we compute the combination of the fuzzy preferences (equal to v_k) for each d_k assignment, supposing that the speaker chooses word b. Each listener sends back to a_s a feedback message according to the following two cases:

- *Failure.* If $u > \max_k(v_k)$ there is a *failure*, and the listener feedbacks a failure message containing the maximum value and the corresponding assignment for l, **Fail**$\langle \max_k(v_k) \rangle$. This corresponds to a failure because the value proposed by the speaker is better than an upper preference threshold for the same word, computed from the point of view of the listener instead.
- *Success.* If $u \leq \max_k(v_k)$ we are in *success* conditions, the listener feedbacks **Succ** only.

Update. The listener feedback determines the update of a_s and of each a_l that has participated to the interaction. When a listener a_l feedbacks a **Succ**, and if it has an preference value for $d_k = b$ higher than u, then it lowers the preference level for d_k to u. If a_s receives only **Succ** feedback messages from all its listeners, then it does not need to update.

Otherwise, a_s may receive a number $h \geq 1$ of **Fail**$\langle v_j \rangle$ feedback messages. In this case, the speaker selects the worst fuzzy preference v_w, s.t. $\forall j, v_w \leq v_j$. As a consequence, a_s sends to all its listeners a **FailUpdate**$\langle v_w \rangle$. Thus, the speaker changes the preference for b of its unary constraint $c_{\{s\}}$ with the worst fuzzy level among the failure feedback messages, i.e., $c_{\{s\}}\eta[s := b] = v_w$. In words, it adapts the value of its variable s in accordance to its neighborhood, since fuzzy preferences are composed with the min operator. In addition, each listener a_l sets its preference for word b to v_w, i.e., $c_{\{l\}}\eta[s := b][l := d_l] = v_w$. In words, the feedback of the "worst" listener is propagated to all the listeners of a_s.

4.2   Theorems

In this section we report the lemmas and theorems that lead to the convergence property of the algorithm described in Sec. 4.1: we formally prove that the algorithm always terminates with the best solution, that is the word with the highest fuzzy preference. With Lemma 1 we state that a subset of constraints $C' \subseteq C$ has a higher fuzzy preference w.r.t. C. We say that a fuzzy constraint problem is α-consistent if it can be solved with a level of satisfiability of at least α (see also [2]), that is if a there exists a solution with a preference better than (or equal to) threshold α (with $\alpha \in [0..1]$). Lemma 1 holds because min is a monotonically decreasing function.

Lemma 1 ([2]). *Consider a set of constraints C and any subset C' of C. Then we have $\bigotimes C \leq \bigotimes C'$.*

The speaker selection-rule defines a probability distribution function F that tells us the probability that a certain domain assignment is selected. In Lemma 2 we relate F to the convergence of the algorithm with probability 1, related to the level of satisfiability of the problem.

Lemma 2. *If function F selects only the domain elements with preference level greater then α, then the algorithm converges with probability 1, to a solution with a preference greater than α.*

From [3,4] we know that if function F allows a random exploration of the word domain, then the algorithm converges to the same word, but this word may not be the optimal one. If we choose F in order to select only words with a preference greater than α, then the algorithm converges to a solution with a global preference greater than α.

With Prop. 1 and Prop. 2 we prepare the background for the main theorem of this section, that is Th. 1. Proposition 1 describes how the global state of the agents converges, while Prop. 2 states that the algorithm converges with a probability of 1.

Proposition 1. *For round $r \to +\infty$, the weight associated to the optimal solution is equal for all the agents, and it is equal to the minimum preference level of that word.*

Proposition 2. *For any probability distribution F the algorithm converges with a probability of 1.*

These two propositions can be derived as proposed in [3,4]. At last, we state that the presented algorithm always converges to the best solution of a Fuzzy DCSP.

Theorem 1. *The algorithm described in Sec. 4.1 always converges to the best solution of the represented Fuzzy NG, i.e., it converges to the solution with the highest fuzzy preference.*

The proof comes from the fact that, *i)* according to Prop. 2, the algorithm always converges, and *ii)* we choose a proper function F as described in Lemma 2.

5   Solving Fuzzy Distributed Constraint Satisfaction Problems as Naming Games

In this section we improve the Fuzzy NG algorithm presented in Sec. 4 in order to solve generic Fuzzy DCSPs instances. To accomplish this, we also consider binary fuzzy constraints instead of crisp ones only, as in Sec. 4. In our algorithm we limit ourselves to unary and binary constraints only because any CSP can be translated to an equivalent one, adopting only unary/binary constraints [14].

As proposed in [18], we assign each variable $x_i \in X$ of $P = \langle X, D, C, A \rangle$ to an agent $a_i \in A$. We assume that each agent knows all the constraints that concern its variables [18]. Each agent $i = 1, 2, \ldots, n$ (where $|A| = n$) searches its own variable domain $d_i \in D$ for an assignment that optimizes P. Each agent has an unary constraint c_i, whose support is defined over its managed variable $x_i \in X$; this unary constraints represent the local agent preference for each variable assignment $d_i \in D$. Each agent can interact only with its neighbors:

we may say that the communication network is determined by the network of binary constraints, since we suppose that an agent $a_i \in A$ can communicate only with an $a_j \in A$ agent sharing a binary constraint with it, i.e., $c_{\{i,j\}} \in C$. Any binary constraint $c_{\{i,j\}}$ returns a preference value in the $[0,1]$ interval, which states the combined preference over the assignment of x_i and x_j together.

The algorithm is dived into time intervals (we call it a "round"), during which the agents are able to interact and share information on their variable assignments and the mutual constraints. At each round r, an agent is drawn with uniform probability to be the speaker a_s. As in Sec. 4, each speaker has a set of listeners a_l, each of them sharing a binary constraint with a_s. In this algorithm the agents keep a list of speakers' proposals up to the last failed interaction, this list is composed of agent-assignment tuples $S = \{\langle a_{s_1}, b_{s_1} \rangle, \ldots, \langle a_{s_q}, b_{s_q} \rangle\}$. The phases of the algorithm are three as in Sec. 4: *i) broadcast, ii) feedback* and *iii) update*.

5.1   Interaction Protocol

Broadcast. The speaker a_s executes the broadcast protocol. The speaker computes $top = \{x_s | x_s = \arg\max_x [(\bigotimes c_{V_s} \eta[s := x]) \Downarrow_s]\}$, as in the previous case 4.1. Then, it checks if the marked variable assignment b is in top. If the marked variable assignment is not in top it selects a new variable assignment b with uniform probability from top, and marks it. Then, the agent recalls the value $u = (\bigotimes c_{V_s} \eta[s := b]) \Downarrow_s$, and a_s sends the couple $\langle b, u \rangle$ to all its listeners. In words, the agent composes all the constraints whose scope contains variable s, that is $s \in V_s$, and it sends its preferred assignment.

Feedback. All the $a_l \in A$ listeners receive the broadcast message $\langle b, u \rangle$ from a_s (with $u = \bigotimes c_{V_s} \eta[s := b]$). Each listener a_l adds $\langle b, u \rangle$ to

$$S = \{\langle a_{s_1}, b_{s_1} \rangle, \ldots, \langle a_{s_q}, b_{s_q} \rangle, \langle a_s, b \rangle\}.$$

Then it computes the value $v_k = (\bigotimes c_{V_i} \eta[s := b_1] \ldots [s := b_q][l := d_k]) \Downarrow_l$ for all the possible d_k values, where d_k is any possible assignment for variable l, and c_{V_i} is any constraint with a scope that includes both the speaker s, and the listener l. Then it computes $d_{\max} = \arg\max_{d_k}(v_k)$ and $v_{\max} = \max_{d_k}(v_k)$. Each listener sends back to a_s a feedback message according to the following two cases:

- *Failure.* If $u > v_{\max}$ we obtain a *failure*, and the listener may only feedback **Fail**$\langle \bigotimes c_{V_i} \eta[s := b][l := d_{\max}] \rangle$.
- *Success.* If $u \leq v_{\max}$, we obtain a *success* for this round, and the listener may feedback **Succ** to the speaker.

Notice that this computation is different from the one in the same phase of the algorithm in Sec. 4.1. In this case, the check has to be computed w.r.t. the composition of all the constraints with variable s in their scope. the reason is that in Fuzzy DCSPs we have fuzzy binary constraints either.

Update. As in Sec. 4.1, the feedback of the listeners determines the update of the listeners and of the speaker itself. When a_l feedbacks **Succ**, and if there is a $\bigotimes c_{V_i} \eta[s := b][l := d_k] > u$, then it sets $\bigotimes c_{V_i} \eta[s := b][l := d_k] = u$. If the speaker receives only **Succ** feedback messages from all its listeners, then it does not need to update and the round ends.

Otherwise, that is if the speaker receives a number $h \geq 1$ of **Fail**$\langle v_j \rangle$ feedback messages. In this case, the speaker selects the worst fuzzy preference v_w, s.t. $\forall j, v_w \leq v_j$. As a consequence, a_s sends to all its listeners a **FailUpdate**$\langle v_w \rangle$.

then the speaker sets $\bigotimes c_s \eta[s := b] = v_w$, as performed in Sec. 4.1. In addition, each listener a_l sets its preference for $s := b$ and $l := d_l$ to v_w, i.e., $c_{\{s,l\}} \eta[s := b][l := d_l] = v_w$. In words, the feedback of the "worst" listener is propagated to all the listeners of a_s. Finally, the speaker and the listeners set $S = \emptyset$.

6   An Example of Algorithm Execution

In this section we show a sample execution of the algorithm for Fuzzy DCSP presented in Sec. 5.1. We consider a problem $P = \langle X, D, C, A \rangle$ with three agents (i.e., $a_1, a_2, a_3 \in A$) and both unary and binary constraints, as defined by the network represented in Fig. 1a. The domain for the variables $x_1, x_2, x_3 \in X$ is $D = \{\triangle, \bigcirc\}$.

When we start executing the algorithm, at round $r = 1$ (whose final state is represented in Fig. 1b) we suppose a_1 is the first agent to be randomly chosen as a speaker. It computes the elements with the highest preference over the constraints c_{V_s}, and fills its list *top* with them (which was previously empty). Since this is the first interaction among the agents, the speaker has no marked element, thus it may only draw an element from *top* with uniform probability. As already introduced, agent a_1 computes $\bigotimes c_{V_{x_1}} \eta$ for all $\forall d \in D$, obtaining that $\bigotimes c_{V_{x_1}} \eta[x_1 := \triangle] = 0.1$, and $\bigotimes c_{V_{x_1}} \eta[x_1 := \bigcirc] = 0.2$. Thus, it marks $\bigcirc$ (marked with an asterisk in Fig. 1b), and choses to broadcast $\langle \bigcirc, 0.2 \rangle$ to its neighbors a_2 and a_3 (the broadcast is underlined in Fig. 1b).

Listener a_2 updates the successful speaker-assignment list $S = \{(a_1, \bigcirc)\}$, then it computes $v_k = \bigotimes c_{V_{x_1, x_2}} \eta[x_1 := \bigcirc][x_2 := d_k]$. For $d_k = \triangle$ it finds $v_1 = \bigotimes c_{V_{x_1, x_2}} \eta[x_1 := \bigcirc][x_2 := \triangle] = 0.3$, and for $d_k = \bigcirc$ it finds $v_2 = \bigotimes c_{V_{x_1, x_2}} \eta[x_1 := \bigcirc][x_2 := \bigcirc] = 0.7$. Thus, a_2 returns **Succ**, since $0.2 \leq max(0.3, 0.7)$.

Simultaneously, listener a_3 updates the successful speaker-assignment list $S = \{(a_1, \bigcirc)\}$, and computes $v_k = \bigotimes c_{V_{x_1, x_3}} \eta[x_1 := \bigcirc][x_3 := d_k]$. For $d_k = \triangle$ it finds $v_1 = \bigotimes c_{V_{x_1, x_3}} \eta[x_1 := \bigcirc][x_3 := \triangle] = 0.5$, and for $d_k = \bigcirc$ it finds $v_2 = \bigotimes c_{V_{x_1, x_3}} \eta[x_1 := \bigcirc][x_3 := \bigcirc] = 0.4$. Thus, it returns **Succ**, since $0.2 \leq max(0.5, 0.4)$.

In the update phase the listeners a_2 and a_3 change the preference levels of all the $v_k > 0.2$ to $v_k = 0.2$, i.e., the value broadcast by a_1 in this round (the changed values are represented in bold in Fig. 1b).

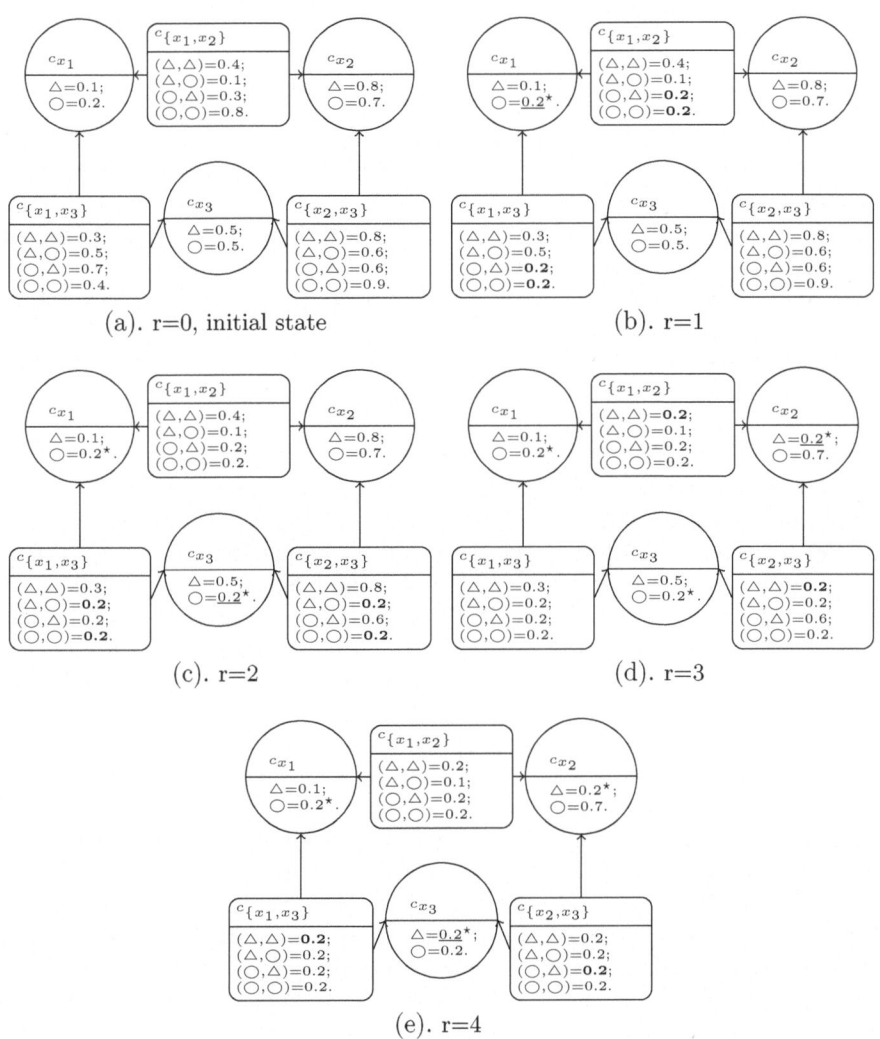

Fig. 1. Example of algorithm run on simple Fuzzy DCSP problem

At $r = 2$ (whose final state is represented in Fig. 1c), agent a_3 is randomly selected. It finds that $\bigotimes c_{V_{x_3}} \eta[x_3 := \triangle] = 0.3$, and $\bigotimes c_{V_{x_3}} \eta[x_3 := \bigcirc] = 0.5$. Thus, it marks $\bigcirc$, and it broadcasts $\langle \bigcirc, 0.5 \rangle$ to its listeners a_1 and a_2. Listener a_1 updates the successful speaker-assignment list $S = \{(a_3, \bigcirc)\}$, and computes $v_k = \bigotimes c_{V_{x_1,x_3}} \eta[x_3 := \bigcirc][x_1 := d_k]$. For $d_k = \triangle$ it finds $v_1 = \bigotimes c_{V_{x_1,x_3}} \eta[x_3 := \bigcirc][l := \triangle] = 0.1$, and for $d_k = \bigcirc$ it finds $v_2 = \bigotimes c_{V_{x_1,x_3}} \eta[x_3 := \bigcirc][x_1 := \bigcirc] = 0.2$. Thus, since $0.5 > max(0.1, 0.2)$, a_1 returns **Fail**$\langle \bigcirc, 0.2 \rangle$.

Simultaneously, listener a_2 updates the successful speaker-assignment list $S = \{(a_1, \bigcirc), (a_3, \bigcirc)\}$, then computes $v_k = \bigotimes c_{V_{x_1, x_2, x_3}} \eta[x_1 := \bigcirc][x_2 := d_k][x_3 := \bigcirc]$. For $d_k = \triangle$ it finds $v_1 = \bigotimes c_{V_{x_1, x_2, x_3}} \eta[x_1 := \triangle][x_2 := \triangle][x_3 := \bigcirc] = 0.4$, and for $d_k = \bigcirc$ it finds $v_2 = \bigotimes c_{V_{x_1, x_2, x_3}} \eta[x_1 := \bigcirc][x_2 := \bigcirc]\eta[x_3 := \bigcirc] = 0.2$. Thus, since $0.2 \leq max(0.5, 0.2)$, a_2 feedbacks **Succ**.

Since a_3 receives a failure feedback, it calls **FailUpdate(0.2)**. Then, the speaker update its preference level, $\bigcirc = 0.2$. The listeners a_1 and a_2 change their preference levels $v_k = 0.2$ (colored in blue in Fig. 1c). a_1, a_2, and a_3 update their successful speaker-assignment lists $S = \emptyset$.

At round $r = 3$ (whose final state is represented in Fig. 1d), a_2 is the third agent to speak. It finds that $\bigotimes c_{V_{x_2}} \eta[x_2 := \triangle] = 0.4$, and $\bigotimes c_{V_{x_2}} \eta[x_2 := \bigcirc] = 0.2$. Thus, it marks $\triangle$, and it broadcasts $\langle \triangle, 0.4 \rangle$ to agents a_1 and a_3. Listener a_1 updates the successful speaker-assignment list $S = \{(a_2, \triangle)\}$, then computes $v_k = \bigotimes c_{V_{x_1, x_2}} \eta[x_1 := d_k][x_2 := \triangle]$. For $d_k = \triangle$ it finds $v_1 = \bigotimes c_{V_{x_1, x_2}} \eta[x_1 := \triangle][x_2 := \triangle] = 0.1$, and for $d_k = \bigcirc$ it finds $v_2 = \bigotimes c_{V_{x_1, x_2}} \eta[x_1 := \bigcirc][x_2 := \triangle] = 0.2$. Thus, it returns **Fail(b,0.2)**.

Listener a_3 updates the successful speaker-assignment list $S = \{(a_2, \triangle)\}$, then computes $v_k = \bigotimes c_{V_{x_2, x_3}} \eta[x_2 := \triangle][x_3 := d_k]$. For $d_k = \triangle$ it finds $v_1 = \bigotimes c_{V_{x_2, x_3}} \eta[x_2 := \triangle][x_3 := \triangle] = 0.3$, and for $d_k = \bigcirc$ it finds $v_2 = \bigotimes c_{V_{x_2, x_3}} \eta[x_2 := \triangle][x_3 := \bigcirc] = 0.2$. Thus, it returns **Succ**. Since a_2 receives a failure feedback, it calls **FailUpdate(0.2)**. Then, the speaker update its preference level, $\triangle = 0.2$, and the listeners a_1 and a_2 change their preference levels $v_k = 0.2$.

At round $r = 4$ (see Fig. 1e), a_3 is the fourth agent to speak. It finds that $\bigotimes c_{V_{x_3}} \eta[x_3 := \triangle] = 0.3$, and $\bigotimes c_{V_{x_3}} \eta[x_3 := \bigcirc] = 0.2$. Thus, it marks $\triangle$, and it broadcasts $\langle \triangle, 0.3 \rangle$ to a_1 and a_2.

Listener a_1 updates the successful speaker-assignment list $S = \{(a_3, \triangle)\}$, then computes $v_k = \bigotimes c_{V_{x_1, x_3}} \eta[x_1 := d_k][x_3 := \triangle]$. For $d_k = \triangle$ it finds $v_1 = \bigotimes c_{V_{x_1, x_3}} \eta[x_1 := \triangle][x_3 := \triangle] = 0.1$, and for $d_k = \bigcirc$ it finds $v_2 = \bigotimes c_{V_{x_1, x_3}} \eta[x_1 := \bigcirc][x_3 := \triangle] = 0.2$. Thus, it returns **Fail(b,0.2)**. Listener a_2 updates the successful speaker-assignment list $S = \{(a_3, \triangle)\}$, then computes $v_k = \bigotimes c_{V_{x_2, x_3}} \eta[x_3 := \triangle][x_2 := d_k]$. For $d_k = \triangle$ it finds $v_1 = \bigotimes c_{V_{x_2, x_3}} \eta[x_3 := \triangle][x_2 := \triangle] = 0.2$, and for $d_k = \bigcirc$ it finds $v_2 = \bigotimes c_{V_{x_2, x_3}} \eta[x_3 := \triangle][x_2 := \bigcirc] = 0.2$. Thus, it returns **Fail(b,0.2)**. Since a_3 receives two failure feedbacks, it calls **FailUpdate(0.2)**. Then, the speaker updates its preference level, $\triangle = 0.2$, and listeners a_1 and a_2 change their preference levels $v_k = 0.2$.

At round $r = 5$, a_2 is the fifth agent to speak. It finds that $\bigotimes c_{V_{x_2}} \eta[x_2 := \triangle] = 0.2$, and $\bigotimes c_{V_{x_2}} \eta[x_2 := \bigcirc] = 0.2$, thus, $\triangle$ is in top. Then a_2 broadcasts $\langle \triangle, 0.2 \rangle$ to a_1 and a_3. Listener a_1 computes $v_k = \bigotimes c_{V_{x_1, x_2}} \eta[x_2 := \triangle][x_3 := d_k]$. For $d_k = \triangle$ it finds $v_1 = \bigotimes c_{V_{x_1, x_2}} \eta[x_2 := \triangle][x_3 := \triangle] = 0.1$, and for $d_k = \bigcirc$ it finds $v_2 = \bigotimes c_{V_{x_1, x_2}} \eta[x_2 := \triangle][x_3 := \bigcirc] = 0.2$. Thus, it returns **Succ**. Listener a_3 computes $v_k = \bigotimes c_{V_{x_2, x_3}} \eta[x_2 := \triangle][x_3 := d_k]$. For $d_k = \triangle$ it finds $v_1 = \bigotimes c_{V_{x_2, x_3}} \eta[x_2 := \triangle][x_3 := \triangle] = 0.2$, and for $d_k = \bigcirc$ it finds $v_2 = \bigotimes c_{V_{x_2, x_3}} \eta[x_2 := \triangle][x_3 := \bigcirc] = 0.2$. Thus, it returns **Succ**. Since all interactions are successful the speaker calls a success update, the listeners a_1 and a_3 do not change the preference levels, because $v_k \leq 0.2$.

From $r = 6$ the system converges to an absorbing state in which all interactions are success, and the preference levels do not change. This state is also a solution of the fuzzy DCSP.

7   Experimental Results

7.1   Fuzzy NG Benchmarks

In this subsection we show the performance results related to the algorithm presented in Sec. 4. To evaluate different executions we define the probability of a successful interaction at round r, i.e., $P_r(succ)$, given the state of the system in that turn. Notice that with r we mean the current round of speaker/listener interaction: if $r = 2$ it means that we are at the second round. $P_r(succ)$ is determined by the probability that an agent is a speaker s at round r (i.e., $P(s = a_i)$), and by the probability that the agent interaction is successful (i.e., $P_r(succ \mid s = a_i)$). This is computed considering all the n agents participating to the distributed computation:

$$P_r(succ) = \sum_{i=1}^{n} P_r(succ \mid s = a_i)P(s = a_i)$$

The probability $P_r(succ \mid s = a_i)$ depends on the state of the agent at round r. In particular, it depends on the variable assignment (or word) b selected. Given an algorithm execution, at each round r we can compute $P_r(succ \mid s = a_i)$ over the states of all agents, before that the interaction is performed. Since we have that $P(s = a_i) = 1/n$, we can compute the probability of being in a successful state as:

$$P_r(succ) = \frac{1}{n} \sum_{i=1}^{n} P_r(succ \mid s = a_i)$$

To set up our benchmark, we generate *Random Fuzzy NG* instances (*RFNGs*). To generate such problems, we assign to each agent the same domain of names D, and for each agent and each name in the agent's domain we draw a preference level in the interval $[0, 1]$, by using an uniform distribution. Moreover, RFNGs can only have crisp binary equality-constraints (as defined in Sec. 4). Then, we set the network of agents to be fully connected, in this way, any agent can speak to any agent. We call this kind of problem as *completely connected RFNG instance*, which represents the first set of problems that we use as benchmark. Clearly, by using a completely connected network, the successful global state (where the system is stabilized and a solution is found) is reached very quickly, as it can be seen in Fig. 2a (we discuss this figure in the following).

For the first round of tests, we generate 5 completely connected RFNG instances, with 10 agents and 10 words each (each agent has a word). For each one of these instances, we compute the best preference level and the word associated to this solution, by using a brute-force algorithm. Then, we execute this algorithm 10 times on each instance. To decide when the algorithm finds the solution, a graph crawler checks marked word of each agent, and the related preference value. If all the agents agree on the marked variable, this means they find an agreement on the name. Then, the graph crawler checks if the shared word has a preference level equal to the best preference (found through the brutal force initial-phase), in such case we conclude that the algorithm has found the optimal solution. In Fig. 2a we can see that the average number of rounds for each of the 5 instances is less than $r = 16$, i.e., within 16 speaker/listeners rounds we can solve all the completely connected RFNG instances.

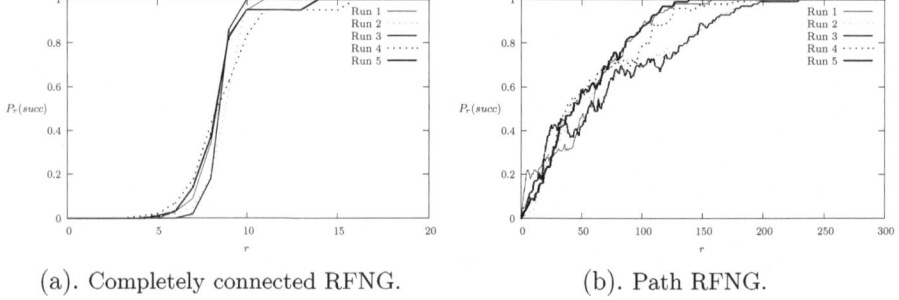

(a). Completely connected RFNG.   (b). Path RFNG.

Fig. 2. Evolution of the average $P_r(succ)$ over 5 different completely connected RFNG instances (2a) and 5 different path RFNG instances (2b). For each instance, we computed the mean $P_r(succ)$ over 10 different runs. We set $n = 10$, and the number of words to 10.

As a second round of tests, we change the topology of our agent networks by defining *Path RFNG* instances [4], which are RFNG instances where the constraint network corresponds to a *path graph*. A path graph (or linear graph) is a particularly simple example of a tree, which has two terminal vertices (vertices that have degree 1), while all others (if any) have degree 2.

In Fig. 2b we report the performance in terms of $P_r(succ)$ for such instances. The instances have been generated following the same guidelines as before: 5 instances with 10 agents and 10 words, and 10 executions for each instance; each preference value in taken from the interval $[0, 1]$, by using an uniform distribution.

As for Fig. 2a, even in Fig. 2b when $P_r(succ) = 1$ the system is in an absorbing state, which we know is also a solution (see Th. 1). As we can notice in Fig. 2b, the network topology among agents strongly influences the performance: having a path graph significantly delays reaching the absorbing state, since we obtain a solution between 140 and 230 speaker/listeners rounds.

In Fig. 3 we show how the *Mean Number of Messages* (*MNM*) needed to find a solution scales over different numbers n of variables in path RFNG instance. For each value n, the *MNM* is measured over 5 different path RFNG instances. We notice that the points approximately overlap the function $cN^{1.8}$.

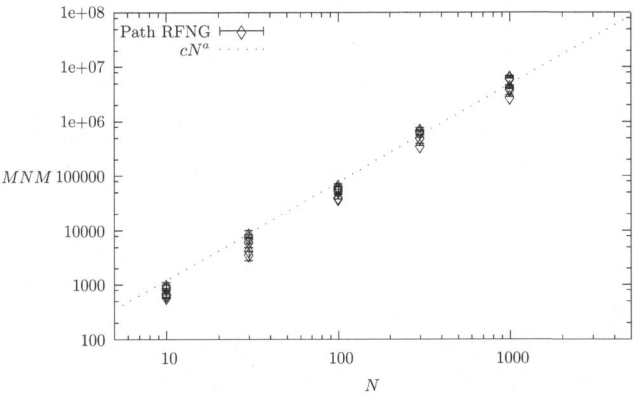

Fig. 3. Scaling of the *MNM* needed to the system to find a solution for different numbers n of variables. For each value n, the *MNM* is measured over 5 different path RFNG instances. We notice that the points approximately overlap the function $cN^{1.8}$.

7.2 Fuzzy CSP Benchmark

For the first fuzzy CSP benchmark, we generate *Random Fuzzy CSP* instances (*RFCSP*). To generate such problems, we consider 10 variables and we assign to each agent a domain of variables D of size 5, and for each assignment we draw a preference level in the interval $[0, 1]$, by using an uniform distribution. Then, we set the binary constraints in such a way that they form a path graph, and we randomly drawn form a uniform distributions in the interval $[0, 1]$ the all the possible fuzzy values of each binary constraint. We call instance a *path RFCSP instance*. In Fig. 4 we show the evolution of the preference level of the solution proposals. In this execution, our algorithm found the best solution after 264 rounds. The level of this solution is 0.4135. We are certain that this is the best solution to the path RFCSP instance because we used a brute-force algorithm to find all the best solutions in advance. It is important to point out that we did not have to set a threshold level, and the algorithm found the best solution autonomously.

For the second fuzzy CSP benchmark we consider the $n \times (n-1)$-queens problem. The $n \times (n-1)$-queens problem [9] is a modification of the n-queens problem in which our objective is to place n queens on a $n \times (n-1)$ chessboard. Because, this board misses a row it is impossible to find a configuration of the queens such that there dos not exist a couple of queens that attack each other. Therefore, we consider a fuzzy version of this problem in which if two queen do not attack each other, their constraint returns a fuzzy preference of one.

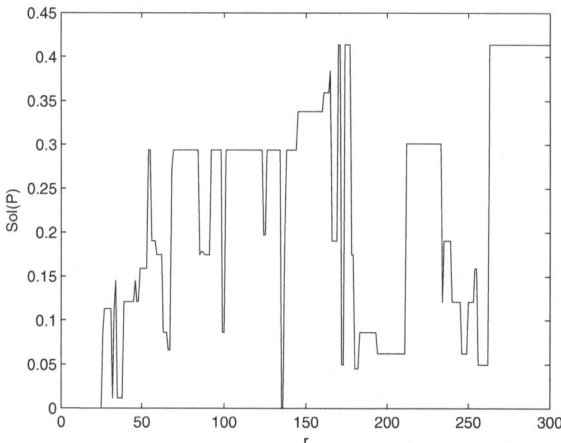

Fig. 4. This graph shows the evaluation of the value of the current solution proposal at each round r for a single algorithm run on a path RFCSP problem, where $n = 10$ and domain size 5

Otherwise, the preference level is proportional to the distance of the queens, according to the formula:

$$\frac{|i_2 - i_1| - 1}{n - 1} \tag{1}$$

Where i_1 is the column of the first queen and i_2 is the column of the second queen. First, as in [17], we search an assignment of the variables in the $n \times (n-1)$-queens problem that has a preference level greater then 0.8.

Table 1. Results on $n \times (n - 1)$-queens problem with a threshold of 0.8. The table shows the mean number of rounds MNR, and the mean number of messages MNM necessary to solve the $n \times (n - 1)$-queens problem at different values of n.

n	MNR	MNM
10	756	20,401
20	1,870	106,590
30	2,130	185,310
40	2,300	269,100
50	2,600	382,200

In Tab. 1, we present the mean number of rounds MNR, and the mean number of messages MNM necessary to find a solution with a threshold of 0.8 to the $n \times (n - 1)$-queens problem. We notice that the algorithm appears to scale well with regards to the increase in the instance size.

Next, Fig. 5 shows the evaluation of the proposed solution at each round r for two algorithms runs on $n \times (n - 1)$-queens problem for $n = 8$. Where we did not set a threshold and the algorithm searches for the best possible solution.

We notice that in both executions the algorithm found optimal solutions greater then 0.8. Unfortunately, the algorithm fails to settle on this solution, because we did not set a threshold level and because the algorithm in unable to infer that the optimal solution is lower the 1. To understand that the $n \times (n-1)$-queens problem has global solution smaller then one the algorithm would have compute not only the binary constraint among its variable and its neighbor variable, but also the combination of the binary constraints among the variables of its neighbors. A complete version of this algorithm would consider this constraint or find a way to propagate this constraints as in the Asynchronous Backtracking algorithm [18]. In future work, we intend to implement such complete version. For now it is important to notice that it is unclear if similar algorithms that do not share a variable ordering are able to solve this problem, because in [17] the authors do not consider this situation. Moreover,it is important to point out that in undistributed CSPs it is reasonable to consider various runs at different threshold level to find the best solution. But in a distributed CSP this would require an other level of coordination among the agent that in some circumstances may require costly or unnecessary assumptions on the communication network.

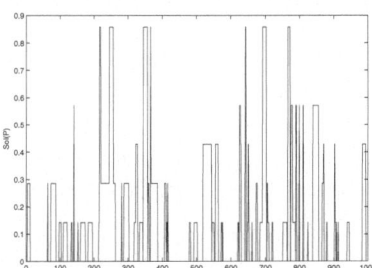 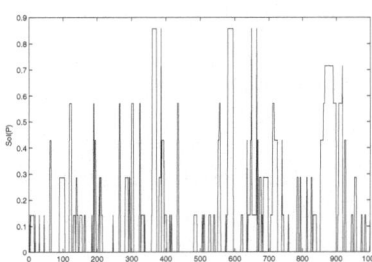

Fig. 5. These two graphs show the evaluation of value of the current solution proposal at each round r for two algorithms runs on $n \times (n-1)$-queens problem with $n = 8$

8   Conclusions and Future Work

In this paper we have shown two main contributions: first we have extended the NG problem [15,1,13,10] to take into account fuzzy preferences over words. Secondly, we have also further extended this algorithm in order to solve a generic instance of Fuzzy DCSPs [14,18,11,12,17], by allowing the solution of binary fuzzy constraints.

Our algorithm is based on the random exploration of the system state-space: our method travels through the possible states until it finds the absorbing state, where it stabilizes. These goals are achieved through the merging of ideas coming from two different fields, and respectively addressed by statistical physics (i.e., NGs), and the computational framework posed by constraint solving (i.e., DCSPs).

The algorithm proposed in Sec. 5 positively answers to an important question: can a distributed uniform probabilistic-algorithm solve general Fuzzy DCSP instances? In other words, we show that a Fuzzy DCSP algorithm may work without a predetermined agent/variable ordering, and it can probabilistically solve instances by taking into account changes to the problem, e.g. deletion/addition of agents during the execution.

Moreover, in the real world, a predetermined agent ordering may be a quite restrictive assumption. For example, we may consider our agents to be corporations, regions in a nation, states in a federation, or independent government agencies. In all of these cases, a predetermined order may not be acceptable for many reasons. Hence, we think it is very important to explore and understand how such distributed systems may work, and what problems may arise.

In the future, we intend to evaluate in depth an asynchronous version of this algorithm, and to test it using comparison metrics, such as a communication cost (number of messages sent) and the *Number of Non-Concurrent Constraint Checks* (*NCCCs*). We would also like to compare our algorithm against other distributed and asynchronous algorithms, such as the *Distributed Stochastic Search Algorithm* (*DSA*) [8], and the *Distributed Breakout Algorithm* (*DBA*) [18]. In addition, we intend to investigate the "fairness" in the loss of privacy between algorithms with no pre-agreed agent/variable ordering, and algorithms with pre-agreed agent/variable ordering. We also plan to develop other functions used to select the speaker in the broadcast phase, and to study the convergence by comparing the performance with the function F used in this paper (see Sec. 4.1).

Finally, we will try to generalise the proposed method to generic semiring-based CSP instances [2], extending the preference from fuzzy to weighted or probabilistic schemes.

References

1. Baronchelli, A., Felici, M., Caglioti, E., Loreto, V., Steels, L.: Sharp transition towards shared vocabularies in multi-agent systems. CoRR, abs/physics/0509075 (2005)
2. Bistarelli, S.: Semirings for Soft Constraint Solving and Programming. LNCS, vol. 2962. Springer, Heidelberg (2004)
3. Bistarelli, S., Gosti, G.: Solving CSPs with Naming Games. In: Oddi, A., Fages, F., Rossi, F. (eds.) CSCLP 2008. LNCS, vol. 5655, pp. 16–32. Springer, Heidelberg (2009)
4. Bistarelli, S., Gosti, G.: Solving distributed CSPs probabilistically. Fundam. Inform. 105(1-2), 57–78 (2010)
5. Bistarelli, S., Gosti, G., Santini, F.: Solving fuzzy DCSPs with naming games. In: IEEE 23rd International Conference on Tools with Artificial Intelligence, ICTAI 2011, pp. 930–931 (2011)
6. Collin, Z., Dechter, R., Katz, S.: On the feasibility of distributed constraint satisfaction. In: IJCAI, pp. 318–324 (1991)
7. Dijkstra, E.W.: Self-stabilizing systems in spite of distributed control. Commun. ACM 17, 643–644 (1974)

8. Fitzpatrick, S., Meertens, L.: An Experimental Assessment of a Stochastic, Anytime, Decentralized, Soft Colourer for Sparse Graphs. In: Steinhöfel, K. (ed.) SAGA 2001. LNCS, vol. 2264, pp. 49–64. Springer, Heidelberg (2001)

9. Guan, Q., Friedrich, G.: Extending Constraint Satisfaction Problem Solving in Structural Design. In: Belli, F., Radermacher, F.J. (eds.) IEA/AIE 1992. LNCS, vol. 604, pp. 341–350. Springer, Heidelberg (1992)

10. Komarova, N.L., Jameson, K.A., Narens, L.: Evolutionary models of color categorization based on discrimination. Journal of Mathematical Psychology 51(6), 359–382 (2007)

11. Luo, X., Jennings, N.R., Shadbolt, N., Leung, H., Lee, J.H.: A fuzzy constraint based model for bilateral, multi-issue negotiations in semi-competitive environments. Artif. Intell. 148, 53–102 (2003)

12. Nguyen, X.T., Kowalczyk, R.: On solving distributed fuzzy constraint satisfaction problems with agents. In: Proceedings of the 2007 IEEE/WIC/ACM International Conference on Intelligent Agent Technology, IAT 2007, pp. 387–390. IEEE Computer Society, Washington, DC (2007)

13. Nowak, M.A., Plotkin, J.B., Krakauer, D.C.: The evolutionary language game. Journal of Theoretical Biology 200(2), 147–162 (1999)

14. Rossi, F., van Beek, P., Walsh, T.: Handbook of Constraint Programming (Foundations of Artificial Intelligence). Elsevier Science Inc., New York (2006)

15. Steels, L.: A self-organizing spatial vocabulary. Artificial Life 2(3), 319–332 (1995)

16. Wong, J., Ng, K., Leung, H.: A Stochastic Approach to Solving Fuzzy Constraint Satisfaction Problems. In: Freuder, E.C. (ed.) CP 1996. LNCS, vol. 1118, pp. 568–569. Springer, Heidelberg (1996)

17. Wong, J.H.Y., Leung, H.: Extending GENET to solve fuzzy constraint satisfaction problems. In: Proceedings of the Fifteenth National/Tenth Conference on Artificial Intelligence/Innovative Applications of Artificial Intelligence, AAAI 1998 IAAI 1998, Menlo Park, CA, USA, pp. 380–385. American Association for Artificial Intelligence (1998)

18. Yokoo, M., Hirayama, K.: Algorithms for distributed constraint satisfaction: A review. Autonomous Agents and Multi-Agent Systems 3, 185–207 (2000)

Commitment Protocol Generation

Akın Günay[1,*], Michael Winikoff[2], and Pınar Yolum[1]

[1] Computer Engineering Department, Bogazici University, Istanbul, Turkey
{akin.gunay,pinar.yolum}@boun.edu.tr
[2] Department of Information Science, University of Otago, Dunedin, New Zealand
michael.winikoff@otago.ac.nz

Abstract. Multiagent systems contain agents that interact with each other to carry out their activities. The agents' interactions are usually regulated with protocols that are assumed to be defined by designers at design time. However, in many settings, such protocols may not exist or the available protocols may not fit the needs of the agents. In such cases, agents need to generate a protocol on the fly. Accordingly, this paper proposes a method that can be used by an agent to generate commitment protocols to interact with other agents. The generation algorithm considers the agent's own goals and capabilities as well as its beliefs about other agents' goals and capabilities. This enables generation of commitments that are more likely to be accepted by other agents. We demonstrate the workings of the algorithm on a case study.

1 Introduction

Interaction is a key element of many multiagent systems. Agents need to interact for various reasons such as coordinating their activities, collaborating on tasks, and so on. These interactions are generally regulated by interaction protocols that define the messages that can be exchanged among agents. Traditionally, agents are supplied with interaction protocols at design time. Hence, they do not need to worry about which protocol to use at run time and can just use the given protocol as they see fit.

However, in open agent systems, where agents enter and leave, an agent may need to interact with another agent for which no previous interaction protocol has been designed. For example, a buyer may know of interaction protocols to talk to a seller, but may not be aware of an interaction protocol to talk to a deliverer. If these two agents meet, they need to figure out a protocol to complete their dealing. Additionally, even if there is an existing interaction protocol, the interaction protocols that are designed generically may make false assumptions about agents' capabilities, which would make the interaction protocol unusable in a real setting. For example, assume that an e-commerce protocol specifies that a buyer can pay by credit card upon receiving goods from a seller. If the buyer does not have the capability to pay by credit card, this protocol will not achieve its purpose. Even when the capabilities of the agents are aligned with those expected by the interaction protocol, the current context of the agents may not be appropriate to engage in the protocol. Following the previous example, an agent who

---

* Akın Günay is partially supported by TÜBİTAK Scholarships 2211 and 2214 and Pınar Yolum is partially supported by a TÜBİTAK Scholarship 2219.

M. Baldoni et al. (Eds.): DALT 2012, LNAI 7784, pp. 136–152, 2013.

can pay by credit card might have a current goal of minimizing bank transactions for that month and thus may find it more preferable to pay cash. That is, based on its current goals and existing commitments, the interactions that it is willing to engage in may differ. Therefore an interaction protocol that is blind to agents' current needs would not be applicable in many settings.

Accordingly, we argue that an agent needs to generate appropriate interaction protocols itself at run time. Since the agent would know its own capabilities, goals, and commitments precisely, it can generate an interaction protocol that respects these. However, for the interaction protocol to be successful, it should also take into account the participating agents' context.

Many times, even though the goals, commitments, or the capabilities of the other agents may not be known in full, partial information will exist. For example, agents may advertise their capabilities especially if they are offering them as services (e.g., selling goods). Existing commitments of the other agents may be known if the agent itself is part of those commitments (e.g., the agent has committed to deliver, after payment). The partial goal set of the participating agents may be known from previous interactions (e.g., the agent is interested in maximizing cash payments), or from domain knowledge (e.g. merchants in general have the goal of selling goods and/or services). Hence, the other agents' context can be approximated and using this approximate model a set of possible interaction protocols can be generated.

To realize this, we propose a framework in which agents are represented with their capabilities, goals, and commitments. The interactions of the agents are represented using commitments [3,14] and the interaction protocols are modeled as commitment protocols. Commitments offer agents flexibility in carrying out their interactions and enable them to reason about them [9,19,21]. An agent that wants to engage in an interaction considers its own goals, makes assumptions about the other agents' goals, and proposes a set of commitments such that, if accepted by the other agent, will lead the initial agent to realize its goal. While doing this generation, the agent also considers its own capabilities, so that it generates commitments that it can realize. Note that even with a good approximation of the other agent, the proposed protocol may not be acceptable. For this reason, the agent generates a set of alternative protocols rather than a single one. The exact protocol that will be used is chosen after deliberations with other agents. Having alternative protocols is also useful for recoverability. That is, if a protocol is chosen by the agents, but if one of the agents then violates a commitment, the goals will not be realized as expected. In this case, agents can switch to an alternative protocol. This work is novel in that it situates commitment-based protocols in the larger context of agents by relating commitments to the agents goals, capabilities, and their knowledge of other agents' goals and capabilities.

The rest of this paper is organized as follows. Section 2 describes our technical framework in depth. Section 3 introduces our algorithm for generating commitment protocols based on agents' goals and capabilities. Section 4 applies the algorithm to a case study. Section 5 explains how our approach can be used in a multiagent system. Finally, Section 6 discusses our work in relation to recent work.

2 Technical Framework

In this section we define formally the necessary concepts: agents which have goals that they want to fulfill, and certain capabilities (formalized as propositions that they are able to bring about). We also define the notion of a social commitment between agents (in line with existing approaches, e.g. [21]). The concepts are captured using the following syntax, where *prop* is a proposition, and *agent* is an agent identifier.

$$
\begin{aligned}
commitment &\rightarrow C(agent, agent, prop, prop)^{cstate} \\
goal &\rightarrow G_{agent}(prop, prop, prop)^{gstate} \\
service &\rightarrow S_{agent}(prop, prop) \\
belief &\rightarrow BG_{agent}(agent, prop, prop) \mid BS_{agent}(agent, prop, prop) \\
cstate &\rightarrow Null \mid Requested \mid Active \mid Conditional \mid Violated \mid Fulfilled \mid Terminated \\
gstate &\rightarrow Inactive \mid Active \mid Satisfied \mid Failed
\end{aligned}
$$

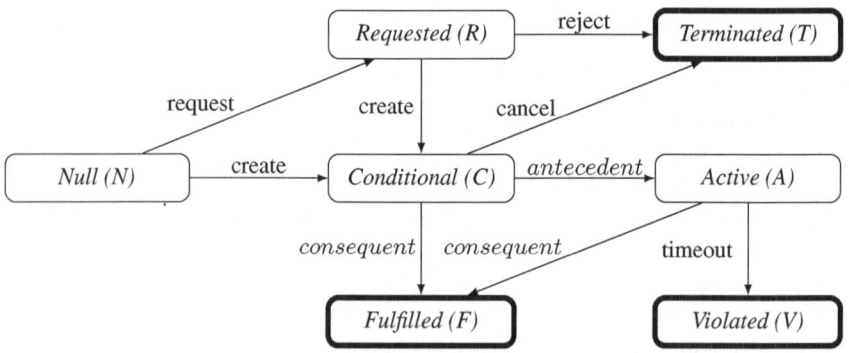

Fig. 1. Life cycle of a commitment

Commitments. A *commitment* $C(debtor, creditor, antecedent, consequent)^{state}$ expresses the social contract between the agents *debtor* and *creditor*, such that if the *antecedent* holds, then the *debtor* is committed to the *creditor* to bring about the *consequent*. Each commitment has a *state* that represents the current state of the commitment in its life cycle. The state of a commitment evolves depending on the state of the antecedent and the consequent and also according to the operations performed by the debtor and the creditor of the commitment. We show the life cycle of a commitment in Fig. 1. In this figure, the rectangles represent the states of the commitment and the directed edges represent the transitions between the states. Each transition is labeled with the name of the triggering event. A commitment is in *Null* state before it is created. The create operation is performed by the *debtor* to create the commitment and the state of the commitment is set to *Conditional*. If the *antecedent* already holds while creating the commitment, the state of the commitment becomes *Active* immediately. It is also possible for the *creditor* of a commitment in *Null* state to make a request to the *debtor* to create the commitment. In this case, the state of the commitment is *Requested*. The *debtor* is free to create the requested commitment or reject it, which makes the commitment *Terminated*. A *Conditional* commitment becomes *Active* if the *antecedent* starts to hold, *Fulfilled* if the *consequent* starts to hold or *Terminated* if the *debtor* cancels the commitment. An *Active* commitment becomes *Fulfilled* if the *consequent* starts to hold, *Violated* if the *debtor* cancels the commitment or *Terminated* if the *creditor* releases the *debtor* from its commitment. *Fulfilled*, *Violated* and *Terminated* states are terminal states (depicted with thicker borders in Fig. 1)

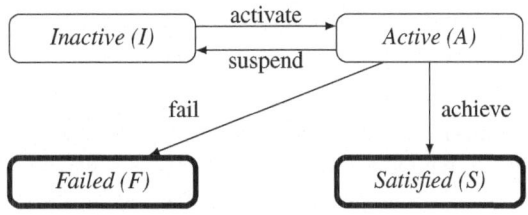

Fig. 2. Life cycle of a goal

Goals. A *goal* $G_{agent}(precondition, satisfaction, failure)^{state}$ represents an aim of an agent such that the *agent* has a goal to achieve *satisfaction* if *precondition* holds and the goal fails if *failure* occurs (adapted from [20]). The state of the goal is represented by *state*. We show the life cycle of a goal in Fig. 2. A goal is in *Inactive* state if its *precondition* does not hold. An inactive goal is not pursued by the agent. A goal is in *Active* state if its *precondition* holds and neither *satisfaction* nor *failure* holds. An active goal is pursued by the agent. A goal is *Satisfied*, if *satisfaction* starts to hold while in the *Active* state. A goal is *Failed*, if *failure* occurs while in the *Active* state. An active goal may also be suspended, if the precondition ceases to hold. The *Satisfied* and *Failed* states are terminal states.

Capabilities. A *capability* $S_{agent}(precondition, proposition)$ states that an agent has the capability of performing an action (or actions) that will make *proposition* true. However, this is only possible if the *precondition* holds. Note that we use the terms **"capability"** and **"service"** interchangeably: in a context where an agent does something for itself "capability" makes more sense, but when an agent acts for another agent, then "service" is more appropriate.

Beliefs. Agents have their own *beliefs* about other agents' goals and capabilities. $BG_{agent_i}(agent_j, condition, satisfaction)$ represents that $agent_i$ believes $agent_j$ has the goal *satisfaction* if *condition* holds. Note that beliefs about other agents' goals do not include information about the failure conditions. Similarly $BS_{agent_i}(agent_j, condition, proposition)$ represents that $agent_i$ believes $agent_j$ is able to bring about the *proposition*, if the *condition* holds. Beliefs about other agents' capabilities essentially correspond to services provided by other agents and interpreted as $agent_i$ believes that $agent_j$ provides a service to bring about *proposition*, if *condition* is brought about (most probably by an effort of $agent_i$). As discussed in Section 1, although in general other agents' goals and capabilities are private, some information will be available. Although it is possible that advertised services may differ from the actual capabilities of the agent. For example, certain capabilities may not be advertised, or some advertised services may in fact be realized by a third party (e.g. a merchant delegating delivery to a courier).

Agents and **Multiagent system**. An *agent* is a four tuple $A = \langle \mathcal{G}, \mathcal{S}, \mathcal{C}, \mathcal{B} \rangle$, where $\mathcal{G}$ is a set of goals that agent A has, $\mathcal{S}$ is a set of services (aka capabilities) that agent A can provide, $\mathcal{C}$ is a set of commitments that agent A is involved in and $\mathcal{B}$ is a set of beliefs that agent A has about other agents. A *multiagent system* $\mathcal{A}$ is a set of agents $\{A_1, \ldots, A_n\}$. We write $a.X$ to denote the X component of the agent, e.g. writing $a.\mathcal{G}$ to denote the agent's goals, $a.\mathcal{C}$ to denote its commitments etc.

Protocol. We adopt the definition of commitment protocols [7,21] in which a *protocol* P is a set of (conditional) commitments. Hence, we do not have explicit message orderings. Each agent can manipulate the commitments as it sees fit. The manipulations of the commitments lead to state changes in the lifecycles of the commitments as depicted in Fig. 1. Unlike traditional approaches to capturing protocols, such as AUML, this approach, using social commitments, aims to provide minimal constraints on the process by which the interaction achieves its aims [15]. We emphasise that a set of commitments is a protocol in the sense that it allows for a range of possible concrete interactions, unlike the notion of contract used by Alberti *et al.* [1] which represents a single specific concrete interaction.

Definition 1 (Proposition Support). *Given a set Γ of propositions that hold, and a proposition p, the agent $a = \langle \mathcal{G}, \mathcal{S}, \mathcal{C}, \mathcal{B} \rangle$ supports p, denoted as $a \Vdash p$, iff at least one of the following cases holds:*

- *base case: $\Gamma \models p$, i.e. p already holds*
- *capability: $\exists S_a(pre, prop) \in \mathcal{S} : \{prop \rightarrow p \wedge a \Vdash pre\}$, i.e. the agent is able to bring about p (more precisely, a condition prop which implies p) itself, and the required condition is also supported*
- *commitment: $\exists C(a', a, \top, cond)^A \in \mathcal{C} : \{cond \rightarrow p\}$, i.e. there is an active commitment from another agent to bring about p*
- *conditional: $\exists C(a', a, ant, cond)^C \in \mathcal{C} : \{cond \rightarrow p \wedge a \Vdash ant\}$, i.e. there is a conditional commitment from another agent to bring about p, and the antecedent of the commitment is supported by agent a*

The *capability* case states that p can be made true by agent a if p is one of the agent's capabilities. This is the strongest support for p, since p can be achieved by the agent's own capabilities. The *commitment* case states that the agent has a commitment in which it expects p to become true (because it is the creditor of an active commitment). Note that this is weaker than the *capability* condition since the commitment may be violated by its debtor. In the *conditional* case, the agent first needs to realize the antecedent for p to be achieved.

Definition 2 (Goal Support). *A goal $g = G_a(pre, sat, fail)^A$ is supported by the agent $a = \langle \mathcal{G}, \mathcal{S}, \mathcal{C}, \mathcal{B} \rangle$, denoted as $a \Vdash g$, if $a \Vdash sat$.*

Theorem 1. *If a proposition p (respectively goal g) is supported by agent a, then the agent is able to act in such a way that p (resp. g) eventually becomes true (assuming all active commitments are eventually fulfilled).*

Proof: *Induction over the cases in Definition 2 (details omitted).*

3   Commitment Protocol Generation Algorithm

We present an algorithm that uses the agent's capabilities, commitments and also beliefs about other agents, to generate a set of alternative commitment protocols[1] such that each generated protocol supports the given agent's set of goals. That is, for each given goal of the agent, either the agent is able to achieve the goal by using its own capabilities, or the agent is able to ensure that the goal is achieved by relying appropriately on a commitment from another agent which has the goal's satisfaction condition as its consequent. More precisely, if an agent a cannot achieve a desired proposition p using its own capabilities, then the algorithm generates a proposed commitment such as $C(a', a, q, p)^R$ (ensuring q is supported by a) to obtain (conditional) proposition support for p, which implies goal support for goal $g \equiv G_a(pre, p, fail)$.

Note that in general, we can only expect to be able to obtain *conditional* support (in terms of Definition 1). Obtaining *capability* support amounts to extending the agent's capabilities, and obtaining *commitment* support amounts to getting an active commitment $C(a', a, \top, q)^A$ which, in general, another agent a' would not have any reason to accept. Thus, the algorithm proposes commitments that are likely to be attractive to a' by considering its beliefs about the goals of a' and creating a candidate commitment $C(a', a, q, p)^R$ where q is a proposition that is believed to be desired by a' (i.e. satisfies one of its goals). Clearly, there are situations where a given goal cannot be supported (e.g. if no other agents have the ability to bring it about, or if no suitable q can be found to make the proposed commitments attractive), and hence the algorithm may not always generate a protocol.

We divide our algorithm into four separate functions (described below) for clarity:

- *generateProtocols* takes an agent and the set of proposition that hold in the world as arguments, and returns a set of possible protocols $\mathcal{P} = \{P_1, \ldots, P_n\}$, where each protocol is a set of proposed commitments (i.e. it returns a set of sets of commitments).
- *findSupport* takes as arguments an agent, a queue of goals, a set of propositions that are known to hold, and a set of commitments that are known to exist (initially empty); and does the actual work of computing the possible protocols, returning a set of possible protocols $\mathcal{P}$.
- *isSupported* takes as arguments an agent, a proposition, a set of propositions known to hold, and a set of commitments known to exist; and determines whether the proposition is supported, returning a Boolean value.
- *updateGoals* is an auxiliary function used by the main algorithm, and is explained below.

The *generateProtocols* function (see Algorithm 1) is the entry point of the algorithm. It has as parameters an agent a and a set of propositions Γ that hold in the world. Γ is meant to capture a's current world state. The algorithm finds possible, alternative protocols such that when executed separately, each protocol ensures that all of the goals of that agent are achievable.

---

[1] In practice, we may want to generate the set incrementally, stopping when a suitable protocol is found.

Algorithm 1. $\mathcal{P}$ generateProtocols(a, Γ)

Require: a, the agent that the algorithm runs for
Require: Γ, set of propositions known to be true
1: **queue** $\mathcal{G}' \leftarrow \{g | g \in a.\mathcal{G} \wedge g.state = Active\}$
2: **return** findSupport($a, \mathcal{G}', \Gamma, \emptyset$)

The *generateProtocols* function copies the agent's active goals into a queue structure $\mathcal{G}'$ for further processing and then calls the recursive function *findSupport* providing a (the agent), $\mathcal{G}'$ (its currently active goals), Γ (the propositions that currently hold), and $\emptyset$ (initial value for Δ) as arguments. The *generateProtocols* function returns the result of *findSupport*, which is a set of commitment protocols ($\mathcal{P}$), i.e. a set of sets of commitments. Recall that we use $a.\mathcal{G}$ to denote the goals $\mathcal{G}$ of agent a, and that for goal g we use $g.state$ to denote its state.

The main function is *findSupport* (see Algorithm 2). The function recursively calls itself to generate alternative commitment protocols which support every given goal of the agent a. The function takes as arguments an agent a, the queue of the agent's goals $\mathcal{G}'$ that need to be supported, a set Γ of propositions that are known to be true, and a set Δ of commitments that are known to exist. The function first defines sets $\mathcal{BG}$ and $\mathcal{BS}$ of (respectively) the beliefs of agent a about the goals and the services of other agents. It then pops the next goal g from the goal queue $\mathcal{G}'$ (Line 3). If all goals are considered (i.e. $g =$ Null), then there is no need to generate extra commitments. Hence, the algorithm simply returns one protocol: the set of the commitments already proposed. This corresponds to the base case of the recursion (Lines 4–5). If the agent already supports g (determined by *isSupported* function, see Algorithm 3), then the algorithm ignores g and calls itself for the next goal in $\mathcal{G}'$ (Line 8).

Otherwise, the function searches for one or more possible sets of commitments that will support the goal g. It first initializes the set of alternative protocols $\mathcal{P}$ to the empty set (Line 10). Then the algorithm searches for candidate commitments that will support g. As a first step it checks whether it has any capabilities that would support this goal if the precondition of the capability could be achieved through help from other agents (Line 11). Note that if the preconditions could be achieved by the agent itself then the algorithm would have detected this earlier in Line 3. Hence, here the specific case being handled is that the precondition of a capability cannot be achieved by the agent itself, but if it were achieved through other agents, then the capability would enable the agent to reach its goal g. For each such capability, we make the precondition pre a new goal for the agent, add it to the list of goals $\mathcal{G}'$ that it wants to achieve, and recursively call *findSupport* to find protocols.

After checking its own capabilities for achieving g, the agent then also starts looking for another agent with a known service $s' \in \mathcal{BS}$ such that s' achieves the satisfaction condition of the goal g (Line 14). For any such service s', we generate a proposed commitment of the form $C(a', a, sat', prop)^R$ (Line 16), where a' is the agent that is believed to be provide the service s', a is the agent being considered by the call to the function (its first argument), $prop$ implies the satisfaction condition of the desired goal g (i.e. $prop \rightarrow sat$), and sat' is an "attractive condition" to the proposed debtor agent (a'). The notion of "attractive to agent a'" is defined in line 15: we look for a condition

Algorithm 2. $\mathcal{P}$ findSupport$(a, \mathcal{G}', \Gamma, \Delta)$

Require: a, the agent that the algorithm runs for
Require: $\mathcal{G}'$, queue of agent's (active) goals
Require: Γ, set of propositions known to be true
Require: Δ, set of commitments already generated (initially called with $\emptyset$)
 1: **define** $\mathcal{BG} \equiv \{b | b \in a.\mathcal{B} \wedge b = BG_a(a', gc, s)\}$
 2: **define** $\mathcal{BS} \equiv \{b | b \in a.\mathcal{B} \wedge b = BS_a(a', c, p)\}$
 3: $g \leftarrow \text{pop}(\mathcal{G}')$
 4: **if** $g = \text{Null}$ **then**
 5:     **return** $\{\Delta\}$
 6:     // else $g = G_a(gpre, sat, fail)^A$
 7: **else if** isSupported(a, sat, Γ, Δ) **then**
 8:     **return** findSupport$(a, \mathcal{G}', \Gamma, \Delta)$
 9: **else**
10:     $\mathcal{P} = \emptyset$
11:     **for all** $\{s \mid S_a(pre, prop) \in a.\mathcal{S} \wedge prop \rightarrow sat\}$ **do**
12:         $\mathcal{P} \leftarrow \mathcal{P} \cup$ findSupport$(a, \{G_a(\top, pre, \bot)^A\} \cup \mathcal{G}', \Gamma, \Delta)$
13:     **end for**
14:     **for all** $\{s' \mid BS_a(a', cond, prop) \in \mathcal{BS} \wedge prop \rightarrow sat\}$ **do**
15:         **for all** $\{g' \mid BG_a(a', pre', sat') \in \mathcal{BG} \wedge$ isSupported$(a, pre', \Gamma, \Delta)\}$ **do**
16:             $c \leftarrow C(a', a, sat', prop)^R$
17:             $\mathcal{G}'' \leftarrow$ updateGoals$(sat', prop, a.\mathcal{G}, \mathcal{G}')$
18:             **if** $\neg$isSupported$(a, sat', \Gamma, \Delta)$ **then**
19:                 $\mathcal{G}'' \leftarrow \{G_a(\top, sat', \bot)^A\} \cup \mathcal{G}''$
20:             **end if**
21:             **if** $\neg$ isSupported$(a, cond, \Gamma, \Delta)$ **then**
22:                 $\mathcal{G}'' \leftarrow \{G_a(\top, cond, \bot)^A\} \cup \mathcal{G}''$
23:             **end if**
24:             $\mathcal{P} \leftarrow \mathcal{P} \cup$ findSupport$(a, \mathcal{G}'', \Gamma, \Delta \cup \{c\})$
25:         **end for**
26:     **end for**
27:     **return** $\mathcal{P}$
28: **end if**

sat' that is believed to be a goal of agent a'. Specifically, we consider the known goals $\mathcal{BG}$ of other agents, and look for a $g' \in \mathcal{BG}$ such that $g' = BG_a(a', pre', sat')$ where pre' is already supported by agent a.

Next, having generated a potential commitment $C(a', a, sat', prop)^R$ where the debtor, a', has a service that can achieve the desired condition $prop$ and has a goal to bring about sat' (which makes the proposed commitment attractive), we update the goals of the agent (discussed below) and check whether (1) the promised condition sat' is supported by agent a, and (2) the precondition $cond$ for realizing $prop$ is supported by agent a. If they are supported, then a does not need to do anything else. Otherwise, it adds the respective proposition to the list of goals $\mathcal{G}''$ (Lines 19 and 22), so that appropriate support for these propositions can be obtained.

Finally, the agent calls the function recursively to deal with the remainder of the goals in the updated goal queue $\mathcal{G}''$. When doing this, it adds the currently created commitment c to the list of already generated commitments Δ. The result of the function call is added to the existing set of possible protocols $\mathcal{P}$ (line 24). Once the agent has completed searching for ways of supporting g, it returns the collected set of protocols $\mathcal{P}$. Note that if the agent is unable to find a way of supporting its goals, then $\mathcal{P}$ will be empty, and the algorithm returns the empty set, indicating that no candidate protocols could be found.

Algorithm 3. $\{$**true** | **false**$\}$ isSupported(a, p, Γ, Δ)

Require: a, agent to check for support of p
Require: p, property to check for support
Require: Γ, set of propositions known to be true
Require: Δ, set of commitments already generated
 1: **if** $\Gamma \models p$ **then**
 2:     **return true**
 3: **end if**
 4: **for all** $s = S_a(pre, prop) \in a.\mathcal{S}$ **do**
 5:     **if** $prop \rightarrow p \wedge$ isSupported(a, pre, Γ, Δ) **then**
 6:         **return true**
 7:     **end if**
 8: **end for**
 9: **for all** $\{c \mid C(a', a, cond, prop) \in (a.\mathcal{C} \cup \Delta)\}$ **do**
10:     **if** $c.state = Active \wedge prop \rightarrow p$ **then**
11:         **return true**
12:     **else if** $(c.state = Conditional \vee c.state = Requested) \wedge prop \rightarrow p \wedge$ isSupported$(a, cond, \Gamma, \Delta)$ **then**
13:         **return true**
14:     **end if**
15: **end for**
16: **return false**

Algorithm 3 defines the *isSupported* function. This algorithm corresponds to Definition 1 and returns true if the given proposition p is supported by the given agent a, and false otherwise. The first case (line 1) checks whether the proposition is known to be true. The second case checks capability support. That is, whether p is supported by a capability s of the agent. More precisely, if the proposition $prop$ of s implies p and the precondition pre of s is supported by the agent (Lines 4-8). The third case checks commitment support by checking whether a has (or will have) an active commitment c, in which a is the creditor and the consequent $prop$ implies p (Lines 10-11). In the last case, the algorithm checks conditional support by checking whether a has (or will have) a conditional commitment c, in which a is the creditor, the consequent $prop$ implies p and a supports the antecedent $cond$ (Lines 12-14). If none of the above cases hold, then the algorithm returns false, indicating that p is not supported by a.

Algorithm 4 defines the *updateGoals* function. This function is called when a new commitment is generated to support goal g of agent a. It takes propositions ant and $cons$ corresponding respectively to the antecedent and consequent of the new commitment. The function also takes as arguments the goals $\mathcal{G}$ of agent a, and the queue of

Algorithm 4. $\mathcal{G}''$ updateGoals($ant, cons, \mathcal{G}, \mathcal{G}'$)

Require: ant, the antecedent of the new commitment
Require: $cons$, the consequent of the new commitment
Require: $\mathcal{G}$, set of agent's goals
Require: $\mathcal{G}'$, the current queue of (potentially) unsupported goals
 1: **create new queue** $\mathcal{G}''$
 2: $\mathcal{G}'' \leftarrow$ copy of $\mathcal{G}'$
 3: **for all** $\{g \mid G_a(pre, sat, fail) \in \mathcal{G}\}$ **do**
 4:    **if** $g.state = Inactive \wedge (ant \rightarrow pre \vee cons \rightarrow pre)$ **then**
 5:       $g.state \leftarrow Active$
 6:       push($\mathcal{G}'', g$)
 7:    **end if**
 8: **end for**
 9: **return** $\mathcal{G}''$

currently unsupported goals $\mathcal{G}'$. The algorithm assumes that both ant and $cond$ will be achieved at some future point due to the generated commitment. Accordingly, the algorithm assumes that currently inactive goals which have ant or $cond$ as their precondition will be activated at some future point. Hence, these goals also need to be able to be achieved, i.e. to be supported by agent a. The algorithm thus generates these additional goals, and adds them to a (new queue) $\mathcal{G}''$. The algorithm first creates a new queue $\mathcal{G}''$ and copies into it the current contents of $\mathcal{G}'$ (Line 2). Then the goals in $\mathcal{G}$ that are inactive but will be activated are pushed into $\mathcal{G}''$ as active goals (Lines 3-8). Finally, $\mathcal{G}''$ is returned. Instead of pushing the goals that are assumed to be activated directly into $\mathcal{G}'$, the algorithm creates a new queue. This is done because every recursive call in line 24 of Algorithm 2 is related to a different commitment, which activates different goals depending on its antecedent and consequent. Hence each recursive call requires a different goal queue.

The algorithms presented are sound in the sense of Theorem 1: for any generated protocol, the agent is able to act in such a way as to ensure that the desired goal becomes achieved, without making any assumptions about the behaviour of other agents, other than that they fulfill their active commitments. The algorithms in this section have been implemented (available from http://mas.cmpe.boun.edu.tr/akin/ cpgen.html), and have been used to generate protocols for a number of case studies, including the one we present next, which took 0.6 seconds to generate protocols (on a 2.7GHz Intel Core i7 machine with 4 GB RAM running Ubuntu Linux).

4 Case Study

We illustrate our commitment generation algorithm's progress through an e-commerce scenario. In this scenario there is a customer (Cus), a merchant (Mer) and a bank ($Bank$). The goal of the customer is to buy some product from the merchant. The customer also has a goal of being refunded by the merchant, if the purchased product is defective. The customer is capable of making payment orders to the bank to pay to the merchant. The customer can also use a gift card, instead of payment. The merchant's goal is to be paid or to receive a gift card and the bank's goal is to get payment orders to earn commissions. We discuss the scenario from the customer's point of view, who runs our algorithm to generate a protocol in order to satisfy her goals. We first describe the propositions that we use and their meanings:

- *Delivered*: The purchased product is delivered to the customer.
- *Paid*: The merchant is paid.
- *HasGiftCard*: The customer has a gift card.
- *GiftCardUsed*: The customer uses the gift card.
- *Defective*: The delivered product is defective.
- *Returned*: The delivered product is returned to the merchant.
- *Refunded*: The customer is refunded.
- *PaymentOrdered*: The bank receives a payment order.

The customer has the following goals and capabilities: g_1 states that the goal of the customer is to have the product be delivered (without any condition) and g_2 represents the goal of the customer to be refunded, if the delivered product is defective, s_1 states that the customer is able to make payment orders (without any condition), and s_2 states that the customer is able to use a gift card (instead of payment), if she has one. Finally, s_3 states that the customer is capable of returning a product, if it is defective.

- $g_1 = G_{Cus}(\top, Delivered, \neg Delivered)$
- $g_2 = G_{Cus}(Defective, Refunded, \neg Refunded)$
- $s_1 = S_{Cus}(\top, PaymentOrdered)$
- $s_2 = S_{Cus}(HaveGiftCard, GiftCardUsed)$
- $s_3 = S_{Cus}(Defective, Returned)$

The customer has the following beliefs about the other agents: b_1 and b_2 state that the customer believes that the merchant provides a service to deliver a product, if the merchant is paid or a gift card is used, respectively. b_3 represents the belief that the merchant will give a refund, if a product is returned, and b_4 is the belief about the service of the bank to perform a money transaction for payment, if the bank receives such a request. The customer also believes that the goal of the merchant is to be paid (b_5) or to receive a gift card (b_6) and refund the customer if a sold product is defective (b_7), in order to ensure customer satisfaction. The goal of the bank is to receive payment orders (b_8), so that it can earn a commission from payment orders.

- $b_1 = BS_{Cus}(Mer, Paid, Delivered)$
- $b_2 = BS_{Cus}(Mer, GiftCardUsed, Delivered)$
- $b_3 = BS_{Cus}(Mer, Returned, Refunded)$
- $b_4 = BS_{Cus}(Bank, PaymentOrdered, Paid)$
- $b_5 = BG_{Cus}(Mer, \top, Paid)$
- $b_6 = BG_{Cus}(Mer, \top, GiftCardUsed)$
- $b_7 = BG_{Cus}(Mer, Defective, Returned)$
- $b_8 = BG_{Cus}(Bank, \top, PaymentOrdered)$

Figure 3 summarises the case study. Ovals are used to denote services, and rectangles denote propositions. Solid arrows (e.g. between the proposition $Paid$ and the service $Delivered$ in the Merchant) indicate the preconditions of a service. Dashed arrows show where a service in one agent is able to bring about a precondition that is desired by another agent.

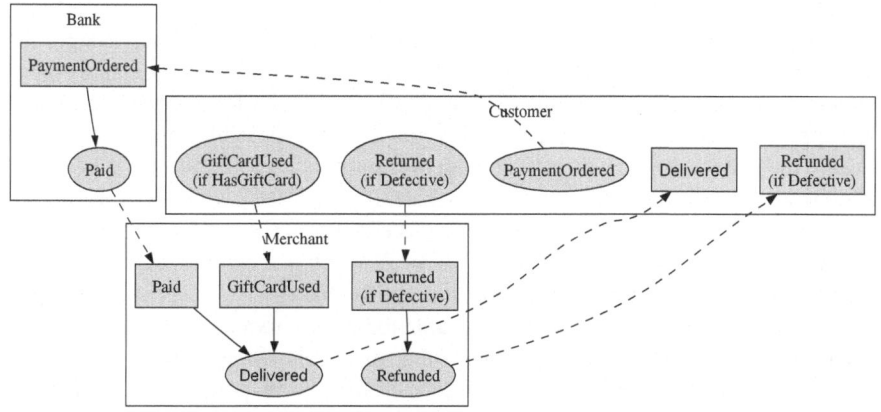

Fig. 3. Case Study

Let us first discuss the states of the merchant's goals g_1 and g_2. The algorithm considers both goals as active. g_1 is active, since its condition is $\top$. On the other hand, $Defective$ actually does not hold initially, which means g_2 should not be active. However, the algorithm assumes that $Defective$ holds, since its truth value is not controlled by any agent and therefore may or may not be true while executing the protocol. Using this assumption, the algorithm aims to create necessary commitments to capture all potential future situations during the execution of the protocol.

Let us walk through the protocol generation process. The algorithm starts with g_1. To support $Delivered$, which is the satisfaction condition of g_1, the algorithm generates the commitment $c_1 = C(Mer, Cus, Paid, Delivered)^R$ using the belief b_1, which is about the service to provide $Delivered$ and b_5, which is the goal of the merchant. However, the antecedent $Paid$ of c_1 is not supported by the customer. Hence, the algorithm considers $Paid$ as a new goal of the customer and starts to search for support for it. It finds the belief b_4, which indicates that the bank can bring about $Paid$ with a condition $PaymentOrdered$, which is also a goal of the bank due to b_8. $PaymentOrdered$ is already supported, since it is a capability of the customer (s_1). Hence, the algorithm generates the commitment $c_2 = C(Bank, Cus, PaymentOrdered, Paid)^R$. At this point, everything is supported to achieve g_1. The algorithm continues for g_2, which is achieved, if $Refunded$ holds. $Refunded$ can be achieved by generating the commitment $c_3 = C(Mer, Cus, Returned, Refunded)^R$ using the service b_3 and the goal b_7 of the merchant. The antecedent $Returned$ is a capability of the customer with a supported condition $Defective$. Hence, everything is supported to achieve g_2 and the algorithm returns the protocol that contains commitments c_1, c_2, and c_3.

Let us examine the protocol. c_1 states that the merchant is committed to deliver the product if the customer pays for it. However, the customer is not capable of payment (cannot bring about $Paid$ by itself). c_2 handles this situation, since the bank is committed to make the payment if the customer orders a payment. Finally, c_3 guarantees a refund, if the customer returns the product to the merchant. Note that the customer returns the product only if it is defective (s_2), hence there is no conflict with the goal (b_5) of the merchant.

Although the above protocol supports all the goals of the customer, the algorithm continues to search for other alternative protocols, since our aim is to generate all possible protocols to achieve the goals. Hence, it starts to search for alternative protocols that support the goals of the customer. It finds that it is possible to support g_1 also by using the service b_2. Accordingly, the algorithm initiates a new alternative protocol and generates the commitment $c_{2-1} = C(Mer, Cus, GiftCardUsed, Delivered)^R$ using the beliefs b_2 and b_6. However, the antecedent $GiftCardUsed$ of c_{2-1} is not supported by the customer, since $HasGiftCard$, which is the condition of service s_2, does not hold. The algorithm searches for support for $HasGiftCard$, but it fails, since neither the customer nor any other agent is able to bring it about.

Note that our algorithm also generates other protocols, which, due to information about other agents not being complete or correct, may be inappropriate. For instance, such a protocol may include a commitment such as $C(Mer, Cus, Paid, Refunded)^R$. This happens because the algorithm considers all believed goals of the other agents while creating commitments. Specifically, to satisfy her goal $Refunded$, the customer considers the known goals of the merchant, and finds three options to offer to the merchant in return: $Paid$, $GiftCardUsed$ and $Returned$. Hence the algorithm creates three alternative commitments using each of these three goals of the merchant and each commitment is considered as an alternative protocol. Another example of this is a situation where the merchant actually replaces a defective product instead of refunding money (i.e. b_2 is incorrect). We deal with inappropriate protocols by requiring all involved agents to agree to a proposed protocol (see below). Specifically in this case when the customer requests the commitment from the merchant, the merchant would not accept the request.

5   Using Generated Protocols

The algorithm presented in the previous section generates candidate protocols, i.e. possible sets of proposed commitments that, if accepted, support the achievement of the desired propositions. In this section we consider the bigger picture and answer the question: *how are the generated candidate protocols used?*

The process is described in Algorithm 5, which uses two variables: the set of candidate protocols ($\mathcal{P}$), and the set of commitments (in the current candidate protocol, P) that agents have already accepted ($\mathcal{C}$). We begin by generating the set of protocols $\mathcal{P}$ (line 1). Next, we need to select one of the protocols[2] (line 2). The selected protocol is removed from $\mathcal{P}$. We then propose each commitment in the protocol to its debtor.

---

[2] For the present we assume that the selection is done based on the simple heuristic that fewer commitments are preferred.

Algorithm 5. generateAndUseProtocols(a, Γ)

Require: a, the agent that the algorithm runs for
Require: Γ, set of propositions known to be true
1: $\mathcal{P} \leftarrow generateProtocols(a, \Gamma)$
2: select $P \in \mathcal{P}$
3: $\mathcal{P} \leftarrow \mathcal{P} \setminus \{P\}$
4: $\mathcal{C} \leftarrow \emptyset$
5: **for all** $C(x, y, p, q)^R \in P$ such that $x \neq a$ **do**
6:    Propose $C(x, y, p, q)^R$ to agent x
7:    **if** Agent x declines **then**
8:       **for all** $C(x, y, p, q)^R \in \mathcal{C}$ **do**
9:          Release agent x from the commitment $C(x, y, p, q)^R$
10:       **end for**
11:       Go to line 2
12:    **else**
13:       $\mathcal{C} \leftarrow \mathcal{C} \cup \{C(x, y, p, q)^R\}$
14:    **end if**
15: **end for**
16: Execute Protocol P

This is needed because, as noted earlier, domain knowledge about other agents' goals may not be entirely correct or up-to-date. If any agent declines the proposed commitment then we cannot use the protocol, and so we clean up by releasing agents from their commitments in the protocol, and then try an alternative protocol. If all agents accept the commitments, then the protocol is executed.

Note that, since agents may not always fulfill their active commitments, we need to monitor the execution (e.g. [10]), and in case a commitment becomes violated, initiate action to recover. There are a range of possible approaches for recovery including simply abandoning the protocol and generating new protocols in the new state of the world; and using compensation [18].

6   Discussion

We developed an approach that enables agents to create commitment protocols that fit their goals. To achieve this, we proposed to represent agents' capabilities and commitments in addition to their goals. Agents reason about their goals as well as their beliefs about other agents' capabilities and goals to generate commitments. Our experiments on an existing case study showed that an agent can indeed generate a set of commitment protocols that can be used among agents. Hence, even agents who do not have any prior protocols among them can communicate to carry out their interactions.

While we primarily discuss how our approach can be used at runtime, many of the underlying ideas can be used at design time as well. That is, a system designer who is aware of some of the goals and capabilities of the agents that will interact at runtime, can use the algorithm to generate protocols for them. This will enable a principled approach for designing commitment-based protocols.

Goals and commitments have been both widely studied in the literature. On the goals side, Thangarajah *et al.* [17] study relations and conflicts between goals. van Riemsdijk *et al.* [13] study different types of goals and propose to represent them in a unifying framework. On the commitments side, El-Menshawy *et al.* [8] study new semantics for commitments. Chopra and Singh [5,6] study the interoperability and alignment of commitments. However, the interaction between goals and commitments has started to receive attention only recently.

Chopra *et al.* [4] propose a formalization of the semantic relationship between agents' goals and commitment protocols. Their aim is to check whether a given commitment protocol can be used to realize a certain goal. To do this, they define a capability set for each agent and first check if an agent can indeed carry out the commitments it participates in. This is important and can be used by agents to choose among possible commitment protocols. Chopra *et al.* assume that the commitment protocols are already available for agents. By contrast, in our work, we are proposing a method for the agents to generate a commitment protocol that they can use to realize their goals from scratch.

Işıksal [11] studies how an agent can create a single commitment to realize its goal with the help of other agents' in the system. She proposes reasoning rules that can be applied in various situations and she applies these rules on an ambient intelligence setting. She does not generate a set of alternative protocols and does not consider beliefs about other agents' goals as we have done here.

Desai *et al.* [7] propose Amoeba, a methodology to design commitment based protocols for cross-organizational business processes. This methodology enables a system designer to specify business processes through the participating agents' commitments. The methodology accommodates useful properties such as composition. Desai *et al.* model contextual changes as exceptions and deal with them through metacommitments. Their commitment-based specification is developed at design time by a human, based on the roles the agents will play. In this work, on the other hand, we are interested in agents generating their commitments themselves at run time. This will enable agents to interact with others even when an appropriate protocol has not been designed at design time.

Telang *et al.* [16] develop an operational semantics for goals and commitments. They specify rules for the evolution of commitments in light of agents' goals. These practical rules define when an agent should abandon a commitment, when it should negotiate, and so on. These rules are especially useful after a commitment protocol has been created and is in use. In this respect, our work in this paper is a predecessor to the execution of the approach that is described by Telang *et al.*, that is, after the protocol has been generated, the agents can execute it as they see fit, based on their current goals.

The work of Marengo *et al.* [12] is related to this work. Specifically, our notion of support (Definition 1) is analogous to their notion of control: intuitively, in order for an agent to consider a proposition to be supported, it needs to be able to ensure that it is achieved, i.e. be able to control its achievement. However, whereas the aim of their work is to develop a framework for reasoning about control and safety of given protocols, our aim is to derive protocols.

There are a number of directions for future work:

- A key direction is the development of means for ranking generated alternative protocols.
- A second direction is to explore how well our algorithms manage to generate appropriate protocols in situations where the agent's beliefs about other agents' goals and capabilities are incomplete or inconsistent.
- When generating protocols, it may be possible to reduce the search space by interleaving protocol generation with checking the acceptability of the protocol. Rather than waiting until a complete protocol is constructed, whenever a commitment is proposed, we could check with the proposed debtor whether that commitment is acceptable. In general, a commitment's acceptability may depend on the rest of the protocol, but there may be some commitments that are clearly unacceptable regardless of context, and in these cases we can terminate the generation of protocols including that commitment.
- Our representation of protocols follows the "traditional" approach to commitment-based protocols. It has been argued that the representation ought to be extended with the ability to represent regulative temporal constraints [2], and one direction for future work is to extend our protocol generation framework and algorithm to support such constraints.

References

1. Alberti, M., Cattafi, M., Chesani, F., Gavanelli, M., Lamma, E., Mello, P., Montali, M., Torroni, P.: A Computational Logic Application Framework for Service Discovery and Contracting. International Journal of Web Services Research (IJWSR) 8(3), 1–25 (2011)
2. Baldoni, M., Baroglio, C., Capuzzimati, F., Marengo, E., Patti, V.: A Generalized Commitment Machine for 2CL Protocols and its Implementation. In: Baldoni, M., Dennis, L., Mascardi, V., Vasconcelos, W. (eds.) DALT 2012. LNCS (LNAI), vol. 7784, pp. 96–115. Springer, Heidelberg (2013)
3. Castelfranchi, C.: Commitments: From Individual Intentions to Groups and Organizations. In: Lesser, V.R., Gasser, L. (eds.) ICMAS, pp. 41–48. The MIT Press (1995)
4. Chopra, A.K., Dalpiaz, F., Giorgini, P., Mylopoulos, J.: Reasoning about Agents and Protocols via Goals and Commitments. In: International Conference on Autonomous Agents and Multiagent Systems, AAMAS, pp. 457–464 (2010)
5. Chopra, A.K., Singh, M.P.: Constitutive Interoperability. In: International Conference on Autonomous Agents and Multiagent Systems, AAMAS, pp. 797–804 (2008)
6. Chopra, A.K., Singh, M.P.: Multiagent Commitment Alignment. In: International Conference on Autonomous Agents and Multiagent Systems, AAMAS, pp. 937–944 (2009)
7. Desai, N., Chopra, A.K., Singh, M.P.: Amoeba: A Methodology for Modeling and Evolving Cross-organizational Business Processes. ACM Transactions on Software Engineering and Methodology 19, 6:1–6:45 (2009)
8. El-Menshawy, M., Bentahar, J., Dssouli, R.: A New Semantics of Social Commitments Using Branching Space-Time Logic. In: WI-IAT 2009: Proceedings of the 2009 IEEE/WIC/ACM International Joint Conference on Web Intelligence and Intelligent Agent Technology, pp. 492–496 (2009)
9. Fornara, N., Colombetti, M.: Operational Specification of a Commitment-Based Agent Communication Language. In: International Conference on Autonomous Agents and Multiagent Systems, AAMAS, pp. 536–542 (2002)

10. Günay, A., Yolum, P.: Detecting Conflicts in Commitments. In: Sakama, C., Sardina, S., Vasconcelos, W., Winikoff, M. (eds.) DALT 2011. LNCS, vol. 7169, pp. 51–66. Springer, Heidelberg (2012)
11. Işıksal, A.: Use of Goals for Creating and Enacting Dynamic Contracts in Ambient Intelligence. Master's thesis, Bogazici University (2012)
12. Marengo, E., Baldoni, M., Baroglio, C., Chopra, A.K., Patti, V., Singh, M.P.: Commitments with Regulations: Reasoning about Safety and Control in REGULA. In: International Conference on Autonomous Agents and Multiagent Systems, AAMAS, pp. 467–474 (2011)
13. van Riemsdijk, M.B., Dastani, M., Winikoff, M.: Goals in Agent Systems: A Unifying Framework. In: International Conference on Autonomous Agents and Multiagent Systems, AAMAS, pp. 713–720 (2008)
14. Singh, M.P.: An Ontology for Commitments in Multiagent Systems. Artificial Intelligence and Law 7(1), 97–113 (1999)
15. Singh, M.P.: Information-Driven Interaction-Oriented Programming: BSPL, the Blindingly Simple Protocol Language. In: International Conference on Autonomous Agents and Multiagent Systems, AAMAS, pp. 491–498 (2011)
16. Telang, P.R., Yorke-Smith, N., Singh, M.P.: A Coupled Operational Semantics for Goals and Commitments. In: 9th International Workshop on Programming Multi-Agent Systems, ProMAS (2011)
17. Thangarajah, J., Padgham, L., Winikoff, M.: Detecting & Avoiding Interference Between Goals in Intelligent Agents. In: Proceedings of the 18th International Joint Conference on Artificial Intelligence, pp. 721–726 (2003)
18. Torroni, P., Chesani, F., Mello, P., Montali, M.: Social Commitments in Time: Satisfied or Compensated. In: Baldoni, M., Bentahar, J., van Riemsdijk, M.B., Lloyd, J. (eds.) DALT 2009. LNCS, vol. 5948, pp. 228–243. Springer, Heidelberg (2010)
19. Winikoff, M., Liu, W., Harland, J.: Enhancing Commitment Machines. In: Leite, J., Omicini, A., Torroni, P., Yolum, p. (eds.) DALT 2004. LNCS (LNAI), vol. 3476, pp. 198–220. Springer, Heidelberg (2005)
20. Winikoff, M., Padgham, L., Harland, J., Thangarajah, J.: Declarative & procedural goals in intelligent agent systems. In: KR, pp. 470–481 (2002)
21. Yolum, P., Singh, M.P.: Flexible Protocol Specification and Execution: Applying Event Calculus Planning using Commitments. In: International Conference on Autonomous Agents and Multiagent Systems, AAMAS, pp. 527–534 (2002)

Goal-Based Qualitative Preference Systems

Wietske Visser, Koen V. Hindriks, and Catholijn M. Jonker

Interactive Intelligence Group, Delft University of Technology, The Netherlands
{wietske.visser,k.v.hindriks,c.m.jonker}@tudelft.nl

Abstract. Goals are not only used to identify desired states or outcomes, but may also be used to derive qualitative preferences between outcomes. We show that Qualitative Preference Systems (QPSs) provide a general, flexible and succinct way to represent preferences based on goals. If the domain is not Boolean, preferences are often based on orderings on the possible values of variables. We show that QPSs that are based on such multi-valued criteria can be translated into equivalent goal-based QPSs that are just as succinct. Finally, we show that goal-based QPSs allow for more fine-grained updates than their multi-valued counterparts. These results show that goals are very expressive as a representation of qualitative preferences and moreover, that there are certain advantages of using goals instead of multi-valued criteria.

Keywords: Qualitative multi-criteria preferences, goals.

1 Introduction

In planning and decision making, goals are used to identify the desired states or outcomes. Essentially, goals provide a binary distinction between those states or outcomes that satisfy the goal and those that do not [1]. Outcomes that satisfy all goals are acceptable. However, it may happen that such outcomes are not available, but a decision still has to be made. Or there may be multiple outcomes that satisfy all goals and only one can be chosen. In these situations, goals provide no guidance to choose between the available alternatives [1,2].

Instead of using goals in an absolute sense, it would be more convenient to use them to derive preferences between outcomes. There are multiple approaches to doing this in the literature, for example comparing the number of goals that are satisfied, or taking the relative importance of the (un)satisfied goals into account. We show in Section 2 that Qualitative Preference Systems [3] provide a general, flexible and succinct way to represent preferences based on goals. In this approach goals are modelled as criteria that can be combined to derive a preference between outcomes. We show that the best-known qualitative approaches to interpret goals as a representation of preferences are all expressible in a QPS.

Most goal-based approaches in the literature define outcomes as propositional models, i.e. all variables are Boolean, either true or false. In real-world applications, not all variables are Boolean. For example, variables may be numeric (e.g. cost, length, number, rating, duration, percentage) or nominal (e.g. destination, colour, location). Qualitative Preference Systems typically express preferences, in a compact way, based on

M. Baldoni et al. (Eds.): DALT 2012, LNAI 7784, pp. 153–169, 2013.

preference orderings on the possible values of variables. In Section 3 we show that such QPSs can be translated into equivalent goal-based QPSs, i.e. QPSs that express preferences based solely on goals. Such a translation requires at most polynomially more space, and hence is just as succinct as the original QPS. This result shows that goals are very expressive as a representation of qualitative preferences among outcomes. In [3], we discussed in detail the relation between Qualitative Preference Systems and two well-known frameworks that are representative for a large number of purely qualitative approaches to modelling preferences, namely Logical Preference Description language [4] and CP-nets [5]. We showed that for both of these approaches, a corresponding QPS can be defined straightforwardly. Since a QPS can be translated to a goal-based QPS, this result also holds for the goal-based QPSs that are the topic of the current paper.

In Section 4 we show that goal-based criterion trees also have some added value compared to trees with multi-valued criteria. We introduce basic updates on a QPS and show that goal-based QPSs allow for more fine-grained updates than their multi-valued counterparts. This is due to the different structure of goal-based criteria. We suggest a top-down approach to preference elicitation that starts with coarse updates and only adapts the criterion structure if more fine-grained updates are needed. Finally, Section 5 concludes the paper.

2   Modelling Goals as Criteria in a QPS

Several approaches to derive preferences over outcomes from goals can be found in the literature. Goals are commonly defined as some desired property that is either satisfied or not. As such, it is naturally represented as a propositional formula that can be true or false. Hence outcomes are often defined as propositional models, i.e. valuations over a set of Boolean variables $p, q, r, \ldots$. Sometimes all theoretically possible models are considered, sometimes the set of outcomes is restricted by a set of constraints. In the latter case, it is possible to specify which outcomes are actually available, or to use auxiliary variables whose values are derived from the values of other variables.

In [3] we introduced a framework for representing qualitative multi-criteria preferences called Qualitative Preference Systems (QPS). With this framework we aim to provide a generic way to represent qualitative preferences that are based on multiple criteria. A criterion can be seen as a preference from one particular perspective. We first summarize the general definition of a QPS from [3] in Section 2.1. We then propose in Section 2.2 that a goal can be straightforwardly modelled as a criterion in a QPS, thus providing the means to derive preferences over outcomes from multiple goals. In Section 2.3 we show that QPSs based on goal criteria can express different interpretations of what it means to have a goal p, such as absolute, ceteris paribus, leximin and discrimin preferences, and provide the possibility to state goals in terms of more fundamental interests.

2.1   Qualitative Preference Systems

The main aim of a QPS is to determine preferences between *outcomes* (or *alternatives*). An outcome is represented as an assignment of values to a set of relevant variables.

Every variable has its own domain of possible values. Constraints on the assignments of values to variables are expressed in a knowledge base. Outcomes are defined as variable assignments that respect the constraints in the knowledge base.

The preferences between outcomes are based on multiple *criteria*. Every criterion can be seen as a *reason* for preference, or as a preference from one particular *perspective*. A distinction is made between simple and compound criteria. Simple criteria are based on a single variable. Multiple (simple) criteria can be combined in a compound criterion to determine an overall preference. There are two kinds of compound criteria: cardinality criteria and lexicographic criteria. The subcriteria of a cardinality criterion all have equal importance, and preference is determined by counting the number of subcriteria that support it. In a lexicographic criterion, the subcriteria are ordered by priority and preference is determined by the most important subcriterion.

Definition 1. (Qualitative preference system [3]) *A qualitative preference system* (QPS) *is a tuple* $\langle Var, Dom, K, \mathcal{C} \rangle$. *Var is a finite set of* variables. *Every variable* $X \in Var$ *has a domain* $Dom(X)$ *of possible values.* K *(a knowledge base) is a set of constraints on the assignments of values to the variables in Var. A constraint is an equation of the form* $X = Expr$ *where* $X \in Var$ *is a variable and Expr is an algebraic expression that maps to* $Dom(X)$. *An* outcome α *is an assignment of a value* $x \in Dom(X)$ *to every variable* $X \in Var$, *such that no constraints in* K *are violated.* Ω *denotes the set of all outcomes:* $\Omega \subseteq \prod_{X \in Var} Dom(X)$. α_X *denotes the value of variable* X *in outcome* α. $\mathcal{C}$ *is a finite, rooted tree of criteria, where leaf nodes are simple criteria and other nodes are compound criteria. Child nodes of a compound criterion are called its subcriteria. The root of the tree is called the top criterion. Weak preference between outcomes by a criterion* c *is denoted by the relation* $\succeq_c$. $\succ_c$ *denotes the strict subrelation,* $\approx_c$ *the indifference subrelation.*

Definition 2. (Simple criterion [3]) *A simple criterion* c *is a tuple* $\langle X_c, \succeq_c \rangle$, *where* $X_c \in Var$ *is a variable, and* $\succeq_c$, *a preference relation on the possible values of* X_c, *is a preorder on* $Dom(X_c)$. $\succ_c$ *is the strict subrelation,* $\doteq_c$ *is the indifference subrelation. We call* c *a* Boolean simple criterion *if* X_c *is Boolean and* $\top \succ_c \bot$. *A simple criterion* $c = \langle X_c, \succeq_c \rangle$ *weakly prefers an outcome* α *over an outcome* β, *denoted* $\alpha \succeq_c \beta$, *iff* $\alpha_{X_c} \succeq_c \beta_{X_c}$.

Definition 3. (Cardinality criterion [3]) *A cardinality criterion* c *is a tuple* $\langle C_c \rangle$ *where* C_c *is a nonempty set of Boolean simple criteria (the* subcriteria *of* c*). A cardinality criterion* $c = \langle C_c \rangle$ *weakly prefers an outcome* α *over an outcome* β, *denoted* $\alpha \succeq_c \beta$, *iff* $|\{s \in C_c \mid \alpha \succ_s \beta\}| \geq |\{s \in C_c \mid \alpha \not\succeq_s \beta\}|$.

Note that a cardinality criterion can only have Boolean simple subcriteria. This is to guarantee transitivity of the preference relation induced by a cardinality criterion [3].

Definition 4. (Lexicographic criterion [3]) *A lexicographic criterion* c *is a tuple* $\langle C_c, \triangleright_c \rangle$, *where* C_c *is a nonempty set of criteria (the* subcriteria *of* c*) and* $\triangleright_c$, *a priority relation among subcriteria, is a strict partial order (a transitive and asymmetric relation) on* C_c. *A lexicographic criterion* $c = \langle C_c, \triangleright_c \rangle$ *weakly prefers an outcome* α *over an outcome* β, *denoted* $\alpha \succeq_c \beta$, *iff* $\forall s \in C_c (\alpha \succeq_s \beta \vee \exists s' \in C_c (\alpha \succ_{s'} \beta \wedge s' \triangleright_c s))$.

This definition of preference by a lexicographic criterion is equivalent to the priority operator as defined by [6]. It generalizes the familiar rule used for alphabetic ordering

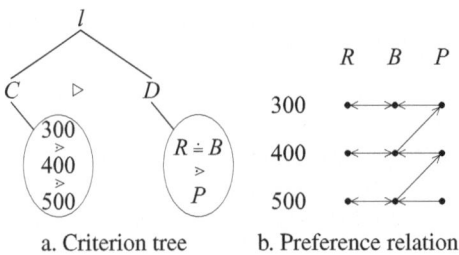

a. Criterion tree   b. Preference relation

Fig. 1. Qualitative Preference System

of words, such that the priority can be any partial order and the combined preference relations can be any preorder.

Example 1. To illustrate, we consider a QPS to compare holidays. Holidays (outcomes) are defined by two variables: C (cost) and D (destination). $Dom(C) = \{300, 400, 500\}$ and $Dom(D) = \{R, B, P\}$ (Rome, Barcelona and Paris). For the moment, we do not use any constraints. We use the notation '300B', '500R' etc. to refer to outcomes. Preferences are determined by a lexicographic criterion l with two simple subcriteria: $\langle C, \geq_C \rangle$ such that $300 \succ_C 400 \succ_C 500$ and $\langle D, \geq_D \rangle$ such that $R \doteq_D B \succ_D P$. We slightly abuse notation and refer to these criteria by their variable, i.e. C and D. C has higher priority than D: $C \rhd_l D$. The criterion tree is shown in Figure 1a, the induced preference relation in Figure 1b. The black dots represent the outcomes, and the arrows represent preferences (arrows point towards more preferred outcomes). Superfluous arrows (that follow from reflexivity and transitivity of the preference relation) are left out for readability.

Priority between subcriteria of a lexicographic criterion ($\rhd$) is a strict partial order (a transitive and asymmetric relation). This means that no two subcriteria can have the same priority. If two criteria have the same priority, they have to be combined in a cardinality criterion, which can then be a subcriterion of the lexicographic criterion. To simplify the representation of such a lexicographic criterion with cardinality subcriteria, we define the following alternative specification.

Definition 5. (Alternative specification of a lexicographic criterion) *A tuple* $\langle C'_c, \unrhd'_c \rangle$, *where* C'_c *is a set of criteria and* $\unrhd'_c$ *is a preorder, specifies a lexicographic criterion* $c = \langle C_c, \rhd_c \rangle$ *as follows.*

- *Partition* C'_c *into priority classes based on* $\unrhd'_c$.
- *For every priority class P, define a criterion* c_P. *If P contains only a single criterion s, then* $c_P = s$. *Otherwise* c_P *is a cardinality criterion such that for all* $s \in P$: $s \in C_{c_P}$.
- *Define* $c = \langle C_c, \rhd_c \rangle$ *such that* $C_c = \{c_P \mid P \text{ is a priority class}\}$ *and* $c_P \rhd_c c_{P'}$ *iff for all* $s \in P, s' \in P'$: $s \rhd'_s s'$.

For example, the specification $l = \langle \{g_1, g_2, g_3\}, \unrhd \rangle$ such that $g_1 \unrhd g_2 \doteq g_3$ is short for $l = \langle \{g_1, c\}, \rhd \rangle$ such that $g_1 \rhd c$ and $c = \langle \{g_2, g_3\} \rangle$.

2.2 Goals in a QPS

In general, the variables of a QPS can have any arbitrary domain and simple criteria can be defined over such variables. Example 1 contains two such multi-valued simple criteria. In the goal-based case however, we define outcomes as propositonal models, and hence all variables are Booleans. Goals are defined as Boolean simple criteria, i.e. simple criteria that prefer the truth of a variable over falsehood.

Definition 6. (Goal) *A QPS goal is a Boolean simple criterion* $\langle X, \{(\top, \bot)\} \rangle$ *for some* $X \in Var$. *For convenience, we denote such a goal by its variable* X.

This is straightforward when goals are atomic, e.g. p. If goals are complex propositional formulas, e.g. $(p \vee q) \wedge \neg r$, an auxiliary variable s can be defined by the constraint $s = (p \vee q) \wedge \neg r$ (see [3] for details on auxiliary variables). As this is a purely technical issue, we will sometimes use the formula instead of the auxiliary variable in order not to complicate the notation unnecessarily.

Multiple goals can be combined in order to derive an overall preference. If multiple goals are equally important and it is the number of satisfied goals that determines preference, a cardinality criterion can be used. Actually, every cardinality criterion is already goal-based, since the subcriteria are restricted to Boolean simple criteria which are the same as goals. If there is priority between goals (or if goals have incomparable priority), they can be combined in a goal-based lexicographic criterion. Such a criterion can also be used to specify priority between sets of equally important goals (goal-based cardinality criteria).

Definition 7. (Goal-based lexicographic criterion) *A* goal-based lexicographic criterion *is a lexicographic criterion all of whose subcriteria are either goals, goal-based cardinality criteria, or goal-based lexicographic criteria.*

Note that in the goal-based case, multi-valued simple criteria do not occur anywhere in the criterion tree; that is, all simple criteria are goals. The criterion tree in Figure 1a is not goal-based. However, we will see later that it can be translated to an equivalent goal-based criterion tree.

Example 2. Anne is planning to go on holiday with a friend. Her overall preference is based on three goals: that someone (she or her friend) speaks the language (*sl*), that it is sunny (*su*) and that she has not been there before (¬*bb*). The set of variables is $Var = \{sl, su, bb\}$. Since every variable is propositional, the domain for each variable is $\{\top, \bot\}$ and there are eight possible outcomes. For the moment we do not constrain the outcome space and do not use auxiliary variables ($K = \varnothing$). Two goals (*sl* and *su*) are based on atomic propositions, the third (¬*bb*) on a propositional formula that contains a negation. The overall preference between outcomes depends on the way that the goals are combined by compound criteria. In the next section we discuss several alternatives.

2.3 Expressivity of QPS as a Model of Goal-Based Preferences

What does it mean, in terms of preferences between outcomes, to have a goal p? Different interpretations can be found in the literature. We give a short overview of the best-known ones and show that QPSs can express the same preferences by means of some small examples.

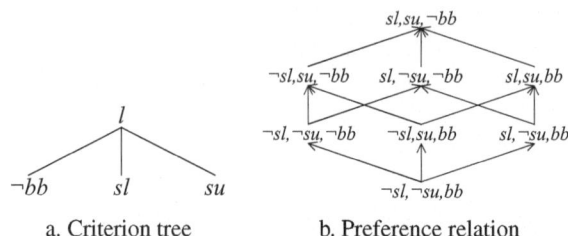

a. Criterion tree   b. Preference relation

Fig. 2. Ceteris paribus preference

Ceteris Paribus Preference. One interpretation of having a goal p is that p is preferred to $\neg p$ ceteris paribus (all other things being equal) [7,1,5]. The main question in this case is what the 'other things' are. Sometimes [5,7], they are the other variables (atomic propositions) that define the outcomes. Wellman and Doyle [1] define ceteris paribus preferences relative to framings (a factorisation of the outcome space into a cartesian product of attributes). The preference relation over all outcomes is taken to be the transitive closure of the preferences induced by each ceteris paribus preference. So if we have p and q as ceteris paribus goals, then $p \wedge q$ is preferred to $\neg p \wedge \neg q$ since $p \wedge q$ is preferred to $\neg p \wedge q$ (by goal p) and $\neg p \wedge q$ is preferred to $\neg p \wedge \neg q$ (by goal q).

Example 3. Consider a lexicographic criterion l that has the three goals as subcriteria, and there is no priority between them, i.e. $l = \langle \{sl, su, \neg bb\}, \varnothing \rangle$ (Figure 2a). The resulting preference relation (Figure 2b) is a ceteris paribus preference.

This is a general property of qualitative preference systems: a lexicographic criterion with only goals as subcriteria and an empty priority relation induces a ceteris paribus preference, where the other things are defined by the other goals (see also [8]). The main advantage of the ceteris paribus approach is that it deals with multiple goals in a natural, intuitive way. However, the resulting preference relation over outcomes is always partial since there is no way to compare $p \wedge \neg q$ and $\neg p \wedge q$. This is why [1] claim that goals are inadequate as the sole basis for rational action. One way to solve this is to introduce relative importance between goals, which is done in the prioritized goals approach.

Prioritized Goals. In e.g. [4], preferences are derived from a set of goals with an associated priority ordering (a total preorder). That is, there are multiple goals, each with an associated rank. There may be multiple goals with the same rank. Various strategies are possible to derive preferences from such prioritized goals. For example, the ⊆ or discrimin strategy prefers one outcome over another if there is a rank where the first satisfies a strict superset of the goals that the second satisfies, and for every more important rank, they satisfy the same goals. The # or leximin strategy prefers one outcome over another if there is a rank where the first satisfies more goals than the second, and for every more important rank, they satisfy the same number of goals.

   The prioritized goals strategies discrimin and leximin can also be expressed in a QPS. An exact translation is given in [3]. Here we just illustrate the principle. In the

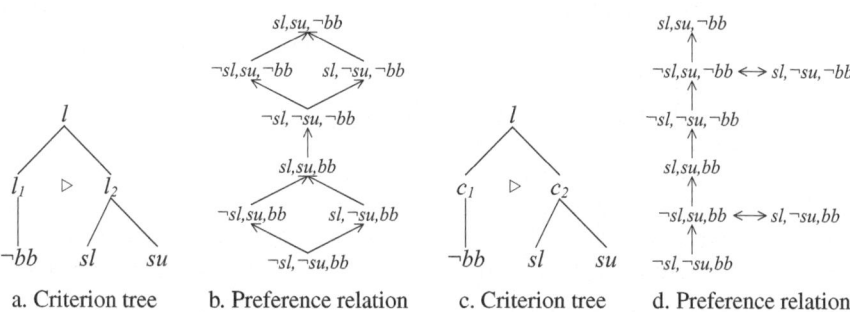

a. Criterion tree   b. Preference relation   c. Criterion tree   d. Preference relation

Fig. 3. (a, b) Discrimin preference (c, d) Leximin preference

prioritized goals approach, priority between goals is a total preorder, which can be expressed by assigning a rank to every goal. A QPS can model a discrimin or leximin preference with a lexicographic criterion that has one subcriterion for every rank. These subcriteria are compound criteria that contain the goals of the corresponding rank, and they are ordered by the same priority as the original ranking. For the discrimin strategy, the subcriteria are lexicographic criteria with no priority ordering between the goals. The leximin strategy uses the number of satisfied goals on each rank to determine overall preference. Therefore, each rank is represented by a cardinality criterion.

Example 4. Suppose that $\neg bb$ has the highest rank, followed by sl and su that have the same rank. The discrimin criterion tree for the example is shown in Figure 3a, where l is the top criterion and l_1 and l_2 the lexicographic criteria corresponding to the two ranks. The resulting preference relation is shown in Figure 3b. The leximin criterion tree for the example is shown in Figure 3c, where l is the top criterion and c_1 and c_2 the cardinality criteria corresponding to the two ranks. The resulting preference relation is shown in Figure 3d. The difference is that the outcomes that are incomparable according to the discrimin strategy are equally preferred according to the leximin strategy.

Preferential Dependence. The above approaches all assume that goals are preferentially independent, that is, goalhood of a proposition does not depend on the truth value of other propositions. There are several options if goals are not preferentially independent. One is to specify conditional goals or preferences, as is done in e.g. [5,2]. Another is to achieve preferential independence by restructuring the outcome space or expressing the goal in terms of more fundamental attributes [1,9] or underlying interests [8].

Example 5. Actually, the variables sl and bb that we chose for the example already relate to some of Anne's underlying interests. It may have been more obvious to characterize the outcome holidays by the destination (where Anne may or may not have been before) and the accompanying friend (who may or may not speak the language of the destination country). In that case we would have had to specify that Anne would prefer Juan if the destination was Barcelona, but Mario if the destination was Rome. Instead of specifying several conditional preferences, we can just say that she prefers to go with someone who speaks the language. In this case, knowledge is used to create an abstraction level that allows one to specify more fundamental goals that are only indirectly related to the most obvious variables with which to specify outcomes [8].

3   Modelling Multi-valued Criteria as Goals

Preferences in a QPS are ultimately based on simple criteria, i.e. preferences over the values of a single variable. In general, the domain of such a variable may consist of many possible values. In the goal-based case, simple criteria are based on binary goals. In this section we show that the goal-based case is very expressive, by showing that every QPS can be translated into an equivalent goal-based QPS (provided that the domains of the variables used in the original QPS are finite). Moreover, we show that this translation is just as succinct as the original representation. In order to do this, we must first formalize the concept of equivalence between QPSs.

3.1   Equivalence

An obvious interpretation of equivalence between criteria is the equivalence of the preference relations they induce. I.e. two criteria c_1 and c_2 are equivalent if for all outcomes α, β, we have $\alpha \succeq_{c_1} \beta$ iff $\alpha \succeq_{c_2} \beta$. However, this definition only works if the criteria are defined with respect to the same outcome space, i.e. the same set of variables Var, the same domains Dom and the same constraints K. Since we will make use of auxiliary variables, we cannot use this definition directly. Fortunately, this is a technical issue that can be solved in a straightforward way.

Definition 8. (Equivalence of outcomes) *Let $S_1 = \langle Var_1, Dom_1, K_1, C_1 \rangle$ and $S_2 = \langle Var_2, Dom_2, K_2, C_2 \rangle$ be two QPSs such that $Var_1 \subseteq Var_2$, $\forall X \in Var_1 (Dom_1(X) \subseteq Dom_2(X))$ and $K_1 \subseteq K_2$. Let Ω_1 and Ω_2 denote the outcome spaces of S_1 and S_2, respectively. Two outcomes $\alpha \in \Omega_1$ and $\beta \in \Omega_2$ are equivalent, denoted $\alpha \equiv \beta$, iff $\forall X \in Var_1 : \alpha_X = \beta_X$.*

In the following, the only variables that are added are auxiliary variables. Such variables do not increase the outcome space because their value is uniquely determined by the values of (some of) the existing variables. We use special variable names of the form '$X = v$' to denote a Boolean variable that is true if and only if the value of variable X is v. For example, the variable $C = 300$ is true in outcomes $300R$, $300B$ and $300P$, and false in the other outcomes. When only auxiliary variables are added, every outcome in Ω_1 has exactly one equivalent outcome in Ω_2. We will represent such equivalent outcomes with the same identifier.

Definition 9. (Equivalence of criteria) *Let $S_1 = \langle Var_1, Dom_1, K_1, C_1 \rangle$ and $S_2 = \langle Var_2, Dom_2, K_2, C_2 \rangle$ be two QPSs such that $Var_1 \subseteq Var_2$, $\forall X \in Var_1 (Dom_1(X) \subseteq Dom_2(X))$ and $K_1 \subseteq K_2$. Let Ω_1 and Ω_2 denote the outcome spaces of S_1 and S_2, respectively. Two criteria c in C_1 and c' in C_2 are called equivalent iff $\forall \alpha, \beta \in \Omega_1, \forall \alpha', \beta' \in \Omega_2$, if $\alpha \equiv \alpha'$ and $\beta \equiv \beta'$, then $\alpha \succeq_c \beta$ iff $\alpha' \succeq_{c'} \beta'$.*

Definition 10. (Equivalence of QPSs) *Let $S_1 = \langle Var_1, Dom_1, K_1, C_1 \rangle$ and $S_2 = \langle Var_2, Dom_2, K_2, C_2 \rangle$ be two QPSs. S_1 and S_2 are equivalent if the top criterion of C_1 is equivalent to the top criterion of S_2.*

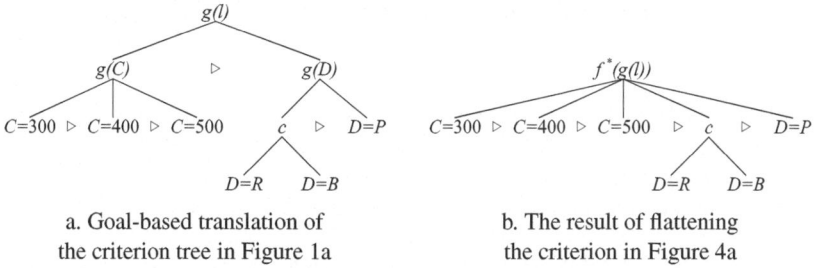

a. Goal-based translation of
the criterion tree in Figure 1a

b. The result of flattening
the criterion in Figure 4a

Fig. 4. Goal-based translation and flattening

3.2   From Simple Criteria to Goals

A simple criterion on a variable with a finite domain can be translated to an equivalent goal-based criterion in the following way.

Definition 11. (Goal-based translation) *Let $c = \langle X, \geqslant \rangle$ be a simple criterion such that $Dom(X)$ is finite. The translation of c to a goal-based criterion, denoted $g(c)$, is defined as follows. If c is already a Boolean simple criterion, then $g(c) = c$. Otherwise:*

- *For every $x \in Dom(X)$, define a goal (Boolean simple criterion) c_x on variable $X = x$ with $\top \geqslant_{c_x} \bot$.*
- *Define a lexicographic criterion $g(c) = \langle C_{g(c)}, \trianglerighteq_{g(c)} \rangle$ such that $C_{g(c)} = \{c_x \mid x \in Dom(x)\}$ and $c_x \trianglerighteq_{g(c)} c_{x'}$ iff $x \geqslant_c x'$.*

Example 6. To illustrate, Figure 4a displays the translation of the criterion tree in Figure 1a. The simple criteria C and D have been replaced by their translations $g(C)$ and $g(D)$. These lexicographic criteria have a subgoal for every value of C resp. D. The priority between these goals corresponds to the value preferences of the original simple criteria.

Theorem 1. *Let $c = \langle X, \geqslant \rangle$ be a simple criterion such that $Dom(X_c)$ is finite. The goal-based translation $g(c)$ of c as defined in Definition 11 is equivalent to c.*

Proof. We distinguish five possible cases and show that in every case, c's preference between α and β is the same as $g(c)$'s preference between α and β.

1. If $\alpha_X = \beta_X$ then (a) $\alpha \approx_c \beta$ and (b) $\alpha \approx_{g(c)} \beta$.
2. If $\alpha_X \doteq_c \beta_X$ but $\alpha_X \neq \beta_X$ then (a) $\alpha \approx_c \beta$ and (b) $\alpha \approx_{g(c)} \beta$.
3. If $\alpha_X >_c \beta_X$ then (a) $\alpha >_c \beta$ and (b) $\alpha >_{g(c)} \beta$.
4. If $\beta_X >_c \alpha_X$ then (a) $\beta >_c \alpha$ and (b) $\beta >_{g(c)} \alpha$.
5. If $\alpha_X \not\geqslant_c \beta_X$ and $\beta_X \not\geqslant_c \alpha_X$ then (a) $\alpha \not\geqslant_c \beta$ and $\beta \not\geqslant_c \alpha$ and (b) $\alpha \not\geqslant_{g(c)} \beta$ and $\beta \not\geqslant_{g(c)} \alpha$.

1-5(a). This follows directly from the definition of simple criteria. **1(b).** If $\alpha_X = \beta_X$ then $\forall x \in Dom(X) : \alpha_{X=x} = \beta_{X=x}$, so also $\forall x \in Dom(X) : \alpha \approx_{c_x} \beta$. Hence, by the definition of a lexicographic criterion: $\alpha \approx_{g(c)} \beta$. **2-5(b).** If $\alpha_X \neq \beta_X$ then $\forall x \in Dom(X) \backslash \{\alpha_X, \beta_X\}$: $\alpha_{X=x} = \beta_{X=x}$ and $\alpha \approx_{g(c)} \beta$. Since a subcriterion s of a compound criterion such that $\alpha \approx_s \beta$ does not influence that compound criterion's preference between α and β, the only criteria that can influence $g(c)$'s preference between α and β are c_{α_X} and c_{β_X}. Since $\alpha >_{c_{\alpha_X}} \beta$ and $\beta >_{c_{\beta_X}} \alpha$, preference between α and β by $g(c)$ is determined by the priority between c_{α_X} and c_{β_X}. **2(b).** If $\alpha_X \geq_c \beta_X$ then $c_{\alpha_X} \triangleq_{g(c)} c_{\beta_X}$, so they are together in a cardinality criterion and we have $\alpha \approx_{g(c)} \beta$. **3(b).** If $\alpha_X > \beta_X$ then $c_{\alpha_X} \triangleright_{g(c)} c_{\beta_X}$ so by the definition of a lexicographic criterion $\alpha >_{g(c)} \beta$. **4(b).** Analogous to 3(b). **5(b).** If $\alpha_X \nleq_c \beta_X$ and $\beta_X \nleq_c \alpha_X$ then $c_{\alpha_X} \ntriangleright_{g(c)} c_{\beta_X}$ and $c_{\beta_X} \ntriangleright_{g(c)} c_{\alpha_X}$ and $c_{\alpha_X} \not\triangleq_{g(c)} c_{\beta_X}$, so by the definition of a lexicographic criterion $\alpha \nleq_{g(c)} \beta$ and $\beta \nleq_{g(c)} \alpha$.   □

By replacing every simple criterion c in a criterion tree with its goal-based translation $g(c)$, an equivalent goal-based criterion tree is obtained.

Definition 12. (Relative succinctness) $g(c)$ *is at least as succinct as c iff there exists a polynomial function p such that $size(g(c)) \leq p(size(c))$. (Adapted from [10].)*

Theorem 2. *Let $c = \langle X, \geq \rangle$ be a simple criterion such that $Dom(X_c)$ is finite. The translation $g(c)$ of c as defined in Definition 11 is just as succinct as c.*

Proof. The goal-based translation just replaces variable values with goals, and the preference relation between them with an identical priority relation between goals, so the translation is linear.   □

The above two theorems are very important as they show that goals are very expressive as a way to represent qualitative preferences, and moreover, that this representation is just as succinct as a representation based on multi-valued criteria.

4   Updates in a QPS

In this section we show that goal-based criterion trees also have some added value compared to trees with multi-valued criteria. We introduce updates on a criterion tree as changes in the value preference of simple criteria or in the priority of lexicographic criteria. The number of updates of this kind that are possible depends on the structure of the tree. In general, the flatter a criterion tree, the more updates are possible. It is possible to make criterion tree structures flatter, i.e. to reduce the depth of the tree, by removing intermediate lexicographic criteria. The advantage of goal-based criterion trees is that they can be flattened to a greater extent than their equivalent non-goal-based counterparts. We first formalize the concept of flattening a criterion tree. Then we define what we mean by basic updates in a criterion tree and show the advantages of flat goal-based QPSs compared to other flat QPSs.

4.1   Flattening

Simple criteria are terminal nodes (leaves) and cannot be flattened. Cardinality criteria have only Boolean simple subcriteria and cannot be flattened either. Lexicographic criteria can have three kinds of subcriteria: simple, cardinality and lexicographic. They can be flattened by replacing each lexicographic subcriterion by that criterion's subcriteria and adapting the priority accordingly (as defined below).

Definition 13. (Removing a lexicographic subcriterion) *Let* $c = \langle C_c, \rhd_c \rangle$ *be a lexicographic criterion and* $d = \langle C_d, \rhd_d \rangle \in C_c$ *a lexicographic criterion that is a subcriterion of* c. *We now define a lexicographic criterion* $f(c,d) = \langle C_{f(c,d)}, \rhd_{f(c,d)} \rangle$ *that is equivalent to* c *but does not have* d *as a subcriterion. To this end, we define* $C_{f(c,d)} = C_c \backslash \{d\} \cup C_d$ *and* $\forall i, j \in C_{f(c,d)} : i \rhd_{f(c,d)} j$ *iff* $i, j \in C_c$ *and* $i \rhd_c j$, *or* $i, j \in C_d$ *and* $i \rhd_d j$, *or* $i \in C_c$, $j \in C_d$ *and* $i \rhd_c d$, *or* $i \in C_d$, $j \in C_c$ *anf* $d \rhd_c j$.

Theorem 3. $f(c,d)$ *is equivalent to* c, *i.e.* $\alpha \succeq_c \beta$ *iff* $\alpha \succeq_{f(c,d)} \beta$.

Proof. $\Rightarrow$. Suppose $\alpha \succeq_c \beta$. Then $\forall s \in C_c(\alpha \succeq_s \beta \vee \exists s' \in C_c(\alpha >_{s'} \beta \wedge s' \rhd_c s))$. We need to show that also $\forall s \in C_{f(c,d)}(\alpha \succeq_s \beta \vee \exists s' \in C_{f(c,d)}(\alpha >_{s'} \beta \wedge s' \rhd_{f(c,d)} s))$. We do this by showing that $\alpha \succeq_s \beta \vee \exists s' \in C_{f(c,d)}(\alpha >_{s'} \beta \wedge s' \rhd_{f(c,d)} s)$ holds for every possible origin of $s \in C_{f(c,d)}$. We have $\forall s \in C_{f(c,d)}$, either $s \in C_c \backslash \{d\}$ or $s \in C_d$.

- If $s \in C_c \backslash \{d\}$, we know that $\alpha \succeq_s \beta \vee \exists s' \in C_c(\alpha >_{s'} \beta \wedge s' \rhd_c s)$. If $\alpha \succeq_s \beta$, trivially also $\alpha \succeq_s \beta \vee \exists s' \in C_{f(c,d)}(\alpha >_{s'} \beta \wedge s' \rhd_{f(c,d)} s)$ and we are done. If $\exists s' \in C_c(\alpha >_{s'} \beta \wedge s' \rhd_c s)$, then either $s' \in C_c \backslash \{d\}$ or $s' = d$. If $s' \in C_c \backslash \{d\}$, then $s' \in C_{f(c,d)}$ and $s' \rhd_{f(c,d)} s$, so also $\alpha \succeq_s \beta \vee \exists s' \in C_{f(c,d)}(\alpha >_{s'} \beta \wedge s' \rhd_{f(c,d)} s)$ and we are done. If $s' = d$, then (since $\alpha >_{s'} \beta$) $\exists i \in C_{s'}$ (and hence $\in C_{f(c,d)}$): $\alpha >_i \beta$. Since $s' \rhd_c s$, we have $i \rhd_{f(c,d)} s$ and so also $\alpha \succeq_s \beta \vee \exists i \in C_{f(c,d)}(\alpha >_i \beta \wedge i \rhd_{f(c,d)} s)$ and we are done.
- Now consider the case that $s \in C_d$. Since $d \in C_c$, we know that either $\alpha \succeq_d \beta$ or $\exists s' \in C_c(\alpha >_{s'} \beta \wedge s' \rhd_c d)$. If $\alpha \succeq_d \beta$, we know $\alpha \succeq_s \beta \vee \exists s' \in C_d(\alpha >_{s'} \beta \wedge s' \rhd_d s)$ and hence $\alpha \succeq_s \beta \vee \exists s' \in C_{f(c,d)}(\alpha >_{s'} \beta \wedge s' \rhd_{f(c,d)} s)$ and we are done. If $\exists s' \in C_c(\alpha >_{s'} \beta \wedge s' \rhd_c d)$ then $\exists s' \in C_{f(c,d)}(\alpha >_{s'} \beta \wedge s' \rhd_{f(c,d)} s)$ so trivially also $\alpha \succeq_s \beta \vee \exists s' \in C_{f(c,d)}(\alpha >_{s'} \beta \wedge s' \rhd_{f(c,d)} s)$ and we are done.

$\Leftarrow$. Suppose $\alpha \nsucceq_c \beta$. Then $\exists s \in C_c(\alpha \nsucceq_s \beta \wedge \forall s' \in C_c(s' \rhd_c s \to \alpha \nsucc_{s'} \beta))$. We need to show that also $\exists t \in C_{f(c,d)}(\alpha \nsucceq_t \beta \wedge \forall t' \in C_{f(c,d)}(t' \rhd_{f(c,d)} t \to \alpha \nsucc_{t'} \beta))$. Either $s \neq d$ or $s = d$.

- If $s \neq d$, then $s \in C_{f(c,d)}$ and we know that $\alpha \nsucceq_s \beta$ and $\forall s' \in C_{f(c,d)} \backslash C_d(s' \rhd_{f(c,d)} s \to \alpha \nsucc_{s'} \beta)$. If $d \nrhd_c s$, then $\forall s' \in C_{c*}(s' \rhd_{f(c,d)} s \to s' \in C_{f(c,d)} \backslash C_d)$. So we have $\exists s \in C_{f(c,d)}(\alpha \nsucceq_s \beta \wedge \forall s' \in C_{f(c,d)}(s' \rhd_{f(c,d)} s \to \alpha \nsucc_{s'} \beta))$. Take $t = s$ and we are done. If $d \rhd_c s$, then $\alpha \nsucceq_d \beta$, i.e. $\alpha \nsucceq_d \beta$ or $\beta \succeq_d \alpha$. If $\alpha \nsucceq_d \beta$, then $\exists u \in C_d(\alpha \nsucceq_u \beta \wedge \forall u' \in C_d(u' \rhd_d u \to \alpha \nsucc_{u'} \beta))$. Since $\forall s' \in C_c(s' \rhd_c s \to \alpha \nsucc_{s'} \beta)$ and $d \rhd_c s$, we also have $\exists u \in C_{f(c,d)}(\alpha \nsucceq_u \beta \wedge \forall u' \in C_{f(c,d)}(u' \rhd_{f(c,d)} u \to \alpha \nsucc_{u'} \beta))$. Take $t = u$ and we are done. If $\beta \succeq_d \alpha$, then $\forall v \in C_d(\beta \succeq_v \alpha \vee \exists v' \in C_d(\beta >_{v'} \alpha \wedge v' \rhd_d v))$. This means that either $\forall u \in C_d(\beta \succeq_u \alpha)$ or $\exists u \in C_d(\beta >_u \alpha \wedge \neg \exists u' \in C_d(u' \rhd_d u))$. If $\forall u \in C_d(\beta \succeq_u \alpha)$, then $\forall u \in C_d(\alpha \nsucc_u \beta)$. Take $t = s$ and we are done. If $\exists u \in C_d(\beta >_u \alpha \wedge \neg \exists u' \in C_d(u' \rhd_d u))$, then $\exists u \in C_d(\alpha \nsucceq_u \beta \wedge \forall u' \in C_d(u' \rhd_d u \to \alpha \nsucc_{u'} \beta))$. Take $t = u$ and we are done.
- If $s = d$, then $\alpha \nsucceq_d \beta$, so $\exists u \in C_d(\alpha \nsucceq_u \beta \wedge \forall u' \in C_d(u' \rhd_d u \to \alpha \nsucc_{u'} \beta))$. Since $\forall s' \in C_c(s' \rhd_c d \to \alpha >_{s'} \beta)$, we have $\forall s' \in C_c(s' \rhd_c u \to \alpha >_{s'} \beta)$. Take $t = u$ and we are done. $\square$

Theorem 4. $f(c,d)$ *is just as succinct as* c.

Proof. When a lexicographic subcriterion is removed according to Definition 13, the total number of criteria decreases with 1: the subcriteria of d become direct subcriteria of

c and d itself is removed. The priority between the original subcriteria of c (i.e. $C_c\backslash\{d\}$) and the priority between the original subcriteria of d (i.e. C_d) remains unaltered. Just the priority between the subcriteria in $C_c\backslash\{d\}$ and d is replaced by priority between the subcriteria in $C_c\backslash\{d\}$ and the subcriteria in C_d. Since $|C_d|$ is finite, the increase in size is linear. □

Definition 14. (Flat criterion) *All simple and cardinality criteria are flat. A lexicographic criterion is flat if all its subcriteria are either simple or cardinality criteria.*

Definition 15. (Flattening) *The flat version of a non-flat lexicographic criterion c, denoted $f^*(c)$, is obtained as follows. For an arbitrary lexicographic subcriterion $d \in C_c$, get $f(c,d)$. If $f(c,d)$ is flat, $f^*(c) = f(c,d)$. Otherwise, $f^*(c) = f^*(f(c,d))$.*

Example 7. (Flattening) The original criterion tree in Figure 1 is already flat. Its goal-based translation in Figure 4a can be flattened further, as shown in Figure 4b. Here the lexicographic subcriteria $g(C)$ and $g(D)$ have been removed.

4.2   Updates

Criterion trees can be updated by leaving the basic structure of the tree intact but changing the priority between subcriteria of a lexicographic criterion ($\unrhd$) or the value preferences of a multi-valued simple criterion ($\geq$). By performing these basic operations, the induced preference relation also changes. Therefore, such updates can be used to 'fine-tune' a person's preference representation.

Definition 16. (Update) *An update of a criterion tree is a change in (i) the preference between values ($\geq$) of a multi-valued simple criterion; and/or (ii) the priority ($\unrhd$) between (in)direct subcriteria of a lexicographic criterion (in the alternative specification). The changed relations still have to be preorders.*

Theorem 5. *For every update on a criterion tree c, there exists an equivalent update on the goal-based translation $g(c)$ and vice versa.*

Proof. Every change in a value preference $\geq$ between two values x and y corresponds one-to-one to a change in priority between c_x and c_y. Every change in priority between two subcriteria s and s' corresponds one-to-one to a change in priority between $g(s)$ and $g(s')$. □

Example 8. Consider for example the criterion tree in Figure 1a. On the highest level, there are three possibilities for the priority: $C \rhd D$, $D \rhd C$ or incomparable priority. On the next level, each simple criterion has preferences over three possible values, which can be ordered in 29 different ways (this is the number of different preorders with three elements, oeis.org/A000798). So in total there are $3 \times 29 \times 29 = 2523$ possible updates of this tree. For the goal-based translation of this tree (in Figure 4a) this number is the same. Figure 5 shows one alternative update of the original criterion tree in Figure 1 as well as its goal-based translation in Figure 4a.

Flattening a criterion tree influences the updates that can be performed; all updates that are possible on the non-flat tree can also be performed on the flattened version, but not vice versa. That is, flattening a criterion tree introduces more possible updates.

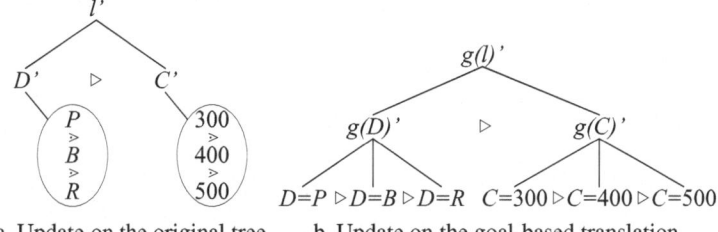

a. Update on the original tree   b. Update on the goal-based translation

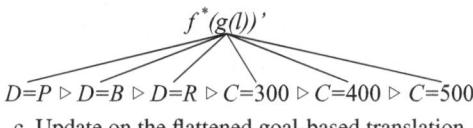

$D{=}P \triangleright D{=}B \triangleright D{=}R \triangleright C{=}300 \triangleright C{=}400 \triangleright C{=}500$

c. Update on the flattened goal-based translation

Fig. 5. Updates on criterion trees

Theorem 6. *For every update on a criterion tree c, there exists an equivalent (set of) update(s) on the flattened criterion tree $f^*(c)$.*

Proof. *Since simple criteria are not altered in the flattening process, every change in a value preference $\geq$ between two values x and y can also be applied in the flattened version. Every change in priority between two subcriteria s and s' corresponds to a change in priority between all of the (in)direct subcriteria of s that are flat and all of the (in)direct subcriteria of s' that are flat.*

Example 9. Figure 5c shows an update on the flat goal-based criterion tree in Figure 4b that is equivalent to the updates in Figure 5a and 5b.

Theorem 7. *If a criterion tree c is not flat, there exist updates on $f^*(c)$ that do not have equivalent updates on c.*

We show this by means of an example.

Example 10. The goal-based tree in Figure 4a can be flattened to the equivalent flat tree in Figure 4b. This flattened tree can be updated in 209527 different ways (the number of different preorders with 6 elements, oeis.org/A000798), thereby allowing more preference relations to be represented by the same tree structure. Figure 6 shows an alternative flat goal-based tree that can be obtained from the previous one by updating it. It is not possible to obtain an equivalent criterion tree by finetuning the original criterion tree or its goal-based translation. This is because goals relating to different variables are 'mixed': the most important goal is that the cost is 300, the next most important goal is that the destination is Rome or Barcelona, and only after that is the cost considered again. This is not possible in a criterion tree that is based on simple criteria that are defined directly on the variables C and D.

We have seen that the same updates are possible on a multi-valued criterion tree and its goal-based translation. If, however, both trees are flattened, more updates are possible on the flattened goal-based tree.

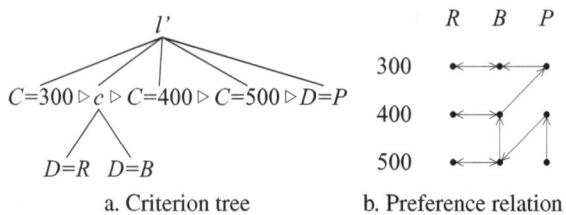

a. Criterion tree   b. Preference relation

Fig. 6. Alternative flat goal-based tree obtained by updating the tree in Figure 4b

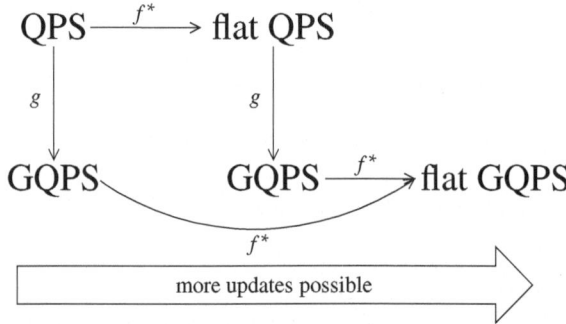

Fig. 7. Effects of goal-based translation and flattening on possible updates

Theorem 8. *Let c be a non-goal-based criterion. Then there exist updates on $f^*(g(c))$ that do not have equivalent updates on $f^*(c)$.*

In general, the flatter a criterion tree, the more different updates are possible. Since a goal-based tree can be made flatter than an equivalent criterion tree that is based on multi-valued simple criteria, the goal-based case allows more updates. This is visualized in Figure 7.

Example 11. This example shows how goals can be used for compensation between variables. The subcriteria of a cardinality criterion must be Boolean, to avoid intransitive preferences. So, for example, the criterion in Figure 8a is not allowed. It would result in $400B \approx 500R$ and $500R \approx 300B$, but $300B > 400B$. However, the underlying idea that the variables C and D are equally important is intuitive. Using goals we can capture it in a different way, as displayed in Figure 8b. This criterion tree results in a total preorder of preference between outcomes, where for instance $300B > 500R > 400B$.

The results above show that every update that can be applied on a criterion tree can also be applied on its flattened goal-based translation, and that this last criterion tree even allows more updates. However, if we look at the size of the updates, we can see that for equivalent updates, more value preference or priority relations have to be changed when the structure is flatter. For example, a simple inversion of the priority between $g(C)$ and $g(D)$ in Figure 4a corresponds to the inversion of priority between all of

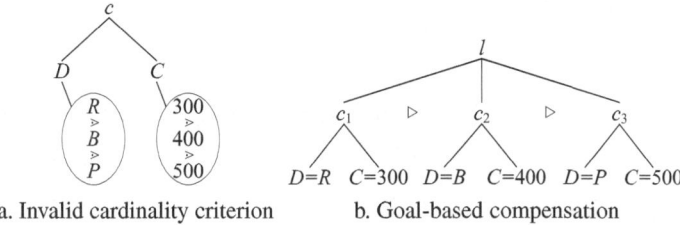

a. Invalid cardinality criterion   b. Goal-based compensation

Fig. 8. Preferences where C and D are equally important

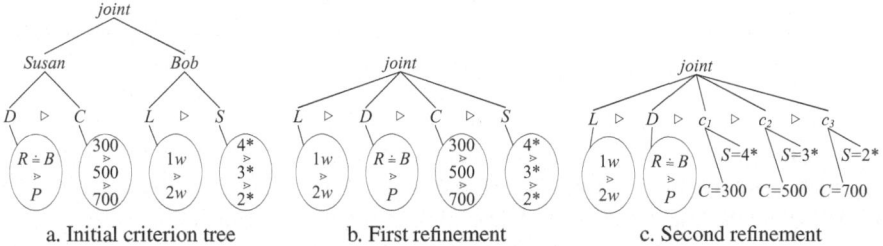

a. Initial criterion tree   b. First refinement   c. Second refinement

Fig. 9. Successive criterion trees for Susan and Bob

$C = 300$, $C = 400$ and $C = 500$ and all of $D = R$, $D = B$ and $D = P$ in Figure 4b. This suggests the following approach to finetuning a given preference representation during the preference elicitation process. First, one can fine-tune the current criterion tree as well as possible using (coarse) updates. If the result does not match the intended preferences well enough, one can start flattening, which will create more, fine-grained possibilities to update the tree. If this still does not allow to express the correct preferences, one can make a goal-based translation and flatten it. This allows for even more possible updates on an even lower level.

Example 12. Susan and Bob are planning a city trip together. Susan would like to go to a city that she has not been to before, and hence prefers Rome or Barcelona to Paris. She also does not want to spend too much money. Bob is a busy businessman who only has a single week of holiday and would like some luxury, expressed in the number of stars of the hotel. There is no priority between Susan's and Bob's preferences. The initial criterion tree for Susan and Bob's joint preferences is displayed in Figure 9a. Susan and Bob decide that Bob's criterion on the length of the trip should be the most important, because he really does not have time to go for two weeks. They also decide that luxury is less important than the other criteria. In order to update the tree, it is first flattened by removing the subcriteria of Susan and Bob. The new tree, after flattening and updating, is shown in Figure 9b. However, Bob feels that luxury can compensate for cost. To represent this, the criteria for cost and number of stars are translated to goals and combined into three cardinality criteria, as shown in Figure 9c. At this point, the travel agent's website is able to make a good selection of offers to show and recommend to Susan and Bob.

5   Conclusion

We have shown that the QPS framework can be used to model preferences between outcomes based on goals. It has several advantages over other approaches. First, the QPS framework is general and flexible and can model several interpretations of using goals to derive preferences between outcomes. This is done by simply adapting the structure of the criterion tree. It is possible to specify an incomplete preference relation such as the ceteris paribus relation by using an incomplete priority ordering. But if a complete preference relation is needed, it is also easy to obtain one by completing the priority relation between subcriteria of a lexicographic criterion, or using cardinality criteria. Second, goals do not have to be independent. Multiple goals can be specified using the same variable. For example, there is no problem in specifying both p and $p \wedge q$ as a goal. Third, goals do not have to be consistent. It is not contradictory to have both p preferred to $\neg p$ (from one perspective) and $\neg p$ preferred to p (from another). This possibility is also convenient when combining preferences of multiple agents, who may have different preferences. Preferences of multiple agents can be combined by just collecting them as subcriteria of a new lexicographic criterion. Fourth, background knowledge can be used to express constraints and define abstract concepts. This in turn can be used to specify goals on a more fundamental level.

When the variables that define the outcomes are not Boolean, preferences are usually based on orderings of the possible values of each variable. We have shown that such multi-valued criteria can be translated to equivalent goal-based criteria. Such a translation requires at most polynomially more space, and hence is just as succinct as the original QPS. This result shows that goals are very expressive as a representation of qualitative preferences among outcomes.

Goal-based criterion trees also have some added value compared to trees with multi-valued criteria. We introduced basic updates on a QPS and showed that goal-based QPSs allow for more fine-grained updates than their multi-valued counterparts. This is due to the different structure of goal-based criteria. In general, the flatter a criterion tree, the more updates are possible. It is possible to make criterion tree structures flatter, i.e. to reduce the depth of the tree, by removing intermediate lexicographic criteria. The advantage of goal-based criterion trees is that they can be flattened to a greater extent than their equivalent non-goal-based counterparts, and hence provide more possible updates.

We proposed a procedure to fine-tune a criterion tree during the preference elicitation process. Essentially, this is a top-down approach where a criterion tree is first updated as well as possible in its current state, and is only flattened and/or translated to a goal-based tree if more updates are necessary. This procedure gives rise to a more fundamental question. If it is really necessary to take all these steps, then maybe the original criteria were not chosen well in the first place. It may have been better to choose more fundamental interests as criteria. This is still an open question that we would like to address in the future.

Acknowledgements. This research is supported by the Dutch Technology Foundation STW, applied science division of NWO and the Technology Program of the Ministry of Economic Affairs. It is part of the Pocket Negotiator project with grant number VICI-project 08075.

References

1. Wellman, M.P., Doyle, J.: Preferential semantics for goals. In: Proc. AAAI, pp. 698–703 (1991)
2. Boutilier, C.: Toward a logic for qualitative decision theory. In: Proc. KR, pp. 75–86 (1994)
3. Visser, W., Aydoğan, R., Hindriks, K.V., Jonker, C.M.: A framework for qualitative multi-criteria preferences. In: Proc. ICAART (2012)
4. Brewka, G.: A rank based description language for qualitative preferences. In: Proc. ECAI, pp. 303–307 (2004)
5. Boutilier, C., Brafman, R.I., Domshlak, C., Hoos, H.H., Poole, D.: CP-nets: A tool for representing and reasoning with conditional ceteris paribus preference statements. Journal of Artificial Intelligence Research 21, 135–191 (2004)
6. Andréka, H., Ryan, M., Schobbens, P.Y.: Operators and laws for combining preference relations. Journal of Logic and Computation 12(1), 13–53 (2002)
7. Von Wright, G.H.: The Logic of Preference: An Essay. Edinburgh University Press (1963)
8. Visser, W., Hindriks, K.V., Jonker, C.M.: Interest-based preference reasoning. In: Proc. ICAART, pp. 79–88 (2011)
9. Keeney, R.L.: Analysis of preference dependencies among objectives. Operations Research 29(6), 1105–1120 (1981)
10. Chevaleyre, Y., Endriss, U., Lang, J.: Expressive power of weighted propositional formulas for cardinal preference modelling. In: Proc. KR (2006)

SAT-Based BMC for Deontic Metric Temporal Logic and Deontic Interleaved Interpreted Systems[*]

Bożena Woźna-Szcześniak and Andrzej Zbrzezny

IMCS, Jan Długosz University
Al. Armii Krajowej 13/15, 42-200 Częstochowa, Poland
{b.wozna,a.zbrzezny}@ajd.czest.pl

Abstract. We consider multi-agent systems' (MASs) modelled by deontic interleaved interpreted systems and we provide a new SAT-based bounded model checking (BMC) method for these systems. The properties of MASs are expressed by means of the metric temporal logic with discrete semantics and extended to include epistemic and deontic operators. The proposed BMC approach is based on the state of the art solutions to BMC. We test our results on a typical MASs scenario: train controller problem with faults.

1 Introduction

By *agents* we usually mean rational, independent, intelligent and high-tech entities that act autonomously on behalf of their users, across open and distributed environments, to solve a growing number of complex problems. *A multi-agent system* (MAS) [27] is a system composed of multiple interacting (communicating, coordinating, cooperating, etc.) agents which can be used to solve problems that are beyond the individual capacities or knowledge of a single agent.

Deontic interpreted systems (DISs) [18] are models of MASs that make possible reasoning about epistemic and correct functioning behaviour of MASs. They provide a computationally grounded semantics on which it is possible to interpret the $\mathcal{O}_i \alpha$ modality, representing the fact "in all correct functioning executions of agent i, α holds", as well as a traditional epistemic modalities and temporal operators. By *deontic interleaved interpreted systems* (DIISs) we mean a restriction of DISs that enforce the executions of agents to be interleaved. Thus we assume that agents act as network of synchronised automata; note that one can see DIISs as a deontic extension of the formalism of interleaved interpreted systems [17]. We consider DIISs since they allow for the distinction between correct (or ideal, normative, etc.) and incorrect states, and they enable more efficient verification of MASs, the behaviour of which is as the behaviour of synchronised automata. Note that although our method is described for DIISs, it can be applied to DISs [10] as well; as it will be clear below the main difference between DIISs and DISs is in the definition of the global evolution function. Thus, to apply our method to DISs it is enough to change the definition a propositional formula that encodes the transition relation. However, only DIISs can be combined with partial order reductions allowing for more efficient verification of MASs that are not so loosely coupled.

---

[*] Partly supported by National Science Center under the grant No. 2011/01/B/ST6/05317.

M. Baldoni et al. (Eds.): DALT 2012, LNAI 7784, pp. 170–189, 2013.

Model checking [6,24] has been developed as a method for automatic verification of finite state concurrent systems, and impressive strides have been made on this problem over the past thirty years. The main aim of model checking is to provide an algorithm determining whether an abstract model - representing, for example, a software project - satisfies a formal specification expressed as a modal formula. Moreover, if the property does not hold, the method discovers a counterexample execution that shows the source of the problem. The practical applicability of model checking in MASs settings requires the development of algorithms hacking the state explosion problem. In particular, to avoid this problem the following approaches have been developed: BDD-based bounded [13,19,20] and unbounded [26,25] model checking, SAT-based bounded [22,23,29,31,30] and unbounded [14] model checking.

To express the requirements of MASs, various extensions of temporal [9] or real time [2] temporal logics with epistemic (to represent knowledge) [10], doxastic (to represent beliefs) [16], and deontic (to represent norms and prescriptions) [18,3] components have been proposed. In this paper we consider a deontic and epistemic extension of Metric Temporal Logic (MTL) [15], which we call MTLKD, and interpret over discrete-time models; note that over the adopted discrete-time model, MTL is simply LTL, but with an exponentially succinct encoding [11]. MTLKD allows for the representation of the quantitative temporal evolution of epistemic states of the agents, as well as their correct and incorrect functioning behaviour. It can express multiple timing constraints on computations, which is really interesting for writing specifications. For example, MTLKD allows to express property asserting that whenever the system finds itself in a p-state, then agent c knows that the system will be in a q-state precisely one time unit later; note that this can be specified by the formula $G_{[0,\infty)}(p \Rightarrow K_c F_{[1,1]}q)$.

In our past research we have provided a theoretical underpinnings of a preliminary bounded model checking (BMC) algorithm for DIS and an existential part of a computation tree logic extended to include an epistemic and deontic modalities (ECTLKD) [29]. However, the method have not been implemented and experimentally evaluated. Moreover, it was not tailored to the DIISs settings, and it was not based on the state-of-the art BMC method for an existential part of a computation tree logic (ECTL) [32], which uses a reduced number of paths, what results in significantly smaller and less complicated propositional formulae that encode the ECTLKD properties. In [30] we have defined and experimentally evaluated a BMC algorithm for the existential part of an epistemic and deontic extension of real time CTL (RTCTLKD) [8] by means of which we can automatically verify not only epistemic and temporal properties but also deontic and quantitative temporal properties that express compliance of a MAS, modelled by DIIS, with respect to specifications.

The main contributions of the paper are as follows. First, we introduce the MTLKD language. Second, we propose a SAT-based BMC technique for DIISs and the existential part of MTLKD. This is the first time when the BMC method for linear time epistemic (and deontic) logics uses a reduced number of paths to evaluate epistemic and deontic components what results in significantly smaller and less complicated propositional formulae that encode the MTLKD properties. Third, we implement the proposed BMC method and evaluate it experimentally. To the best of our knowledge, this is the first work which provides a practical (bounded) model checking algorithm for the MTLKD language, and the MTL itself.

The structure of the paper is the following. In Section 2 we shortly introduce DIISs and the MTLKD language. In Section 3 we define a bounded semantics for EMTLKD (the existential part of MTLKD) and prove that there is a bound such that both bounded and unbounded semantics for EMTLKD are equivalent. In Section 4 we define a BMC method for MTLKD. In Section 5 we present performance evaluation of our newly developed SAT-based BMC algorithm. In Section 6 we conclude the paper.

2   Preliminaries

DIIS. We assume that a MAS consists of n agents, and by $Ag = \{1, \ldots, n\}$ we denote the non-empty set of agents; note that we do not consider the environment component because this may be added with no technical difficulty at the price of heavier notation. We assume that each agent $c \in Ag$ is in some particular local state at a given point in time, and that a set L_c of local states for agent $c \in Ag$ is non-empty and finite (this is required by the model checking algorithms). We assume that for each agent $c \in Ag$, its set L_c can be partitioned into *faultless (green)* and *faulty (red)* states. For n agents and n mutually disjoint and non-empty sets $\mathcal{G}_1, \ldots, \mathcal{G}_n$ we define the set S of all possible *global states* as the Cartesian product $\prod_{c=1}^{n} L_c$, such that $L_c \supseteq \mathcal{G}_c$. The set $\mathcal{G}_c$ represents the set of green states for agent c. The complement of $\mathcal{G}_c$ with respect to L_c (denoted by $\mathcal{R}_c$) represents the set of red states for agent c. Note that for any agent c, $L_c = \mathcal{G}_c \cup \mathcal{R}_c$. Further, by $l_c(s)$ we denote the local component of agent $c \in Ag$ in a global state $s = (\ell_1, \ldots, \ell_n)$.

With each agent $c \in Ag$ we associate a finite set of *possible actions* Act_c such that a special "null" action (ϵ_c) belongs to Act_c; as it will be clear below the local state of agent c remains the same, if the null action is performed. We do not assume that the sets Act_c (for all $c \in Ag$) are disjoint. Next, with each agent $c \in Ag$ we associate a protocol that defines rules, according to which actions may be performed in each local state. The protocol for agent $c \in Ag$ is a function $P_c : L_c \to 2^{Act_c}$ such that $\epsilon_c \in P_c(\ell)$ for any $\ell \in L_c$, i.e., we insist on the null action to be enabled at every local state. For each agent c, there is a (partial) evolution function $t_c : L_c \times Act_c \to L_c$ such that for each $\ell \in L_c$ and for each $a \in P_c(\ell)$ there exists $\ell' \in L_c$ such that $t_c(\ell, a) = \ell'$; moreover, $t_c(\ell, \epsilon_c) = l$ for each $\ell \in L_c$. Note that the local evolution function considered here differs from the standard one (see [10]) by having the local action instead of the join action as the parameter. Further, we define the following sets $Act = \bigcup_{c \in Ag} Act_c$ and $Agent(a) = \{c \in Ag \mid a \in Act_c\}$.

The *global interleaved evolution function* $t : S \times \prod_{i=1}^{n} Act_i \to S$ is defined as follows: $t(s, a_1, \ldots, a_n) = s'$ iff there exists an action $a \in Act \setminus \{\epsilon_1, \ldots, \epsilon_n\}$ such that for all $c \in Agent(a)$, $a_c = a$ and $t_c(l_c(s), a) = l_c(s')$, and for all $c \in Ag \setminus Agent(a)$, $a_c = \epsilon_c$ and $t_c(l_c(s), a_c) = l_c(s)$. In brief we write the above as $s \xrightarrow{a} s'$.

Note that similarly to blocking synchronisation in automata, the above insists on all agents performing the same non-null action in a global transition; additionally, note that if an agent has the action being performed in its repertoire, it must be performed, for the global transition to be allowed. This assumes that the local protocols are defined to permit this; if a local protocol does not allow it, then the local action cannot be performed and therefore the global transition does not comply with the definition of interleaving above. As we formally clarify below, we only consider interleaved transitions here.

Now, for a given set of agents Ag and a set of propositional variables $\mathcal{PV}$ we define a *deontic interleaved interpreted system* DIIS as a tuple $(\iota, \{L_c, \mathcal{G}_c, Act_c, P_c, t_c\}_{c \in Ag}, V)$, where $\iota \in S$ is an initial global state, and $V : S \to 2^{\mathcal{PV}}$ is a valuation function. With such a DIIS we associate a Kripke *model* $M = (\iota, S, T, \{\sim_c\}_{c \in Ag}, \{\bowtie_c\}_{c \in Ag}, V)$, where ι is the initial global state; S is the set of global states; $T \subseteq S \times S$ is a global transition (temporal) relation defined by: $(s, s') \in T$ iff there exists an action $a \in Act \setminus \{\epsilon_1, \ldots, \epsilon_n\}$ such that $s \xrightarrow{a} s'$ (we assume that the relation is total, i.e., for any $s \in S$ there exists an $a \in Act \setminus \{\epsilon_1, \ldots, \epsilon_n\}$ such that $s \xrightarrow{a} s'$ for some $s' \in S$); $\sim_c \subseteq S \times S$ is an indistinguishability relation for agent c defined by: $s \sim_c s'$ iff $l_c(s') = l_c(s)$; $\bowtie_c \subseteq S \times S$ is a deontic relation for agent c defined by: $s \bowtie_c s'$ iff $l_c(s') \in \mathcal{G}_c$; $V : S \to 2^{\mathcal{PV}}$ is the valuation function of DIIS. V assigns to each state a set of propositional variables that are assumed to be true at that state.

Syntax of MTLKD. Let $p \in \mathcal{PV}$, $c, d \in Ag$, $\Gamma \subseteq Ag$, and I be an interval in $\mathbb{N} = \{0, 1, 2, \ldots\}$ of the form: $[a, b)$ and $[a, \infty)$, for $a, b \in \mathbb{N}$ and $a \neq b$; note that the remaining forms of intervals (i.e., $[a, a]$, $[a, b]$, (a, b), $(a, b]$, and (a, ∞)) can be defined by means of $[a, b)$ and $[a, \infty)$. Hereafter, let $left(I)$ denote the left end of the interval I (i.e., $left(I) = a$), and $right(I)$ the right end of the interval I (i.e., $right([a, b)) = b - 1$ and $right([a, \infty)) = \infty$). The MTLKD formulae are defined by the following grammar:

$$\alpha := \textbf{true} \mid \textbf{false} \mid p \mid \neg\alpha \mid \alpha \wedge \alpha \mid \alpha \vee \alpha \mid X\alpha \mid \alpha U_I \alpha \mid$$
$$G_I\alpha \mid \overline{K}_c\alpha \mid \overline{D}_\Gamma\alpha \mid \overline{E}_\Gamma\alpha \mid \overline{C}_\Gamma\alpha \mid \overline{\mathcal{O}}_c\alpha \mid \widehat{\underline{K}}_c^d\alpha$$

The derived basic modalities are defined as follows: $\alpha R_I \beta \overset{def}{=} \beta U_I(\alpha \wedge \beta) \vee G_I\beta$, $F_I\alpha \overset{def}{=} \textbf{true}U_I\alpha$, $\mathcal{O}_c\alpha \overset{def}{=} \neg\overline{\mathcal{O}}_c\neg\alpha$, $K_c\alpha \overset{def}{=} \neg\overline{K}_c\neg\alpha$, $\widehat{K}_c^d\alpha \overset{def}{=} \neg\widehat{\underline{K}}_c^d\neg\alpha$, $D_\Gamma\alpha \overset{def}{=} \neg\overline{D}_\Gamma\neg\alpha$, $E_\Gamma\alpha \overset{def}{=} \neg\overline{E}_\Gamma\neg\alpha$, $C_\Gamma\alpha \overset{def}{=} \neg\overline{C}_\Gamma\neg\alpha$, where $c, d \in \mathcal{AG}$, and $\Gamma \subseteq \mathcal{AG}$.

Intuitively, X, U_I and G_I are the operators, respectively, for "neXt time", "bounded until", and "bounded always". $X\alpha$ is true in a computation if α is true at the second state of the computation, $\alpha U_I \beta$ is true in a computation if β is true in the interval I at least in one state and always earlier α holds, and $G_I\alpha$ is true in a computation if α is true at all the states of the computation that are in the interval I. $\overline{K}_c$ is the operator dual for the standard epistemic modality K_c ("agent c knows"), so $\overline{K}_c\alpha$ is read as "agent c does not know whether or not α holds". Similarly, the modalities $\overline{D}_\Gamma, \overline{E}_\Gamma, \overline{C}_\Gamma$ are the dual operators for $D_\Gamma, E_\Gamma, C_\Gamma$ representing distributed knowledge in the group Γ, everyone in Γ knows, and common knowledge among agents in Γ. Further, we use the (double) indexed modal operators $\mathcal{O}_c$, $\overline{\mathcal{O}}_c$, $\widehat{K}_c^d$ and $\widehat{\underline{K}}_c^d$ to represent the *correctly functioning circumstances of agent* c. The formula $\mathcal{O}_c\alpha$ stands for "for all the states where agent c is functioning correctly, α holds". The formula $\overline{\mathcal{O}}_c\alpha$ can be read as "there is a state where agent c is functioning correctly, and in which α holds". The formula $\widehat{K}_c^d\alpha$ is read as "agent c knows that α under the assumption that agent d is functioning correctly". $\widehat{\underline{K}}_c^d$ is the operator dual for the modality $\widehat{K}_c^d$. We refer to [18] for a discussion of this notion; note that the operator $\overline{\mathcal{O}}_c$ is there referred to as $\mathcal{P}_c$.

The existential fragment of MTLKD (denoted by EMTLKD) is defined by the following grammar:

$$\alpha := \textbf{true} \mid \textbf{false} \mid p \mid \neg p \mid \alpha \wedge \alpha \mid \alpha \vee \alpha \mid X\alpha \mid \alpha U_I \alpha \mid$$
$$G_I \alpha \mid \overline{K}_c \alpha \mid \overline{D}_\Gamma \alpha \mid \overline{E}_\Gamma \alpha \mid \overline{C}_\Gamma \alpha \mid \overline{O}_c \alpha \mid \widehat{K}_c^d \alpha$$

Semantics of MTLKD. Let $M = (\iota, S, T, \{\sim_c\}_{c \in Ag}, \{\bowtie_c\}_{c \in Ag}, \mathcal{V})$ be a model for DIIS. A *path* in M is an infinite sequence $\pi = (s_0, s_1, \ldots)$ of states such that $(s_m, s_{m+1}) \in T$ for each $m \in \mathbb{N}$. For a path π and $m \in \mathbb{N}$, we take $\pi(m) = s_m$. Moreover, the m-th suffix of the path π is defined in the standard way: $\pi^m = (s_m, s_{m+1}, \ldots)$, and the m-th prefix of π is also defined in the standard way: $\pi[..m] = (s_0, s_1, \ldots, s_m)$. By $\Pi(s)$ we denote the set of all the paths starting at $s \in S$. For the group epistemic modalities we define the following. If $\Gamma \subseteq Ag$, then $\sim_\Gamma^E \overset{def}{=} \bigcup_{c \in \Gamma} \sim_c$, $\sim_\Gamma^C \overset{def}{=} (\sim_\Gamma^E)^+$ (the transitive closure of $\sim_\Gamma^E$), and $\sim_\Gamma^D \overset{def}{=} \bigcap_{c \in \Gamma} \sim_c$. Given the above, the semantics of MTLKD is the following.

Definition 1. *Let I be an interval in $\mathbb{N}$ of the form: $[a, b)$ or $[a, \infty)$ for $a, b \in \mathbb{N}$, and $m \in \mathbb{N}$. Then, $I + m \overset{df}{=} [a + m, b + m)$ if $I = [a, b)$, and $I + m \overset{df}{=} [a + m, \infty)$ if $I = [a, \infty)$. A MTLKD formula φ is true (valid) along the path π (in symbols $M, \pi \models \varphi$) iff $M, \pi^0 \models \varphi$, where*

$M, \pi^m \models \textbf{true}, \quad M, \pi^m \not\models \textbf{false},$

$M, \pi^m \models p$ *iff* $p \in \mathcal{V}(\pi(m)), \quad M, \pi^m \models \neg \alpha$ *iff* $M, \pi^m \not\models \alpha,$

$M, \pi^m \models \alpha \wedge \beta$ *iff* $M, \pi^m \models \alpha$ *and* $M, \pi^m \models \beta,$

$M, \pi^m \models \alpha \vee \beta$ *iff* $M, \pi^m \models \alpha$ *or* $M, \pi^m \models \beta,$

$M, \pi^m \models X\alpha$ *iff* $M, \pi^{m+1} \models \alpha,$

$M, \pi^m \models \alpha U_I \beta$ *iff* $(\exists i \geqslant m)[i \in I + m$ *and* $M, \pi^i \models \beta$ *and* $(\forall m \leqslant j < i) M, \pi^j \models \alpha],$

$M, \pi^m \models G_I \alpha$ *iff* $(\forall i \in I + m)[M, \pi^i \models \alpha],$

$M, \pi^m \models \overline{K}_c \alpha$ *iff* $(\exists \pi' \in \Pi(\iota))(\exists i \geqslant 0)[\pi(m) \sim_c \pi'(i)$ *and* $M, \pi'^i \models \alpha],$

$M, \pi^m \models \overline{O}_c \alpha$ *iff* $(\exists \pi' \in \Pi(\iota))(\exists i \geqslant 0)[\pi(m) \bowtie_c \pi'(i)$ *and* $M, \pi'^i \models \alpha],$

$M, \pi^m \models \widehat{K}_c^d \alpha$ *iff* $(\exists \pi' \in \Pi(\iota))(\exists i \geqslant 0)[\pi(m) \sim_c \pi'(i)$ *and* $\pi(m) \bowtie_d \pi'(i)$ *and* $M, \pi'^i \models \alpha],$

$M, \pi^m \models \overline{Y}_\Gamma \alpha$ *iff* $(\exists \pi' \in \Pi(\iota))(\exists i \geqslant 0)[\pi(m) \sim_\Gamma^Y \pi'(i)$ *and* $M, \pi'^i \models \alpha],$
    where $Y \in \{D, E, C\}.$

A MTLKD formula φ holds in the model M (denoted $M \models \varphi$) iff $M, \pi \models \varphi$ for all the paths $\pi \in \Pi(\iota)$. An EMTLKD formula φ holds in the model M, denoted $M \models^\exists \varphi$, iff $M, \pi \models \varphi$ for some path $\pi \in \Pi(\iota)$. The *existential model checking problem* asks whether $M \models^\exists \varphi$.

3   Bounded Semantics for EMTLKD

The proposed bounded semantics is the backbone of the SAT-based BMC method for EMTLKD, which is presented in the next section. The temporal part of this semantics is based on the bounded semantics presented in [28,33]. As usual, we start by defining k-*paths* and *loops*.

Let $M = (\iota, S, T, \{\sim_c\}_{c \in Ag}, \{\bowtie_c\}_{c \in Ag}, \mathcal{V})$ be a model for DIIS, $k \in \mathbb{N}$, and $0 \leqslant l \leqslant k$. A k-*path* π_l is a pair (π, l), where π is a finite sequence $\pi = (s_0, \ldots, s_k)$ of states such that $(s_j, s_{j+1}) \in T$ for each $0 \leqslant j < k$. A k-path π_l is a *loop* if $l < k$ and $\pi(k) = \pi(l)$. Note that if a k-path π_l is a loop, then it represents the infinite path of the form uv^ω, where $u = (\pi(0), \dots, \pi(l))$ and $v = (\pi(l+1), \dots, \pi(k))$. We denote this unique path by $\varrho(\pi_l)$. Note that for each $j \in \mathbb{N}$, $\varrho(\pi_l)^{l+j} = \varrho(\pi_l)^{k+j}$. By $\Pi_k(s)$ we denote the set of all the k-paths starting at s in M.

Let $k \in \mathbb{N}$ be a bound, $0 \leqslant m \leqslant k$, $0 \leqslant l \leqslant k$, and φ an EMTLKD formula. As in the definition of semantics we need to define the satisfiability relation on suffixes of k-paths, we denote by π_l^m the pair (π_l, m), i.e., the k-path π_l together with the designated starting point m. Further, $M, \pi_l^m \models_k \varphi$ denotes that the formula φ is k-true along the suffix $(\pi(m), \dots, \pi(k))$ of π.

Definition 2. *An EMTLKD formula φ is k-true along the k-path π_l (in symbols $M, \pi_l \models_k \varphi$) iff $M, \pi_l^0 \models_k \varphi$, where*

$M, \pi_l^m \models_k$ **true**, $M, \pi_l^m \not\models_k$ **false**,

$M, \pi_l^m \models_k p$ *iff* $p \in \mathcal{V}(\pi(m))$, $M, \pi_l^m \models_k \neg p$ *iff* $p \notin \mathcal{V}(\pi(m))$,

$M, \pi_l^m \models_k \alpha \wedge \beta$ *iff* $M, \pi_l^m \models_k \alpha$ *and* $M, \pi_l^m \models_k \beta$,

$M, \pi_l^m \models_k \alpha \vee \beta$ *iff* $M, \pi_l^m \models_k \alpha$ *or* $M, \pi_l^m \models_k \beta$,

$M, \pi_l^m \models_k \mathrm{X}\alpha$ *iff* $(m < k$ *and* $M, \pi_l^{m+1} \models_k \alpha)$ *or*
$\qquad\qquad\qquad (m = k$ *and* $l < k$ *and* $\pi(k) = \pi(l)$ *and* $M, \pi_l^{l+1} \models_k \alpha)$,

$M, \pi_l^m \models_k \alpha \mathrm{U}_I \beta$ *iff* $(\exists m \leqslant j \leqslant k)(j \in I+m$ *and* $M, \pi_l^j \models_k \beta$ *and* $(\forall m \leqslant i < j)$
$\qquad\qquad\qquad M, \pi_l^i \models_k \alpha)$ *or* $(l < m$ *and* $\pi(k) = \pi(l)$ *and* $(\exists l < j < m)$
$\qquad\qquad\qquad (j+k-l \in I+m$ *and* $M, \pi_l^j \models_k \beta$ *and* $(\forall l < i < j)M, \pi_l^i \models \alpha$
$\qquad\qquad\qquad$ *and* $(\forall m \leqslant i \leqslant k)M, \pi_l^i \models_k \alpha))$,

$M, \pi_l^m \models_k \mathrm{G}_I \alpha$ *iff* $(k \geqslant right(I+m)$ *and* $(\forall j \in I + m)\,(M, \pi_l^j \models_k \alpha))$ *or*
$\qquad\qquad\qquad (k < right(I+m)$ *and* $\pi(k) = \pi(l)$ *and* $(\forall max \leqslant j < k)$
$\qquad\qquad\qquad M, \pi_l^j \models_k \alpha$ *and* $(\forall l \leqslant j < max)\,(j + k - l \in I + m$ *implies*
$\qquad\qquad\qquad M, \pi_l^j \models_k \alpha))$, *where* $max = max(left(I + m), m)$,

$M, \pi_l^m \models_k \overline{\mathrm{K}}_c \alpha$ *iff* $(\exists \pi'_{l'} \in \Pi_k(\iota))(\exists 0 \leqslant j \leqslant k)\,(M, \pi'_{l'}{}^{j} \models_k \alpha$ *and* $\pi(m) \sim_c \pi'(j))$,

$M, \pi_l^m \models_k \overline{\mathrm{Y}}_\Gamma \alpha$ *iff* $(\exists \pi'_{l'} \in \Pi_k(\iota))\,(\exists 0 \leqslant j \leqslant k)\,(M, \pi'_{l'}{}^{j} \models_k \alpha$ *and* $\pi(m) \sim_\Gamma^Y \pi'(j))$,

$M, \pi_l^m \models_k \overline{\mathrm{O}}_c \alpha$ *iff* $(\exists \pi'_{l'} \in \Pi_k(\iota))\,(\exists 0 \leqslant j \leqslant k)\,(M, \pi'_{l'}{}^{j} \models_k \alpha$ *and* $\pi(m) \bowtie_c \pi'(j))$,

$M, \pi_l^m \models_k \widehat{\underline{\mathrm{K}}}_c^d \alpha$ *iff* $(\exists \pi'_{l'} \in \Pi_k(\iota))\,(\exists 0 \leqslant j \leqslant k)\,(M, \pi'_{l'}{}^{j} \models_k \alpha$ *and* $\pi(m) \sim_c \pi'(j)$
$\qquad\qquad\qquad$ *and* $\pi(m) \bowtie_d \pi'(j))$.

Let M be a model, and φ an EMTLKD formula. We use the following notations: $M \models_k^\exists$ φ iff $M, \pi_l \models_k \varphi$ for some $\pi_l \in \Pi_k(\iota)$. The *bounded model checking problem* asks whether there exists $k \in \mathbb{N}$ such that $M \models_k^\exists \varphi$.

Equivalence of the Bounded and Unbounded Semantics. Now, we show that for some particular bound the bounded and unbounded semantics are equivalent.

Lemma 1. *Let M be a model, φ an EMTLKD formula, $k \geqslant 0$ a bound, π_l a k-path in M, and $0 \leqslant m \leqslant k$. Then, $M, \pi_l^m \models_k \varphi$ implies*
1. if π_l is not a loop, then $M, \rho^m \models \varphi$ for each path $\rho \in M$ such that $\rho[..k] = \pi$.
2. if π_l is a loop, then $M, \varrho(\pi_l)^m \models \varphi$.

Proof. (Induction on the length of φ) The lemma follows directly for the propositional variables and their negations. Assume that $M, \pi_l^m \models_k \varphi$ and consider the following cases:

1. $\varphi = \alpha \wedge \beta \mid \alpha \vee \beta \mid X\alpha$. See the proof of Lemma 2.1 of [33].

2. $\varphi = \alpha U_I \beta$. Assume that π_l is not a loop. Then $(\exists m \leqslant j \leqslant k)(j \in I + m$ and $M, \pi_l^j \models_k \beta$ and $(\forall m \leqslant i < j)(M, \pi_l^i \models_k \alpha))$. By inductive hypothesis, for every path ρ in M such that $\rho[..k] = \pi$, $(\exists m \leqslant j \leqslant k)(j \in I + m$ and $M, \rho^j \models \beta$ and $(\forall m \leqslant i < j)M, \rho^i \models \alpha)$. Thus, for every path ρ in M such that $\rho[..k] = \pi$, $M, \rho^m \models \varphi$.

   Now assume that π_l is a loop. Then $l < m$ and $\pi(k) = \pi(l)$ and $(\exists l < j < m)$ $(j+k-l \in I+m$ and $M, \pi_l^j \models_k \beta$ and $(\forall l < i < j)M, \pi_l^i \models \alpha$ and $(\forall m \leqslant i \leqslant k)$ $M, \pi_l^i \models_k \alpha)$. By inductive hypothesis, $(\exists l < j < m)(j + k - l \in I + m$ and $M, \varrho(\pi_l)^j \models \beta$ and $(\forall l < i < j)$ $M, \varrho(\pi_l)^i \models \alpha$ and $(\forall m \leqslant i \leqslant k)$ $M, \varrho(\pi_l)^i \models \alpha)$. Since for each $n \in \mathbb{N}$, $\varrho(\pi_l)^{l+n} = \varrho(\pi_l)^{k+n}$, it follows that $M, \varrho(\pi_l)^{j+k-l} \models \beta$ and $(\forall k < i < j+k-l)$ $(M, \varrho(\pi_l)^i \models \alpha)$ and $(\forall m \leqslant i \leqslant k)$ $(M, \varrho(\pi_l)^i \models \alpha)$. Hence, $\varrho(\pi_l)^{j+k-l} \models \beta$ and $(\forall m \leqslant i < j + k - l)$ $(M, \varrho(\pi_l)^i \models \alpha)$. Thus, $M, \varrho(\pi_l)^m \models \varphi$.

3. $\varphi = G_I \alpha$. Assume that π_l is not a loop. Then $k \geq right(I+m)$ and $(\forall j \in I + m)$ $(M, \pi_l^j \models_k \alpha)$. By inductive hypothesis, for every path ρ in M such that $\rho[..k] = \pi$, $(\forall j \in I + m)(M, \rho^j \models \alpha)$. Thus, for every path ρ in M such that $\rho[..k] = \pi$, $M, \rho^m \models \varphi$.

   Now assume that π_l is a loop, and $max = max(left(I + m), m)$. Then, $k < right(I + m)$ and $\pi(k) = \pi(l)$ and $(\forall max \leqslant j < k)$ $M, \pi_l^j \models_k \alpha$ and $(\forall l \leqslant j < max)$ $(j + k - l \in I + m$ implies $M, \pi_l^j \models_k \alpha)$. By inductive hypothesis, $(\forall max \leqslant j < k)$ $M, \varrho(\pi_l)^j \models \alpha$ and $(\forall l \leqslant j < max)$ $(j + k - l \in I + m$ implies $M, \varrho(\pi_l)^j \models \alpha)$. Since for each $n \in \mathbb{N}$, $\varrho(\pi_l)^{l+n} = \varrho(\pi_l)^{k+n}$, it follows that $(\forall n \in \mathbb{N})$ $(\forall j \geqslant l + n)$ $(j + k - l \in I + m$ implies $M, \varrho(\pi_l)^j \models \alpha)$. Thus, $M, \varrho(\pi_l)^m \models \varphi$.

4. $\varphi = \overline{K}_c \alpha$. From $M, \pi_l^m \models_k \varphi$ it follows that $(\exists \pi_{l'}' \in \Pi_k(\iota))(\exists 0 \leqslant j \leqslant k)$ $(M, \pi_{l'}'^j \models_k \alpha$ and $\pi(m) \sim_c \pi'(j))$. Assume that both π_l and $\pi_{l'}'$ are not loops. By inductive hypothesis, for every path ρ' in M such that $\rho'[..k] = \pi'$, $(\exists 0 \leqslant j \leqslant k)$ $(M, \rho'^j \models \alpha$ and $\pi(m) \sim_c \rho'(j))$. Further, for every path ρ in M such that $\rho[..k] = \pi$, we have that $\rho(m) \sim_c \rho'(j))$. Thus, for every path ρ in M such that $\rho[..k] = \pi$, $M, \rho^m \models \varphi$.

   Now assume that $\pi_{l'}'$ is not a loop, and π_l is a loop. By inductive hypothesis, for every path ρ' in M such that $\rho'[..k] = \pi'$, $(\exists 0 \leqslant j \leqslant k)(M, \rho'^j \models \alpha$ and $\pi(m) \sim_c \rho'(j))$. Further, observe that $\varrho(\pi_l)(m) = \pi(m)$, thus $M, \varrho(\pi_l)^m \models \varphi$.

   Now assume that both π_l and $\pi_{l'}'$ are loops. By inductive hypothesis, $(\exists 0 \leqslant j \leqslant k)$ $(M, \varrho(\pi_{l'}')^j \models \alpha$ and $\pi(m) \sim_c \varrho(\pi_{l'}')(j))$. Further, observe that $\varrho(\pi_l)(m) = \pi(m)$, thus $M, \varrho(\pi_l)^m \models \varphi$.

   Now assume that $\pi_{l'}'$ is a loop, and π_l is not a loop. By inductive hypothesis, $(\exists 0 \leqslant j \leqslant k)$ $(M, \varrho(\pi_{l'}')^j \models \alpha$ and $\pi(m) \sim_c \varrho(\pi_{l'}')(j))$. Further, for every path ρ in M such that $\rho[..k] = \pi$, we have that $\rho(m) \sim_c \varrho(\pi_{l'}')(j))$. Thus, for every path ρ in M such that $\rho[..k] = \pi$, $M, \rho^m \models \varphi$.

5. Let $\varphi = \overline{Y}_\Gamma \alpha$, where $Y \in \{D, E, C\}$, or $\varphi = \overline{\mathcal{O}}_c \alpha$, or $\varphi = \widehat{\underline{K}}_c^d \alpha$. These cases can be proven analogously to the case 4.

Lemma 2. (Theorem 3.1 of [4]) *Let M be a model, α an LTL formula, and π a path. Then, the following implication holds: $M, \pi \models \alpha$ implies that for some $k \geqslant 0$ and $0 \leqslant l \leqslant k$, $M, \rho_l \models_k \alpha$ with $\pi[..k] = \rho$.*

Since MTL is simply LTL with an exponentially succinct encoding ([11]), every MTL formula γ can be translated into an LTL formula α_γ. Thus, by Lemma 2 we have that the following lemma holds:

Lemma 3. *Let M be a model, α an MTL formula, and π a path. Then, the following implication holds: $M, \pi \models \alpha$ implies that for some $k \geqslant 0$ and $0 \leqslant l \leqslant k$, $M, \rho_l \models_k \alpha$ with $\pi[..k] = \rho$.*

Lemma 4. *Let M be a model, α an MTL formula, $Y \in \{\overline{K}_c, \overline{D}_\Gamma, \overline{E}_\Gamma, \overline{C}_\Gamma, \overline{O}_c, \widehat{\overline{K}}_c^d\}$, and π a path. Then, the following implication holds: $M, \pi \models Y\alpha$ implies that for some $k \geqslant 0$ and $0 \leqslant l \leqslant k$, $M, \rho_l \models_k Y\alpha$ with $\pi[..k] = \rho$.*

Proof. Let X^j denote the neXt time operator applied j times, i.e., $X^j = \underbrace{X \ldots X}$.

1. Let $Y = \overline{K}_c$. Then $M, \pi \models \overline{K}_c\alpha$ iff $M, \pi^0 \models \overline{K}_c\alpha$ iff $(\exists \pi' \in \Pi(\iota))$ $(\exists j \geqslant 0)[\pi'(j) \sim_c \pi(0)$ and $M, \pi'^j \models \alpha]$. Since $\pi'(j)$ is reachable from the initial state of M, the checking of $M, \pi'^j \models \alpha$ is equivalent to the checking of $M, \pi'^0 \models X^j\alpha$. Now since $X^j\alpha$ is a pure MTL formula, by Lemma 3 we have that for some $k \geqslant 0$ and $0 \leqslant l \leqslant k$, $M, \rho'^0_l \models_k X^j\alpha$ with $\pi'[..k] = \rho'$. This implies that $M, \rho'^j_l \models_k \alpha$ with $\pi'[..k] = \rho'$, for some $k \geqslant 0$ and $0 \leqslant l \leqslant k$. Now, since $\pi'(j) \sim_c \pi(0)$, we have $\rho'(j) \sim_c \rho(0)$. Thus, by the bounded semantics we have that for some $k \geqslant 0$ and $0 \leqslant l \leqslant k$, $M, \rho_l \models_k \overline{K}_c\alpha$ with $\pi[..k] = \rho$.

2. Let $Y = \overline{D}_\Gamma$. Then $M, \pi \models \overline{D}_\Gamma\alpha$ iff $M, \pi^0 \models \overline{D}_\Gamma\alpha$ iff $(\exists \pi' \in \Pi(\iota))(\exists j \geqslant 0)[\pi'(j) \sim_\Gamma^D \pi(0)$ and $M, \pi'^j \models \alpha]$. Since $\pi'(j)$ is reachable from the initial state of M, the checking of $M, \pi'^j \models \alpha$ is equivalent to the checking of $M, \pi'^0 \models X^j\alpha$. Now since $X^j\alpha$ is a pure MTL formula, by Lemma 3 we have that for some $k \geqslant 0$ and $0 \leqslant l \leqslant k$, $M, \rho'^0_l \models_k X^j\alpha$ with $\pi'[..k] = \rho'$. This implies that $M, \rho'^j_l \models_k \alpha$ with $\pi'[..k] = \rho'$, for some $k \geqslant 0$ and $0 \leqslant l \leqslant k$. Now, since $\pi'(j) \sim_\Gamma^D \pi(0)$, we have $\rho'(j) \sim_\Gamma^D \rho(0)$. Thus, by the bounded semantics we have that for some $k \geqslant 0$ and $0 \leqslant l \leqslant k$, $M, \rho_l \models_k \overline{D}_\Gamma\alpha$ with $\pi[..k] = \rho$.

3. Let $Y = \overline{E}_\Gamma$. Since $\overline{E}_\Gamma\alpha = \bigvee_{c \in \Gamma} \overline{K}_c\alpha$, the lemma follows from the case 1.

4. Let $Y = \overline{C}_\Gamma$. Since $\overline{C}_\Gamma\alpha = \bigvee_{i=1}^n (\overline{E}_\Gamma)^i\alpha$, where n is the size of the model M, the lemma follows from the case 3.

5. Let $Y = \overline{O}_c$. Then $M, \pi \models \overline{O}_c\alpha$ iff $M, \pi^0 \models \overline{O}_c\alpha$ iff $(\exists \pi' \in \Pi(\iota))$ $(\exists j \geqslant 0)[\pi(0) \bowtie_c \pi'(j)$ and $M, \pi'^j \models \alpha]$. Since $\pi'(j)$ is reachable from the initial state of M, the checking of $M, \pi'^j \models \alpha$ is equivalent to the checking of $M, \pi'^0 \models X^j\alpha$. Now since $X^j\alpha$ is a pure MTL formula, by Lemma 3 we have that for some $k \geqslant 0$ and $0 \leqslant l \leqslant k$, $M, \rho'^0_l \models_k X^j\alpha$ with $\pi'[..k] = \rho'$. This implies that $M, \rho'^j_l \models_k \alpha$ with $\pi'[..k] = \rho'$, for some $k \geqslant 0$ and $0 \leqslant l \leqslant k$. Now, since $\pi(0) \bowtie_c \pi'(j)$, we have $\rho(0) \bowtie_c \rho'(j)$ Thus, by the bounded semantics we have that for some $k \geqslant 0$ and $0 \leqslant l \leqslant k$, $M, \rho_l \models_k \overline{O}_c\alpha$ with $\pi[..k] = \rho$.

6. Let $Y = \widehat{\overline{K}}_c^d$. This case can be proven analogously to the case 1 and 5.

Lemma 5. *Let M be a model, φ an* EMTLKD *formula, and π a path. The following implication holds: $M, \pi \models \varphi$ implies that there exists $k \geqslant 0$ and $0 \leqslant l \leqslant k$ such that $M, \rho_l \models_k \varphi$ with $\rho[.\,.\,k] = \pi$.*

Proof. (Induction on the length of φ) The lemma follows directly for the propositional variables and their negations. Assume that the hypothesis holds for all the proper sub-formulas of φ and consider φ to be of the following form:

1. $\varphi = \psi_1 \vee \psi_2 \mid \psi_1 \wedge \psi_2 \mid X\psi \mid \psi_1 U_I \psi_2 \mid G_I \psi$. Straightforward by the induction hypothesis and Lemma 3.

2. Let $\varphi = Y\alpha$, and $Y, Y_1, \ldots, Y_n, Z \in \{\overline{K}_c, \overline{D}_\Gamma, \overline{E}_\Gamma, \overline{C}_\Gamma, \overline{O}_c, \widehat{K}_c^d\}$. Moreover, let $Y_1\alpha_1, \ldots, Y_n\alpha_n$ be the list of all "top level" proper Y-subformulas of α (i.e., each $Y_i\alpha_i$ is a subformula of $Y\alpha$, but it is not a subformula of any subformula $Z\beta$ of $Y\alpha$, where $Z\beta$ is different from $Y\alpha$ and from $Y\alpha_i$ for $i = 1, \ldots, n$).

   If this list is empty, then α is a "pure" MTL formula with no nested epistemic modal-ities. Hence, by Lemma 4 we have $M, \pi \models \varphi$ implies that there exists $k \geqslant 0$ and $0 \leqslant l \leqslant k$ such that $M, \rho_l \models_k \varphi$ with $\rho[.\,.\,k] = \pi$.

   Otherwise, introduce for each $Y_i\alpha_i$ a new proposition q_i, where $i = 1, \ldots, n$. Using first a translation of MTL formulae to LTL formulae, and then a symbolic state labelling algorithm presented in [7] (for LTL modalities) and [26] (for epistemic and deontic modalities), we can augment with q_i the labelling of each state s of M initialising some run along which the epistemic formula $Y_i\alpha_i$ holds, and then translate the formula α to the formula α', which instead of each subformula $Y_i\alpha_i$ contains adequate propositions q_i. Therefore, we obtain "pure" LTL formula. Hence, by Lemma 4 we have $M, \pi \models \varphi$ implies that there exists $k \geqslant 0$ and $0 \leqslant l \leqslant k$ such that $M, \rho_l \models_k \varphi$ with $\rho[.\,.\,k] = \pi$.

The following theorem, whose proof follows directly from Lemma 1 and Lemma 5, states that for a given model and an EMTLKD formula there exists a bound k such that the model checking problem ($M \models^\exists \varphi$) can be reduced to the bounded model checking problem ($M \models_k^\exists \varphi$).

Theorem 1. *Let M be a model and φ an* EMTLKD *formula. Then, the following equiv-alence holds: $M \models^\exists \varphi$ iff there exists $k \geqslant 0$ such that $M \models_k^\exists \varphi$.*

Further, by straightforward induction on the length of an EMTLKD formula φ, we can show that φ is k-true in M if and only if φ is k-true in M with a number of k-paths reduced to $f_k(\varphi)$, where the function $f_k : \text{EMTLKD} \to \mathbb{N}$ gives a bound on the number of k-paths, which are sufficient to validate a given EMTLKD formula.

In the definition of f_k we assume that each EMTLKD formula is preceded by the "path" quantifier E with the meaning "there exists a path in $\Pi_k(\iota)$"; this assumption is only technical and it makes the definition of f_k easy to implement. Note that in the BMC method we deal with the existential validity ($\models^\exists$) only, so the above assumption is just another way to express this fact. More precisely, let φ be an EMTLKD formula. To calculate the value of $f_k(\varphi)$, we first extend the formula φ to the formula $\varphi' = E\varphi$. Next, we calculate the value of f_k for φ' in the following way: $f_k(E\varphi) = f_k(\varphi) + 1$; $f_k(\textbf{true}) = f_k(\textbf{false}) = 0$; $f_k(p) = f_k(\neg p) = 0$ for $p \in \mathcal{PV}$; $f_k(\alpha \wedge \beta) = f_k(\alpha) + f_k(\beta)$; $f_k(\alpha \vee \beta) = max\{f_k(\alpha), f_k(\beta)\}$; $f_k(X\alpha) = f_k(\alpha)$; $f_k(\alpha U_I \beta) = k \cdot f_k(\alpha) +$

$f_k(\beta)$; $f_k(\mathrm{G}_I\alpha) = (k+1) \cdot f_k(\alpha)$; $f_k(\overline{\mathrm{C}}_\Gamma\alpha) = f_k(\alpha) + k$; $f_k(Y\alpha) = f_k(\alpha) + 1$ for $Y \in \{\overline{\mathrm{K}}_c, \overline{\mathrm{O}}_c, \widehat{\underline{\mathrm{K}}}_c^d, \overline{\mathrm{D}}_\Gamma, \overline{\mathrm{E}}_\Gamma\}$.

4   SAT-Based BMC for EMTLKD

Let $M = (\iota, S, T, \{\sim_c\}_{c\in Ag}, \{\bowtie_c\}_{c\in Ag}, \mathcal{V})$ be a model, φ an EMTLKD formula, and $k \geqslant 0$ a bound. The proposed BMC method is based on the BMC encoding presented in [33], and it consists in translating the problem of checking whether $M \models_k^\exists \varphi$ holds, to the problem of checking the satisfiability of the propositional formula

$$[M, \varphi]_k := [M^{\varphi,\iota}]_k \land [\varphi]_{M,k}$$

The formula $[M^{\varphi,\iota}]_k$ encodes sets of k-paths of M, whose size equals to $f_k(\varphi)$, and in which at least one path starts at the initial state of the model M. The formula $[\varphi]_{M,k}$ encodes a number of constraints that must be satisfied on these sets of k-paths for φ to be satisfied. Note that our translation, like the translation from [33], does not require that either all the k-paths used in the translation are loops or none is a loop. Once this translation is defined, checking satisfiability of an EMTLKD formula can be done by means of a SAT-solver.

In order to define the formula $[M, \varphi]_k$ we proceed as follows. We begin with an encoding of states of the given model M. Since the set of states of M is finite, each state s of M can be encoded by a bit-vector, whose length r depends on the number of agents' local states. Thus, each state s of M can be represented by a vector $w = (\mathrm{w}_1, \ldots, \mathrm{w}_r)$ (called a *symbolic state*) of propositional variables (called *state variables*). The set of all the propositional state variables we denote by SV.

Since any k-path (π, l) is a pair consisting of a finite sequence of states of length k and a number $l \leqslant k$, to encode it by propositional formula, it suffices to take a finite sequence of symbolic states of length k and a formula that encodes the position $l \leqslant k$. The designated position l can be encoded as a bit vector of the length $t = max(1, \lceil log_2(k+1)\rceil)$. Thus, the position l can be represented by a valuation of a vector $u = (\mathrm{u}_1, \ldots, \mathrm{u}_t)$ (called a *symbolic number*) of propositional variables (called *propositional natural variables*), which not appear among propositional state variables. The set of all the propositional natural variables we denote by NV, and we assume that $SV \cap NV = \emptyset$. Given the above we can define a *symbolic k-path* as a pair $((w_0, \ldots, w_k), u)$ consisting of a finite sequence of symbolic states of length k and a symbolic number. Since in general we may need to consider more than one symbolic k-path, therefore we introduce a notion of the j-th symbolic k-path $\pi_j = ((w_{0,j}, \ldots, w_{k,j}), u_j)$, where $w_{i,j}$ are symbolic states for $0 \leqslant j < f_k(\varphi)$ and $0 \leqslant i \leqslant k$, and u_j is a symbolic number for $0 \leqslant j < f_k(\varphi)$. Note that the exact number of symbolic k-paths depends on the checked formula φ, and it can be calculated by means of the function f_k.

Let $PV = SV \cup NV$, and $V : PV \to \{0, 1\}$ be a *valuation of propositional variables* (a *valuation* for short). Each valuation induces the functions $\mathbf{S} : SV^r \to \{0, 1\}^r$ and $\mathbf{J} : NV^t \to \mathbb{N}$ defined in the following way: $\mathbf{S}((\mathrm{w}_1, \ldots, \mathrm{w}_r)) = (V(\mathrm{w}_1), \ldots, V(\mathrm{w}_r))$, $\mathbf{J}((\mathrm{u}_1, \ldots, \mathrm{u}_t)) = \sum_{i=1}^{t} V(\mathrm{u}_i) \cdot 2^{i-1}$. Moreover, for a symbolic state w and a symbolic number u, by $SV(w)$ and $NV(u)$ we denote, respectively, the set of all the state variables occurring in w, and the set of all the natural variables occurring in u.

Next, let w and w' be two symbolic states such that $SV(w) \cap SV(w') = \emptyset$, and u be a symbolic number. We define the following auxiliary propositional formulae:

- $I_s(w)$ is a formula over $SV(w)$ that is true for a valuation V iff $\mathbf{S}(w) = s$.
- $p(w)$ is a formula over $SV(w)$ that is true for a valuation V iff $p \in V(\mathbf{S}(w))$ (encodes a set of states of M in which $p \in \mathcal{PV}$ holds).
- $H(w, w')$ is a formula over $SV(w) \cup SV(w')$ that is true for a valuation V iff $\mathbf{S}(w) = \mathbf{S}(w')$ (encodes equality of two global states).
- $H_c(w, w')$ is a formula over $SV(w) \cup SV(w')$ that is true for a valuation V iff $l_c(\mathbf{S}(w)) = l_c(\mathbf{S}(w))$ (encodes equality of local states of agent c).
- $HO_c(w, w')$ is a formula over $SV(w) \cup SV(w')$ that is true for a valuation V iff $l_c(\mathbf{S}(w')) \in \mathcal{G}_c$ (encodes an accessibility of a global state in which agent c is functioning correctly).
- $\widehat{H}_c^d(w, w') := H_c(w, w') \wedge HO_d(w, w')$.
- $\mathcal{T}(w, w')$ is a formula over $SV(w) \cup SV(w')$ that is true for a valuation V iff $(\mathbf{S}(w), \mathbf{S}(w')) \in T$ (encodes the transition relation of M).
- $\mathcal{B}_j^{\sim}(u)$ is a formula over $NV(u)$ that is true for a valuation V iff $j \sim \mathbf{J}(u)$, where $\sim \in \{<, \leqslant, =, \geqslant, >\}$.
- $\mathcal{L}_k^l(\boldsymbol{\pi}_j) := \mathcal{B}_k^{>}(u_j) \wedge H(w_{k,j}, w_{l,j})$.

Moreover, let $j \in \mathbb{N}$, and I be an interval. Then,

$$In(j, I) = \begin{cases} \mathbf{true}, & \text{if } j \in I \\ \mathbf{false}, & \text{if } j \notin I \end{cases}$$

Let $W = \{SV(w_{i,j}) \mid 0 \leq i \leq k \text{ and } 0 \leqslant j < f_k(\varphi)\} \cup \{NV(u_j) \mid 0 \leqslant j < f_k(\varphi)\}$ be a set of propositional variables. The propositional formula $[M^{\varphi, \iota}]_k$ is defined over the set W in the following way:

$$[M^{\varphi, \iota}]_k := I_\iota(w_{0,0}) \wedge \bigwedge_{j=0}^{f_k(\varphi)-1} \bigwedge_{i=0}^{k-1} \mathcal{T}(w_{i,j}, w_{i+1,j}) \wedge \bigwedge_{j=0}^{f_k(\varphi)-1} \bigvee_{l=0}^{k} B_l^{=}(u_j).$$

The next step of the reduction to SAT is the transformation of an EMTLKD formula φ into a propositional formula $[\varphi]_{M,k} := [\varphi]_k^{[0,0,F_k(\varphi)]}$, where $F_k(\varphi) = \{j \in \mathbb{N} \mid 0 \leqslant j < f_k(\varphi)\}$, and $[\varphi]_k^{[m,n,A]}$ denotes the translation of φ along the symbolic path $\boldsymbol{\pi}_{m,n}$ with starting point m by using the set A.

For every EMTLKD formula φ the function f_k determines how many symbolic k-paths are needed for translating the formula φ. Given a formula φ and a set A of k-paths such that $|A| = f_k(\varphi)$, we divide the set A into subsets needed for translating the subformulae of φ. To accomplish this goal we need some auxiliary functions that were defined in [33]. We recall the definitions of these functions.

The relation $\prec$ is defined on the power set of $\mathbb{N}$ as follows: $A \prec B$ iff for all natural numbers x and y, if $x \in A$ and $y \in B$, then $x < y$.

Now, let $A \subset \mathbb{N}$ be a finite nonempty set, and $n, d \in \mathbb{N}$, where $d \leqslant |A|$. Then,

- $g_l(A, d)$ denotes the subset B of A such that $|B| = d$ and $B \prec A \setminus B$.
- $g_r(A, d)$ denotes the subset C of A such that $|C| = d$ and $A \setminus C \prec C$.
- $g_s(A)$ denotes the set $A \setminus \{min(A)\}$.

- if n divides $|A| - d$, then $hp(A, d, n)$ denotes the sequence $(B_0, \ldots, B_n)$ of subsets of A such that $\bigcup_{j=0}^{n} B_j = A$, $|B_0| = \ldots = |B_{n-1}|$, $|B_n| = d$, and $B_i \prec B_j$ for every $0 \leqslant i < j \leqslant n$.

Now let $h_k^U(A, d) \stackrel{df}{=} hp(A, d, k)$ and $h_k^G(A) \stackrel{df}{=} hp(A, 0, k)$. Note that if $h_k^U(A, d) = (B_0, \ldots, B_k)$, then $h_k^U(A, d)(j)$ denotes the set B_j, for every $0 \leqslant j \leqslant k$. Similarly, if $h_k^G(A) = (B_0, \ldots, B_k)$, then $h_k^G(A)(j)$ denotes the set B_j, for every $0 \leqslant j \leqslant k$.

The functions g_l and g_r are used in the translation of the formulae with the main connective being either conjunction or disjunction. For a given EMTLKD formula $\alpha \wedge \beta$, if a set A is used to translate this formula, then the set $g_l(A, f_k(\alpha))$ is used to translate the subformula α and the set $g_r(A, f_k(\beta))$ is used to translate the subformula β; for a given EMTLKD formula $\alpha \vee \beta$, if a set A is used to translate this formula, then the set $g_l(A, f_k(\alpha))$ is used to translate the subformula α and the set $g_l(A, f_k(\beta))$ is used to translate the subformula β.

The function g_s is used in the translation of the formulae with the main connective $Q \in \{\overline{K}_c, \widehat{\underline{K}}_c^j, \mathcal{O}_c, \overline{D}_\Gamma, \overline{E}_\Gamma\}$. For a given EMTLKD formula $Q\alpha$, if a set A is used to translate this formula, then the path of the number $min(A)$ is used to translate the operator Q and the set $g_s(A)$ is used to translate the subformula α.

The function h_k^U is used in the translation of subformulae of the form $\alpha U_I \beta$. If a set A is used to translate the subformula $\alpha U_I \beta$ at the symbolic k-path π_n (with starting point m), then for every j such that $m \leqslant j \leqslant k$, the set $h_k^U(A, f_k(\beta))(k)$ is used to translate the formula β along the symbolic path π_n with starting point j; moreover, for every i such that $m \leqslant i < j$, the set $h_k^U(A, f_k(\beta))(i)$ is used to translate the formula α along the symbolic path π_n with starting point i. Notice that if k does not divide $|A| - d$, then $h_k^U(A, d)$ is undefined. However, for every set A such that $|A| = f_k(\alpha U_I \beta)$, it is clear from the definition of f_k that k divides $|A| - f_k(\beta)$.

The function h_k^G is used in the translation of subformulae of the form $G_I \alpha$. If a set A is used to translate the subformula $G_I \alpha$ along a symbolic k-path π_n (with starting point m), then for every j such that $m \leqslant j \leqslant k$ and $j \in I$, the set $h_k^G(A)(j)$, is used to translate the formula α along the symbolic paths π_n with starting point j; Notice that if $k + 1$ does not divide $|A|$, then $h_k^G(A)$ is undefined. However, for every set A such that $|A| = f_k(G_I \alpha)$, it is clear from the definition of f_k that $k + 1$ divides $|A|$.

Let φ be an EMTLKD formula, and $k \geqslant 0$ a bound. We can define inductively the translation of φ over path number $n \in F_k(\varphi)$ starting at symbolic state $w_{m,n}$ as shown below. Let $A' = min(A)$, $h_k^U = h_k^U(A, f_k(\beta))$ and $h_k^G = h_k^G(A)$, then:

$$[\textbf{true}]_k^{[m,n,A]} := \textbf{true},\ [\textbf{false}]_k^{[m,n,A]} := \textbf{false},$$

$$[p]_k^{[m,n,A]} := p(w_{m,n}),\ [\neg p]_k^{[m,n,A]} := \neg p(w_{m,n}),$$

$$[\alpha \wedge \beta]_k^{[m,n,A]} := [\alpha]_k^{[m,n,g_l(A,f_k(\alpha))]} \wedge [\beta]_k^{[m,n,g_r(A,f_k(\beta))]},$$

$$[\alpha \vee \beta]_k^{[m,n,A]} := [\alpha]_k^{[m,n,g_l(A,f_k(\alpha))]} \vee [\beta]_k^{[m,n,g_l(A,f_k(\beta))]},$$

$$[X\alpha]_k^{[m,n,A]} := [\alpha]_k^{[m+1,n,A]}, \text{ if } m < k$$

$$\bigvee_{l=0}^{k-1} (\mathcal{L}_k^l(\pi_n) \wedge [\alpha]_k^{[l+1,n,A]}), \text{ if } m = k$$

$$[\alpha U_I \beta]_k^{[m,n,A]} := \bigvee_{j=m}^{k} (In(j, I+m) \wedge [\beta]_k^{[j,n,h_k^U(k)]} \wedge \bigwedge_{i=m}^{j-1} [\alpha]_k^{[i,n,h_k^U(i)]}) \vee$$

$$(\bigvee_{l=0}^{m-1} (\mathcal{L}_k^l(\pi_n)) \wedge \bigvee_{j=0}^{m-1} (\mathcal{B}_j^>(u_n) \wedge [\beta]_k^{[j,n,h_k^U(k)]} \wedge$$

$$(\bigvee_{l=0}^{m-1} (\mathcal{B}_l^=(u_n) \wedge In(j+k-l, I+m)))) \wedge$$

$$\bigwedge_{i=0}^{j-1}(\mathcal{B}_i^>(u_n) \to [\alpha]_k^{[i,n,h_k^U(i)]}) \wedge \bigwedge_{i=m}^{k}[\alpha]_k^{[i,n,h_k^U(i)]})),$$

$$[\mathsf{G}_I\alpha]_k^{[m,n,A]} := \text{if } right(I+m) \leqslant k, \text{ then } \bigwedge_{j=max}^{right(I+m)}[\alpha]_k^{[j,n,h_k^G(j)]},$$

$$\text{if } right(I+m) > k, \text{ then } \bigvee_{l=0}^{k-1}(\mathcal{L}_k^l(\pi_n)) \wedge \bigwedge_{j=max}^{k-1}[\alpha]_k^{[j,n,h_k^G(j)]} \wedge$$

$$\bigwedge_{j=0}^{max-1}((\mathcal{B}_j^{\geqslant}(u_n) \wedge (\bigvee_{l=0}^{max-1}(\mathcal{B}_l^=(u_n) \wedge In(j+k-l,I+m))))$$

$$\to [\alpha]_k^{[j,n,h_k^G(j)]}), \text{ where } max = max(left(I+m),m)$$

$$[\overline{\mathsf{K}}_c\alpha]_k^{[m,n,A]} := I_\iota(w_{0,A'}) \wedge \bigvee_{j=0}^{k}([\alpha]_k^{[j,A',g_s(A)]} \wedge H_c(w_{m,n},w_{j,A'})),$$

$$[\overline{\mathcal{O}}_c\alpha]_k^{[m,n,A]} := I_\iota(w_{0,A'}) \wedge \bigvee_{j=0}^{k}([\alpha]_k^{[j,A',g_s(A)]} \wedge HO_c(w_{m,n},w_{j,A'})),$$

$$[\widehat{\mathsf{K}}_c^d\alpha]_k^{[m,n,A]} := I_\iota(w_{0,A'}) \wedge \bigvee_{j=0}^{k}([\alpha]_k^{[j,A',g_s(A)]} \wedge \widehat{H}_c^d(w_{m,n},w_{j,A'})),$$

$$[\overline{\mathsf{D}}_\Gamma\alpha]_k^{[m,n,A]} := I_\iota(w_{0,A'}) \wedge \bigvee_{j=0}^{k}([\alpha]_k^{[j,A',g_s(A)]} \wedge \bigwedge_{c\in\Gamma} H_c(w_{m,n},w_{j,A'})),$$

$$[\overline{\mathsf{E}}_\Gamma\alpha]_k^{[m,n,A]} := I_\iota(w_{0,A'}) \wedge \bigvee_{j=0}^{k}([\alpha]_k^{[j,A',g_s(A)]} \wedge \bigvee_{c\in\Gamma} H_c(w_{m,n},w_{j,A'})),$$

$$[\overline{\mathsf{C}}_\Gamma\alpha]_k^{[m,n,A]} := [\bigvee_{j=1}^{k}(\overline{\mathsf{E}}_\Gamma)^j\alpha]_k^{[m,n,A]}.$$

Now, let α be an EMTLKD formula. For every subformula φ of α, we denote by $[\varphi]_k^{[\alpha,m,n,A]}$ the propositional formula $[M]_k^{F_k(\alpha)} \wedge [\varphi]_k^{[m,n,A]}$, where $[M]_k^{F_k(\alpha)} = \bigwedge_{j=0}^{f_k(\alpha)-1}\bigwedge_{i=0}^{k-1} \mathcal{T}(w_{i,j},w_{i+1,j}) \wedge \bigwedge_{j=0}^{f_k(\alpha)-1}\bigvee_{l=0}^{k} B_l^=(u_j)$. We write $V \Vdash \xi$ to mean that the valuation V satisfies the propositional formula ξ. Moreover, we write $s_{i,j}$ instead of $\mathbf{S}(w_{i,j})$, and l_j instead of $\mathbf{J}(u_j)$.

The lemmas below state the correctness and the completeness of the presented translation respectively.

Lemma 6. *Correctness of the translation Let M be a model, α an EMTLKD formula, and $k \in \mathbb{N}$. For every subformula φ of the formula α, every $(m,n) \in \{0,\ldots,k\} \times F_k(\alpha)$, every $A \subseteq F_k(\alpha) \setminus \{n\}$ such that $|A| = f_k(\varphi)$, and every valuation V, the following condition holds: $V \Vdash [\varphi]_k^{[\alpha,m,n,A]}$ implies $M,((s_{0,n},\ldots,s_{k,n}),l_n)^m \models_k \varphi$.*

Proof. Let $n \in F_k(\alpha)$, A be a set such that $A \subseteq F_k(\alpha) \setminus \{n\}$ and $|A| = f_k(\varphi)$, m be a natural number such that $0 \leqslant m \leqslant k$ and V a valuation. Suppose that $V \Vdash [\varphi]_k^{[\alpha,m,n,A]}$ and consider the following cases:

1. Let $\varphi = p \mid \neg p \mid \psi_1 \vee \psi_2 \mid \psi_1 \wedge \psi_2 \mid \mathsf{X}\psi$ with $p \in \mathcal{PV}$. See Lemma 3.1. of [33].
2. $\varphi = \psi_1\mathsf{U}_I\psi_2$. Denote by A_1 the propositional formula $\bigvee_{j=m}^{k}\big(In(j,I+m) \wedge [\psi_2]_k^{[j,n,h_k^U(A,f_k(\psi_2))(k)]} \wedge \bigwedge_{i=m}^{j-1}[\psi_1]_k^{[i,n,h_k^U(A,f_k(\psi_2))(i)]}\big)$, and by A_2 the propositional formula $\bigvee_{l=0}^{m-1}(\mathcal{L}_k^l(\pi_n)) \wedge \bigvee_{j=0}^{m-1}\big(\mathcal{B}_j^>(u_n) \wedge [\beta]_k^{[j,n,h_k^U(A,f_k(\beta))(k)]} \wedge (\bigvee_{l=0}^{m-1}(\mathcal{B}_l^=(u_n) \wedge In(j+k-l,I+m))) \wedge \bigwedge_{i=0}^{j-1}(\mathcal{B}_i^>(u_n) \to [\alpha]_k^{[i,n,h_k^U(A,f_k(\beta))(i)]}) \wedge \bigwedge_{i=m}^{k}[\alpha]_k^{[i,n,h_k^U(A,f_k(\beta))(i)]}\big)$. Observe that $V \Vdash [\psi_1\mathsf{U}_I\psi_2]_k^{[\alpha,m,n,A]}$ iff $V \Vdash A_1 \vee A_2$ iff $V \Vdash A_1$ or $V \Vdash A_2$. Let us denote by π_l the k-path $((s_{0,n},\ldots,s_{k,n}),l_n)$, and consider two cases:

    (a) $V \Vdash A_1$. From this we get: $(\exists m \leqslant j \leqslant k)$ $(j \in I+m$ and $M,\pi_l^j \models_k \psi_2$ and $(\forall m \leqslant i < j)M,\pi_l^i \models_k \psi_1)$. Hence $M,\pi_l^m \models_k \psi_1\mathsf{U}_I\psi_2$.

    (b) $V \Vdash A_2$. From this we get: $l < m$ and $\pi(k) = \pi(l)$ and $(\forall m \leqslant i \leqslant k)M,\pi_l^i \models_k \psi_1$ and $(\exists l < j < m)(j+k-l \in I+m$ and $M,\pi_l^j \models_k \psi_2$ and $(\forall l < i < j)M,\pi_l^i \models \psi_1)$. Hence $M,\pi_l^m \models_k \psi_1\mathsf{U}_I\psi_2$.

3. $\varphi = \mathrm{G}_I \psi$. If $right(I + m) \leqslant k$, then by B_1 we denote the propositional formula:
$\bigwedge_{j=max(left(I+m),m)}^{right(I+m)} [\psi]_k^{[j,n,h_k^G(A)(j)]}$. If $right(I + m) > k$, then by B_2 we denote
the propositional formula: $\bigvee_{l=0}^{k-1}(\mathcal{L}_k^l(\pi_n)) \wedge \bigwedge_{j=max(left(I+m),m)}^{k-1}[\psi]_k^{[j,n,h_k^G(A)(j)]} \wedge$
$\bigwedge_{j=0}^{max(left(I+m),m)-1} ((\mathcal{B}_j^{\geqslant}(u_n) \wedge (\bigvee_{l=0}^{max(left(I+m),m)-1}(\mathcal{B}_l^{=}(u_n) \wedge In(j+k-l, I+$
$m)))) \rightarrow [\psi]_k^{[j,n,h_k^G(A)(j)]})$. Observe that $V \Vdash [\mathrm{G}_I\psi]_k^{[\alpha,m,n,A]}$ iff $V \Vdash B_1 \vee B_2$ iff
$V \Vdash B_1$ or $V \Vdash B_2$. Let us denote by π_l the k-path $((s_{0,n}, \ldots, s_{k,n}), l_n)$, and consider two cases:

(a) $V \Vdash B_1$. From this we get: $k \geqslant right(I+m)$ and $(\forall j \in I+m)(M, \pi_l^j \models_k \psi)$.
Thus $M, \pi_l^m \models_k \mathrm{G}_I\psi$.

(b) $V \Vdash B_2$. From this we get: $k < right(I+m)$ and $\pi(k) = \pi(l)$ and $(\forall max \leqslant j < k)\ M, \pi_l^j \models_k \psi$ and $(\forall l \leqslant j < max)(j + k - l \in I+m$ implies $M, \pi_l^j \models_k \psi)$, where $max = max(left(I+m), m)$. Thus $M, \pi_l^m \models_k \mathrm{G}_I\psi$.

4. Let $\varphi = \overline{\mathrm{K}}_c\psi$. Let $n' = min(A)$, and $\widetilde{\pi}_{l'}$ denotes the k-path $((g_{0,n'}, \ldots, g_{k,n'}), l_{n'})$.
By the definition of the translation we have $V \Vdash [\overline{\mathrm{K}}_c\psi]_k^{[\alpha,m,n,A]}$ implies $V \Vdash I_t(w_{0,n'})$
$\wedge \bigvee_{j=0}^k ([\psi]_k^{[\alpha,j,n',g_s(A)]} \wedge H_c(w_{m,n}, w_{j,n'}))$. Since $V \Vdash H_c(w_{m,n}, w_{j,n'})$ holds, we
have $g_{m,n} \sim_c g'_{j,n'}$, for some $j \in \{0, \ldots, k\}$. Therefore, by inductive hypothe-
ses we get $(\exists 0 \leqslant j \leqslant k)(M, \widetilde{\pi}_{l'}^j \models_k \psi$ and $g_{m,n} \sim_c g'_{j,n'})$. Thus we have
$M, ((g_{0,n}, \ldots, g_{k,n}), l_n)^m \models_k \overline{\mathrm{K}}_c\psi$.

5. Let $\varphi = \overline{\mathrm{Y}}_\Gamma\psi$, where $Y \in \{\mathrm{D, E, C}\}$, or $\varphi = \overline{\mathcal{O}}_c\psi$, or $\varphi = \widehat{\underline{\mathrm{K}}}_c^d\psi$. These can be
proven analogously to Case 4.

Let B and C be two finite sets of indices. Then, by $Var(B)$ we denote the set of all the
state variables appearing in all the symbolic states of all the symbolic k-paths whose
indices are taken from the set B. Moreover, for every valuation V and every set of
indices B, by $V \uparrow B$ we denote the restriction of the valuation V to the set $Var(B)$.
Notice that if $B \cap C = \emptyset$, then $Var(B) \cap Var(C) = \emptyset$. This property is used in the
proof of the following lemma.

Lemma 7. *Completeness of the translation Let M be a model, $k \in \mathbb{N}$, and α an
EMTLKD formula such that $f_k(\alpha) > 0$. For every subformula φ of the formula α, every
$(m, n) \in \{(0, 0)\} \cup \{0, \ldots, k\} \times F_k(\alpha)$, every $A \subseteq F_k(\alpha) \setminus \{n\}$ such that $|A| = f_k(\varphi)$,
and every k-path π_l, the following condition holds: $M, \pi_l^m \models_k \varphi$ implies that there ex-
ists a valuation V such that $\pi_l = ((s_{0,n}, \ldots, s_{k,n}), l_n)$ and $V \Vdash [\varphi]_k^{[\alpha,m,n,A]}$.*

Proof. First, note that given an EMTLKD formula α, and natural numbers k, m, n with
$0 \leqslant m \leqslant k$ and $n \in F_k(\alpha)$, there exists a valuation V such $V \Vdash [M]_k^{F_k(\alpha)}$. This is
because M has no terminal states. Now we proceed by induction on the complexity
of φ. Let $n \in F_k(\alpha)$, A be a set such that $A \subseteq F_k(\alpha) \setminus \{n\}$ and $|A| = f_k(\varphi)$, ρ_l
be a k-path in M, and m be a natural number such that $0 \leqslant m \leqslant k$. Suppose that
$M, \pi_l^m \models_k \varphi$ and consider the following cases:

1. Let $\varphi = p \mid \neg p \mid \psi_1 \vee \psi_2 \mid \psi_1 \wedge \psi_2 \mid \mathrm{X}\psi$ with $p \in \mathcal{PV}$. See the proof of Lemma
3.3. of [33].

2. $\varphi = \psi_1 \mathrm{U}_I \psi_2$. Let $A_j = h_k^U(A, f_k(\psi_2))(j)$, for each $0 \leqslant j \leqslant k$. We have to consider
two cases:

(a) $(\exists m \leqslant j \leqslant k)(j \in I + m$ and $M, \pi_l^j \models_k \psi_2$ and $(\forall m \leqslant i < j)M, \pi_l^i \models_k \psi_1)$. By inductive hypothesis, there exist valuations $V_0, V_1, \ldots, V_k$, such that $(\exists m \leqslant j \leqslant k)(V_k \Vdash [\psi_2]_k^{[\alpha,j,n,A_k]}$ and $(\forall m \leqslant i < j)V_i \Vdash [\psi_2]_k^{[\alpha,i,n,A_i]})$. Since the family of sets $\{A_j\}_{0 \leqslant j \leqslant k}$ is pairwise disjoint and the formula $In(j, I + m)$ has always a constant value equal to **true** or **false**, then there exists a valuation V such that $(\exists m \leqslant j \leqslant k)(V \Vdash In(j, I+m) \wedge [\psi_2]_k^{[\alpha,j,n,A_k]}$ and $(\forall m \leqslant i < j)V \Vdash [\psi_2]_k^{[\alpha,i,n,A_i]})$. From this we get that $(\exists m \leqslant j \leqslant k)$ $(V \Vdash In(j, I + m) \wedge [\psi_2]_k^{[\alpha,j,n,A_k]}$ and $V \Vdash \bigwedge_{i=m}^{j-1}[\psi_1]_k^{[\alpha,i,n,A_i]})$. Hence, $V \Vdash \bigvee_{j=m}^k(In(j, I + m) \wedge [\psi_2]_k^{[\alpha,j,n,A_k]} \wedge \bigwedge_{i=m}^{j-1}[\psi_2]_k^{[\alpha,i,n,A_i]})$. Thus, $V \Vdash [\psi_1 U_I \psi_2]_k^{[\alpha,m,n,A]}$.

(b) $(\exists l < j < m)(j + k - l \in I + m$ and $M, \pi_l^j \models_k \psi_2$ and $(\forall l < i < j)M, \pi_l^i \models \psi_1)$ and $(\forall m \leqslant i \leqslant k)M, \pi_l^i \models_k \psi_1$ and $l < m$ and $\pi(k) = \pi(l)$. By inductive hypothesis, there exist valuations $V_0, V_1, \ldots, V_k$, such that $(\exists l < j < m)(V_k \Vdash [\psi_2]_k^{[\alpha,j,n,A_k]}$ and $(\forall m \leqslant i < j)V_i \Vdash [\psi_2]_k^{[\alpha,i,n,A_i]})$ and $(\forall m \leqslant i \leqslant k)V_i \Vdash [\psi_2]_k^{[\alpha,i,n,A_i]}$. Since the family of sets $\{A_j\}_{0 \leqslant j \leqslant k}$ is pairwise disjoint, and the formula $In(j + k - l, I + m)$ has always a constant value equal to **true** or **false**, there exists a valuation V such that $(\exists l < j < m)(V \Vdash In(j + k - l, I + m) \wedge [\psi_2]_k^{[\alpha,j,n,A_k]}$ and $(\forall l < i < j)V \Vdash [\psi_2]_k^{[\alpha,i,n,A_i]})$ and $(\forall m \leqslant i \leqslant k)V \Vdash [\psi_2]_k^{[\alpha,i,n,A_i]}$. Moreover, $V \Vdash \mathcal{L}_k^l(\pi_n)$. From this we get: $V \Vdash \bigvee_{j=0}^{m-1}(\mathcal{B}_j^>(u_n) \wedge [\psi_2]_k^{[j,n,h_k^U(A,f_k(\psi_2))(k)]} \wedge (\bigvee_{l=0}^{m-1}(\mathcal{B}_l^=(u_n) \wedge In(j + k - l, I + m))))$ $\wedge \bigwedge_{i=0}^{j-1}(\mathcal{B}_i^>(u_n) \to [\psi_1]_k^{[i,n,h_k^U(A,f_k(\psi_2))(i)]}) \wedge \bigwedge_{i=m}^k[\psi_1]_k^{[i,n,h_k^U(A,f_k(\psi_2))(i)]})$ and $V \Vdash \bigvee_{l=0}^{m-1}\mathcal{L}_k^l(\pi_n)$. Hence, $V \Vdash [\psi_1 U_I \psi_2]_k^{[\alpha,m,n,A]}$.

3. $\varphi = G_I \psi$. Let $A_j = h_k^G(A)(j)$, for each $0 \leqslant j \leqslant k$. We have to consider two cases:

(a) $k \geq right(I + m)$ and $(\forall j \in I + m)(M, \pi_l^j \models_k \alpha)$. By inductive hypothesis, there exist valuations $V_0, V_1, \ldots, V_k$, such that $(\forall j \in I+m)V_j \Vdash [\psi]_k^{[\alpha,j,n,A_j]}$. Since the family of sets $\{A_j\}_{0 \leqslant j \leqslant k}$ is pairwise disjoint, there exists a valuation V such that $(\forall j \in I + m)V \Vdash [\psi]_k^{[\alpha,j,n,A_j]}$. From this we get: $V \Vdash \bigwedge_{j=max(left(I+m),m)}^{right(I+m)}[\alpha]_k^{[j,n,h_k^G(A)(j)]}$. Hence, $V \Vdash [G_I \psi]_k^{[\alpha,m,n,A]}$.

(b) $k < right(I + m)$ and $\pi(k) = \pi(l)$ and $(\forall max \leqslant j < k)M, \pi_l^j \models_k \alpha$ and $(\forall l \leqslant j < max)(j + k - l \in I + m$ implies $M, \pi_l^j \models_k \alpha)$, where $max = max(left(I + m), m)$. By inductive hypothesis, there exist valuations $V_0, V_1, \ldots, V_k$, such that $(\forall max \leqslant j < k)V_j \Vdash [\psi]_k^{[\alpha,j,n,A_j]}$ and $(\forall l \leqslant j < max)(j + k - l \in I + m$ implies $V_j \Vdash [\psi]_k^{[\alpha,j,n,A_j]})$. Since the family of sets $\{A_j\}_{0 \leqslant j \leqslant k}$ is pairwise disjoint, there exists a valuation V such that $(\forall max \leqslant j < k)V \Vdash [\psi]_k^{[\alpha,j,n,A_j]}$ and $(\forall l \leqslant j < max)(j + k - l \in I + m$ implies $V \Vdash [\psi]_k^{[\alpha,j,n,A_j]})$. Moreover, $V \Vdash \mathcal{L}_k^l(\pi_n)$. From this we get: $V \Vdash \bigvee_{l=0}^{k-1}(\mathcal{L}_k^l(\pi_n)) \wedge \bigwedge_{j=max}^{k-1}[\psi]_k^{[j,n,h_k^G(A)(j)]} \wedge \bigwedge_{j=0}^{max-1}((\mathcal{B}_j^\geqslant(u_n) \wedge (\bigvee_{l=0}^{max-1}(\mathcal{B}_l^=(u_n) \wedge In(j + k - l, I + m)))) \to [\psi]_k^{[j,n,h_k^G(A)(j)]})$. Hence, $V \Vdash [G_I \psi]_k^{[\alpha,m,n,A]}$.

4. Let $\varphi = \overline{K}_c\psi$. Since $M, \pi_l^m \models_k \overline{K}_c\psi$, we have that $(\exists \pi'_{l'} \in \Pi_k(\iota))(\exists 0 \leqslant j \leqslant k)$ $(M, \pi'^j_{l'} \models_k \psi$ and $\pi(m) \sim_c \pi'(j))$. Let $n' = \min(A)$ and $B = g_s(A)$. By the inductive hypothesis and the definition of the formula H_c, there exists a valuation V' such that $V' \Vdash [M]_k^{F_k(\alpha)}$ and $V' \Vdash [\psi]_k^{[j,n',B]} \wedge H_c(w_{m,n}, w_{j,n'})$ for some $j \in \{0, \ldots, k\}$. Hence we have $V' \Vdash \bigvee_{j=0}^k ([\psi]_k^{[j,n',B]} \wedge H_c(w_{m,n}, w_{j,n'}))$. Further, since $\pi'_{l'} \in \Pi_k(\iota)$, $\pi'_{l'}(0) = \iota$. Thus, by the definition of the formula I, we get that $V' \Vdash I_\iota(w_{0,n'})$. Therefore we have $V' \Vdash I_\iota(w_{0,n'}) \wedge \bigvee_{j=0}^k ([\psi]_k^{[j,n',B]} \wedge H_c(w_{m,n}, w_{j,n'}))$, which implies that $V' \Vdash [\overline{K}_c\psi]_k^{[m,n,A]}$. Since $n' \notin B$ and $n \notin A$, there exists a valuation V such that $V \uparrow B = V' \uparrow B$ and moreover $V \Vdash [M]_k^{F_k(\alpha)}$ and $V \Vdash [\overline{K}_c\psi]_k^{[m,n,A]}$. Therefore we get $V \Vdash [\overline{K}_c\psi]_k^{[\alpha,m,n,A]}$.

5. Let $\varphi = \overline{Y}_\Gamma\psi$, where $Y \in \{D, E, C\}$, or $\varphi = \overline{O}_c\psi$, or $\varphi = \widehat{K}_c^d\psi$. These can be proven analogously to Case 4.

Theorem 2. *Let M be a model, and φ an EMTLKD formula. Then for every $k \in \mathbb{N}$, $M \models_k^\exists \varphi$ if, and only if, the propositional formula $[M, \varphi]_k$ is satisfiable.*

Proof. ($\Longrightarrow$) Let $k \in \mathbb{N}$ and $M, \pi_l \models_k \varphi$ for some $\pi_l \in \Pi_k(\iota)$. By Lemma 7 it follows that there exists a valuation V such that $\pi_l = ((s_{0,0}, \ldots, s_{k,0}), l_0)$ with $\mathbf{S}(w_{0,0}) = s_{0,0} = \iota$ and $V \Vdash [\varphi]_k^{[\varphi,0,0,F_k(\varphi)]}$. Hence, $V \Vdash I(w_{0,0}) \wedge [M]_k^{F_k(\varphi)} \wedge [\varphi]_k^{[0,0,F_k(\varphi)]}$. Thus $V \Vdash [M, \varphi]_k$.

($\Longleftarrow$) Let $k \in \mathbb{N}$ and $[M, \varphi]_k$ is satisfiable. It means that there exists a valuation V such that $V \Vdash [M, \varphi]_k$. So, $V \Vdash I(w_{0,0})$ and $V \Vdash [M]_k^{F_k(\varphi)} \wedge [\varphi]_k^{[0,0,F_k(\varphi)]}$. Hence, by Lemma 6 it follows that $M, ((s_{0,0}, \ldots, s_{k,0}), l_0) \models_k \varphi$ and $\mathbf{S}(w_{0,0}) = s_{0,0} = \iota$. Thus $M \models_k^\exists \varphi$.

Now, from Theorems 1 and 2 we get the following.

Corollary 1. *Let M be a model, and φ an EMTLKD formula. Then, $M \models^\exists \varphi$ if, and only if, there exists $k \in \mathbb{N}$ such that the propositional formula $[M, \varphi]_k$ is satisfiable.*

5 Experimental Results

Our SAT-base BMC method for EMTLKD is, to our best knowledge, the first one formally presented in the literature, and moreover there is no any other model checking technique for the considered EMTLKD language. Further, our implementation of the presented BMC method uses Reduced Boolean Circuits (RBC) [1] to represent the propositional formula $[M, \varphi]_k$. An RBC represents subformulae of $[M, \varphi]_k$ by fresh propositions such that each two identical subformulae correspond to the same proposition[1]. For the tests we have used a computer with Intel Core i3-2125 processor,

---

[1] Following van der Meyden at al. [12], instead of using RBCs, we could directly encode $[M, \varphi]_k$ in such a way that each subformula ψ of $[M, \varphi]_k$ occurring within a scope of a k-element disjunction or conjunction is replaced with a propositional variable p_ψ and the reduced formula $[M, \varphi]_k$ is conjuncted with the implication $p_\psi \Rightarrow \psi$. However, in this case our method, as the one proposed in [12], would not be complete.

8 GB of RAM, and running Linux 2.6. We set the timeout to 5400 seconds, and memory limit to 8GB, and we used the state of the art SAT-solver MiniSat 2. The specifications for the described benchmark are given in the universal form, for which we verify the corresponding counterexample formula, i.e., the formula which is negated and interpreted existentially.

To evaluate our technique, we have analysed a scalable multi-agent system, which is a faulty train controller system (FTC). Figure 1 presents a DIIS composed of three agents: a controller and two trains, but in general the system consists of a controller, and n trains (for $n \geqslant 2$) that use their own circular tracks for travelling in one direction (states Away (A)). At one point, all trains have to pass through a tunnel (states Tunnel 'T'), but because there is only one track in the tunnel, trains arriving from each direction

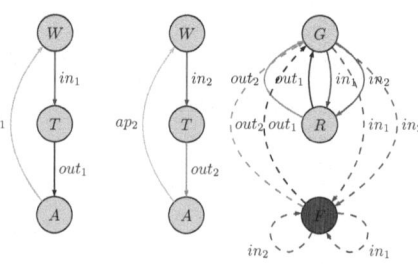

Fig. 1. An DIIS of FTC for two trains. Null actions are omitted.

cannot use it simultaneously. There are colour light signals on both sides of the tunnel, which can be either red (state 'R') or green (state 'G'). All trains notify the controller when they request entry to the tunnel or when they leave the tunnel. The controller controls the colour of the colour light signals, however it can be faulty (state 'F'), i.e., a faulty traffic light remains green when a train enters the tunnel, and thereby it does not serve its purpose. In the figure, the initial states of the controller and the trains are 'G' and 'W' (Waiting in front of the tunnel) respectively, and the transitions with the same label are synchronised.

Let $\mathcal{PV} = \{inT_1, \dots inT_n, Red\}$ be a set of propositional variables, which we find useful in analysis of the scenario of the FTC system. A valuation function $\mathcal{V} : S \to 2^{\mathcal{PV}}$ is defined as follows. Let $Ag = \{Train1\ (T1), \dots, TrainN\ (TN), Controller\ (C)\}$. Then, $inT_c \in \mathcal{V}(s)$ if $l_c(s) = T$ and $c \in Ag \setminus \{C\}$; $Red \in \mathcal{V}(s)$ if $l_C(s) = R$. The specifications are the following:

$\varphi_1 = \mathrm{G}_{[0,\infty]}\ \mathcal{O}_C(\bigwedge_{i=1}^{n-1} \bigwedge_{j=i+1}^{n} \neg(InT_i \wedge InT_j))$. "Always when *Controller* is functioning correctly, trains have exclusive access to the tunnel".

$\varphi_2 = \mathrm{G}_{[0,\infty]}(inT_1 \Rightarrow \widehat{\mathrm{K}}_{T1}^C(\bigwedge_{i=2}^{n}(\neg inT_i)))$. "Always when *Train1* is in the tunnel, it knows under assumption that *Controller* is functioning correctly that none of the other trains is in the tunnel".

$\varphi_3 = \mathrm{G}_{[0,\infty]}(inT_1 \Rightarrow \widehat{\mathrm{K}}_{T1}^C(Red))$. "Always when *Train1* is in the tunnel, it knows under assumption that *Controller* is functioning correctly that the colour of the light signal for other trains is red".

$\varphi_4 = \mathrm{G}_{[0,\infty]}(InT_1 \Rightarrow \mathrm{K}_{T1}(\mathrm{F}_{[1,n+1]}(\bigvee_{i=1}^{n} InT_i)))$. "Always when *Train1* is in the tunnel, it knows that either it or other train will be in the tunnel during the next $n + 1$ time units".

$\varphi_5 = \mathrm{G}_{[0,\infty]}(InT_1 \Rightarrow \mathrm{K}_{T1}(\mathrm{G}_{[3m-2,3m-2]}InT_1 \vee \mathrm{F}_{[1,n+1]}(\bigvee_{i=2}^{n} InT_i)))$, where $m \geqslant 2$. "Always when *Train1* is in the tunnel, it knows that either he is in the tunnel every $3m - 2$ time units or other train will be in the tunnel during the next $n + 1$ time units".

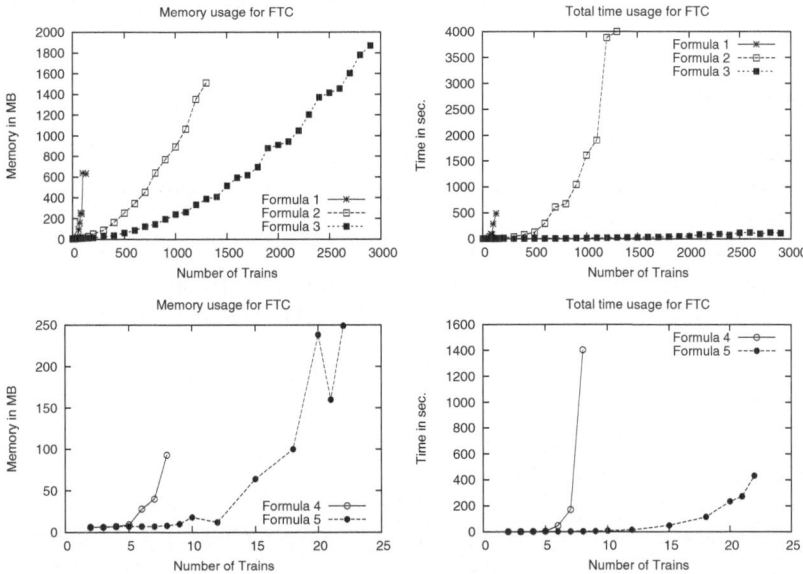

All the above properties are false in our DIIS model of the FTC system. Since there is no model checker that supports the EMTLKD properties, we were not able to compare our results with others for the above formulae; McMAS [25] is the only model checker that supports deontic modalities, however it is designated for branching time logics only. Thus, we present results of our method only. An evaluation is given by means of the running time and the memory used, and it is presented on the included line-charts. It can be observed that for φ_1, φ_2, φ_3, φ_4 and φ_5 we managed to compute the results for 130, 1300, 2900, 8, and 22 trains, respectively, in the time of 5400 seconds. The exact data for the mentioned maximal number of trains are the following:

φ_1: $k = 4$, $f_k(\varphi_1) = 2$, bmcT is 5.44, bmcM is 14.00, satT is 483.61, satM is 632.00, bmcT+satT is 489.05, max(bmcM,satM) is 632.00;

φ_2: $k = 4$, $f_k(\varphi_2) = 2$, bmcT is 148.02, bmcM is 909.00, satT is 3850.09, satM 1511.00, bmcT+satT is 3998.11, max(bmcM,satM) is 1511.00;

φ_3: $k = 1$, $f_k(\varphi_3) = 2$, bmcT is 98.89, bmcM is 1114.00, satT is 9.69, satM 1869.00, bmcT+satT is 108.58, max(bmcM,satM) is 1869.00;

φ_4: $k = 24$, $f_k(\varphi_4) = 2$, bmcT is 2.00, bmcM is 3.57, satT is 1401.24, satM 93.00, bmcT+satT is 1403.24, max(bmcM,satM) is 93.00;

φ_5: $k = 65$, $f_k(\varphi_5) = 2$, bmcT is 281.50, bmcM is 18.13, satT is 149.59, satM 249.00, bmcT+satT is 431.10, max(bmcM,satM) is 249.00,

where k is the bound, $f_k(\varphi)$ is the number of symbolic paths, bmcT is the encoding time, bmcM is memory use for encoding, satT is satisfiability checking time, satM is memory use for satisfiability checking.

The formulae φ_1, φ_2 and φ_3 corroborates the efficiency of the SAT-based BMC methods when the length of the counterexamples does not grow with the number of agents (trains). On the other hand the formulae φ_4 and φ_5 demonstrate that SAT-based

BMC becomes inefficient when the the the length of the counterexamples grows with the number of agents (trains).

6   Conclusions

We have proposed, implemented, and experimentally evaluated a BMC method for EMTLKD interpreted over deontic interleaved interpreted systems. The experimental results show that the method is very promising.

In [21] it has been shown that the BDD- and SAT-based BMC approaches for ELTLK (an existential part of LTL that is extended with epistemic operators) are complementary. This result is consistent with comparisons for pure temporal logics [5]. Thus, in the future we are going to check whether the same results we can get for DIIS and EMTLKD. Therefore, we are going to define and implement a BDD-based BMC algorithm for EMTLKD, and compare it with the method presented in this paper.

In [20] the semantics of interpreted systems (IS) and interleaved interpreted systems (IIS) were experimentally evaluated by means of the BDD-based bounded model checking method for LTLK. IIS restrict IS by enforcing asynchronous semantics. The paper shows that the modelling approach has a very strong impact on the efficiency of verification by means of BMC. Thus, our future work will involve an implementation of the method for deontic interpreted systems and a comparison of the SAT-based BMC for DIS with the method presented in this paper.

References

1. Abdulla, P.A., Bjesse, P., Eén, N.: Symbolic Reachability Analysis Based on SAT-Solvers. In: Graf, S. (ed.) TACAS 2000. LNCS, vol. 1785, pp. 411–425. Springer, Heidelberg (2000)
2. Alur, R., Henzinger, T.A.: Logics and Models of Real Time: A Survey. In: Huizing, C., de Bakker, J.W., Rozenberg, G., de Roever, W.-P. (eds.) REX 1991. LNCS, vol. 600, pp. 74–106. Springer, Heidelberg (1992)
3. Aqvist, L.: Deontic logic. In: Handbook of Philosophical Logic. Extensions of Classical Logic, vol. II, pp. 605–714. Reidel, Dordrecht (1984)
4. Biere, A., Heljanko, K., Junttila, T., Latvala, T., Schuppan, V.: Linear encodings of bounded LTL model checking. Logical Methods in Computer Science 2(5:5), 1–64 (2006)
5. Cabodi, G., Camurati, P., Quer, S.: Can BDD compete with SAT solvers on bounded model checking? In: Proceedings of DAC 2002, pp. 117–122 (2002)
6. Clarke, E.M., Allen Emerson, E.: Design and Synthesis of Synchronization Skeletons for Branching-Time Temporal Logic. In: Kozen, D. (ed.) Logic of Programs 1981. LNCS, vol. 131, pp. 52–71. Springer, Heidelberg (1982)
7. Clarke, E., Grumberg, O., Hamaguchi, K.: Another Look at LTL Model Checking. In: Dill, D.L. (ed.) CAV 1994. LNCS, vol. 818, pp. 415–427. Springer, Heidelberg (1994)
8. Sistla, A.P., Emerson, E.A., Mok, A.K., Srinivasan, J.: Quantitative temporal reasoning. Real-Time Systems 4(4), 331–352 (1992)
9. Emerson, E.A.: Temporal and modal logic. In: Handbook of Theoretical Computer Science, vol. B, ch. 16, pp. 996–1071. Elsevier Science Publishers (1990)
10. Fagin, R., Halpern, J.Y., Moses, Y., Vardi, M.Y.: Reasoning about Knowledge. MIT Press, Cambridge (1995)
11. Furia, C.A., Spoletini, P.: Tomorrow and All our Yesterdays: MTL Satisfiability over the Integers. In: Fitzgerald, J.S., Haxthausen, A.E., Yenigun, H. (eds.) ICTAC 2008. LNCS, vol. 5160, pp. 126–140. Springer, Heidelberg (2008)

12. Huang, X., Luo, C., van der Meyden, R.: Improved Bounded Model Checking for a Fair Branching-Time Temporal Epistemic Logic. In: van der Meyden, R., Smaus, J.-G. (eds.) MoChArt 2010. LNCS, vol. 6572, pp. 95–111. Springer, Heidelberg (2011)

13. Jones, A., Lomuscio, A.: A BDD-based BMC approach for the verification of multi-agent systems. In: Proceedings of CS&P 2009, vol. 1, pp. 253–264. Warsaw University (2009)

14. Kacprzak, M., Lomuscio, A., Lasica, T., Penczek, W., Szreter, M.: Verifying Multi-agent Systems via Unbounded Model Checking. In: Hinchey, M.G., Rash, J.L., Truszkowski, W.F., Rouff, C.A. (eds.) FAABS 2004. LNCS (LNAI), vol. 3228, pp. 189–212. Springer, Heidelberg (2004)

15. Koymans, R.: Specifying real-time properties with metric temporal logic. Real-Time Systems 2(4), 255–299 (1990)

16. Levesque, H.: A logic of implicit and explicit belief. In: Proceedings of the 6th National Conference of the AAAI, pp. 198–202. Morgan Kaufman (1984)

17. Lomuscio, A., Penczek, W., Qu, H.: Partial order reduction for model checking interleaved multi-agent systems. In: AAMAS, pp. 659–666. IFAAMAS Press (2010)

18. Lomuscio, A., Sergot, M.: Deontic interpreted systems. Studia Logica 75(1), 63–92 (2003)

19. Męski, A., Penczek, W., Szreter, M.: Bounded model checking linear time and knowledge using decision diagrams. In: Proceedings of CS&P 2011, pp. 363–375 (2011)

20. Męski, A., Penczek, W., Szreter, M.: BDD-based Bounded Model Checking for LTLK over Two Variants of Interpreted Systems. In: Proceedings of LAM 2012, pp. 35–50 (2012)

21. Męski, A., Penczek, W., Szreter, M., Woźna-Szcześniak, B., Zbrzezny, A.: Two Approaches to Bounded Model Checking for Linear Time Logic with Knowledge. In: Jezic, G., Kusek, M., Nguyen, N.-T., Howlett, R.J., Jain, L.C. (eds.) KES-AMSTA 2012. LNCS, vol. 7327, pp. 514–523. Springer, Heidelberg (2012)

22. Penczek, W., Lomuscio, A.: Verifying epistemic properties of multi-agent systems via bounded model checking. In: Proceedings of AAMAS 2003, pp. 209–216. ACM (2003)

23. Penczek, W., Woźna-Szcześniak, B., Zbrzezny, A.: Towards SAT-based BMC for LTLK over interleaved interpreted systems. Fundamenta Informaticae 119(3-4), 373–392 (2012)

24. Quielle, J.P., Sifakis, J.: Specification and Verification of Concurrent Systems in CESAR. In: Dezani-Ciancaglini, M., Montanari, U. (eds.) Programming 1982. LNCS, vol. 137, pp. 337–351. Springer, Heidelberg (1982)

25. Raimondi, F., Lomuscio, A.: Automatic Verification of Deontic Properties of Multi-agent Systems. In: Lomuscio, A., Nute, D. (eds.) DEON 2004. LNCS (LNAI), vol. 3065, pp. 228–242. Springer, Heidelberg (2004)

26. Raimondi, F., Lomuscio, A.: Automatic verification of multi-agent systems by model checking via OBDDs. Journal of Applied Logic 5(2), 235–251 (2005)

27. Wooldridge, M.: An introduction to multi-agent systems. John Wiley, England (2002)

28. Woźna, B.: Bounded Model Checking for the universal fragment of CTL*. Fundamenta Informaticae 63(1), 65–87 (2004)

29. Woźna, B., Lomuscio, A., Penczek, W.: Bounded model checking for deontic interpreted systems. In: Proceedings of LCMAS 2004. ENTCS, vol. 126, pp. 93–114. Elsevier (2005)

30. Woźna-Szcześniak, B., Zbrzezny, A.: SAT-Based Bounded Model Checking for Deontic Interleaved Interpreted Systems. In: Jezic, G., Kusek, M., Nguyen, N.-T., Howlett, R.J., Jain, L.C. (eds.) KES-AMSTA 2012. LNCS, vol. 7327, pp. 494–503. Springer, Heidelberg (2012)

31. Woźna-Szcześniak, B., Zbrzezny, A., Zbrzezny, A.: The BMC Method for the Existential Part of RTCTLK and Interleaved Interpreted Systems. In: Antunes, L., Pinto, H.S. (eds.) EPIA 2011. LNCS, vol. 7026, pp. 551–565. Springer, Heidelberg (2011)

32. Zbrzezny, A.: Improving the translation from ECTL to SAT. Fundamenta Informaticae 85(1-4), 513–531 (2008)

33. Zbrzezny, A.: A new translation from ECTL* to SAT. Fundamenta Informaticae 120(3-4), 377–397 (2012)

Some Thoughts about Commitment Protocols
(Position Paper)

Matteo Baldoni and Cristina Baroglio

Università degli Studi di Torino
Dipartimento di Informatica
c.so Svizzera 185, I-10149 Torino, Italy
{matteo.baldoni,cristina.baroglio}@unito.it

Abstract. From the seminal paper by Singh [22], commitment protocols
have been raising a lot of attention. The key feature of commitment
protocols is their *declarative nature*, which allows specifying them in a
way which abstracts away from any reference to the actual behavior of
the agents. By doing so, commitment protocols respect the autonomy of
agents. After more than ten years from the introduction of commitments,
it is time to ask (*i*) if a "commitment to do something" is *the only kind
of regulative norm*, that we need in order to give a social semantics to
a physical action, and (*ii*) if they realize what they promised. In this
position paper we discuss these points.

1 Introduction

Practical commitments lie at the level of *regulative* (or *preservative*) norms that,
in turn, impact on the agents' behavior, creating social expectations, that should
not be frustrated. By a practical commitment, in fact, an actor (*debtor*) is committed towards another actor (*creditor*) to bring about something [9,20], i.e. to
act either directly or by persuading others so as to make a condition of interest
become true. Due to their *social nature*, practical commitments are a powerful
tool that helps to overcome the controversial assumptions of the mentalistic approach that mental states are verifiable and that agents are sincere. Moreover,
they support an *observational semantics* for communication that allows verifying
an agent's compliance with its commitments based on observable behavior.

From the seminal paper by Singh [22], commitment protocols have been raising a lot of attention, see for instance [27,17,25,12,24,14,6]. The key feature of
commitment protocols is their *declarative nature*, which allows specifying them
in a way which abstracts away from any reference to the actual behavior of the
agents, thus avoiding to impose useless execution constraints [28]. By doing so,
commitment-based protocols respect the autonomy of agents because whatever
action they decide to perform is fine as long as they accomplished their commitments, satisfying each others' expectations. Now, after more than ten years
from the introduction of commitments, it is time to ask (*i*) if a "commitment
to do something" is *the only kind of regulative norm*, that we need in order to
give a social semantics to a physical action, and (*ii*) if they realize what they

M. Baldoni et al. (Eds.): DALT 2012, LNAI 7784, pp. 190–196, 2013.

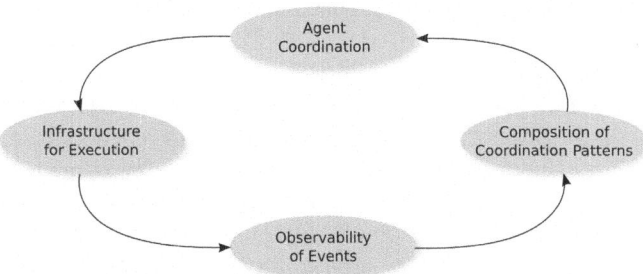

Fig. 1. The four considered intertwined aspects

promised. To this aim, we think that there are four intertwined aspects to be considered (see Figure 1):

1. *Agent Coordination*: how to account for coordination patterns?
2. *Infrastructure for Execution*: which is the reference execution infrastructure?
3. *Observability of Events*: are events really observable by all agents?
4. *Composition of Coordination Patterns*: is composition influenced by the previous aspects?

2   Agent Coordination

Commitment protocols leave the choice of which action to execute and when, totally up to the single agents. From a more general perspective, they do not impose constraints on the possible evolutions of the social state. However, in many practical cases there is the need to capture regulative aspects of *agent coordination*. For instance, a customer and a merchant may *agree* that payment should be done before shipping but how to represent this socially agreed constraint in commitment protocols? When a similar coordination is desired by the parties, one feels the lack of the means for capturing them *as regulations* inside the protocol. Notice that the desired coordination patterns, though restricting the choices up to the agents, would not prevent flexibility because, for instance, it is not mandatory that payment and shipping are one next to the other. What matters is their relative order. More importantly, an agreed coordination pattern establishes the boundaries within which each party can exercise his/her own autonomy without compromising the aims for which the agreement was taken. Citing Dwight Eisenhower (State of the Union Address, Feb. 2, 1953) *"To be true to one's own freedom is, in essence, to honor and respect the freedom of all others."* As long as agents respect such constraints, they are free to customize the execution at their will, e.g. by interleaving the two actions with others (like sending a receipt or asking a quote for another item). This need is felt by the research community, see [4,5,6] for an overview.

When regulations are expressed, agents can individually check whether their behavior conforms to the specification [2]. But in order to guarantee to the others that one will act in a way that conforms to the regulation, an agent should *formally bind* its behavior to the regulation itself. The proposal in [3,6], for instance, allows the representation of temporal regulations imposed on the evolution of the social state, however, it does not supply a deontic semantics to the constraints. Therefore the agents' behavior is not formally bound to them. On the other hand, the REGULA framework [19] uses precedence logic to express temporal patterns that can be used as antecedent (or consequent) conditions inside commitments. Since patterns may involve various parties, the framework also introduces a notion of condition control and of commitment safety, in order to allow agents to reason about the advisability of taking a commitment. However, patterns are not generally expressed on the evolution of the social state but are limited to events.

3   Infrastructure for Execution and Observability of Events

Commitments were introduced to support *run-time verification* in contrast to the mentalistic approach but despite this, they still lack of a *reference infrastructure* that practically enables such a verification. Verification is supported by proposals like [1,10], although the authors do not draft an infrastructure, while commitment machines [28,25,23] have mainly been used to provide an operational semantics. Normative approaches, e.g. institutions [16,17], provide an answer but with some limitations. Indeed, they tend to implicitly assume a centralized vision, often realized by introducing a new actor, whose task is to monitor the interaction: the institution itself. This assumption is coherent with the fact that commitment protocols tend to assume that events are *uniformly observed* by all the agents although in the real world this seldom happens; for instance, communications tend to be point-to-point. For instance, consider an e-commerce seller, a supplier, and a client: the seller communicates with both the supplier and the client, who do not interact with one another. In other words, the interaction between each pair of actors is point-to-point and cannot be observed by the third party. We need the infrastructure to support *this* kind of interaction and to monitor, in *this* context, the on-going enactment, checking whether it respects all the regulative aspects – that the designer identified as relevant or that the agents agreed.

Chopra and Singh [11] addressed the issue of realizing an architecture that relaxes the centralization constraint by incorporating the notion of *commitment alignment*. In this way it becomes possible to answer questions like "how to decide whether agents are acting in a way that complies to the regulations or not?", "How to know that an agent satisfied one of its commitments?" in contexts where events are not uniformly observable. Nevertheless, they relegated commitment alignment to the middleware, shielding the issue of *observability of events* from the agents and from the designer. Our claim is that this is a limitation and that in many real-world situations it is more desirable to have the means of making clear who can access what information and who is accountable for reporting what event. This is especially true when the protocol allows the representation of coordination patterns: there is the need of mechanisms for expressing who can observe what, tracking which part of a pattern was already followed, which is left to be performed, who is in charge of the next moves, and so on. As a consequence, we think that the specification of the coordination patterns and the design of the infrastructure cannot leave out the *observability of events*, which plays a fundamental role *at the level of the protocol specification* and, for this reason, it should be captured by *first-class abstractions* and appropriate regulations. Such abstractions/regulations should be represented in a way that makes them *directly manipulable* by the agents [7].

4   Composition of Coordination Patterns

Most of the works concerning software engineering aspects of commitment protocol specification focus on the formal verification to help the protocol designer to get rid of or to enforce given behaviors, [26,18,8,15,14]. An aspect that is not to be underestimated is the realization of a development methodology for commitment protocols. The most relevant representative is the Amoeba methodology [13], which allows the design of commitment protocols and their composition into complex business processes. With respect to the aspects that we are discussing, this methodology, however, has two main limits. On the one hand, when two or more protocols are composed, the designer is requested to define a set of temporal constraints among events and of data flow constraints to combine the various parts. However, such constraints have neither a regulatory flavor nor a deontic characterization. On the other hand, since a wider number of roles are involved, which among actors of one protocol is entitled to (and physically can) observe events generated inside another protocol? The methodology does not explicitly account for this problem in the description of the various steps that compose it. For instance, suppose of composing a protocol that allows a merchant and a supplier to interact with one that allows the same merchant to interact with a customer. It is unrealistic to suppose that the client can observe events involving the supplier, even though after the composition both actors will play in the same protocol. Actually, it would be useful to incorporate in the protocol the means for letting the merchant tell the client that it received items from the supplier in a way that makes it accountable for its declarations.

5   Conclusive Remarks

Commitments [21] are a powerful tool for creating communication and interaction standards with a solid and verifiable semantics, which is extremely important for dealing with open worlds, but to this aim there is the need of solving the issues that we have discussed.

1. *Agent Coordination: how to account for coordination patterns?* We claim that for accounting for coordination patterns there is the need of enriching the language for expressing commitment conditions (both antecedents and

consequents) with temporal expressions in a way that shapes the desired interactions.

2. *Infrastructure for Execution: which is the reference execution infrastructure?* In our opinion, there is the need of reifying interaction protocols as first-class elements that can be manipulated and inspected by agents, rather than relegating them to the middleware.

3. *Observability of Events: are events really observable by all agents?* In the real world events are not uniformly observable by all the interacting parties. The seller-shipper-client example shows this fact in practice and proves that inside commitment protocols there is the need of specifying and managing objects like *claims, assertions, declarations, statements*, so typical in every day life as well as in programming languages. Indeed, by stating something about a state of things that the client cannot observe directly, the seller took a commitment, though not a practical one. A crucial limitation of the interaction protocols literature is that here the used commitments are always *practical*, meaning that they describe what the roles involved would bring about (e.g. a buyer commits to paying for some item). Practical commitments are limited to the debtor's own capabilities and powers (including persuading others), however, real scenarios often require the *account of some event*, without delegating the burden of making it happen to the agent who gives the account.

4. *Composition of Coordination Patterns: is composition influenced by the previous aspects?* All the above aspects should be supported by appropriate software engineering methodologies. This will have a positive impact on the acceptance of declarative approaches inside industrial settings.

References

1. Alberti, M., Gavanelli, M., Lamma, E., Chesani, F., Mello, P., Torroni, P.: Compliance verification of agent interaction: a logic-based software tool. Applied Artificial Intelligence 20(2-4), 133–157 (2006)
2. Baldoni, M., Baroglio, C., Chopra, A.K., Desai, N., Patti, V., Singh, M.P.: Choice, Interoperability, and Conformance in Interaction Protocols and Service Choreographies. In: Proc. of AAMAS 2009, pp. 843–850. IFAAMAS (2009)
3. Baldoni, M., Baroglio, C., Marengo, E.: Behavior-Oriented Commitment-based Protocols. In: Proc. of ECAI, pp. 137–142. IOS Press (2010)
4. Baldoni, M., Baroglio, C., Marengo, E.: Constraints among Commitments: Regulative Specification of Interaction Protocols. In: Proc. of Int. Workshop on Agent Communication, AC 2010, Toronto, Canada, pp. 2–18 (May 2010)
5. Baldoni, M., Baroglio, C., Marengo, E.: Commitment-Based Protocols with Behavioral Rules and Correctness Properties of MAS. In: Omicini, A., Sardina, S., Vasconcelos, W. (eds.) DALT 2010. LNCS (LNAI), vol. 6619, pp. 60–77. Springer, Heidelberg (2011)
6. Baldoni, M., Baroglio, C., Marengo, E., Patti, V.: Constitutive and Regulative Specifications of Commitment Protocols: a Decoupled Approach. ACM TIST, Spec. Iss. on Agent Communication 4(2) (2013)

7. Baldoni, M., Baroglio, C., Marengo, E., Patti, V., Ricci, A.: Back to the future: An interaction-oriented framework for social computing. In: First Int. Workshop on Req. Eng. for Social Computing, RESC, pp. 2–5. IEEE (2011)

8. Bentahar, J., Meyer, J.-J.C., Wan, W.: Model checking communicative agent-based systems. Knowl.-Based Syst. 22(3), 142–159 (2009)

9. Castelfranchi, C.: Commitments: From Individual Intentions to Groups and Organizations. In: Proc. of ICMAS, pp. 41–48 (1995)

10. Chesani, F., Mello, P., Montali, M., Torroni, P.: Commitment Tracking via the Reactive Event Calculus. In: Proc. of IJCAI, pp. 91–96 (2009)

11. Chopra, A.K., Singh, M.P.: An Architecture for Multiagent Systems: An Approach Based on Commitments. In: Proc. of ProMAS. LNCS (LNAI), vol. 5919, pp. 148–162. Springer, Heidelberg (2009)

12. Chopra, A.K.: Commitment Alignment: Semantics, Patterns, and Decision Procedures for Distributed Computing. PhD thesis, NCSU, Raleigh, NC (2009)

13. Desai, N., Chopra, A.K., Singh, M.P.: Amoeba: A methodology for modeling and evolving cross-organizational business processes. ACM TSEM 19(2) (2009)

14. El-Menshawy, M., Bentahar, J., Dssouli, R.: Verifiable Semantic Model for Agent Interactions Using Social Commitments. In: Dastani, M., El Fallah Segrouchni, A., Leite, J., Torroni, P. (eds.) LADS 2009. LNCS, vol. 6039, pp. 128–152. Springer, Heidelberg (2010)

15. El-Menshawy, M., Bentahar, J., Dssouli, R.: Symbolic Model Checking Commitment Protocols Using Reduction. In: Omicini, A., Sardina, S., Vasconcelos, W. (eds.) DALT 2010. LNCS (LNAI), vol. 6619, pp. 185–203. Springer, Heidelberg (2011)

16. Fornara, N.: Interaction and Communication among Autonomous Agents in Multiagent Systems. PhD thesis, Univ. della Svizzera italiana (June 2003)

17. Fornara, N., Colombetti, M.: Defining Interaction Protocols using a Commitment-based Agent Communication Language. In: Proc. of AAMAS, pp. 520–527. ACM (2003)

18. Mallya, A., Singh, M.: An algebra for commitment protocols. Autonomous Agents and Multi-Agent Systems 14(2), 143–163 (2007)

19. Marengo, E., Baldoni, M., Baroglio, C., Chopra, A.K., Patti, V., Singh, M.P.: Commitments with Regulations: Reasoning about Safety and Control in REGULA. In: Proc. of AAMAS, pp. 467–474 (2011)

20. Singh, M.P.: An Ontology for Commitments in Multiagent Systems. Artificial Intelligence and Law 7(1), 97–113 (1999)

21. Singh, M.P.: Community Standards for Agent Communication. Unpublished Draft (July 2010), http://www.csc.ncsu.edu/faculty/mpsingh/papers/drafts/Singh-AC-Manifesto.pdf

22. Singh, M.P.: Agent communication languages: Rethinking the principles. IEEE Computer 31(12), 40–47 (1998)

23. Singh, M.P.: Formalizing Communication Protocols for Multiagent Systems. In: Proc. of IJCAI, pp. 1519–1524 (2007)

24. Torroni, P., Chesani, F., Mello, P., Montali, M.: Social Commitments in Time: Satisfied or Compensated. In: Baldoni, M., Bentahar, J., van Riemsdijk, M.B., Lloyd, J. (eds.) DALT 2009. LNCS (LNAI), vol. 5948, pp. 228–243. Springer, Heidelberg (2010)

25. Winikoff, M., Liu, W., Harland, J.: Enhancing Commitment Machines. In: Leite, J., Omicini, A., Torroni, P., Yolum, P. (eds.) DALT 2004. LNCS (LNAI), vol. 3476, pp. 198–220. Springer, Heidelberg (2005)
26. Yolum, P.: Design time analysis of multiagent protocols. Data Knowl. Eng. 63(1), 137–154 (2007)
27. Yolum, P., Singh, M.P.: Designing and Executing Protocols Using the Event Calculus. In: Agents, pp. 27–28. ACM, New York (2001)
28. Yolum, p., Singh, M.P.: Commitment Machines. In: Meyer, J.-J.C., Tambe, M. (eds.) ATAL 2001. LNCS (LNAI), vol. 2333, pp. 235–247. Springer, Heidelberg (2002)

Semantic Web and Declarative Agent Languages and Technologies: Current and Future Trends* (Position Paper)

Viviana Mascardi[1], James Hendler[2], and Laura Papaleo[3]

[1] DIBRIS, University of Genova, Italy
viviana.mascardi@unige.it
[2] Rensselaer Polytechnic Institute, Troy, NY, USA
hendler@cs.rpi.edu
[3] ICT Department, Provincia di Genova, Genova, Italy
laura.papaleo@gmail.com

1 Introduction

One of the first discussions about a Web enriched with semantics and its relationships with artificial intelligence (and hence, with intelligent agents) dates back to 1998 [3], but it was only ten years ago that the idea of a Semantic Web on top of which agent-based computing would have allowed computer programs to interact with non-local web-based resources, became familiar to a wide audience of scientists [4,18].

Whereas in the beginning the Semantic Web was conceived as something that inevitably required some extra effort from the final users, it became soon clear that the exploitation of semantic features should have been less intrusive as possible, making semantic markup a by-product of normal computer use.

Agents and ontologies are recognized as the right tools for managing information on the Web both by academic researchers [17], and by experts from the industry [27], and agent-based applications have been successfully deployed on top of the Semantic Web in many domains including multi-site software development [40], health care [39], cultural heritage, education and learning[1].

The integration of Semantic Web concepts as first class entities inside agent languages, technologies, and engineering methodologies has different levels of maturity: many AOSE methodologies [20],[23],[22],[38], organizational models [10],[12],[16],[24],[37] and MAS architectures (for example the FIPA Ontology Service Specification, www.fipa.org/specs/fipa00086/) seamlessly integrate them, but few languages do.

In this position paper we review the state of the art in the integration of semantic web concepts in declarative agent languages and technologies and outline what we expect to be the future trends of this research topic.

---

* The work of the first author has been partially supported by the "Indiana MAS and the Digital Preservation of Rock Carvings" FIRB 2010 project, funded by the Italian Ministry of Education, Universities and Research.
[1] Applications developed by the Finnish Semantic Computing Research Group (SeCo), http://www.seco.tkk.fi/.

M. Baldoni et al. (Eds.): DALT 2012, LNAI 7784, pp. 197–202, 2013.

2   State of the Art

Agent Communication Languages (ACLs). In agent communication, the assumption that ontologies should be used to ensure interoperability had been made since the very beginning of the work on ontologies, even before they made the basis for the Semantic Web effort. Both KQML [31] and FIPA-ACL [14] allow agents to specify the ontology they are using, although none of them forces that. ACLs were born with the Semantic Web in mind, and the exploitation of Semantic Web languages to represent both the content of an ACL message and the meaning of the whole message is still a topical research issue [13], [36].

Differently from ACLs, agent programming languages started only recently to address ontologies as first class objects, thus demonstrating how the two research fields need a strong integration and cross-fertilization.

Agent Programming Languages. AgentSpeak [34] underwent many extensions over time. However, what was considered only with the work [32] discussing AgentSpeak-DL, is that ontological reasoning could facilitate the development of AgentSpeak agents. The implementation of AgentSpeak-DL concepts is given in JASDL [25]. CooL-AgentSpeak [30], the "Cooperative Description-Logic Agent-Speak" language integrating Coo-BDI [1] and AgentSpeak-DL and enhancing them with *ontology matching capabilities* [11] is a further effort on this subject.

In CooL-AgentSpeak, the search for a plan takes place not only in the agent's local plan library but also in the other agents' libraries, according to the cooperation strategy as in Coo-BDI. However, handling an event is more flexible as it is not based solely on unification and on the subsumption relation between concepts as in AgentSpeak-DL, but also on ontology matching. Belief querying and updating take advantage of ontological matching as well. The paper [15] stems from [32] and proposes the core of a logic agent-oriented programming language based on DL-Lite [6], taking efficiency issues into account.

The authors of [7] and [8] explore the use of a formal ontology as a constraining framework for the belief store of a rational agent and show the implementation of their proposal in the Go! multi-threaded logic programming language [7]. That work mainly aims at defining a mapping between OWL-Lite constructs and labeled theories in the Go! language, losing references to the external ontologies which define the agents' vocabulary. On the contrary, the works in [32] and [30] implicitly assume that ontologies exist outside the agents' "mind", which is more in line with the Semantic Web philosophy. As far as ontology matching capabilities which characterize the CooL-AgentSpeak language are concerned, neither [15] nor [7,8] take them into account as a means for inferring "cross-ontological knowledge" and none of them consider "cross-ontological reasoning" for exchanging behavioral knowledge.

The support natively given by Jadex [33] and 2APL [9] to ontologies consists in boosting agent communication by allowing messages to refer to concepts defined in the agents' ontologies. This support is hence due to the respect of FIPA-ACL specifications, and not to a true integration of Semantic Web elements into the languages. In a recent paper [28], the implementation of an ontology-based

BDI agent engine able to interpret an ontology describing the agent operations, implemented on top of Jadex, is discussed. Finally, an extension to 3APL [19] to support ontology-based communication is discussed on [29].

Proof and Trust in MASs. Even if the Semantic Web is often incorrectly reduced to reasoning on semantic markups, it actually goes far beyond that, coping with proof and trust as well. Both these topics are extremely hot within the agent community, and on the DALT's one in particular. In the literature we can find dozens of works on trust and reputation in agent societies, and research on formally proving that an agent can enter an organization without damaging it has already produced many valuable results. Model checking declarative agent languages has a long tradition too (see for example the "MCAPL: Model Checking Agent Programming Languages" project,http://cgi.csc.liv.ac.uk/MCAPL/index.php/Main_Page , and [21]). Since these works are well known inside the DALT community, we do not enter into the details here and we limit ourselves to point out that proof and trust are extremely relevant issues both in the agent and in the Semantic Web communities, and that results achieved here, should be timely transferred there and vice-versa.

3   Future Trends

There are many promising directions that the research on integration of Semantic Web technologies and DALTs could take.

Semantic-Web based Proof and Trust. Although the maturity level of the aspects concerned with proof and trust in DALTs is satisfactory, mechanisms that give the developer the real power or putting all together are still missing. For example, to design and build MASs where agents can trust each other, the consistency of the agents' beliefs represented as ontologies should be always preserved, and formally demonstrated if required by the application.

Semantic-Web based Mediation. In [2], a semantic mediation going beyond the integration of ontologies within traditional message-based communication was envisaged. Mediation should occur at the level that characterizes the social approach where it is required to bind the semantics of the agent actions with their meaning in social terms (ontology-driven count-as rules).

Semantic Representation of the Environment. Although not yet formalized in published papers, the A&A model [35] is moving towards integrating semantic web concepts as first class objects for semantically representing the environment and the artifacts available to the agents[2]. This line of research should be pursued by other declarative approaches as well, where the environments is explicitly represented. Formally proving the consistency of the "Environment Ontology" should be possible, as well as evolving it, and learning it from sources of semi-structured information.

---

[2] Private communication of one of the authors of this paper with the authors of the A&A model.

Adoption of Semantic-Web enriched DALTs for Real Applications. Many real applications involve scenarios where procedural rules for achieving a goal are expressed in an informal and fully declarative way, may require to achieve sub-goals, and the domain knowledge is hard-wired within the rules themselves, making them barely re-usable in other domains, even if they could. Think of the rules for getting a new identity card issued by Genova Municipality, which are declaratively defined by conditions to be met [5], other documents to be obtained before, and exactly the same as those for obtaining the document in another municipality, but nevertheless would be hard to compare. Expressing procedural rules of this kind using declarative agent languages fully integrated with semantic web concepts might help comparing and composing them in an automatic way, moving a step forward the automation of many services that are still completely performed by human agents.

Discussion. The first problem that the Semantic Web and Declarative Agent Languages and Technologies communities should struggle to solve together, is bringing usability to the world. Forthcoming technologies should be not only secure, efficient, self-*, etc. It is mandatory that *they will be usable* by average computer scientists, average professionals and even average users. *"Making intelligent software agents both powerful and easy to construct, manage, and maintain will require a very rich semantic infrastructure"* [26], and the rich semantic infrastructure seething with agents, must be there for anyone. In a few years, it must become a commodity, clearing the boundaries of academic research once and for all.

References

1. Ancona, D., Mascardi, V.: Coo-BDI: Extending the BDI Model with Cooperativity. In: Leite, J., Omicini, A., Sterling, L., Torroni, P. (eds.) DALT 2003. LNCS (LNAI), vol. 2990, pp. 109–134. Springer, Heidelberg (2004)
2. Baldoni, M., Baroglio, C., Bergenti, F., Marengo, E., Mascardi, V., Patti, V., Ricci, A., Santi, A.: An Interaction-Oriented Agent Framework for Open Environments. In: Pirrone, R., Sorbello, F. (eds.) AI*IA 2011. LNCS, vol. 6934, pp. 68–79. Springer, Heidelberg (2011)
3. Berners-Lee, T.: An parenthetical discussion to the web architecture at 50,000 feet and the semantic web roadmap (1998), www.w3.org/DesignIssues/RDFnot.html (accessed on November 20, 2012)
4. Berners-Lee, T., Hendler, J., Lassila, O.: The Semantic Web. Scientific American, 29–37 (May 2001)
5. Bozzano, M., Briola, D., Leone, D., Locoro, A., Marasso, L., Mascardi, V.: MUSE: MUltilinguality and SEmantics for the Citizens of the World. In: Fortino, G., Badica, C., Malgeri, M., Unland, R. (eds.) Intelligent Distributed Computing VI. SCI, vol. 446, pp. 97–102. Springer, Heidelberg (2013)
6. Calvanese, D., De Giacomo, G., Lemho, D., Lenzerini, M., Rosati, R.: DL-Lite: tractable description logics for ontologies. In: Proc. of Nat. Conf. on Artificial Intelligence, vol. 2, pp. 602–607. AAAI Press (2005)

7. Clark, K.L., McCabe, F.G.: Go! a multi-paradigm programming language for implementing multi-threaded agents. Ann. Math. Artif. Intell. 41, 171–206 (2004)
8. Clark, K.L., McCabe, F.G.: Ontology schema for an agent belief store. Int. J. Hum.-Comput. Stud. 65, 640–658 (2007)
9. Dastani, M.: 2APL: a practical agent programming language. Autonomous Agents and Multi-Agent Systems 16(3), 214–248 (2008)
10. Dignum, V.: Ontology support for agent-based simulation of organizations. Multi-agent and Grid Systems 6(2), 191–208 (2010)
11. Euzenat, J., Shvaiko, P.: Ontology Matching. Springer (2007)
12. Fornara, N., Colombetti, M.: Representation and monitoring of commitments and norms using OWL. AI Commun. 23(4), 341–356 (2010)
13. Fornara, N., Okouya, D., Colombetti, M.: Using OWL 2 DL for Expressing ACL Content and Semantics. In: Cossentino, M., Kaisers, M., Tuyls, K., Weiss, G. (eds.) EUMAS 2011. LNCS, vol. 7541, pp. 97–113. Springer, Heidelberg (2012)
14. Foundation for Intelligent Physical Agents. FIPA ACL message structure specification. Approved for standard (December 6, 2002)
15. Fuzitaki, C., Moreira, Á., Vieira, R.: Ontology Reasoning in Agent-Oriented Programming. In: da Rocha Costa, A.C., Vicari, R.M., Tonidandel, F. (eds.) SBIA 2010. LNCS, vol. 6404, pp. 21–30. Springer, Heidelberg (2010)
16. Grossi, D., Aldewereld, H., Vázquez-Salceda, J., Dignum, F.: Ontological aspects of the implementation of norms in agent-based electronic institutions. Computational & Mathematical Organization Theory 12(2-3), 251–275 (2006)
17. Hadzic, M., Wongthongtham, P., Dillon, T., Chang, E.: Ontology-Based Multi-Agent Systems. SCI, vol. 219. Springer, Heidelberg (2009)
18. Hendler, J.A.: Agents and the semantic web. IEEE Intelligent Systems 16(2), 30–37 (2001)
19. Hindriks, K.V., de Boer, F.S., van der Hoek, W., Meyer, J.-J.C.: Agent programming in 3APL. Autonomous Agents and Multi-Agent Systems 2(4), 357–401 (1999)
20. Jeroudaih, L.M., Hajji, M.S.: Extensions to some AOSE methodologies. World Academy of Science, Engineering and Technology 64, 383–388 (2010)
21. Jongmans, S.-S.T.Q., Hindriks, K.V., van Riemsdijk, M.B.: Model Checking Agent Programs by Using the Program Interpreter. In: Dix, J., Leite, J., Governatori, G., Jamroga, W. (eds.) CLIMA XI. LNCS, vol. 6245, pp. 219–237. Springer, Heidelberg (2010)
22. Kardas, G., Göknil, A., Dikenelli, O., Topaloglu, N.Y.: Metamodeling of semantic web enabled multiagent systems. In: Multiagent Systems and Software Architecture, the Special Track at Net.ObjectDays, pp. 79–86 (2006)
23. Kardas, G., Goknil, A., Dikenelli, O., Topaloglu, N.Y.: Model Transformation for Model Driven Development of Semantic Web Enabled Multi-Agent Systems. In: Petta, P., Müller, J.P., Klusch, M., Georgeff, M. (eds.) MATES 2007. LNCS (LNAI), vol. 4687, pp. 13–24. Springer, Heidelberg (2007)
24. Katasonov, A., Terziyan, V.Y.: Semantic approach to dynamic coordination in autonomous systems. In: Proc. of the 5th Int. Conf. on Autonomic and Autonomous Systems, pp. 321–329. IEEE Computer Society (2009)
25. Klapiscak, T., Bordini, R.H.: JASDL: A Practical Programming Approach Combining Agent and Semantic Web Technologies. In: Baldoni, M., Son, T.C., van Riemsdijk, M.B., Winikoff, M. (eds.) DALT 2008. LNCS (LNAI), vol. 5397, pp. 91–110. Springer, Heidelberg (2009)

26. Krupansky, J.: Richness of semantic infrastructure (2011),
    http://semanticabyss.blogspot.com/2011/06/
    richness-of-semantic-infrastructure.html
    (accessed on November 20, 2012)
27. Lewis, D.J.: Semantic web – developing an intelligent web (2008),
    www.ibm.com/developerworks/web/library/wa-intelligentage/ (accessed on
    November 20, 2012)
28. Liu, C.-H., Chen, J.J.-Y.: Using ontology-based BDI agent to dynamically cus-
    tomize workflow and bind semantic web service. JSW 7(4), 884–894 (2012)
29. Liu, C.-H., Lin, Y.-F., Chen, J.J.-Y.: Using agent to coordinate web services. In:
    Proc. of the 2008 Int. Conference on Software Engineering Research & Practice,
    pp. 317–322. CSREA Press (2008)
30. Mascardi, V., Ancona, D., Bordini, R.H., Ricci, A.: CooL-AgentSpeak: Enhancing
    AgentSpeak-DL agents with plan exchange and ontology services. In: Proc. of the
    Int. Conf. on Intelligent Agent Technology, pp. 109–116. IEEE Computer Society
    (2011)
31. Mayfield, J., Labrou, Y., Finin, T.: Evaluation of KQML as an Agent Communi-
    cation Language. In: Tambe, M., Müller, J., Wooldridge, M.J. (eds.) IJCAI-WS
    1995 and ATAL 1995. LNCS, vol. 1037, pp. 347–360. Springer, Heidelberg (1996)
32. Moreira, Á.F., Vieira, R., Bordini, R.H., Hübner, J.F.: Agent-Oriented Pro-
    gramming with Underlying Ontological Reasoning. In: Baldoni, M., Endriss, U.,
    Omicini, A., Torroni, P. (eds.) DALT 2005. LNCS (LNAI), vol. 3904, pp. 155–170.
    Springer, Heidelberg (2006)
33. Pokahr, A., Braubach, L., Lamersdorf, W.: Jadex: A BDI reasoning engine. In:
    Multi-Agent Programming: Languages, Platforms and Applications. Multiagent
    Systems, Artificial Societies, and Simulated Organizations, vol. 15, pp. 149–174.
    Springer (2005)
34. Rao, A.S.: AgentSpeak(L): BDI Agents Speak Out in a Logical Computable Lan-
    guage. In: Perram, J., Van de Velde, W. (eds.) MAAMAW 1996. LNCS (LNAI),
    vol. 1038, pp. 42–55. Springer, Heidelberg (1996)
35. Ricci, A., Viroli, M., Omicini, A.: Programming MAS with Artifacts. In: Bordini,
    R.H., Dastani, M., Dix, J., El Fallah Seghrouchni, A. (eds.) PROMAS 2005. LNCS
    (LNAI), vol. 3862, pp. 206–221. Springer, Heidelberg (2006)
36. Schiemann, B., Schreiber, U.: OWL-DL as a FIPA-ACL content language. In: Proc.
    of the Int. Workshop on Formal Ontology for Communicating Agents (2006)
37. Smith, B.L., Tamma, V.A.M., Wooldridge, M.: An ontology for coordination. Ap-
    plied Artificial Intelligence 25(3), 235–265 (2011)
38. Tran, Q.-N.N., Low, G.: Mobmas: A methodology for ontology-based multi-agent
    systems development. Information & Software Technology 50(7-8), 697–722 (2008)
39. Wang, M.-H., Lee, C.-S., Hsieh, K.-L., Hsu, C.-Y., Acampora, G., Chang, C.-
    C.: Ontology-based multi-agents for intelligent healthcare applications. Journal on
    Ambient Intelligence and Humanized Computing 1(2), 111–131 (2010)
40. Wongthongtham, P., Chang, E., Dillon, T.: Ontology-based multi-agent system
    to multi-site software development. In: Proc. of the Workshop on Quantitative
    Techniques for Software Agile Process, pp. 66–75. ACM Press (2004)

Designing and Implementing a Framework for BDI-Style Communicating Agents in Haskell
(Position Paper)

Alessandro Solimando* and Riccardo Traverso*

Dipartimento di Informatica, Bioingegneria, Robotica e Ingegneria dei Sistemi,
Università di Genova, Italy
{alessandro.solimando,riccardo.traverso}@unige.it

Abstract. In this position paper we present the design and prototypical implementation of a framework for BDI-style agents defined as Haskell functions, supporting both the explicit representation of beliefs and back-tracking (at the level of individual agents), and asynchronous communication via message passing. The communication layer is separated from the layers implementing the features of individual agents through different stacked monads, while beliefs are represented through atomic or structured values depending on the user's needs. Our long-term goal is to develop a framework for purely functional BDI agents, which is currently missing, in order to take advantage of the features of the functional paradigm, combined with the flexibility of an agent-oriented approach.

1 Introduction

The Belief-Desire-Intention (BDI) model is a well-known software model for programming intelligent rational agents [11]. Only a few frameworks that implement the BDI approach are developed directly on top of logical languages [7], while most of them are built using imperative or object oriented languages. For example, Jason [2] is developed in Java and exploits inheritance and overriding to define selection functions and the environment in a convenient and flexible way. The drawback is that many features natively available in the logic programming paradigm have to be re-implemented from scratch, resulting in a more onerous mixed-paradigm code. For instance, in Jason, unification is needed to find plans relevant to a triggering event, and to resolve logical goals in order to verify that the plan context is a logical consequence of the belief base. BDI-style agents are usually described in a declarative way, no matter how the language interpreter is implemented. The functional paradigm supports pattern matching for free and gives all the advantages of declarativeness; moreover, the use of types for typing communication channels may provide great benefits to guarantee correctness properties both a priori, and during the execution. Nevertheless, to the best of our knowledge no functional frameworks for BDI-style communicating agents have been proposed so far.

---

* Both authors of this paper are Ph. D. students at the University of Genova, Italy.

M. Baldoni et al. (Eds.): DALT 2012, LNAI 7784, pp. 203–207, 2013.
© Springer-Verlag Berlin Heidelberg 2013

In order to fill this gap, we propose a framework for functional agents taking inspiration from the BDI model (although not implementing all of its features), and supporting communication and backtracking. A generic and easily composable architecture should partition the agents' functionalities into several well-separated layers, and in functional programming monads are a powerful abstraction to satisfy these needs. Intuitively, in our solution agents are monadic actions provided with local backtracking features and point-to-point message passing primitives. Their local belief base is stored within variables that are passed down through execution steps. Goals are defined with functions from beliefs to booleans. When it comes to monadic computations, Haskell [3], being strongly based on them, is the best fit. However, even though we focus on a specific architecture, our purpose is not to propose a definitive implementation, but rather to show that this kind of integration is indeed possible without sacrificing or reimplementing fundamental features of different programming paradigms.

Our work is a generalization of [12], where the authors describe a single-agent monadic BDI implementation relying on CHR [6]; we share with [12] the idea of a BDI architecture based on monads, but instead of relying on CHR to represent beliefs and their evolution, the aim of our work is to provide a better integration with the language by handling them directly as Haskell values and expressions.

In [14] agents executing abstract actions relative to deontic specifications (prohibition, permission, and obligation) are simulated in Haskell. Although close to our approach up to some extent, that work does not take the BDI model into account. We are not aware of other proposals using functional languages to represent BDI-style agents.

2   Preliminaries: Haskell

In this section we provide a very brief overview of Haskell's syntax [9], to allow the reader to understand our design choices.

The keyword `data` is used to declare new, possibly polymorphic, data types. A new generic type may be, e.g., `data MyType a b = MyType a a b`: `a` and `b` are two type variables, and the constructor for new values takes (in the order) two `a` arguments and one `b`. A concrete type for `MyType` could be, e.g., `MyType Int String`. A type signature for `f` is written `f :: a`, where `a` is a type expression; an arrow → is a right-associative infix operator for defining domain and codomain of functions. A type class is a sort of interface or abstract class that data types may support by declaring an `instance` for it. A special type (), called unit, acts as a tuple with arity 0; its only value is also written ().

Further information on Haskell and monads can be found in [4,8,3] and in the freely available book [9].

3   Our Framework

In our framework, we split the definition of the capabilities of the agents in different layers by means of monads. The innermost one, `Agent`, provides support for the reasoning that an agent may accomplish in isolation from the rest of the system, that is without any need to communicate. On top of it we build another monad `CAgent` for communicating agents that provides basic message-passing features.

```
data Agent s a = Agent (s → (s,a))
instance Monad (Agent s) where {- omitted -}
```

The declaration of `Agent` follows the definition of the well-known state monad [4]. It is parameterized on two types: the state `s` of the agent, containing its current beliefs, and the return type `a` of the action in the monad. Each action is a function from the current state to the (possibly modified) new one, together with the return value.

At this layer it is safe to introduce goal-directed backtracking support, because computations are local to the agent and no interaction is involved. In Haskell, one could provide a basic backtracking mechanism for a monad `m` by defining an instance of the `MonadPlus` type class. `MonadPlus m` instances must define two methods, `mzero :: m a` and `mplus :: m a → m a → m a`, that respectively represent failure and choice. Infinite computations, i.e. with an infinite number of solutions, can not be safely combined within `MonadPlus` because the program could diverge. In order to address this problem the authors of [5] propose a similar type class – along with a comparison between different implementations – where its operators behave fairly, e.g. solutions from different choices are selected with a round robin policy. In our work we plan to exploit their solutions to give `Agent` the possibility to handle backtracking even in such scenarios. Goals can be defined as predicates `pred :: Agent s Bool` to be used in guards that may stop the computation returning `mzero` whenever the current state does not satisfy `pred`. It is worth noting how this concept of goals fits well into Haskell: such guards are the standard, natural way to use `MonadPlus`.

```
type AgentId = String
data Message a = Message AgentId AgentId a
data AgentChan a = {- omitted -}
```

Another building block for our MAS architecture is the FIFO channel `AgentChan`. We omit the full definition for the sake of brevity: it is sufficient to know that messages have headers identifying sender and receiver agents and a payload of arbitrary type `a`.

```
data CAgentState a = CAgentState AgentId (AgentChan a)
data CAgent s a b = CAgent (CAgentState a → Agent s (CAgentState a, b))
instance Monad (CAgent s a) where {- omitted -}
```

A `CAgent` is, just like before, defined by means of a state monad. It only needs to know its unique identifier and the communication channel to be used for interacting with other agents. This is why, unlike before, the type that holds the state is fixed as `CAgentState`. The function wrapped by `CAgent`, thanks to its codomain `Agent s (CAgentState a, b)`, is able to merge an agent computation within a communicating agent. Intuitively, a `CAgent` can be executed by taking in input the initial `CAgentState` and beliefs base `s`, producing at each intermediate step a value b and the new `CAgent` and `Agent` states. The execution flow of a `CAgent` may use functionalities from `Agent`; once the computation moves to the inner monad we gain access to the beliefs base, goals, and backtracking, but all the interaction capabilities are lost until the execution reaches `CAgent` again. Both monads may be concisely defined through the use of the Monad Transformer Library [4], thus many type class instances and utility functions are already given.

A `CAgent` may interact using point-to-point message exchange. The communication interface is summarized below; all functions are blocking and asynchronous, with the exception of `tryRecvMsg` that is non-blocking.

```
myId        :: CAgent s a AgentId
sendMsg     :: AgentId → a → CAgent s a ()
recvMsg     :: CAgent s a (Message a)
tryRecvMsg :: CAgent s a (Maybe (Message a))
```

Given a set of communicating agents, it is straightforward to define a simple module that manages the threads and the synchronization between them.

4   Conclusion and Future Work

We presented a basic architecture based on monads for MAS composed of Haskell agents. Similarly to other solutions, our system provides backtracking capabilities, even if they are limited to the decisions taken between two communication acts.

We have been able to show how the concepts behind MAS can be naturally instantiated in a purely functional language without any particular influence from other paradigms or solutions that may undermine the integration of the framework with the Haskell standard library.

This is still a preliminary work, as the architecture may change to better address the objectives and the prototype of this framework needs to be developed further in order to provide full support for all the described features. Some ideas for future extensions are (1) integrating the backtracking capabilities described in [5], (2) supporting event-based selection of plans, (3) adding communication primitives (e.g. broadcast, multicast), and (4) enriching the communication model with session types [13] in order to check the correctness of ongoing communication along the lines of [1] and [10].

References

1. Ancona, D., Drossopoulou, S., Mascardi, V.: Automatic Generation of Self-Monitoring MASs from Multiparty Global Session Types in Jason. In: Baldoni, M., Dennis, L., Mascardi, V., Vasconcelos, W. (eds.) DALT 2012. LNCS (LNAI), vol. 7784, pp. 76–95. Springer, Heidelberg (2013)
2. Bordini, R.H., Hübner, J.F., Wooldridge, M.: Programming multi-agent systems in AgentSpeak using Jason, vol. 8. Wiley-Interscience (2008)

3. Hudak, P., Hughes, J., Jones, S.P., Wadler, P.: A history of Haskell: being lazy with class. In: HOPL III: Proceedings of the Third ACM SIGPLAN Conference on History of Programming Languages, pp. 12-1–12-55 (2007)
4. Jones, M.: Functional Programming with Overloading and Higher-Order Polymorphism. In: Jeuring, J., Meijer, E. (eds.) AFP 1995. LNCS, vol. 925, pp. 97–136. Springer, Heidelberg (1995)
5. Kiselyov, O., Shan, C., Friedman, D.P., Sabry, A.: Backtracking, interleaving, and terminating monad transformers (functional pearl). In: Proceedings of the Tenth ACM SIGPLAN International Conference on Functional Programming, ICFP 2005, pp. 192–203. ACM, New York (2005)
6. Lam, E.S.L., Sulzmann, M.: Towards agent programming in CHR. CHR 6, 17–31 (2006)
7. Mascardi, V., Demergasso, D., Ancona, D.: Languages for programming BDI-style agents: an overview. In: Proceedings of WOA 2005, pp. 9–15. Pitagora Editrice Bologna (2005)
8. Moggi, E.: Notions of computation and monads. Inf. Comput. 93(1), 55–92 (1991)
9. O'Sullivan, B., Stewart, D.B., Goerzen, J.: Real World Haskell. O'Reilly Media (2009)
10. Pucella, R., Tov, J.A.: Haskell session types with (almost) no class. In: Haskell, pp. 25–36 (2008)
11. Rao, A.S.: AgentSpeak(L): BDI Agents Speak Out in a Logical Computable Language. In: Perram, J., Van de Velde, W. (eds.) MAAMAW 1996. LNCS, vol. 1038, pp. 42–55. Springer, Heidelberg (1996)
12. Sulzmann, M., Lam, E.S.L.: Specifying and Controlling Agents in Haskell
13. Takeuchi, K., Honda, K., Kubo, M.: An Interaction-based Language and its Typing System. In: Halatsis, C., Philokyprou, G., Maritsas, D., Theodoridis, S. (eds.) PARLE 1994. LNCS, vol. 817, pp. 398–413. Springer, Heidelberg (1994)
14. Wyner, A.Z.: A Functional Program for Agents, Actions, and Deontic Specifications. In: Baldoni, M., Endriss, U. (eds.) DALT 2006. LNCS (LNAI), vol. 4327, pp. 239–256. Springer, Heidelberg (2006)

Author Index